From One Life
to the Next

Lampis D. Anagnostopoulos, M.D.

"From One Life to the Next," by Lampis Anagnostopoulos. ISBN 978-1-949756-11-1.

Dedication

To the memory of my parents.

Acknowledgments

I would like to thank Peter Nenhaus for his comments and inspiration. My deep appreciation to Ms. Patty Apostolides for her comments and editing.

Contents

Preface

"IF SOMEONE TOLD YOU that you have only six months to live, what would you do?" Peter asked. He was my closest friend.

We sipped Metaxa, Peter's favorite brandy, at one-thirty in the morning, in Peter's fragrant backyard. We'd been sitting there for about two hours, exchanging stories and thoughts that we had started at dinner, at a restaurant, earlier in the evening. The quiet of the night was punctuated irregularly by a distant humming of a passing car. The soft rustling of the leaves of the Hickory in the playful breeze, the scattered stars across the sky, and the plaintive meowing of a cat on the other side of the fence, all reminded us to keep our voices low and our laughter subdued.

"What would you do?" Peter asked again, after taking another slow, sensual sip.

I thought about it. The silence helped.

"Well, Peter," I began, "if I had six months to live, I would write about my life. Writing requires concentration; concentration in retrieving memories will make me relive my past in full. Passing through for the second time will give me a chance to refocus on my thoughts at every encounter and from every stimulus. That way, my life may seem twice as long."

After a long moment's silence, before the next sip, Peter said, "What I would do is…"

Fortunately, we both had a lot longer to live and much more to do. But that's how it started. It took me about fourteen years to write my memoir. I wrote mostly while traveling; while waiting to board planes, on the planes, and in the lobbies of hotels. I wrote occasionally in hotel rooms, and in the final stretch, at home.

I was surprised, and more importantly, gratified in realizing how I relived my past, by discovering that images, dialogues, and fantasies remained indelible, and through re-experiencing my emotions in their full intensity. Unavoidably, and unexpectedly, the events with the stronger impacts were easier to restore. Those with the weaker influence were weaned, and some painful ones resurfaced incidentally and were left out to avoid disrupting the sequence.

To the women and men whom I failed to give tribute for their influence in molding my personality or igniting an inspiration, I extend my apologies. To those who may remember events or encounters differently, I must appeal to keep in mind that my memories were engraved with my emotions and my emotions were generated by my personal and subjective reactions and actions.

I hope and pray that my friends and relatives who shared some of my experiences or judged me with their standards would be more understanding.

CHAPTER 1
The Voyage

ON THIS CLEAR, BRIGHT DAY IN GREECE, the blue, gently heaving waters reflected the majesty and mission of the ocean liner. Leisurely and disciplined traffic moved along and away from the shore boulevard. Pedestrians waited obediently for the green light. The unevenly undulating hum was pierced occasionally by the horn of a taxi or the clanging of the tram. Flat and tiled sloping rooftops stretched from the shore to the crest of the hill on the left, halfway up the mountain slope on the right. Boats and ships of all sizes glided smoothly in and out of the harbor.

Lampis watched the elderly couple and young woman in black, with candles in their hands, ascend slowly up the steps to the entrance of St. Nicholas, the protector of seafarers. Silent, resigned crowds stood along the pier. Women and girls wiped their eyes and men gazed in the distance for an escape or for relief. The Greek flag rested on the pole for a respite.

Lampis turned to his friend across the little round, marble-top table, at the sidewalk café. "I hope they make it. I need to hear their farewells, to draw some strength from their last embraces," he said, gratefully and imploringly.

"They'll be here," his friend assured him, reaching for his hand. The usually talkative friend looked away and remained silent, thinking who knows what.

Lampis checked his papers again and arranged them in the expected order of presenting them between crossing the gate to the harbor and boarding the ship. He held them tightly in his right hand, against his chest, and retraced the events of the day.

He remembered the squeezing embrace and soft kisses of Aunt Nikki at the door of her humble and warm home, and the promise to call, as he rushed off at four o'clock. He prayed for deliverance at the frustratingly slow tram and subway train rides and had dashed along the deserted streets from the Subway Station to the American Consulate (there were about twenty people ahead of him). He had handed his application and documents to the young, attractive woman who scrutinized them, and afterwards, rose and wished him "The best of luck," with a warm handshake and a genuine smile.

Then he had rushed madly to the Headquarters of the Security Police while engrossed in all-consuming apprehension about bureaucratic snags. There were interminable delays by the slow-moving, nonchalant officers at the Police Station.

He had waited in line to use the public telephone, which tried his patience, and called Uncle Vasiles, then his sister, to tell them that he would be boarding the ship in about one and one-half hours and pleaded with them to start now, if they wished to see him off.

"They should be here any moment. What's taking them so long?" his friend asked, checking his watch.

The silence that followed blanked even the incessant hum of the traffic.

"We can't miss them from this spot," his friend continued. "Remember this place. We'll meet again, here, after you graduate from Medical School."

"Here is your sister, helping Aunt Nikki off the tram," his friend announced, jumping off his chair.

Lampis waved to attract their attention and waited for them to cross the street.

He held his sister tightly in his arms. "I love you. I love you."

Then Aunt Nikki burst into sobs and kept kissing him on the cheeks several times. "This is from your mother. This is from your father. This is from me, and the rest of the people that love you."

"The others should be here any minute," his friend reassured them and called the waiter. "Have a piece of galactoboureko (custard pastry) or whatever you like," he said to them.

Lampis was flanked by his sister and aunt. His sister held his hand with her right hand and ate with the left, and his aunt held his other hand with her left and ate with the right.

His friend, holding all his papers, assured and reassured them that Lampis would return.

Uncle Vasiles and his family arrived a few minutes later. The children broke away and rushed to Lampis. He picked them up and swirled them, holding the year-old baby girl until they reached the gates.

"*Kalo taxeidi.* (Safe voyage) *Kalee tyche (*Good luck*),*" the waiter shouted.

Lampis turned around and acknowledged him with a grateful smile. His sister and Aunt Violetta, his uncle's wife, clung to his arms; the rest walked behind them.

"Let's take some pictures before it's too late," Uncle Vasiles implored, and directed them to the steps of the Church of St. Nicholas.

Everybody clustered around Lampis. Smiling was hard, with the thought that he might never see them again, but he managed.

The surge of the crowd toward the gates confirmed, after a furtive gland, that the gates were open and embarking was starting.

His sister threw her arms around his neck and sobbed violently. "I'll miss you. I love you. Write to me often," she stuttered.

The others waited their turns, declaring their love with and after their embraces. Their tears and sobs burdened his heart. His four-year-old cousin's appeal, "Will you take me to the park tomorrow?" pierced it.

Lampis picked up his light suitcase and held a bouquet of thyme with his other hand. He followed the beckoning Fates and the surging crowd. He turned for one last, close look at his family, and continued with heavy steps.

"All in order," the check-man at the gate said, with an ambivalent smile, and repeated his wishes to the man before him. "Bon voyage, good luck, don't forget us."

Lampis heard nothing else and saw nothing, until he started climbing the ladder on the side of the ship. He had stepped off the glorious, blood-saturated soil of Greece. He stopped halfway up, scanned the horizon, and tried to store all within sight: the sidewalk cafes; the white-washed building lining the shore boulevard; the fluttering flags; the cross on the dome of St. Nicholas church; the distant mountain ridges of Hymetos. The man behind him waited respectfully.

Lampis resumed his ascent, slowly, deliberately, almost passively. After a quick look at the flag at the top of the mast and at the sky above, he acknowledged the steward's motioning.

The descent into the bowels of the ship, as he silently followed the steward reminded him of the Souls of the departed following *Charon* (death); the walk along the long corridors, of the approach for the final judgment; his small cabin, with two tiers of two bunks across each other, of the sleeping quarters for slaves in the Roman galleys.

He flung his suitcase on the upper bunk next to the porthole to claim it, and rushed out and up the stairs, like Orpheus escaping. The decks were crowded. Those farther back from the railings stood on their toes or jumped for another glimpse of those left behind. His heart throbbed for another look at his family, but he thought it unfair to try to worm his way through the crowd to the front. The solution to his problem became obvious when he looked at the mast.

Lampis climbed about ten meters above the deck, braced with his right arm, suspended in mid-air and started waving his bouquet of Thyme in his left hand furiously. A member of the crew raised his right hand as if to command "come down from there," but waved instead, "I understand," and walked away with a rueful smile.

Nearby, a young woman smiled at him, and in that smile, he read approval, envy, and deep appreciation of his sentiments.

After scanning the pier, Lampis spotted his sister, this side of the gate, leaning against his trusted friend of many years, now a soldier. A few meters away, on the other side of the fence, Aunt Violetta waved her scarf above her head, holding her little girl in her arm. She had given him the bouquet of Thyme, having picked it in a field excursion a few days earlier, in premonition of his departure, as a symbol of the purity of her family's love. Aunt Nikki was comforted by her all-pure and devoted husband, Uncle George, and Uncle Vasiles cuddled his two boys who were waving their little hands

The void from his parent's absence was filled, partly, with flashing images of their crossing themselves, side-by-side, before the Holy Icons; of leaning on the rails of the balcony, side-by-side again, to disperse their anguish and to send their blessings over the mountain-tops; and of fortifying their aching hearts by repeating, "Thy will be done, Oh Lord."

He heard the tune, "Anchors aweigh and start full speed, away from the deserted poor village, to other ports, to foreign lands, the breeze shall carry us safely." He thought how it would stir the emotions of the determined and give courage to the reluctant. Those on the pier, hearing the tune, broke out in sobs, soaking with tears the handkerchiefs meant for waving. Through moist eyes, he focused on his sobbing sister whose shoulders were held by his trusted friend.

Lampis's anticipation of "reaching other ports and observing foreign people," from the tune that repeatedly played, conflicted with his apprehension and sadness of leaving the familiarity of his land and the warmth of his family. It kept the tears from his cheeks and gave a new expression to his smile, as he kept waving his bouquet.

The resolute whistle by the ocean liner resounded across the port, echoed from the buildings that lined the shore boulevards, and resonated against the mast and chest walls.

The ropes from the tug boats stretched and strained. The blue-brown waters churned and bubbled around the midget pulling at the giant, and the majestic ocean liner *Nea Hellas* (New Greece), slowly pulled away from the pier.

Still perched high on the mast, Lampis kept the same view until the ship turned about two hundred seventy degrees. For a last glimpse of his sister, relatives, and friends, who came to see him off, he slid down from the mast, ran to the stern and resumed waving the bouquet. He blew kisses to those he left behind and to the land of his birth.

Gradually, the figures became less distinct and eventually, he recognized only a vague movement in the crowd.

The line of people blended with the horizon, and eventually he walked slowly toward the tourist class lounge, wondering whether he could recognize his three cabinmates, whom he met briefly when the steward took him and his cardboard suitcase to the cabin. He would have to share his cabin with them for the next fifteen or sixteen nights; he should make their acquaintance now. He hoped that they would be polite, understanding, and deferential.

He spoke to the young woman who had smiled at him earlier when he had climbed the mast. After she learned his name and told him hers, she walked by his side. He prayed that they would be seated at the same table, at the same sitting.

Maybe he could share his thoughts with her. She looked serene, sweet, and understanding. For the moment, they chose to keep their thoughts to themselves.

They had reached the lounge. "I see my mother. I must go to her," she said, smiling. She gave him her hand. "Had I seen in a movie what you did, climbing the mast, I would have thought that could happen only in a movie. I hope to see you later."

Lampis wandered through the lounge, found his cabinmates, and introduced himself. He decided, without much deliberation, that he did not have much in common with them. They were older and appeared disappointed that he was younger, and probably immature or indiscreet. One looked to his left, in his brief and condescending introduction. The second hardly acknowledged his presence with a limp handshake, and the third inquired, looking at him and the other two successively, whether he snored.

He met Demetri, a boy from his hometown, who was headed for Canada. Demetri looked to him for guidance and support. In his youth and innocence, and not having left the confines of the village before, he thought of Lampis as "cosmopolitan." He clung to Lampis and asked questions uninhibitedly and trustingly, seeking approval of, or corrections, in his manners.

Demetri's presence, and discreetness, promised the forging of a pure friendship and a strong link to the past twenty years. He assumed his charge would give the journey an additional meaning. He would talk with him about his plans, his anticipations and his dreams. He would also warn Demetri about choosing his friends and about the dangers of falling into the habits of smoking, drinking and gambling, echoing Aunt Katerina's advice. He would tell him about self-respect and about separating good from evil and remind him of his parent's expectations.

Lampis discovered an old schoolmate, Peter and his sister, Maria, as they strolled the opposite way. They were mere acquaintances in the past and were glad to see each other. He hoped to enjoy talking with them about his plans and sharing a laugh. Peter had the charge of his sister and suggested that his friend dance with her from time to time. Maria, like Demetri, was trusting and pure. Her timid smile displayed the purity of her heart and thoughts.

Maria and Peter added two more links to the chain of security stretching back to the lost horizon. He was grateful for their presence, not doubting or questioning their decency, sincerity, or discretion. He would spend as much time with them as they would allow.

The dinner bell sounded.

"Dinner served, second sitting," the steward cried.

Lampis had chosen the second sitting. It added a new memorable and romantic experience, reminding him that he was on board a ship. He had decided that this voyage would be to a destiny, not a destination.

He found the others, at the dinner table, preoccupied with their thoughts. The silence, interrupted only with the customary polite amenities, accentuated the pervasive sadness.

A few tables away, Kalliope, the girl who had walked alongside him on the deck after the last look at the familiar horizon, lifted her glass and toasted him with a smile on her lips and in her large, brown eyes.

"Would you like to join us?" she asked, with a slight raising of her eyebrows and a tilt of her head at the empty chair next to her.

She introduced him to her mother, a lady of classical beauty and deportment, and to her little brother, a very bright boy of twelve. The easy smiles and the absence of sadness contrasted with the rest of the passengers.

"We are going to join my two older brothers in New York," Kalliope said. She halted for a moment, as if reaching for strength or ensuring that she was not transgressing. "My father had died in combat against the German Paratroopers in the battle of Crete."

"I admire your father's heroism. He is an example for imitation or inspiration to all who cherish and long for freedom," Lampis said.

"And you? When did you decide to go to the United States?" Kalliope asked.

"I decided to emigrate two months ago, which meant there was much scurrying to get all the documents that I needed." He told her about his last-minute acquisition of the final papers.

"And your parents? Did they see you off at the dock?"

"No," he said, and paused. "I left without a farewell embrace by my parents, although my sister and relatives saw me off." Kalliope's attentiveness and response convinced him of her genuine sensitivity and refined manners.

"Would you like to meet in the lounge, after supper, to get better acquainted?" she asked.

He nodded. Her suggestions promised the beginning of a needed friendship.

Lampis stood at the rail, watching the blinking lights studding the shores of the homeland and its islands, trying to store these last images in detail.

A middle-aged man leaned next to him against the rail. "You are a very good-looking young man. Are you traveling alone?" he said.

Lampis nodded. "Yes."

The man began talking. "I appreciate music. It is my obsession, and all the fine arts."

As Lampis listened politely, his tolerance was taxed, especially when some of the man's inquiries and overtures suggested subtle erotic designs. The repeated comments about his good looks were disturbing and resented.

Lampis drew the line, clearly and tactfully, discouraging further overtures.

When he arrived at the lounge, he realized that he was late. Kalliope was sitting there. He felt guilty for keeping her waiting.

After the dance, they walked the length of the deck, mostly in silence, leaning frequently against the rails and gazing for long intervals at the distant gray shores, isolated blinking lights or flashes of the lonely light houses, and the dark, undulating waters or the whiteness fanning out behind the ship. The gentle splashing of the waves, in caressing the sides of the ship, stirred a new awareness of life in the silence of the night, under the canopy of stars, and the scattered whitecaps. He took her to her cabin about one o'clock in the morning and returned on deck, where under a weak light, he condensed his thoughts of the previous night.

The previous night, Lampis had talked to his sister for half the night, mostly about his thoughts of his parents' and two younger brothers' reaction to his leaving, perhaps forever, without an embracing farewell or a chance to exchange vows of "eternal" remembrance and love. The risk of postponing his departure for the next trip of *Nea Hellas* seemed too high, with his approaching military age to serve the "fatherland" before emigrating. Also, he had anticipated, from one day to the next, an order from the Ministry of Military Affairs forbidding emigration from his class, "the class of 1951."

His heart would remain heavy, he knew, until the day he saw them again, in spite of his faith in their understanding and love. While writing, he thought, "Maybe I'll read it to Kalliope. She would understand."

When he returned to his cabin, the aloof cabinmate was sighing heavily. The frivolous one, who had asked whether any of his cabinmates snored, was snoring sonorously. The third one was quietly sleeping or praying.

Keeping pace with the overlapping events of the day and harnessing his emotions, had left little room for reflection or contemplation. Lampis lay in his bunk, retracing his actions and reaction, and reassessing his reserves and his vulnerabilities. He prayed that his parents would find solace in their faith and in their other three children, and remember that seven years ago, they had parted with him, not knowing whether they would see him again or whether he would ever reach his destination.

CHAPTER 2

AS LAMPIS LAY IN HIS BUNK, the fleeting and overlapping memories resurfaced and regained all the vividness of the early morning of April 28, 1944, and the next two days.

Their home and the rest of the village, had been burned on March 14, by the German Army. They had been crowded, all six of them, in a tiny room. It was an extension of the house that they had managed to salvage after the Germans withdrew. They had tried to survive on what little his mother's heroic and superhuman efforts had managed to save from the fire and the pillage. The alms from the nearby villages stopped after the continuing plunder and destruction.

Uncle Vasiles's offer to take him, the oldest, to lighten their burden, was weighed carefully by his parents, before reaching the painful decision that his and their chances of survival may be better if he went.

Lampis left at three o'clock the following morning by mule. He traveled one and one-half hours to Uncle Thanases's village. Uncle Thanases, a distant relative, had gotten a permit from the German authorities to have a boy stay with him, and he had promised Lampis's parents to deliver him to Uncle Vasiles in Athens

The parting with his father at the village square, after a prolonged tight embrace and an unrestrained torrent of sobs, made the darkness of the night even more foreboding and oppressive. The deliberate pace of the mule, with the occasional stumble, the monotony of the water current in the creek, his mother's silence and frequent heavy sighs, and his surrender to the mercy of the Fates stretched the journey to endlessness. Their safety in their steep ascent along the winding path, known as the 'Donkey Precipice,' was trusted to the sense and strength of the mule.

They arrived at Agriacona. He could hardly trace the outline of his village, Kaltezai, across the deep gorge and narrow valley stretching before it. It might have been easier to see it before the burning when all the houses were still white-washed in lime, he reasoned.

Lampis's aching heart was warmed by the caresses of old *Yiayia* (grandmother) Villiena. His anguish was softened by the sweet glances of her daughter, Aunt Giannoula. He clung to his mother for the next fifteen minutes before he was smothered with her kisses and prayers.

"May God and the all-Holy Virgin Mary protect you and bring you safely back to us," she said, in her last embrace.

Lampis left shortly with Uncle Thanases and his wife.

His first ride on a truck, or any self-propelled vehicle, seemed as if he were on the ferry traveling across the Styx. The arrival in Tripoli and the wait for clearance by the German authorities and their Collaborator Security Battalions was scary, like the approach to the gates of Hell and the scrutiny by the devils. Lampis dipped deep into his young soul to resolve the drowning hopes and to push his fear out of recognition. They stopped on the other side of Tripoli for another search and inspection. He did not resent the delay, because his motion sickness had reached its peak.

The slow travel along the worn-out road, up and down the hills, forced them to spend the night in Achladocampos (Pear-plane). Traveling at night was forbidden. They slept on the floor of a near-empty general store. His lying next to a pretty seventeen-year-old girl kept him awake through most of the night fearing embarrassment in inadvertently touching her.

The next day, they traveled slowly again, even in the plains with straight roads. Not knowing when he might be ordered to stop for another search and check by the patrols, or at what turn the next roadblock might appear, the driver kept his speed to where a good horse or mule could overtake it at a trot. The landscape appeared desolate. Lampis could not decide whether the silhouettes along the distant ridges or slopes were of trees or soldiers.

People in the streets of Argos and Corinth either displayed defiance or evoked pity. The lines of German soldiers along both sides of the bridge, across the canal of Corinth, intensified the weight of oppression. Words and even glances, were scarce, as if the quota of words preassigned for the life of each of them were being depleted.

Lampis looked at the heaving and surging sea on his right and at the steep rocky slopes on his left. His curiosity kept his gaze to the right. He was familiar with the slopes and ridges. The dense, low clouds, and gray, menacing waves, and the truck's groaning engine were so depressingly different from what he had read in poems about the sunlit hills and the blueness of the sky reflecting in the sparkling waters of the Saronic Gulf.

The truck stopped among a few other trucks at a roadblock at Aghioe Theodoroi (St. Theodores). This inspection was not of the cargo or the load on the truck. That was done thoroughly before crossing the canal. This was an inspection of the travelers, for proper "Permits to Travel." Lampis became frightened when he heard the whispers, that those without a permit would have their hands tied behind them and would be thrown into the sea. He looked at the waves and imagined the tossed bodies sinking and floating, face-up, face-down.

How long had he been alone in the truck? Where was his uncle with the permit and the promise to protect him? He looked again at the hellish waves and compressed clouds about thirty meters away. "I am not going to drown in that sea.

17

My soul couldn't make it to heaven through those clouds. I'll run away, up to those mountain slopes," he thought.

He began to descend from the truck when a woman dressed in black came up to him. "Where are you going?" she asked.

"I am going to run. I'd rather die by a bullet than drown in that sea," he answered.

"Don't you have a permit? How are you traveling?" she asked, appearing disturbed.

"My uncle had a permit to take me with him, but I don't know where he is. I don't know what happened to him."

He glanced around to the right, to decide which direction to take, and then he saw his uncle. "There he is, coming out of the building with his wife at his arm."

"He went through inspection without you. Get in the truck," she ordered, after a quick look around.

He obeyed without hesitation.

The woman in black leapt into the truck, as if lifted by an invisible divinity. She pulled down the canvas from the roof in the back of the truck, opened a suitcase and took out a dress. She put it on him, yanking it over his head. She rolled his short pants up to his midthigh and put a kerchief on his head and tied it under his chin. "You are now my daughter. I have a permit for a daughter."

She raised the canvas, took his hand and climbed down from the truck and guided him to the building for inspection.

He followed, with unconditional and absolute trust.

The German officer behind the desk, looked at him and his "mother" and half-smiled, reaching out to caress his cheek gently. Lampis's right hand clutched tightly the hand of his savior. He followed her out of the building, across the square to the truck and looked at her divinely transfigured face for the last time.

The next thing he remembered was a plea from Uncle Thanases's sister-in-law to stop rocking on the chair in her living room. He must have been numb after his narrow escape.

"Where is Uncle Thanases?" he asked.

"He went to find your Uncle Vasiles before the curfew. I hope he finds him."

Uncle Vasiles came, with his brother-in-law, Metsos, to rescue Lampis from confusion and uncertainty.

Lampis felt secure, sitting in the small taxi, on the lap of Uncle Metsos, another "uncle" added to the list, while Uncle Vasiles held his hand.

Someone's coarse snoring interrupted Lampis's thoughts. He realized that he had been lying in his bunk in the cabin, daydreaming. The muffled roar of the engines and the perpetual splashing of the waves hypnotized him. He fell asleep amid the gentle rocking of the ship. His sleep was deep and dreamless. Awakened briefly by the gongs of the first bell for breakfast, he promptly resumed sleep for another hour.

Breakfast at sea, for the first time, with the glasses half-full against spilling by the swaying of the ship, and the plates secured against sliding from side to side or to and fro, was as hearty as it was exciting. Most passengers did not show up for breakfast, nursing their seasickness and/or their sadness in their cabins.

The decks, washed by the waves during the rounding of Cape Maleas, were deserted. Holding on to the rails, Lampis stared at the resentment of the Mediterranean, with its raised and foaming waves. He wondered whether the sea would ever surrender the secrets from its depth or keep teasing man by revealing only a few samples while toying with him on its surface. He wondered if his thoughts, deposited on the waves, would either carry him to his past or to fantasizing. Remembering, thinking, and dreaming, seemed to change with the rise, the ripples, and the sounds of the sea. The rainbows in the splashes of the waves hypnotized and exalted his spirits almost at the same time. He strained to discern the shores. He fixed his gaze on the gliding and diving seagulls and delighted in the playfulness of the escorting dolphins. Lampis lost track of and concern for time. He felt timeless, like the sea.

Lost in his thoughts, he was hardly disturbed by Kalliope's presence.

"Good morning," she said.

"Good morning," he replied.

They gazed and thought separately, side by side, for an inestimable interval before deciding to share their thoughts. Their words, phrases, or sentences served as the connections of their thoughts. Then the memories of the past dominated the conversation.

"Would you like to hear me read last night's condensed thoughts?" he asked.

She nodded.

He left for the cabin and returned with the paper.

Kalliope was still scanning the horizon.

They walked to a bench and sat next to each other. He read:

> *Oh night, do not retreat; do not fold your dark veils;*
> *Do not allow the sun to appear and set the firmament ablaze -*
> *Keep your morning star, do not fade*
> *Keep your twinkling stars, even as the resting clouds*
> *Change to purple in the East,*
> *Announcing the imminent sunrise*
> *And promising to expose all that's hidden;*
> *Do not listen to the commands of the upstart day.*
> *Daylight is jealous, it will drive Dawn away.*
> *It wishes to drive joy from my spinning life.*

Oh, Morning Star, do not blur,
Oh Dawn, do not brighten up,
Oh Sun, do not awaken nature from its dreams,
And do not postpone the day that will take me
From the sacred grounds of my fathers,
The faces that I have loved.
I have lost the desire to smell the flowers of strange lands.
Oh Breeze, keep cooling Dawn against the Sun;
Oh, Night Owl, do not return to the crags of the ruins yet,
You are still hungry.
Oh Night, do not retreat. Stay, stay one moment longer;
Do not roll up my last Dawn in Greece;
Give me another chance to taste the sweetness
Of the land of my birth.
Give me another moment's chance to store
The brightness of Greece's morning star in my heart;
Give me a chance to gather the scents of Dawn
And the purple of the horizon for keepsakes –
For this chance, do not depart yet, I implore you!
Keep the moon bright, do not lift the mist from the ravines and
ridges.
Let me take the ashes of the clash from your battle with the sun –
To pit against the long evenings of the loneliness in the future.
Do not retreat, dear Night,
Hold on to this last Dawn.

After he finished reading it, he waited for her response.

"Did you loathe leaving so much?" she asked, staring at the flag.

He fixed his eyes on his open notebook. "Yes," he answered.

"Then, why did you leave?" she continued, unable or unwilling to look in any other direction.

"I could not resist the call of the Siren to the future, and I wasn't tied to the mast of the present," he said, and stopped.

There was silence.

"And that great love, what will happen to it? Will it be transformed to another object, and wither with time, or be stored for keepsake?"

"It won't change," he replied. "It won't be transferred. It will just become the guide to my dreams and goals, keeping me from turning to simple and transient pleasures, and sustaining me in cultivating another love to match it." He talked slowly, deliberately, almost to himself.

He needed time to reflect.

He walked away after a while, without looking at her, holding on to the rails. He thought of what he had just said, hoping that she understood.

Kalliope walked up to him, placed her hand on his and looked at him with moist eyes. "Thank you for sharing your poem with me," she whispered, even though there was no one around. "I love my mother. She understands me. May I show it to her and tell her what you just said? Maybe she'll help me understand you better."

"You may," he said. "But it isn't a poem. It's more like a prayer, or better yet, a dirge."

"If you write some more, will you? I'd like to read it."

He wanted to change the subject.

"Your brothers will be happy to see you again," he said, speaking rapidly. "They'll be proud of you. How long has it been since they saw you last? You must have been a little girl when they left. Your brothers' friends will be visiting them more often now."

He did not look to see whether she blushed, but it seemed that it worked.

She was silent for a long time, her gaze parallel with his. He could sense that.

"Where are you going to live in America?" she asked.

"My uncles in Chicago sponsored me. I will live there."

"Do you know them well?"

It seemed she was making conversation.

"Not at all. Two of them I have never seen. The other I met twice, once when I was eight and the next time when I was sixteen. I don't expect much understanding or support. They don't even know my mother. They left when she was a little girl."

"You're going to be with strangers. You're strong. You'll reach your goal. I hope your goal is a lofty one," she said, speaking with conviction, and emphasizing each sentence.

They strolled on deck, greeting or nodding at some new acquaintances, and being careful not to bump into each other with the rocking of the ship.

They didn't talk anymore.

She folded her arms tightly across her chest. "I wonder what my mother is doing. I admit that it is cold." She turned and looked at him "Will I see you later? There is a movie in the afternoon."

"I think I'll go to the library and see what they have," he said, hoping that she'd understand that he wished to spend time alone, thinking.

She must have understood. She didn't talk about the movie, nor did she inquire about the library.

Demetri joined Lampis on deck and informed him that Kalliope had gone to the movie with her mother. It seemed that Demetri, fascinated by her, was enjoying a vicarious pleasure with Lampis spending so much time with Kalliope. Lampis secretly wondered whether she knew that he had gone to the piano concert, or whether anybody noticed that something strange had happened to him during the concert (many years later, he would make his own diagnosis of psychomotor epilepsy).

"Demetri, I'll meet you in the lounge in about an hour," he told him. He needed some time alone.

Lampis thought of yesterday, of what lay ahead, of his childhood and tribulations. He thought of his heartbreaks and his determination. He extrapolated from his encounters with the uncle that he knew, that determination was not enough. Obsession must grow and dominate.

He lamented, and was relieved, alternatively, that Kalliope would stay in New York. He wondered what her influence on him would be. He wondered whether he would be comparing others to her, and what made her "special." Did her understanding exceed her knowledge? He thought about how much time or how little time he would share with her. He even wondered how she would be when in love, or what type of man she would likely fall in love with.

What would Kalliope think if he avoided her for a day or two? He'd be courteous, discreet, and distant. He would spend more time with Demetri and socialize more with Peter and Maria. He would make new acquaintances. He'd spend time tomorrow with his frivolous cabinmate in Naples and would ask him if he chose to visit Pompei.

Lampis was uncomfortable in his realization that Kalliope was filling a void or displacing other images too quickly. He'd rather preserve the void for a clearer resonance of the past. He was afraid that her comforting words might be followed by complacency or that her luminous image would blur his memories of yesterday. He had to convince himself that he indeed was on board a ship bound for America, and that he had left his family and country, and that he must not look back. He needed solitude to assert his individuality and uniqueness; to appreciate that he was with and not of this crowd. He needed to search in his past for sustenance and strength.

Kalliope's presence would be a hindrance, for the present. Perhaps in a few days, he could measure her against his memories and dreams of the past, tall and erect in her own strength.

He strolled from one deck to another, watching the smoke from the chimney stretch parallel to the churning waters behind the ship. He looked past the crew performing their tasks and stepped aside when he met other passengers. He estimated the height of the masts, and struggled to discipline his thoughts and memories, traveling in a direction opposite the ship's.

Standing at the bow, gazing ahead, he tried to see behind the horizon, feeling the strong breeze cleaving his face. He returned to the stern, leaning against the rails to watch the effortless gliding of the seagulls. Kalliope glided in his thoughts, much like the seagulls that followed the ship.

He tried to imagine his strong father holding his mother's shoulders, and looking, through moist eyes, directly into her pained soul, telling her, "Wife, our son is following his destiny. Let's pray that God gives him strength to fulfill his dreams. Our love will keep him. He's gone with our blessings."

Lampis pictured his mother agreeing to what his father said, but in private, she would probably curse the fates that took her young son far away from her. She would lament that it was only yesterday that she rocked him in her arms, nursed him through his illnesses, and smiled while he shaved for the first time. She had resolved to never surrender him to the Communist guerillas. She would busy herself to dull the pain and to conceal her sorrow and would watch his father taking off for the field with an axe and hoe to transfer his thoughts from his departed son to his work.

Lampis imagined his brothers talking about returning home from school for the Easter holidays, alternating between excitement and sadness.

"Easter holidays," they'd exclaim. "Lampis will spend them on the ship, alone."

His family would be silent at the dinner table, not daring to ask aloud, "I wonder where he is now?" fearing stimulating the grief of separation, and following up with the inevitable, "We may never see Lampis again."

Lampis knew his family. After some effort, they would raise their glasses and toast to his safe voyage. They would change the subject quickly, and each one would silently pray and wait for the other to leave the table first. Any visitors, any distraction, would be welcomed. During Holy Week, the tolling church bells would summon the faithful to follow Christ's passion, accentuated and appreciated better in the mellow candlelight in the darkness of early night. On Holy Friday, the mourning tolls would silence the voices of Spring, the distant bleating of an impetuous goat, or the crisp chirping of an irreverent sparrow. His brothers would gather wild flowers from the fields to decorate Christ's tomb (*Epitaphios*), challenging the vigor of their adolescence to resist laughing or the temptation to throw stones at an inviting target, lest they inflict pain on Christ. In the child's fantasy, every part of the creation, animate and inanimate, was identified with Christ on that day.

He followed his brothers through the ravines and slopes and stopped short of imagining them grown up.

Then he thought about Demetra and wondered whether her transformation from being defiant and callous to having an awareness of pain at the reality of parting would last longer than it took her to climb from the vantage point where she had ascended to wave goodbye. He contemplated if that last image of her, more human, would prevail over time, or if he would continue rationalizing her behavior.

Did she or did she not love him? If she did, why did she show it in such a strange way? What was she afraid of? And why was he attracted to this apparently untamable, unfathomable girl?

Had she been standing here with him, she would probably have accepted his fascination with the successive rainbows in the arches, formed by the waves that splashed against the sides of the ship. She would probably have listened to his reading of the messages carried by the waves and the drifting clouds, but she would not have let go of the rail and be transported with him to his worlds.

"Some lucky American girls."

Lampis turned and saw the urbane and presumptuous musician. This phrase became suspended somewhere between them, sounding distant, and would have been carried away by the breeze, had the musician's determination to make his presence felt not been pursued with a repetition of the phrase followed by a deep sigh.

Lampis resented the intrusion but switching his thoughts to the present was not unwelcomed. He wondered whether the American girls were all lovely and trusting, as he had seen them in the movies, and whether, one day, he'd be walking hand-in-hand, laughing and running in the meadows with one of them. He wondered whether new dreams and nostalgia would compete with his plans.

"What are your thoughts, plans, and loves?" the musician asked Lampis.

Lampis looked straight ahead at the white-capped waves, and into the future. "I am going to study medicine," he replied. "I took a vow with two other members of "the first triumvirate" to become physicians. We had graduated from high school, and had agreed, late one evening in March of last year, to go out into the country and plan our course."

Lampis thought about the quiet of the dusk on that evening, on a deserted hill, sitting on a rock. They had exchanged idealistic and pragmatic ideas, deliberating and concluding that their mission had been preordained. They had to study medicine."

"What happened to the other two?"

"They were successful in the competitive entrance examination and had matriculated into medical school in Greece," he replied. "I must follow my mission in America. I might take longer, but I will reach my goal, for sure."

Whether the musician or anyone believed him or not, it did not matter.

"Did you leave a girl behind?"

Lampis didn't know how to answer that question. Perhaps Demetra could have been his girl, if he had not left. The images, both from memories and dreams, flashed quickly and blurred, fusing with each other as in a kaleidoscope. He smiled. "No," he replied resolutely. He hoped his companion had picked up the suggestion that he had transgressed propriety.

Being either considerate or using a new approach, the musician asked no more questions, but talked about his love of music. "I am concerned about all those young people, severed from their roots and venturing into the unknown, and I pray for their parents' anguish to be relieved."

During the brief pauses, Lampis's thoughts traveled, unbridled, to some of the other emigrants, and their homes and futures. He wondered who would return and when, and who would have or master the strength to realize his dreams, and who would wander aimlessly and never grow new roots. The thoughts of Kalliope returned and changed into a wish that she would come by his way to rescue him from his whirling emotions.

Lampis and the musician strolled the length of the deck, talking, but hardly looking at each other. They finally parted to their separate worlds, with a polite "au revoir."

Lampis had overtaxed his mind and overcharged his sentiments. He looked for Demetri, who might be lonely and homesick. He would tell him stories about his father's behavior during or after a card game, to make him laugh, and acquaint him with another lovable side to his father. He would tell him how everybody thought that Demetri's mother was the "sweetest lady," and he then would enjoy watching Demetri's show of appreciation and privilege. He hoped that Demetri would resolve to make his parents proud of him and to nurture, or even idealize their affections.

Or perhaps he would find Kostas and listen to his bragging confabulations, pretending he believed his stories and wondering how they would change the next time they were repeated. He would not talk very much to Kostas, just listen, lest Kostas be carried too far with his boasting.

Lampis found Demetri in the lounge, bright-eyed and happy, with some other boys and young girls. They were laughing, apparently enjoying each other's stories or jokes – the laughter of innocence, relief, and escape. Demetri saw him and showed in the gleam of his eyes, his dilemma whether to stay with his new friends or join his older friend.

Their eye contact reiterated the trust and bond between them. He smiled at Demetri, appreciating the purity and strength of his attachment, and left him with his new friends. He would tell him about his parents later, or tomorrow. They would have plenty of time together in the next fifteen days.

Lampis wished to be alone again, to reminisce.

He passed through the lounge. Most people there seemed subdued or numbed. He wondered, for a moment, whether the grief of parting with their families or the apprehension for what was in store for them predominated. He felt stronger than his fellow travelers – he had no apprehension.

He saw Kalliope sitting across from her mother, staring out the window. Peter was serious in his role as the older brother and protector of Maria. Kostas had found some more gullible listeners and was enjoying his bragging with a cigarette in his hand.

Two of Lampis's cabinmates were engaged in a card game. The frivolous one talked constantly, apparently enjoying the game, while the other, the one who sighed heavily during the night, was lost in his thoughts and looking past his cards.

Lampis walked out on deck again, straining to see the coast on the North or other ships going South. He abandoned his attempts to collect his thoughts and allowed flashes of memories, dreams, and images to appear and recede in disorder. The memory of his newborn brother, George, crying in the bassinet was displaced by that of his father winning the foot race. That, in turn, was interrupted by his promise to his friend that he will return to Greece after graduating from medical school.

Someone coughed. Lampis turned and looked. It was an old man with a cigarette in his hand. What in the world was this man going to America for? He tried to imagine how this deeply tanned man, with the sun-bleached hair and calloused hands from working in the fields, would look, after working in a factory or washing dishes in a restaurant. Lampis resolved to work hard to reach his goal.

Oblivious of time, Lampis walked along the deck, exploring, without noticing the different levels, until the dinner bell called for the first sitting. He wondered whether he would be hungry by the time the second sitting was called.

CHAPTER 3

SOMEHOW, THE RINGING OF THE DINNER BELL restored Lampis's strength to gather his wits and made him aware of the stretching links with the past. It positioned him precisely into space and time and unfolded a progressively dimming future into the distance. Whether for security or in search of courage, Lampis chose to reach back into his past, to retrace the development of his self and to sort out the events that set him on this path. He would start now and resume tomorrow, and the next day. He would have plenty of time in the next fifteen days.

Lampis did not remember whether he knew his name, but at the time he was frustrated when the child he saw in the mirror on the wall hid from him, as he ran out to the balcony to play with him. Nor could he recall his sister's birth. She was almost two years younger than him. One day, there she was. His cousin Nick's share in the frustration in not being able to open the snaps of his one-piece blouse-pants was as genuine as his own joy when his all-reliable grandmother "freed" him to answer the call of nature.

Lampis's bewilderment (he was four and one-half years old then) when he unexpectedly walked into the room where his mother had just given birth to his brother, George, was mixed with fright as he screamed, "Why are you killing my mother?" He watched his grandmother washing the baby in a large pan. The same baby aroused neither jealousy or curiosity when at his mother's breast. Lampis was too busy playing priest or soldier with his sister and cousin Nick. By the time that he finished "mass" and gave his sister and Nick "communion" or returned from his "tour of duty," walking to and from the balcony, the baby was forgotten.

His mother was identified with the Madonna on the iconostas in church and his father was a blend of the archangels Michael and Gabriel. The similarities between the prophet Elijah or the "father" of the Holy Trinity icon and his grandfather were too obvious. As for his grandmother, she was what the hen was to the chicks – warm, comforting, protecting, and giving. Hiding in the folds of her long skirts was not just a game, or just finding refuge, it was nurturing and revitalizing. When she opened her arms to gather all three of them in – Nick, his sister, and him – it was like the "wider than heavens" painting of the Almighty at the dome of the monastery.

When *Papou* (Grandfather) would return from the fields, Lampis and the others would hear the distant sound of the bells that hung on the necks of the mule and cows, and they'd run to meet him and be rewarded by being lifted on the back of the mule, one behind the other, with arms tight around each other's waist (whoever arrived first, would sit up front). And they'd be rewarded by a bunch of wild flowers, berries, figs, or roasted corn on the cob. They'd giggle and jump up and down as *Papou* told everybody how he found them; one under a squash plant, and the other under a tomato plant, and the third suckling on a female hare. He didn't know how they got there, but since they seemed pretty and nice he decided their grandmother wouldn't mind having them around for company. The female hare would be looking all over for them, but grandfather would be sure to comfort her the next day.

In bed at night when the *megali* (big ones) threatened or bribed them, they were never tired. Lampis and his siblings asked each other why the dogs barked only at night, and what the children on the other side of the world, behind the mountain on the west, Tsemberou, were doing? They wondered how the sun returned to the mountain on the east, *Aghios Christophoros* (Saint Christopher). Whispering and giggling, they went to sleep, mingling their fantasies of the day with their dreams. In the morning, hearing someone approaching, they pretended to be asleep, and resumed their giggling when awakened. Then they would hang on their mother's or grandmother's neck, proud in their conviction that they had surprised those in whose bosom they felt so secure and loved.

Every day seemed so full, eventful, and long. They imitated the chirping of the birds and the calls of the animals, and smelled the flowers, taking turns. They estimated the distance to the Taygetus Mountains and prayed to God to make them understand the language of the animals and birds; when looking up to the sky, they were convinced that their home was the very center of the world (this conviction caused a great deal of consternation when a long time later, at the age of six years, he looked up to see that the center was also directly above his maternal grandmother's house, in a different village, and finally resolved this paradox by concluding that the center of the world was following him). They wondered why the bee buzzed in its flight and why the butterfly did not, and why the cypress trees grew straight up and the fig tree spread out. They asked why the sparrows and swallows lived in people's homes while the other birds preferred living in the trees and forests. They'd see little faces like their own in the flowers, and they would exclaim how they heard the *neraides* (nymphs) singing. In church, they would strain to see God in the Inner Sanctum and knew that He was watching them and that His angels were guarding them day and night. The priest was one of the Saints, only that he had come off one of the icons during the day and would return at night.

And so, their days would pass, each bringing new excitement and temporarily pushing back the memories of yesterday to make room for the impressions of today. They were not concerned about tomorrow. Grandmother and Mother would be there in the mornings while Grandfather and Father would return in the evenings.

The sweet sound of the ship's bell, announcing the second sitting for dinner, so different from the church bells at vespers, transported Lampis from the doorsteps of his house, where he and his companions were straining to hear the familiar cow and mule bells, to the deck of the ship. Here, he was alone, holding onto the rails, and unwilling to look to the right or to the left, not ready to see faces that did not look like cousin Nick's or his sister's. He would return to the same spot later, or tomorrow, to unfold more memories and "get to know" how he came here and who he was.

Sitting at the dinner table with the same people and being served by the same stewards, was never boring. Their sighs, their small talk, their fears, and their mannerisms would initiate a new series of questions about them and about himself. Invariably, he would find himself, by comparison, stronger and better equipped for the future.

"What are you going to do in America?" one new friend asked him.

"I am going to study medicine," he answered, matter-of-factly. "And you?"

"I am going to be washing dishes," he replied.

"I am going to do that, too," Lampis said.

Lampis knew from his geography, that the distance between Chicago and Boston, or Chicago and New York were great, but he politely and comfortingly agreed with his new friends that they would meet again in America. He listened to their stories of suffering and sacrificing during the war. He decided that they were heroic and durable, and that they had passed the severest test, and would plow ahead, whether under the whip or at the reigns. He didn't know and didn't ask what their ultimate goals were.

Lampis clinked glasses with them and repeated the "Es egyan (to your health), or "Kali patrida (happy return to the fatherland)" - the latter, with a smile about its triteness (it had been used for centuries) and with a silent prayer that it would come true, and the former, meant mostly for the others, since in the vigor of his youth, he had seen his own health as forever robust.

Lampis raised his glass to Kalliope.

She acknowledged his gesture by tipping her glass and touching it to her lips.

One of his new companions smiled benevolently. "Nice girl."

One by one, they left the table, and he remained alone for a few minutes, chatting with the stewards about the life they had chosen and about their aspirations, or he simply compared himself with the canary in the swaying cage.

When his thoughts began to revolve, he left for the deck again, veering right so as to face North. There, he watched for the lights of villages or towns in the distant shores. If there were no mountains behind the shores, the lights of the villages seemed to blend with the stars at the horizon. If there was a space between the lights and the stars, he would try to estimate the height of the mountain by the broadness of the dark space. He would try and imagine life in the towns or villages; youths serenading their girls or displaying pranks; old men telling stories to each other at coffee-houses, or to their grandchildren by the fireside; middle-aged men contemplating plans for the future or cursing their fates. He would think of young girls giggling at each other's fibs, and little children sleeping peacefully in dimly lit rooms. He imagined them to be very similar to the folks in his village and wondered what possessed people like them, or their leaders, to go to war with other populations.

Lampis tried to estimate the time from the moment the village lights appeared on his left, to the moment they dimmed on his right, as the ship sailed westward. He invariably lost track of time, as his thoughts were distracted by memories, people whispering nearby, footsteps behind him, and an occasional polite greeting. He looked at the stars and tried to name the constellations and the bright ones and retracted his thoughts quickly when he ventured to wonder about the space between and beyond the stars.

At times, his thoughts were scattered or receded into vague notions as soon as they were formulated. At other times, Lampis aborted his thoughts as soon as they were conceived, causing his mind to be sterile and blank – so blank, that he was not aware of his existence. He would be startled back by some noise, or voice, or from the chill of the night, or by the fright of non-existence.

Lampis resumed pacing the deck, and stopped at a different spot, just to show that he had some control of his destiny, on this ship in the middle of the sea, and in the middle of the night.

"I chose to board this ship and elected to travel this way, and it was I that had plotted my own course," he told himself angrily. Seeking the company of others, he went looking for Kalliope. When he couldn't find her, he searched for Demetri or Peter. When he didn't find them, either, he searched for his frivolous cabinmate and tried to make sense of his chaotic talk.

Lampis tried to postpone adjourning for the night. He did not wish to be confined in the small cabin, in the bowels of the ship. It made him feel like cargo. He often sought his compartment between 2:00 and 3:00 A.M. when he knew that he would fall asleep instantly.

His sleep, terminated by the sound of the bell and the call, "Breakfast, first sitting," was usually totally dreamless. If dreams came, they were vivid, diverse, and occasionally confusing. The light in his dreams was always bright, and the images, clear and without shadows, were portrayed against a wide, clearly outlined horizon. In his dreams, he'd be mostly alone, or parting from someone, and feeling free but slightly afraid. Often, he would be flying, without wings and without effort. He'd fly over the tree tops of an apple orchard, or across a deep ravine (this recurring dream lasted for many years). He'd leave his parents or his friends, who'd be standing erect, with moist eyes. They'd be submitting to the ordinance of the Fates and drawing strength from the sap of their own roots. When there were no dreams, he found it easy to resume his thoughts of the previous evening.

The second call for breakfast, an hour later, severed him from his thoughts abruptly and made him wonder whether he had fallen asleep after the first bell. He was not concerned about the sequence becoming a routine.

His thoughts, his sustenance throughout the long voyage, never followed a pattern or direction, but were initiated when observing an old man walking slowly, even painfully, up the stairs, or a young boy persistently shouting to capture the adults' attention, or even a young woman gazing fixedly in the distance. His thoughts, linked and branching, delved deep into his past memories or far into the future, with the undulating reflections of his dreams. He was not concerned about storing new memories for a reservoir, or soothing the past, or paving the future. He observed and thought; he thought and reflected; he reflected and became aware of his existence in a stage of transition. He exulted and shuddered at the thought that this stage may not be an ordinary transition, but a literal metamorphosis.

Lampis had never been out of Greece, so the prospect of disembarking at Naples filled him with excitement. He had read about Italy and had seen Mussolini's soldiers, with the feathers on their caps, and toward the end of the war, had observed their helplessness in their numbed faces. He had heard about the mellow light of the land and of the temperament of the people. But his excitement was restrained, or even neutralized, by the realization that he did not have enough money for the fare to visit Pompeii.

He recalled from history, that Naples and Pompeii were founded by his great ancestors. This thought started him on a journey to the past, a journey with leaps over long, blurred or dark intervals of emptiness. He paced frequently, to arrange his thoughts and separate them from his emotions. When feeling spent, he'd make contact with a fellow passenger and with reality. Still, he looked forward to exploring the streets of Naples.

"Be aware of Italians. Look around with four, not just two eyes," one of his fellow travelers told him.

Lampis smiled at the older person's warning. His confidence had not been shaken or compromised.

Fervently wishing to walk the streets of Naples with Kalliope, hand in hand, he looked for her.

"Are you also going to Pompeii?" she asked him.

Lampis felt disappointed. "I'm going to Naples."

"I'll go to Naples with you," his frivolous cabinmate offered.

His cabinmate's imposition seemed neither unwelcome, nor the most desirable.

They had reached Naples. Lampis studied, from the deck, the multitude of people on the pier. He wondered whether it was curiosity or enterprise that brought them to the port so early in the morning. They seemed to move without purpose, like the Brownian movements he had learned in physics, ignoring each other, or occasionally casting hostile glances and exchanging loud and seemingly unfriendly words.

Lampis saw an urchin picking up a cigarette butt and inspecting it as if to decide which end to put between his lips. The boy asked someone for a light, and puffed it, with his cheeks caving in. Lampis watched this display of human degradation, caused by either necessity or rejection, and felt pained, if not shattered, by this experience. The cynicism or barbarity on deck, apparently kindled by this sight, reached unsuspecting proportions. Sinister laughter ensued, followed by someone throwing cigarettes at the waifs, one at a time. Lampis watched this demonstration of decadence, as swarms of urchins, as young as ten and as old as thirty years, scrambling and fighting for the cigarettes.

Lampis saw Kostas throwing cigarettes to the urchins and appearing proud of his generosity. His disgust transformed into anger.

"Stop at once this sadistic and inhuman act," Lampis ordered Kostas.

Kostas appeared stunned and at a loss for words. He moved away and avoided him for the next several days.

Eventually and mercifully this display of sin against the human form came to an end. The mob below resumed its Brownian movements while the horde of Satans on deck scattered to their private or collective mischiefs.

Lampis recalled the pity he had felt when an Italian ex-soldier, without weapons and insignia, rummaged through a garbage can. Retrieving a half rotten orange, he had gulped it with relish, totally oblivious of those watching him. Lampis realized that this behavior was due to an instinct for survival. Another time, having observed a German soldier sharing his meal with a dog, Lampis had rationalized his feelings as contempt for a traitor. But it was impossible to rationalize the behavior of the Greek passengers on the ship. His appreciation that the crew did not participate in this display of baseness was not enough to dull the pain. Unable to swallow, or dissolve with tears, the lump in his throat, Lampis prayed that he be spared of similar experiences in the future.

His cabinmate tugged at his sleeve "Let's go ashore."

Lampis welcomed the rescue and obeyed, not his cabinmate, but his urge to venture into the unknown. They descended the ladder. His cabinmate talked to himself about his days in the Navy and his knowledge of Italian.

Fifty meters away from the ship, Lampis was accosted by an open-shirted, olive-complexioned man in his late twenties or early thirties.

"*Mia sorella, bella, bella, vergine* (my sister, beautiful, beautiful virgin)," the man said.

"Thank you, but I want to walk around and see this city," Lampis replied naively.

The Italian must have been encouraged rather than deterred, for he persisted.

The cabinmate shooed the solicitous man away with a resolute extension of his wrist and explained to Lampis what had happened.

Lampis watched the *fratello* (brother) walking away and shrugging his shoulders.

As they strolled the streets, Lampis listened to the incessant chatter of the cabinmate, who sounded like the rattle of child's wound toy. Lampis concentrated in keeping chronological and spatial orderliness in what he indiscriminately observed. He would retrieve all the impressions for later comparison, contrasts, and explanations. At the tug of the cabinmate or the flow of the crowd, he passively changed directions. The faces in the crowd displayed either daily cares, or a sense of purpose, or self-awareness, or lack of all. These were no different from the faces in the center of Athens.

Somehow, along the way, Lampis had stopped listening to the cabinmate's chatter and had lost him. He knew he was alone only when a tug of his sleeve seemed gentle in contrast to the cabinmate's yank. Lampis was embarrassed when he realized that the voice he was hearing, but not listening to, for a few minutes had a sweet cadence. Turning, he stopped and gazed into the woman's sky-blue bright eyes. He became transfixed, unconscious of his surroundings, separated from the past and future, and lost in the present without boundaries.

She talked and talked in Italian, smiling.

He listened, not understanding a word and hoping she'd never stop.

She held a baby in her arms and had a clear, beautiful face that was fully exposed by her hair pulled back in a knot. She wore a simple dress, with ever changing folds in the light breeze and a little cross on her neck. Her feet were bare. All of this made him wonder, for a moment, if she were simply an apparition. He wished fervently that it would last.

He looked into her eyes. She smiled, took his left hand, and looked at his watch. *She just wants to know what time it is.* She smiled and thanked him but did not let go of his hand. They walked together and held hands. He enjoyed the contact as they gently pressed their hands. She hummed softly, transporting him to a world of fantasy and bliss.

They stopped and looked at each other and smiled. She stepped backward and stretched her arm. He did the same, their hands gliding gently to their fingertips in a last farewell. He walked backward with her a few steps and bumped into someone, unable to break his gaze from hers. He turned and they walked in opposite directions.

As he walked away, he could feel his fingertips tingling and his heart throbbing. He felt the swirling of his essence and the urge to turn around for one last, forever, look. He exhilarated in, and cherished, these feelings. Turning around, he saw that she must have turned at the same time. They smiled again and waved goodbye. *If I could only stretch this moment to infinity.*

The traffic policeman blew his whistle and the crowds crossing the street, separated them. He didn't resent the policeman, nor the crowds. He was glad he had lost the cabinmate. He was happy he had met her. He hadn't asked her for her name. She didn't need a name. She was the symbol of his contact with a world in contrast to the waterfront – pure, simple, beautiful, trusting, and inspiring. Sometime later, he would wonder what course his life would have taken if his impulse had prevailed and he had followed her.

Lampis meandered through the streets, heading toward the ship. He saw her face in the crowds, in the windows of the medieval fortress, in the stained glass of the churches, and in the lens of the photographer when posing for a picture. His smile in the picture, intended for his parents, had never left his face from the moment that he had seen her. Her image remained indelible. He would not tell anyone about this encounter, fearing sacrilege against his soul and sin against Divine Providence. He forgot that he was hungry. He felt fulfilled.

Back on the ship, Lampis listened to Kalliope's description of what she saw and felt at Pompeii. He also heard passengers' stories of their triumphs in bargaining with the Italians, followed by other passengers' infectious laughter about their gullibility and victimization by some Italian sharpies. He watched Italian passengers climbing the ladder to the ship, shaking with sobs and wiping their eyes. He thought about his family and friends as he looked at those on the pier bewailing and tearing at their hair. Thrown against the whirlwind of his emotions and unable to find solace or comfort, Lampis walked to the other side of the deck, facing away from life. He brought back the blueness of *her* misty eyes out of the blueness and mist of the sea. How grateful he was, and would be, for that encounter.

The Vesuvius to the left, hiding its murderous summit in a gray cloud and in silence, could never extinguish such moments in any life. If some of those people, buried in its lava 1900 years ago, had experienced a moment like his, this afternoon, they would have had a full and fulfilled life. He was not disturbed by his greed for more encounters such as this in the future, though he knew that greed was one of the deadly sins.

That evening, as they sailed away from Naples, was quiet and subdued. The barbarians of the morning had turned into silent suppliants to the altars of the Fates, casting their eyes upward in prayer and down in grief, or to the Italian passengers with empathy. They were now united in sorrow and in misery. They reminded Lampis of the souls ferried across the Styx by Charon: kings and beggars, heroes and slaves, beautiful and ugly. All were crowded together and grieving for what they had lost while cursing their fates. Only Charon maintained his serenity. He had been at this for a long time and was accustomed to crying and cursing.

Lampis felt uncomfortable with this parallelism, placing himself in such a crowd. He searched and found a way to separate and set himself apart, by recalling the death of Digenes Acritas:

Mounted on his horse, Charon dragged behind him the screaming and bewailing human flock. Only Digenes, walking with head erect and high, taunted Charon. "You do not intimidate me, Charon, though you tripped me in our struggle at the marble threshing floors. I am Digenes Acritas!"
He was with, but not of the crowd.

Lampis wished that he could lessen the grief of the new Italian passengers and stop the renewed bleeding from the wounds of the Greek passengers, but he trusted that Time would deal with that. Besides, he hadn't forgiven his fellow Greek passengers for their behavior with the urchins, earlier that morning. Maybe in their sorrow, they'd reflect and try to lift themselves out of baseness. He saw Kostas walking alone with cigarette in his hand, as usual, bestowing pleading glances at silent clusters of people, and then continuing on. He probably was more concerned about the next drag on his cigarette than about the others' preoccupation.

The music, clearer than the previous nights, drifted toward Lampis. He enjoyed it at first, and then wondered why. He looked curiously through the windows and saw no one on the dance floor. A few groups of people sat listening to the music or nodding to each other. The people on deck who had looked at the dimming and retreating lights of Naples, were also quiet. Lampis heard an occasional muffled sigh as it was carried away and scattered by the breeze.

He paced the deck that night, reliving all the experiences of that day: his disgust with the cigarettes; his frustration at his inability to handle the guy with the "virgin sister;" his trance with gazing into her blue eyes; and the struggle to set himself apart from the crowd. He touched himself and concluded that he existed. "Who am I? Why am I this way?" he asked himself. To say that he was different, or that he was made of a different concoction, or that he was there for a different purpose, seemed both simplistic and blasphemous. Still, looking around to make certain no one was reading his thoughts, he forged the conviction that, simplistic or blasphemous, that's how it was. He had thought about it before, and he was not changing his mind. He wouldn't divulge it to anybody. *Who would understand?*

There was no one on deck. No one had said "goodnight" within hearing distance. It seemed that no one wished to disturb the other's solitude. Lampis was neither glad nor disappointed. He could not decide whether to go to his cabin or perpetuate his privacy. He had no new thoughts. The same ones from the preceding day kept revolving in his mind, stirring the same emotions.

Tethered to the center of a narrow world, Lampis could not cut the rope to spin off. He wasn't eager to, not this night. Eventually, when half-satisfied and half spent, he let his legs carry him to his cabin down below, but still at the top bunk. He tried not to disturb his cabinmates but did wonder what emotions the day before had stirred in them. He just wondered. He did not try to divine.

CHAPTER 4

THE NEXT MORNING WAS ONLY SLIGHTLY DIFFERENT than the night before. There were no new people, to be sure. The faces were no different from the first morning after leaving Piraeus; bags under the eyes, red eyes, haggard cheeks, furrowed foreheads, and tight lips. Hardly anyone talked. People gave polite acknowledgements when disturbed, and at meal times, made mechanical motions of forks and knives and unobtrusive departures.

Strangely, Kalliope seemed different. She didn't smile at her brother's antics, nor did she talk with her mother.

"How is your health?" Lampis asked her. "Would you like to meet in the lounge after lunch?"

"All right," she answered graciously.

He spied her in the lounge, about two hours later, writing in what seemed to be a diary. Somehow, he felt a bit of guilt and remorse when, walking past her, he was thinking of the moist, blue eyes and the clear bright face. He had not sinned against Kalliope or anyone, but he felt it improper to think of yesterday's encounter in her presence. He wondered whether she would mention him in her diary, and how she would describe him or even whether she had sensed that he had had a momentous encounter. He wanted her to think well of him. He also hoped that the woman (Blue Eyes) whom he had met yesterday, would sparkle when she recalled his ecstasy.

Comparing Kalliope's dark, languid eyes and intellectualizing conversation with the inquiring blue eyes and touch of the strange girl with the baby, seemed inappropriate or even schizophrenic. Kalliope held him to the past. Blue Eyes pulled him to the future. Kalliope, with her writing, was storing memories. Blue Eyes stirred the imagination. He would assert himself in his memories and let his imagination amuse him. Kalliope did not remind him of his sister but memories of his sister unfolded easily after meeting or thinking of Kalliope.

Blue Eyes inevitably helped resurface Demetra's image in his mind and inspired a curious desire for contrast: the smiling sparkle versus the glance of skepticism; the desire for contact versus the readiness for defense; the joy of the moment versus the preparation for encounters in the future; the touching and caressing of the hand versus the restrained handshake; the bare feet versus the elegant shoes; the trust of the baby versus the sterility of the pictures on the wall; the exploitation of the presenting opportunity versus the preoccupation with self and self-aggrandizement. He was rather surprised and amused with his returning to these contrasts and allowing his imagination to follow the evolution of these strikingly different beings through the future. He saw one woman as touching and caressing, or joining with those who shared in her trust, and the other, as ready to fight and defeat whomever crossed her path. He had met one for only a few moments; he had known the other for a few years. He did not think it unfair to contrast and compare, and he had plenty of time to dwell in this type of mental exercising.

Lampis paced the decks aimlessly, thinking, dreaming, and remembering. He looked at the rising waves and followed the smoke as it faded away, allowing his thoughts to scatter. When brought back to consciousness by a greeting or an unexpected sight, Lampis marked the moment in space and time, and sought associations to fasten it with, attempting to give it some significance. Then he drifted back into the emptiness of oblivion to his surroundings and to time.

Eventually, he found himself in the library, looking for books that he had already read, like *Les Miserables* or *The Red Cliff*. He was returning to the past, apparently not satiated with memories and seeking different avenues for these trips.

He did not read. Instead, Lampis held the book open and revived his discussion of *Les Miserables* with his father, and of *The Red Cliff* with the other two members of the "First Triumvirate." He remembered and admired his father's keen intellect and insight into Victor Hugo's characters and ideas. He felt he had witnessed the young woman casting her baby over the cliff, clutching her chest and defying death with her forbidden, unrequited love, as she jumped without a cry off the edge of the cliff. He and his friends had not tried to label her act noble or desperate. They just considered it a crown to her innocence and an impulse of youth, and he wondered whether her cousin, who stirred and aroused her love, would ever have any conscience pangs. The novel had left them wishing that the guilty one would be punished mercilessly by an awakened consciousness.

It seemed that Lampis had placed himself, as a direct and immediate observer, in every novel he had read, and that he had become acquainted with every character and place, and that his life had become different because of them. Although he did not identify with any of the characters, he admired some and envied others, and preferred judging to imitating them. If he judged them to be good, he would pit them against or separate them from the bad. If he found them to be bad, he would identify them with persons he had come across in real life, and those who behaved badly. He would often consult his father to help him decide who was good and who was not.

Lampis had almost forgotten that he had promised to meet Kalliope. He almost wished that he had not planned to meet her or that he had forgotten. He found a strange pleasure, or at least relief, in being transported through time with the weightlessness of abstract thought. He planned to concentrate on just this type of existence for the next twelve days. This was a unique opportunity. He was not exactly comfortable with the thought that his peers, or even his older relatives, had labeled him "serious and older than his years," and that he did not have fun like the other young men, or that they "had to behave" in his presence.

He began to wonder whether Kalliope's responses to him expressed her character or were influenced, if not dictated, by his demeanor. He wondered how she would react if he told a joke, or if he ran to her with open arms and picked her up and whirled her around, or if he laughed uninhibitedly the way he laughed at his father's witty remarks. He wondered how he would respond to her reaction. Or was it character that dictated his deportment when they were together? Perhaps there was a part of her personality the he had not appreciated yet.

They met in the lounge, greeting each other politely and with restraint. Lampis walked with her on the deck, the way they had walked before. They did not talk much, and he wished that she would excuse herself and return to her diary. He knew that he'd be hurt and hoped that she'd feel guilty if she did, but he wished it nevertheless.

When he made an attempt to start a conversation, he felt awkward like an intruder.

She must have sensed it and walked along in silence and seemed to finally find the solution. "Have you been to the library?" she asked.

"Yes."

"What have you read?

"I read *The Red Cliff.*"

"I've read it also." She interpreted the story, its messages and the author's psyche. "I look at the author as being apart from the characters, so he would observe his creations the way the sculptor looks at his works and not in his image, like God with man in the Bible, but like man creating Gods. What do you think about the author?"

"I had reconstructed the author from the characters in the book," he replied.

"I don't see it that way. I see the author's works as an extension of his essence, outside of himself."

"I view the characters as a reflection of his image in the ripples of water, somewhat distorted, blurred at its borders and indistinct, but still his narcissistic image."

Her philosophical analysis seemed similar to his father's view while his was more like that of a poet.

Lampis talked about his father, idealizing him.

Kalliope appeared to enjoy listening to him, sighing occasionally and probably trying to imagine her own relationship with her father, had he lived.

Gradually, or inevitably, they compared notes of their memories. He tried to imagine her father, strong and resolute, and going off to battle knowing that he might never return.

Lampis concluded that her image of her father was that of a hero and of a martyr, a mixture of Heracles and Prometheus, but he did not tell her, lest he reveal to her, her own secret.

Long pauses inserted themselves in their conversation. He tried to read her thoughts, and she probably his. They did not lose touch with each other, though, and resumed talking as if they had never stopped. He was glad that she had not excused herself earlier and prayed that he was not boring her.

As he was deciding whether to ask her to continue after dinner, or leave the initiative to her, she looked at her watch.

"I have to meet my mother and brother before dinner. I'll see you later," she said.

"All right," he said.

Lampis returned to the stern of the ship for solitude and escape. Alone again, he looked straight back, beyond the limits of the "V" on the waves, feeling totally alone at the apex of the "V" and contemplating his aloneness in time, space, and life. He had to admit to himself that he was scared, but also appreciated that he was numb, and grateful that he could find some solace in his numbness.

What if he perished in his climb to his goal? What if his strength failed him and his spirit weakened? What if his promises became nightmares instead of inspirations? Would his family and friends understand? Would he lose his self-esteem? What if a gust of wind blew him overboard? Would his life unfold to his earliest memories before it was extinguished? Would it seem as if it had been worthwhile? Would his soul or his spirit, floating over his body, feel the tear of his flesh by the fish? Would he know the grief of his parents?

The lump in his throat swelled. In trying to swallow it, he bit his lower lip and let out the cry of the wounded wolf, tasting the saltiness of his tears. Unable to check the heaving of his chest, he gripped the rails with his remaining strength, bidding goodbye to the love and happiness he had touched.

Relieved and resigned, after several minutes, Lampis walked to the dining room. He nodded to his table mates. They, and Kalliope, looked at him understandingly. *They seemed to know*. He did not talk much at dinner, only acknowledging requests for passing the salt or pepper, and smiling to show his appreciation of their presence. He ate voraciously, thinking only of the taste of the foods before him. He did not dwell long in these or any other observations. It seemed that, along with his tears earlier, his preoccupation with sentimentality had been wiped away, at least temporarily.

Lampis wondered what Demetri, Peter, and even Kostas were doing, and whether the Italian passengers had come back to life. He wondered what the next course in his dinner would be. He enjoyed the wine, and his older table mates showed some concern as he kept emptying and refilling his glass. He concluded that, to protect him, they drank more to empty the bottle sooner. The rhythmic rocking of the ship lulled him to a twilight of thinking and existence. The surroundings overlapped and faded, creating or leaving a gray amorphous image. The creaking of the hull of the ship, with each rise and fall, displaced all other sounds in his environment. He waved at those who greeted him on their way out of the dining room. When he realized that only the stewards and he were left, he waved to them and walked away, deliberating whether he should go to his cabin or to the lounge.

Lampis caught up with a heavy, old man at the bottom of the stairway, and had to be patient as the old man negotiated each step, holding on to the rails while swaying to-and-fro with the rocking of the ship. The old man's groans with each step, followed by a loud exhaust from below the belt, almost in Lampis's face as he walked behind, made him chuckle.

Later, Lampis entertained Demetri and his friends by relating the incident with the old man, garnishing the story for their amusement. He wondered why Kalliope left her mother and came over.

"Are you all right?" she asked.

"Yes, I am," he said, touching her hand, and barely managing to roll back from his lips the startling, spontaneous, and instantly born phrase, "I love you."

Did she hear it without his pronouncing it? Could it be that her inquiry, "Are you all right," was her way of saying, "I love you?"

Lampis watched Kalliope return to her mother, smiling and blushing, and probably wondering whether he was "all right" or whether he loved her.

Demetri touched his hand and looked him directly in the eye with a sincere, frightened concern. "Are you all right?" he asked him.

"Yes, I'm all right," he replied. "I love you."

Demetri smiled broadly, his eyes moist and glittering, and provided the epilogue, simply and uninhibitedly. "You love Kalliope, too."

Demetri's friends smiled and looked at Lampis in agreement.

With this revelation and his friend's empathy, Lampis walked away to understand and explain to himself his "love" for Kalliope. He went to the deck again. Preoccupied with his thoughts most of the time, he had not become entirely familiar with his surroundings, yet he had become aware of the rows of suspended life boats on the first day. The portholes all looked the same and too monotonous to be distracting. The shuffleboard designs seemed simplistic. He started to count the life boats, but lost count and interest.

As he walked slowly and deliberately, his thoughts revolved around Kalliope. He was not perturbed in concluding that he loved her and wondered why he did not desire her. He could not remember whether he had ever loved anyone else in this way. Why? She seemed so genuinely sincere and at ease with her mother and brother. Her conversation with him was purely and effortlessly proper. She was in control of reality and familiar, or unafraid, of strong emotions. She made him aware of his strengths, his weaknesses, his doubts and even some of his potentials, not by mentioning them, but by making him think.

In her presence, he was totally aware of his existence, at least his intellectual existence. "I think therefore I am," he said aloud.

He was totally aware of her physical presence and therefore his physical presence. She was, in addition, young and beautiful. He was young, and others had said – sometimes - handsome. Why then, did he not desire her? Or was he suppressing his desire with sublimations? Would he run out of, or outgrow, these sublimations? He could not answer these questions. He was content – grateful, to be more accurate- that she had become such a good friend. *That's what she was, a friend*. Now that he had explained his feelings, he could return to counting the life boats and the portholes. He would ask Demetri to count them, too. He found out later that Demetri had done that already.

Lampis passed by the lounge and looked in mechanically. He saw Kalliope's face, and after he walked a few yards, realized that she had been dancing with Kostas, and that Kostas was neither holding her close nor talking. Strange? (Several days later, she told him that Kostas never said more than a few words to her on the dance floor or anywhere, and he seemed stiffly formal and courteous, and that he even tried to hide his cigarette whenever he saw her on deck).

Having concluded that she was totally and perfectly "human," he was neither surprised nor in the least upset that she was dancing with Kostas.

Lampis continued his walk around the upper, middle, and lower decks. He stopped from time to time to gaze at the stars and to listen to a boisterous crew laughing and cursing, and to divine the thoughts of the clustered, silent Italian passengers. He had thought of the Italians as loud and demonstrative, and not like these resigned and passive souls.

A girl with thick blonde curls, somewhere between seventeen and eighteen, cried softly or silently in the middle of the middle deck. He slowed his step, trying to decide whether or not to speak with her, and then quickened his pace, leaving her to her private sorrow. He remembered that, from the first day, she had sought solitude and had smiled timidly and politely whenever approached by passengers of any age or sex. Her moist eyes and hard swallow invited respect for her privacy. He had seen her weep silently practically every day, just like now, touching the rail gently and facing landward. He choked with the lump that developed in his throat, wishing to help her, but unable to think of a way. He decided that leaving her alone was probably the only way to help. He walked away, not turning back. He was certain that she would not look his way.

Lampis didn't know, and never learned the girl's name, though she had become a distinct, separate identity and frequent occupant of his thoughts. Would she abandon herself to her fates? Would she finally discover some inner strength to go on? Or would she muster some courage to not disembark and return by the same ship? She was traveling alone, it seemed, and wished to remain alone. She was quite pretty, with an athletic, feminine figure and apparently well-bred.

He came to the spot where he had wept earlier in the evening. He gripped the rails as if to squeeze his secrets in them and felt a peculiar comfort among the inanimate witnesses of his torment. He would return to this spot every evening at about the same time until he reached New York, he resolved. He suspended himself in this peculiar comfort, until some strong stimulus, either in his thoughts or his senses, retrieved him and deposited him at this finite time at the stern of his westward bound ship named *Nea Hellas*. The chill and dampness of the night numbed his limbs. Caressing his rail goodbye, he walked back to the lounge.

Lampis stayed with Kalliope for a few minutes. After she left for her cabin, he walked out on deck with Peter without keeping track of time. They talked about their plans.

"I don't have any definite plans," Peter admitted. "I am going to school, then work, and will follow my inclinations as they develop. I am quite sure that I would be happy or content in whatever I do."

Peter appeared totally honest and genuinely devoted to his sister, and a good prospect for a true friendship. Perhaps, being in charge of his sister had instilled a sense of responsibility in him that did not allow – or had displaced – dreaming and far-reaching ambitions. Or was it modesty, rather unbecoming of someone his age, that did not permit him to relate his dreams?

They talked about their parents, about the Gymnasium, the school that they both had attended and about their five-hour walk when they were fifteen years old, from Tripoli to Peter's village.

"I remember my legs being cold and wearing those short pants," Peter said.

"Remember how hungry we were, and how we acted grown-up to suppress the discomfort of the cold and hunger?"

"I remember when the Germans burned my house, and I cried in front of the house, hoping to arouse some pity in the stern, detached German officer. He noticed me but kept looking about five feet in front of his steps. The soldiers simply announced that the house was to be set afire and proceeded with their task, pushing my frantic mother aside. It seemed that I was in the midst of hell with the flames shooting from the windows and doors. The smoke from all the burning houses had darkened the day. Then there were the screams of the frantic women and children making the hell of the scriptures a frightening reality."

Peter listened quietly.

"I also remember examples of human compassion, strength and values," Lampis continued. "I saw a German soldier guiding the blind grandmother, Antonena, down the stairs while the others were setting the house afire. He held her left hand with his left hand and placed his other arm around her waist, his rifle slung across his shoulders. Meanwhile, my mother pushed with superhuman strength a chest full of wheat out of the reach of the flames and burning beams, so that we could have some bread to eat."

"Your father?"

"When I told him that my mother and siblings were all right, he told me not to cry, that we would build the house again." Lampis stopped talking. They walked in silence for a few minutes.

"Do you wonder what happened to that German soldier, the one that helped the old grandmother down the stairs?"

They both shuddered at the thought that he may have been killed by a Greek bullet.

"I must go and check on my sister," Peter said, leaving him.

After strolling alone on the deck, Lampis descended the deserted stairway to his cabin and quietly climbed into his bunk. The memory of that fateful day, March 14, 1944, kept revolving in his mind, with flashes of flames, screams, mules and donkeys loaded with loot, piles of chicken heads (the soldiers yanked off the heads of the chickens and threw them in one spot), and the despair of the men returning from their hideouts to smoldering ruins.

Lampis could not sleep.

CHAPTER 5

A STRANGE, DISTANT, CONTINUOUS THUNDER and a peculiar yellow-orange light made Lampis jump out of his bunk and run to the upper deck. The horizon to the south was aflame with an immense pillar of bright orange-red in the center, and a gradually fading orange-yellow spread to the east and the west. The dome looked gray and starless. The north looked dark gray and amorphous. An obtuse angle of mellow light, with its apex at the column of bright orange-red, undulated on the heaving sea's surface. A sudden flash of brighter colors in the center of the column was followed by the spreading of a white-gray umbrella above it, and moments later, a horrendous thunder, punctuated a more or less continuous roar.

"What is happening?" Lampis asked a sailor.

"The volcano, Stromboli, is erupting." The sailor went about his business, unimpressed by the Titan's anger and trusting that Zeus' hex had buried him so deep that, however powerful his fury, Enceladus would never surface again.

Lampis, following his recently acquired habit, gripped the rails as if wishing to insure a firmer hold on this new experience.

The ship changed direction, apparently moving away from the spewing Enceladus.

Lampis kept turning to his left to maintain a constant view, and felt the ship rocking back and forth, instead of the earlier side-to-side. The glow seemed to become brighter and the distance between the fiery pillar and the ship became short rather than longer. The impulse to estimate the height of the column was erased when the ship made a sudden nose dive, followed within a minute, by a nearly vertical rise out of the water. Marveling at the forces and the beauty of nature seemed mundane. Invoking the name of God and contemplating the insignificance of man, as compared to nature, seemed no less than blasphemous to Lampis. He watched in awe, being aware of his presence at this moment separated him from all tangible or even imaginable experiences. He promised himself to retrieve this memory and measure his future experiences against it.

He returned to his cabin only after the ship's rocking became smooth and the southern glow began to resemble the dusk behind Tsemberou, the mountain to the west of his village.

Peter and Kalliope, separately, expressed envy for and disappointment in him, the next day when he related what he had witnessed the previous night. They had been awakened by the strange roar, and both had wondered about the peculiar orange-yellow light coming through their portholes and had gone back to sleep. They remonstrated that he should have awakened them. He had thought of waking up Peter but was reluctant to miss a fraction – any fraction – of this unexpected experience. Also, knocking on Kalliope's cabin door at 2:00 A.M. didn't seem decent.

Lampis thought, or imagined, about the eruptions of Vesuvius and Aetna, of Pompeii buried by the lava, of people running from and overtaken by the flowing wall of liquid fire, of the dark and total devastation left behind. He remembered reading about the cloud of thick dust that spread across the oceans and blocked the sun after the eruption of the volcano in Java. He tried to imagine the tidal waves swallowing cities and tumbling mountains after the eruption of Strongile, now Thera, hundreds of times stronger than that of Java; and he wondered what happened to the plants without sunlight and the animals without plants. He spent most of the day with these thoughts, taking a break, now and then, to gaze at the shores of Spain, or to check on Demetri, or to listen to stories by Alkis (short for Alkibiades), the "Hero" of the war.

Alkis, with the sun-bleached curly hair, the massive arms and perpetual smile, was always surrounded by children and young teenagers whom he either held in utter suspense and silence or made roar with laughter. They followed him on deck and exercised with him, imitating his calisthenics and his jumps, and competed for his recognition. His stories about his exploits, such as parachuting behind the enemy lines, blowing up bridges and factories, planting time bombs on the ships in enemy harbors, and awaiting rescue in mountain caves or desolate coasts were related as if they came from a movie. He showed no malice or hatred toward "the enemy," nor any hints of patriotism. It seemed that he had just been having fun.

One day, in the lounge, Lampis heard the children pleading with Alkis. "Show us your medals! Show us your medals!"

Alkis blushed like a bride and tried to put them off. When he was unable to distract them with stories and games, he gave in. He returned with a box filled with stars and crosses and ribbons. He lifted each medal. "This one is Greek, and this is French, and this is American."

The children admired them and probably imagined him standing stiffly at attention while some king or general hung the medal around his neck. The adults in the lounge stopped their card games to stare at the hero's medals in awe or envy. Some of the Italian passengers twisted and turned in their chairs to also have a look (they had been the enemy – some of these medals were earned for deeds and destructions against them).

Alkis gathered his medals rather hurriedly when he noticed the Italian passengers looking at him. "I'll take this box to my cabin. Then I'll be back, and we'll go out on the deck for some exercise."

The children laughed and started talking all at the same time.

Alkis returned, running up the stairs and summoning them to go outside. The parents seemed grateful that their children were entertained by a war hero who played, laughed, blushed, hugged, and exchanged pranks. Alkis had never shown annoyance or anger or uttered a bad word. He declined offers of cigarettes and drinks and helped old ladies up the stairs. He also mingled with the Italians and listened attentively to their chatting. He walked the decks with his arm around the shoulder of a passenger or crew member in genuine camaraderie or affection.

Kalliope and her mother were infected by their little boy's admiration for Alkis, and Demetri never stopped talking about him. Even Kostas tried ingratiating himself on him. The whole ship seemed captivated by Alkis. Only the blonde girl with the thick curls and tearful eyes seemed to be unaffected by his presence.

Lampis tried to be deferential toward Alkis and thought of him only in terms of his functions either in war or among the surrounding children. He was somewhat surprised that the hero's behavior never changed, and that his self-confidence appeared unshakeable. The image of this remarkable young man would remain vivid in Lampis's mind for the rest of his life.

Reading, strolling the decks, listening to stories, discussing literature and the future with Kalliope, reminiscing with Demetri and Peter, and reaching in the past for inspiration and strength, had already become a pattern for Lampis. Divining the plights, the motivations, and the characters of his fellow passengers, stimulated him unpredictably at mealtime, or in the lounge, and kept him occupied. There were still the times when he'd watch the crests or dips of the waves and fix his gaze upon the distant shores, and he would lose all thought and self in a timeless void. Recollecting his thoughts and reasserting his existence at the end of such times seemed to require a frightful and frightening effort, and invariably led to the panting and pounding of his heart, leaving him exhausted and desperately needing human contact.

The next day, when the shores of Europe and Africa seemed to converge, Lampis spent the whole day on deck, now to the right and then to the left, and sometimes with company, but mostly alone. He drew knowledge of mythology and history to give wings to his imagination. He saw Heracles erecting his pillars to mark the end of his westward travels; he observed the Greek triremes along the coast of Europe; he followed the Phoenician sails on the African shores, and he strained to keep in sight the eastward bound masts of the crusaders.

The sight of tiny, white chapels tucked away at the ends of a bay or gorge, of bobbing fishing boats, of gliding seagulls, and of soaring hawks against or over mountain slopes, brought surging memories of familiar seacoasts and, inevitably, persons he had walked or played with along those seacoasts. The anticipation of going beyond the Pillars of Heracles (presently known as Gibraltar) raised a gripping sensation of determination, fear, and irrevocable commitment. He looked for an escape and ended up in the library, writing hurriedly.

The thunderous sounds in the distance did not disturb him but inescapably stirred some memories of the war. For the present, these memories had to be put aside, yet were kept on the surface. When Lampis finished writing his brief poems, he walked out on deck, facing north, to admire the famous Rock of Gibraltar and to contemplate its role in history. The steep, sheer incline, smoother with the addition of concrete, made it appear invulnerable from the sea and from the air. As if to demonstrate this, an English plane flew low against the precipice, dropped two bombs and veered away. One of the bombs exploded on contact while the other skidded in front of a flurry of sparks and landed in the sea, spewing forth water and smoke. When the smoke cleared on the slope and the waves, nothing had changed. The exercises continued for about one-half hour, appearing to fascinate the passengers, Greek and Italian.

Their ship left the Mediterranean Sea and entered the Atlantic Ocean. Extending in front of him and to his left, as they sailed north to Lisbon, Lampis could see the vastness that separated the old from the new world. He thought of the Mediterranean as the womb and of the Straits as the birth canal. In its confines, he had been nourished and had grown to this stage. He now breathed a deep breath and concluded that he did not need an umbilical cord for nourishment. The mist of the Atlantic, covering the shores, seemed a poor stimulus for contemplation.

Lampis needed to strengthen the connection between the passing images before him and the stirring emotions in his heart before the vastness of monotony across the Atlantic Ocean blurred or distorted these images and dulled or drowned his emotions. He wrote, corrected, and rewrote his poems. He concluded that what was left out would come back whenever he reread these lines:

Abandon
Here, a seagull glides
There, a wave smashes and disintegrates on a rock
Further away, the sun reflects and quivers in the water
A village on a slope inhales the breeze
A flock of birds, revels in the brightness of the day
A lone chapel on a hilltop touches heaven
A city reposes on a plain, at the border of the horizon
The ship overtakes new revelations
Images appear, are replaced, and fade into the past
Nymphs, Nereids, Graces, dance on the crests of the waves
The sun's rays are mixed with sprays of the waves

Rainbows are born, displayed, and erased
The breeze whispers the nuptials of the blue sky with the blue sea

The ship stays on course to foreign lands
The firm hand of the captain follows the commands of his mission
My soul must find a harbor with anchored promises.

The Waves
Tell me, waves, what are you clutching in your crests?
Are you, perchance, concealing among your oracles,
The blessings of a hurting mother?
Muffling the sighs of a burdened father?
Are you, perhaps, submerging the tears and pleas of my sister for a future
delivery?
Or are you, maybe, spraying the sides of the ship with my brother's greetings?
Are you finally swelling with the farewells from old friendships?
Tell me, waves, if you crown your crests in rainbows for divinations
If you do, waves, when you return to repose
On the shores where the Nymphs of Greece revel
Spread your benevolence with your white foam at their feet
And declare to them, crested waves, that my love
For their spirit and song will lure me back.

Chasing Thoughts
A butterfly shaking a dewdrop off a tilting flower
My sweet mother's tear
Further up the creek, the water flowing over a rocky dam
My father's blessings
A young pear-tree shedding its blossom in the breeze
My sister's knitting and embroidered dreams
Two swallows swooping over the surface of the pond
My brothers testing their wings
Sparrows chirping and fluttering in the thick branches of the cypress
My friends' goodbyes and farewells
A honeybee buzzing from blossom to blossom
My spirit in search of sustenance
A flock of white doves flying from East to West
My mother's arms and eyes raised in prayer
The breeze rustling the leaves of the poplar
My grandfather's commandments from beyond.

The memories, put aside while passing by Gibraltar, were pulled to the center of his existence. Lampis relived the prolonged agony of fighting in the streets of Athens, first, between the Germans and the resistance fighters, and later, between the Communists and Nationalists. The rattling of machine guns, the rumbling of the tanks, the thundering of the artillery, and the shouts of charging or of agonizing pain reverberated with the intensity of the time of their occurrences. The sight of gaping holes in the houses, of streets littered with motionless and swollen bodies, and of flares illuminating the night, made life seem most precarious and elusive. The preoccupation of surviving for one more day had reached the point of precluding plans beyond tomorrow. Decisions were made instantly or with truncated deliberation. A moment of joy was spread to engulf one's entire essence and repeating "it could be worse" seemed quite comforting.

When the sound of battle did not fill the air, the silence was oppressive and foreboding, like the calm before the storm for the seafarer. The final escape from the raging war to the quiet and forsaken environment of his charred village was followed by a conscious effort to readjust, to relearn how to deliberate, and to listen to people making plans, however mundane, for the future beyond the next month or the next year. The uneasy truce between the nationalist and the leftist factions in the village dictated civil exchanges, since both sides seemed equally uncertain about which side was going to win the battle of Athens. The uneasiness persisted and nothing seemed to change for several months. After the battle of Athens ended, each side took inventory and plotted its next move.

Then war resumed with light skirmishes. It intensified, spreading hatred, destruction and death. Lampis recalled the frequent sights of the mass burials, to the sound of drums; the soldiers ambushed by the *Andartes* (guerillas); drunken revelries of soldiers after a victorious battle; bell tolls answered by bell tolls; black-clad older women sobbing in solitude; young women bewailing uninhibitedly in the streets; and old men stooping from the weight of age and grief. Vulnerable in his tender age, Lampis and other children and teenagers, were infused with the grief of others and found it unnatural to smile or laugh, at least in public. The children seemed serious and intent, subconsciously, traversing quickly through the natural stages of life – childhood, adolescence, adulthood and old age- lest they be cheated early. The end of the war seemed to jar them back to childhood or adolescence, but they were not accustomed to pranks and exuberance. Instead, they felt guilty and remorseful, or even moralistic, about their expressions of joy in dancing or in flirting.

Ruins were around them and in them.

"Lampis."

He turned and saw Kalliope standing next to him.

"I have been standing here for some time," she said.

Lost in his thoughts, Lampis had not noticed her.

"I had observed your expression changing from sadness to hopelessness and finally, I decided to rescue you," she said. "I didn't know how to intrude until I saw the dolphins leaping out of the waters, parallel to and keeping pace with the ship. They move in graceful arches." She touched his hand and pointed to them.

They watched them together in silence. He cherished the sight, until the last of the school disappeared under the ship, then reappeared on the other side and vanished in the west.

"I am, my mother and I are," she corrected, "worried about you. In the last two days, you seem very preoccupied. You seem to look past people and even have avoided us."

"I confess that I had felt my confidence somewhat shaken," he admitted, "and had plunged into the past in search of strength and answers. I was afraid that I might have imparted my sadness on you and was embarrassed to admit that I needed some support." He continued talking, finding another escape in telling about the forthcoming visit to Lisbon. He talked about the brief explosion of Portuguese power in the fifteenth and sixteenth centuries and the present miserable oppressive State of Salazar.

Her listening and adding her own comments gave him the support or the crutch that he needed – for the present. He was afraid that he had not succeeded in hiding his fears and loneliness and wondered if he had made her feel guilty that she was not alone, like him, and if her feelings were influenced by pity.

Lampis was uncomfortable in his suspicion that she was not listening to his monologue, and that she was aware of his grappling with his anxieties of separation. When he stopped, he expected her to say something like, "don't be afraid," and tried to think of an answer.

Instead, there was a prolonged silence.

They strolled across the deck, each waiting for the other to start.

He gave in first. "What are you thinking?" he asked.

"You," she answered without hesitation. "I think of you constantly. When I don't think about you, I even dream about you. Sometimes I try hard not to, but I end up looking for you. You're a challenge! You're unfathomable. I can't suppress the desire to understand you before we part *forever* in New York. What I wish to retain from our encounter is not a confusion of questions but the positive knowledge that I knew you. Then I can indulge in intellectualizing what made you the way you are. At this stage, you're terribly perplexing to me. Sometimes you frighten me. Just when you've reassured me with your strength and determination, you lose grasp of whatever gave you confidence, and you're adrift with the currents of your past memories and fantasies. You anger me, sometimes, to the point that I wish I had not met you."

Lampis looked at her. The tone of her voice was becoming firmer, more resolute, and finally stern.

"You don't share, really," she continued. "How many times have we talked, stood side by side, and sat across from each other? You let me into some of your inner thoughts; you confide in me, I think, but you never shared! You never wanted to know how I felt about your trust in me. You have never looked into my eyes to see what I feel."

She stopped, gripped his wrist firmly, and commanded, "Look at me. Look into my eyes."

He obeyed. They were large, dark brown, beautiful warm, moist and understanding eyes. He saw a world of purity, free of guile, with a profusion of compassion and light – a world without horizons. He was lost. He looked and looked, unable to shift his focus, and in his helplessness, managed to paraphrase what he really wanted so say. "There is no one like you in the whole world." He couldn't confess that he lacked the courage. "I'll never forget you. I'll always think of you," he added hurriedly and looked away.

"You're frightening me," she responded and let go of his wrist and walked away.

He did not follow her but glanced at her frequently as she walked to the other side. He'd never met anyone like her. She disturbed him. What did she mean by all that? Why couldn't she come out and say what she wanted to say? Maybe he was wrong in letting her into his thoughts and in making her aware of his conflicts. He didn't have the right to burden her with his problems. He should have been more discreet.

"What did Kalliope tell you?"

He turned to see Kalliope's mother standing next to him, her eyes benevolent and sweet, much like Kalliope's eyes. She caressed the back of his hand, invitingly. "What did she say to you?"

"She is the most wonderful girl in the world."

"She *didn't* say that," she said, smiling.

"No, she didn't, but from what she said, that's my conviction."

"Whatever she said, she thinks a lot about you, and so do I."

Lampis thanked her awkwardly and inquired about the little boy.

"He has found a hero, a model. He wants to grow up to be just like him," she said, and nodded at Alkis with his entourage of young boys.

They talked about the dolphins, their anticipated visit to Lisbon, about the long voyage across the Atlantic and about the reunion of her family. His joy in the thought of their happiness outweighed, at least temporarily, the sadness of his separation from his family. Kalliope looked their way and smiled a half-confident smile before walking away.

"I must go to her," her mother thought aloud. "She needs me now. She's probably afraid that she hurt you." She offered her hand.

He took it. "Thank you. She's precious. You both are."

When Lampis was alone, he felt lighter. He remembered Kalliope pushing her wind-blown hair from her face, and he began to whistle the light tune, "Let your hair, uncombed, flutter in the breeze." He wasn't hungry, but impatient for the call to dinner, so he could see her again.

Demetri ran up to Lampis with bright eyes and his usual broad smile. He nodded at Alkis. "I was with them," he said. Then he added spontaneously and disconnectedly, "She loves you. She's very beautiful."

"I love you too, Demetri," Lampis replied, "but don't say things like that about Kalliope."

"Why not?" Demetri protested innocently "It's true. Everybody knows it. Her brother knows it. Alkis knows it, and he says that if we grow up to be beautiful like you, then good girls like Kalliope will love us."

Lampis was about to chastise Demetri but was at a loss.

"He likes you both, very much," Demetri added.

"What stories did he tell you today?" Lampis asked, finding a safe way to change the subject.

Demetri took the bait and went on to relate how Alkis was parachuted in France, before the invasion of Normandy, with six other men, three Englishmen and three Frenchmen, to blow up some bridges. How they were separated from each other after being detected and chased by the Germans. How he was hunted by Germans and collaborators or betrayed by suspicious and frightened peasants, and how he was finally rescued by the British in the Southern coast of France, after wandering for weeks in the forests and surviving on what he could manage to steal from isolated farms or the outskirts of hamlets.

"One day, as Alkis was milking a cow, the cow kicked him hard. He not only got wet with milk, but also got a black eye. He also had a terrible time with the flies until he found a combination of a sunny day and a creek to wash his clothes in."

Lampis laughed with him.

"I'm very excited about going to Lisbon with Alkis to see where he hid during his mission and spreading rumors about an impending allied invasion in the south of France." Demetri paused. "Maybe you and Kalliope could go off by yourselves, just the two of you."

Lampis thought that Demetri said this as a way of apologizing for having chosen to go with Alkis instead of himself. He had trouble dealing with this innocently presumptuous young man. He was quite convinced that Demetri had a "crush" on Kalliope and that he was enjoying a vicarious experience. Still, at times like this, Demetri seemed to be God-sent, rescuing him from his struggles and conflicts.

Dusk came sooner than he had anticipated. Demetri had helped in spanning the interval from Kalliope's confrontation to supper in one leap. He had helped in diminishing the apprehension at the inevitable encounter in the dining room and had buttressed his resolve to let Kalliope know that he appreciated her comments as a sincere expression of unmitigated concern, except that, with this last thought, he tumbled into the uncomfortable realization of "there I go again, with rationalizations and intellectualizations." He still shied from assessing his feelings as "sublimation."

Am I hopeless?

He felt inferior to her.

When Lampis lifted his glass to Kalliope, he read in her genuine and resigned smile, "I accept your ineptitude and hopelessness. I wish you well."

He offered his resignation, but thought it best, in this rationalizing way, to spend the evening in the library writing letters. He will mail them from Lisbon. The letters to his parents, sister, and his friend, George, were long and rambling. To his parents, he wrote about the people he had met and the sights he had seen. To his sister, he conveyed his devotion and the promise of a return. To George, who was boasting that he had never fallen in love, he wrote about the blue-eyed barefooted girl in Naples, and the disconsolate girl on deck, and at great length, about Kalliope, emphasizing how his cousin Demetri was enchanted by her. The letter to George was the longest. After he finished, Lampis sat thinking of his strange, strong friendship with George until the librarian apologetically informed him that she had to lock up.

Lampis resumed thinking about George on deck. His friend was older and was trusted by others more than he was trusting. He was discreet, generous, volatile and devoted to friendship rather than love in the way of the Ancient Greek youth. The combination of tenderness and gruffness in him seemed intertwined, but unnatural, permanent but benevolent, unique but unenviable. George's father had been machine-gunned by the Germans when he had approached them with a white flag. His old grandmother had been hung in front of her house with the women and children forced to watch, and their house in the village had been burned – all in one day. Yet George, in the depths of his grief, had neither cried nor found relief in shedding tears, and his pain did not diminish.

Seven years after his father's death, saying goodbye to Lampis, George felt the warmth on his cheeks and the saltiness on his lips as the tears streamed down his face. He cried as if in joy and relief. "Look! Look at me. I am crying! Look at my tears. I am crying."

They hugged, squeezing each other with all their strength and sobbed together. George was the only friend whom he had real hopes of seeing again and who would return to his native Canada, after his tour of duty in the Greek Army. They would meet again, either in Canada or the United States. Strange how he loved George, in spite of his smoking, and cursing. In their innumerable and lengthy conversations, sometimes until dawn, they exchanged stories, ideas, and dreams.

How many times had they bid "goodnight," and walked away, only to turn around and spend two or more hours exchanging new streams of thoughts as if afraid that these thoughts may escape them forever – and were too profound to let go – if not expressed at that very moment. Standing in a corner under a lamp post, they would talk and talk, mostly in whispers, while the rest of the town slept. They were interrupted only by the occasional cries of an owl or a cat's meowing. Sometimes they'd stroll in the middle of the street, away from sidewalks and half-open windows so that they would not disturb anybody. They had shared, in addition, their food, money and their privations.

His father seemed to have had some reservations about George's influence, but his trust in either George's good qualities and discretion, or his son's character had suppressed his apprehensions. Lampis had had other friends, but in George, he had found what he needed as a mentor in controlling emotions, in rationalizing reverses, and in channeling thinking. He could see nobility behind his friend's light fog of coarseness, and he anticipated a torrent of pure thoughts and deeds by one simple turning on of the faucet of a seemingly dormant mind.

In George's presence, he did not venture to talk about romantic love, either in his dreams and fantasies or in the literature. He respected George's private resolutions or fears about romantic love, remembering how his mother's witnessing of a tender, romantic encounter had embarrassed and outraged him. Lampis often wondered, but never ventured to seriously ask him why.

Following his established routine, Lampis walked around the deck before descending to the bowels of the ship to stretch on his bunk and abandon his taxed mind to the grips of a hopefully restful sleep. He wondered for the first time, why he could not remember anything from the deck to his cabin. This descent had become mechanical and passive, after his first trip with his cardboard suitcase.

The presence of the three strangers in his cabin intensified rather than diminished his growing nostalgia and loneliness. When on deck, he could look at the horizon and contemplate his fateful decision to board this ship and seek new horizons. When in the bowels of the ship, he felt a prisoner of his fates and helpless in an endless drift. He suppressed his sighs and tried not to stir, lest he awakened his cabinmates and betrayed his apprehension.

CHAPTER 6

THE NEXT DAY STARTED WITH THE ANTICIPATION OF DISEMBARKING for the last time before crossing the wide Atlantic Ocean. The dining room was unusually quiet and greetings were exchanged by head nodding. Most eyes were moist. Stepping on European soil, probably for the last time, was almost as painful as stepping off Greek soil for the last time. The walk across the gangplank onto the shore was reminiscent of walking into the cemetery for the burial of someone dear.

The Portuguese faces, displaying their wares on the sidewalks or milling around, appeared mournful, or at least resigned to some all-powerful and none-too-benign fate. The deprivation of freedom and of human dignity had, it seemed, spread a defeatist attitude or servile dependence on Salazar's paternalistic authority. Compassion for these people and their country was quickly replaced by sadness for their hopelessness. They appeared like relics of an evil past, like the victims of the crimes of greed and exploitation, perpetuated by the Crown and the merchants, against the people and lands of Africa, South America, and the coasts of the Indian Ocean.

The church bells pealed to summon the faithful to escape from their present misery and to meditate and hope, the latter for a passage beyond the sins of their ancestors and their own plight. If they stirred memories of hordes of crusaders or explorers, these memories must have faded quickly. Nobody showed any pride or any emotion in pointing to the cathedrals and the palaces – they just pointed to show that they, also the remnants of the past, were there.

Compared to Naples, Lisbon seemed docile. What moved in its streets seemed passive, purposeless as if drawn or tugged by invisible lines and strings. The masonry echoed only short-lived ambitions and sorrows, having outlived its purpose of existence. The people walked and talked as if severed from the future.

As Lampis walked back on the gangplank to the ship he felt as if he were leaving the cemetery after the burial. And for a while, he did not wish to look back, not until the mooring was loosened and the ship began to move away from this port of the past.

Gazing at this forsaken land, mixed emotions, from the brief visit and from the historical background, occupied his thoughts for a while. He pushed back the sentiments he had anticipated, about having stepped off the old and worn European soil and about the long interval until his next step on soil in the New World.

The heavy veil of fog hid the sunset, and the gray murky waves made his thoughts recoil to the confines of the ship. He listened, though distractedly, to Kostas's enthusiastic description of the grass-covered soccer field, of his outwitting the peddlers of souvenirs, and of comparing the plain Portuguese girls with the coquettish Italian women. The cigarette in his gesticulating hand added to his authority over his audience of simpler village boys who seemed to encourage him to go on with his Zarathustrian aphorisms. Though curious to find out how long it would take Kostas to come to the end of his manifesto, Lampis decided that he had heard enough confabulations and moved on to find Peter.

They, Peter and he, agreed that the Portuguese seemed resigned and hardly aware of being individual entities. They also concluded that the vitality of the Greek people, milling among the ruins of a devastating foreign occupation and a catastrophic civil war, in comparison to the Portuguese, was not an expression of their nationalistic pride, since they had observed life with purpose among the Italians of Naples, the enemy until eight years ago.

Their ship did not pick up any passengers in Lisbon. There were no farewell embraces, no bewailing or waving of handkerchiefs when the ship began to pull away.

The dock was deserted except for a few workers with seemingly purposeless movements casting an occasional empty glance in their direction. Leaving this world was not hard. Disembarking in New York was anticipated with greater eagerness.

The dampness of the dark gray dusk and the oppressiveness of the day's memories drove Lampis and others to the lounge. There, people participated in the general and overpowering sadness of silence or subdued whispers. They looked tired and it appeared that they couldn't think of anything to say, or had trouble putting their thoughts in an expressive order. Someone suggested playing cards, but it was dropped. They were not trying to escape boredom. The venture to try Coca-Cola again seemed inappropriate. Even Alkis, the war hero, had lost his zest for storytelling and entertaining.

The hands on the clock moved very slowly and the call to supper was delayed. Though not hungry, Lampis needed an excuse to move. There was not a lot of "no-shows" in the dining room. Everybody was acting mechanically, absent-mindedly. Kalliope and her mother were making small talk, here and there, and the little boy, somewhat ignored, just kept stirring his plate.

After supper, everyone moved to the lounge, and it became crowded early. Lampis felt that the piano sonatas and violin movements were particularly moving that evening, translating the emotions and sentiments of the individuals in the audience into music. The pianist seemed to be in a trance and the violinist rose in mid-air with his notes. Lampis was transfixed and suspended by the music, halfway between the past and his dreams of the future. When he sensed the peculiar salivation, he knew it was too late to stop the loss of continuity.

Peter jarred him. "Are you all right?"

Somewhere between the peculiar taste in his mouth and Peter's inquiry, the music had stopped.

"I am all right," Lampis answered. He felt somewhat weak and had the urge to walk around. "Please stay with Maria. I promise you I am well and will be back."

Later, when he returned, he danced with Maria, an older married woman who clung too closely for his comfort, and with Kalliope, more frequently and silently. During the Greek dancing, he spun his frustrations out in gyrations, shaking his sadness with leaps, and tiring out his aching mind with the fatigue from his legs. Kalliope danced the Pentozale, a spritely Cretan dance, with grace, modesty, and discipline. He hoped he had shown her, in his dance, strength, determination, and endurance.

Kalliope left at 1:00A.M. and they parted with a respectful handshake and a simple "goodnight," – no promises for tomorrow. Lampis stayed behind to talk with the musician. He needed a change. They talked briefly about Lisbon, longer about Italy, and much longer about themselves. He listened more than he talked. He appreciated the musician's devotion to his music and was moved by his sensitivity to the anguish of the passengers he had met. The musician, obviously giving body and soul to his music when he played the piano, had the gift to understand human emotion and passion, and the capacity to translate them into compassion and empathy.

"What do you think of Kalliope?" Lampis asked him.

"I have a high opinion of her," he said, "but am disturbed about the young married woman traveling alone." He also had deep sympathy for the sobbing blonde girl and had an unhappy premonition about Kostas. Not once did he give a derogatory remark about anybody. He was discreet and not inquisitive, civil and direct, but not rude. He moved among the very young and the very old and had made friends among the Greeks and Italians. It seemed that he had given more comfort than he had found.

"Do you have family?" Lampis asked him.

He shook his head. "I am alone. I had not complied with my mother's wishes." He said that he was hoping to find a way to share his feelings with someone who would not defile them.

It was 3:00 A.M. when Lampis left the musician, heavily burdened with the long day, and when he turned to wave goodnight, he saw him walking out to the deck.

Lampis walked slowly to his cabin, climbed into his bunk, and lay thinking, with some sense of guilt, about his previous conclusions about this unusual and admirable musician. Before falling asleep, he prayed that he had been a good listener.

Awakening to the bell-call for breakfast and observing that there were no seagulls gliding behind the ship, Lampis felt a light shudder at the realization of the lessening distance between his beginning and his approaching destiny.

After breakfast, he attended services in the lounge, which had been converted into a chapel for the occasion. Today was Palm Sunday.

His religious cabinmate chanted most melodiously and assertively, standing out in his element and giving the service a most solemn expression. Memories brought tears to practically everybody, and the conclusion brought recognition and gratitude to this man who had remained alone and aloof until now.

The old priest had been entirely inconspicuous until now, and Lampis secretly wondered if he had been privately grieving about being uprooted at his age, yet he had put his feelings aside to answer his call to duty. In commemorating the passion of Christ, the old priest was restoring faith and hope in the foundations of doctrine and tradition; strengthening the link with the past and making the future less frightening. In the next few days, the priest would be almost more important than the captain of the ship, yet he continued to remain inconspicuous between services.

Lampis walked out on deck, avoiding or hoping to avoid any encounters. He traveled back to his childhood, reliving Palm Sunday in his familiar world. The contrast between today's low, gray skies that circled the heaving, dark-gray ocean and his village's bright sun, high in the light blue sky, helped prevent any distraction from the vivid memories. He could still smell the scent of the bay leaves, brought the previous day by the newlyweds, according to the local tradition, from the forest in the mountains. He could still taste the baked cod, allowed on a certain day during the great Lent. He could hear the song of the bird as he perched at the top-most branch of an olive tree.

As Lampis walked, he realized that he was chanting, "Behold the bridegroom is coming," the way he and his brothers would anticipate the evening service. He choked on the verse, "and blessed be the servant," trying to fortify his resolve by the brutal utterance, "That's gone forever," and looked for an escape in the memories of the squabbles and of the merriment with his brothers and sister. In his mind, he roamed the fields with the bright flowers and chased after butterflies; he climbed the trees, looking for bird's nests and watched the lambs and baby goats frolicking at the edge of a terrace. He competed with his cousin in hitting the stump of a tree with stones, and he dreaded his mother's call to come home to eat.

When his escape was blocked by the right angle of the railing at the end of the deck, Lampis sought rescue in the company of Demetri, whose brightly innocent face flashed before him. In the way of half-cowards, he reasoned that Demetri probably needed him.

Demetri had remained in the lounge after services, in the company of Alkis and some other young boys. Alkis had been relating, in his inimitable way, Christ riding the donkey into Jerusalem. The young audience gaped in awe and in total silence, although each of the listeners must have heard the story many times.

Lampis stood silently aside, fascinated by Alkis' version of the story and waited until Alkis ruffled each of the listener's heads before calling Demetri. He didn't dare congratulate Alkis, fearing sacrilege.

"Demetri," Lampis called.

Demetri came to him, chatting animatedly. "Alkis just told us a beautiful story about Christ entering Jerusalem on his donkey." He talked about his father's feverish cleaning of the church and how he shined the candleholders in preparation for Easter, and now about how things were going to be in Canada. When talking about his father, Demetri's voice faltered, and his eyes moistened. He looked at Lampis as if he were begging for reassurance that he would see his father again.

Lampis put his arm around Demetri. "Next time you see your father, he won't have to shine the candleholders. He'll be displaying the new ones that you brought him for his church, from Canada."

Having ignited Demetri's childish imagination, Lampis listened to him talk about the fantasies about the new home he would build in the village when he returned, and the comforts that his parents would enjoy. Demetri talked about the splendor of the church ornaments, the books and maps in the village school, the soccer balls, and all the other things that he would bring with him when he returned from Canada. He appeared to enjoy making others happy.

They strolled while chatting, being transported from the present moment to their parents' or to their new and unknown homes.

Lampis was careful in emphasizing only the New World's dynamic qualities and opportunities. He stressed the likelihood of being rewarded from doing honest, hard work. He had resolved that hard work would soothe or lighten their homesickness and help them grow in confidence and self-esteem. He had assumed the responsibility of protecting and preparing Demetri. Fortunately, he had found a God-sent ally in Alkis, who had made his task much easier. He reflected on this responsibility, distracting him at intervals from his sadness and was thankful for it.

The bell call to dinner reminded Lampis that he was hungry and made him rush off to the dining room. He transferred the sound of the bell call to his grandmother's voice calling him and his sister to lunch from the balcony of their home. They would be so engrossed in building their mud castles, plotting out their estates, and outdoing each other in their future accomplishments that they would forget about being hungry and eating. Half-resentful, half appreciative, they would leave their creations, turning around once or twice to admire them or to inspect them for possible defects and needs for improvement, and then race home to Grandmother's gentle scolding and loving embrace. They would make plans while eating, to go back and expend on their all-important and grandiose creations. More often than not, they'd engage in a new game or fantasy and forget their majestic estates. A few days later, they would start anew, either at the same place, by the village fountain, or by "the old house" or even in the shades of the plane trees by the creek. Whether the distance from the sites of these memories multiplied, by a factor of kilometers, the years from their genesis, he could not decide. They seemed so remote in time that their vividness suggested a story related by someone else. He wondered whether these memories would keep him tied to his past and weigh him down, or serve as sparks to ignite new hopes, or convert their spirit into strength for the struggles ahead.

Lampis looked at the waves again and saw his spirits and hopes crest and plunge endlessly. He was alone, utterly alone, with no one to come to his rescue. Those around him would scatter as soon as they reached New York, and some even before, when they docked at Halifax. Of those left behind, the ones that loved him would pray for him, and the ones that had only made his acquaintance would replace him with other acquaintances. He had only reservations about some of those who would appear in his future. He studied the lifeboats and the lifesavers and concluded that his lifeboat was hope and his lifesaver was work.

He was aware that his voyage through life would be like the voyage of the ship; sometimes calm and smooth, sometime stormy and desperate, following an already plotted course or carried by the waves of the times, riding high on the crest of good fortune or looking up from the depths of desperation, leaving behind places and events to never revisit, or treasuring memories and praying for a return. His beginnings kept receding in the past and his future was obscured by the haziness in the mist of the almost touchable horizon. His present situation was crammed in the confines of this ship with people he did not know until a few days earlier, and with thoughts of "whence" and "whither." The expected "what ifs" either never surfaced or were pushed aside without an answer. Attempting to escape from the present to the future led him to the edge of an unknown place or brought him to the banks of a swift flowing river. He would think of ways to scale the wall and would search for a way to ford the river. He would wonder about what he'd find on the other side and whether he should look back. He tried to sort out his excitement, anticipation, fears, and dreams, but overwhelmed by one or dwelling on another, he drifted into fantasies and frequently lost contact with his identity.

Not infrequently, all thoughts faded, and he was suspended in time and space, when he was jolted back to his self-cognizance, wondering how he had ended up going from one end of the deck to the other.

Escaping to the past served at least two purposes; one, in making his life appear longer by reliving the memories, and the other, in displacing fears of the unknown future. The realization that his past had unrolled to its end and that looking back was fraught with dangers of excessive homesickness frequently frightened him as much as the unknown future did. If he could only find a way to fasten himself on the mast of his ship so that he could listen to the sirens of his memories. If he could muster the strength to row beyond the clashing past and future with losing only a part of his oar. In his weak moments, Lampis found the songs of the past alluring. In his youthful enthusiasm and feelings of indestructibility, he found the future challenging, and in his somber reflections, he braced himself for a hard struggle.

The evening services, attended by every passenger, including the Italians and the crew, brought memories and tears to most. Lampis could hear his father's chanting and the village priest's supplications. He saw the sexton moving silently among the congregants as they lit or extinguished their candles, and he heard Uncle Panos's familiar words, saying, "Kyrie Eleison." Though the old priest's voice was solemn and grave, it could not compare with the celestial quality of the familiar voices in his village's church. The young boys here were quiet and attentive, in contrast with some restless urchins in the village who, now and then, with a candle crack on the head, had to be reminded to keep quiet. Lampis reflected on the admonition of the hymns: "Blessed be the servant who is found alert and ready," and "Unworthy is he who is found loafing."

CHAPTER 7

AFTER THE CONCLUSION OF THE SERVICES, Lampis paced the decks in the dampness and silence of the night, transported back to the time when he ran ahead of his sister from church to home, frightened by the barking of the dog, or when he walked out on the balcony to listen to the callings of the owl and to anticipate the same services for the next few nights.

He pictured his mother coming out on the balcony to remind him that it was late and that he should go to bed. He frequently breached his promise, marveling at the stars and wondering whether they had multiplied since the time of Jesus. The outlines of the hills and the mountains against the starlight invited him to picture himself running along their ridges. The dark ravines and valleys frightened him, but he leapt over them. The rustling of the fresh leaves in the spring breeze carried him, like a scent, over the tree tops. The song of the nightingale stirred his soul. The call of the owl reminded him of the story of how the Gods took pity on the young shepherd and transformed him into the owl who kept perpetually calling his lost brother, Gheones. Lampis lost track of time, and when his mother called him again, he took one last, long look, sighing deeply and reluctantly going to bed.

There was no mother to call him to bed now.

Perhaps she had called him to bed for the last time during his last, hurried visit. He had gone there for the "Certificate of Social Beliefs" and to complete his application for his visa. He recalled how he had leaned against the balcony's rail and listened to the sound, absorbed in the wonders of the night which saturated his soul and kept it from drifting away with the breeze.

His mother came out and stood next to him, touching his hand lightly. She remained silent for several minutes.

"So many stars," she said, as if she had never seen the stars before. She retreated to the sanctity and torment of other thoughts for a few minutes and then kissed him. "Good night, my son. Please don't stay up too long. You have to leave early in the morning."

After she left, Lampis remembered that earlier in the day, she had interpreted the tamed turtledoves' flying away as a bad omen. "My son would also fly away," she had cried, shedding copious tears of helplessness and resignation and lamenting that she had never had a chance to enjoy her "fledglings."

His mother had nursed him, her firstborn, through illnesses and privations; had watched him, painfully, grow at a retarded pace, and had agonized with the thought of his perishing before reaching adolescence. She had sacrificed the most essential of her own needs to send him through school. And now, he was taken from her, pulled by the Fates to the opposite side of the world.

After she closed the door behind her, he heard her light steps receding in the darkness of the house. He remained glued to the rail. His sighs were carried through the rustling of the leaves of the mulberry tree, with the breeze from the east, to be deposited far in the west for a possible future recovery. The distant bleating of an ewe summoning her lamb close to her, registered, but did not transfer his thoughts to the sheepfold. The chill of the night helped his inner numbness overlap with that of his skin. Now and then, he summoned all his reserves to slide his hand to one side or the other, to shift his feet, or to turn his head. He had to assert his separate identity, to convince himself, if only momentarily, that he had a little control of his life. And finally, after he summoned some of his reserves and managed to pull away from the balcony rails, he pushed the door handle slowly, turned around for one more, perhaps last, look at the silhouettes of the hills in the darkness. He stretched out on the bread chest, face up and arms crossed over his chest, with no real hope that sleep may come to him.

Lampis heard his mother whispering, from time to time, through the incomplete partition of their rooms and imagined his father trying to comfort her and himself. If he slept, his dreams must have continued in the same chain with his thoughts – a chain with a wide assortment of links, anchoring him to the early memories of his childhood and stretching out to a foggy, far away, horizon.

When his mother awakened him with a gentle kiss and told him it was time to get ready, he put his arms around her and held her for a long time. He felt her tears on his cheeks and the heaves of her chest through his conscience. He tried desperately to find strength or comfort in reassuring her and himself that he would return after he finished medical school.

Condensing her love for him, she looked into his eyes, saying, "You have never disappointed me."

His father came in and took him in his strong arms, then held his shoulders with stretched arms. With a firm voice, he said, "Wherever you go, wherever you may be, remember, you have God's and our blessings."

The customary bread and cheese breakfast was silent and brief. Swallowing was painful with the lump of sadness stuck in his throat. Lampis did not remember descending the steps of the house, nor turning around for one last look. Aunt Antonia stood on the last step of her stairway, wiping her eyes with her apron. Uncle George descended slowly and reluctantly while Cousin Nick turned the other way to hide his tears and Cousin Tony called for his dog, Azor, for no reason.

Lampis embraced his mother, first and last, and each of them and a few neighbors.

He climbed into the bus after his father. The bus driver nodded, closed the doors and drove slowly away. His father stared straight ahead as Lampis turned to wave. He saw their blurred faces through his moist eyes and fogged windows. He and his father did not talk much. The ride was bumpy on the dirt road, gutted or gullied by the spring rains, but welcome. With each bump, his left shoulder would bounce against his father's right shoulder. He felt that each touch transferred a measure of his father's strength to him. Looking out the window, Lampis was amazed that he knew every tree, bush, and stone on either side of the road. Every flight of a sparrow, every sway of a tree top, every patch of wildflowers, he recognized as parts of his essence. He had assimilated them all in his past and they just sprang up again, without order, to remind him who and what he was, that he was carrying all that with him, that his existence would dissolve without them.

His father's comments, deliberate and disconnected by long pauses, did not encourage conversation, as if he were guarding some of his private thoughts from inadvertently escaping in the form of counseling, prayers, or hopes. By the time these comments had settled in his thoughts, his father seemed to be engrossed in his own struggle of harnessing and reigning his emotions.

"I do not think that I will have everything in order for the next sailing of *Nea Hellas*, Lampis told him. "I should return for Easter, though." He repeated this phrase at least a dozen times, and each time, he wondered whether this was wishful thinking.

His father's answer was the same, "God's will be done."

Lampis never doubted and always admired his father's strength and resolve, but he was convinced that at this stage, the strain could reach breaking point. He was also convinced that these spent reserves would be replaced by faith and that his father would emerge as strong as ever, or even stronger, just as he had in the past with every crisis.

The journey to Tripoli, though familiar in detail with every turn and every stop, seemed in some ways like a totally new experience. The faces and voices of those climbing aboard the bus at the stops of the bus route, he would not have identified in the past, now seemed intimate, integral parts of his life and indispensable elements of a life he was leaving behind. He said "goodbye" to the stone fences, the wild blueberry bushes, the flock of sheep on a distant slope, the dilapidated house with the broken tiles on its roof, and the swift flight of the swallow only inches above the ground.

Lampis did not look at his father very much, afraid that the pain of his uprooting would show in his eyes. Even when his father talked, usually repeating his counsel to maintain a firm grip on his purpose and to fortify his resolve against temptation for the easy road, Lampis gazed out the window to gather all the sights and memories of this, possibly his last, voyage.

The other passengers remained silent, absorbed in their own individual cares, casting an occasional glance in his direction and offering a sad farewell smile. He looked at them, occasionally, having just now realized that they were a part of him, to plead with them to wish him well and to remember him. He felt that the strong need to be remembered overwhelmed all thoughts of present and future as if his very existence depended on whether or how he was remembered. The reassurance that he read in their eyes, that they would remember him well, and his conviction that he could not discard the memory of their existence brightened the hope that he would return.

They traveled the last stretch of the road to Tripoli through the apple orchards in full blossom at a relatively high speed, reviving in him a profusion of images, memories, and emotions. He would rearrange them later when he was alone on the bus from Tripoli to Athens.

"As your works, oh Lord, were glorified," his father said, appearing to be inspired by the sight of the apple blossoms, but probably reflecting on his struggle with his own emotions, punctuated the silence and the train of Lampis's thoughts.

Brought together by this comment, they started talking about the chores in Tripoli – the visits to the Police headquarters, the Prefecture office, Aunt Katerina and "the boys" (his brothers).

"Everything must be finished by two o'clock, when the bus departs for Athens," his father said.

The visits to the Police headquarters and the Prefecture offices were brief. No new emotions. The blank, disinterested faces of the petty clerks, the filling-in of the forms, and the flare of the signature followed by an assertive stamp, made Lampis wonder how far these actions had succeeded in convincing the clerks of their own importance.

Lampis had to go through several clerks before the final approval by the Department Head, at both places.

The Department Head sat behind an impressive desk and under the portraits of King Paul and Queen Frederica. He glanced at Lampis as if to say "I know you. I know everybody and everything." He traced his signature with authority and handed Lampis his papers without looking up.

"You're going to America," he said, as if to suggest, "thanks to me."

"Thank you," Lampis said, tossing the words at this "donkey with a saddle" – one of his father's appropriate expressions – and prayed that he would not have to deal with people of this sort ever again.

He walked away with his father.

"May the devil take them all," his father cursed, expressing disgust at bureaucratic anachronism and attitude.

Aunt Katerina's home was not far. On the way, they greeted some acquaintances and didn't say much to each other. They found her cleaning house, her thoughts apparently occupied with distant subjects. Her usual cheerfulness was absent.

"Oh," she said, appearing flustered when she saw them. "Please excuse me so I can make some coffee and make myself presentable."

When she returned, a few minutes later, she took Lampis in her arms, holding him tightly. "My child, my child, if only you knew, if only you could imagine how much I love you."

He knew that she loved him and how much he loved her.

She looked intently into his eyes. "Take good care of yourself. Stay good and honest. Work hard, and stay faithful to truth, and keep your sights on your goals," she advised. Her tears streamed down her face and neck, but her voice was resolute and even. "My love and faith in you is strong, and I have set you up as an example to my two little ones. I missed you after your graduation from the Gymnasium." She continued, telling him about the traps and obstacles set for him, or any youth, away from home.

The farewell embrace was prolonged as if meant to squeeze into him the love that she could not express in words. She stood at the door, waving. She blew kisses with the right hand and wiped her tears with the left hand. "Go with God's and my blessings, my child."

His throat was tight. His heart was aching. He turned around for one last look at the saintly face, waved, and caught up with his father.

They walked alone in silence on the way to his brothers. After some distance, he told his father, "I have to go somewhere."

His father excused him, continuing alone.

Lampis had walked about two hundred meters, to the middle of the Central Square, when a sense of guilt overwhelmed him and made him turn around and try to catch up with his father. He had left his father, whose love and sacrifices he had received consistently and whom he may not see again, to visit Demetra, a girl whose sentiments and feelings he had never understood. She had probably waved her last goodbye to him and did not expect to see him again and would soon forget him completely while his father would enjoy and cherish every moment of a father-son togetherness.

Lampis did not catch up with his father, who must have hastened his step after his son's choice to see "his girl."

Lampis entered into his brothers' room, just as his father was taking off his coat.

"You're back so soon?" his father asked, looking straight into his eyes.

"Yes," he replied laconically.

"You did not go," his father added, squeezing his shoulders.

"No."

His father said nothing more and walked out into the back yard and wandered among the flower patches, probably contemplating on his son's conflicts and final resolve.

Lampis looked over and arranged his papers and belongings distractedly, caressed his books that had been passed down to his brothers and wondered how much practical service those books would provide for his struggles in the immediate future.

His brothers came from school for their noon break and said very little after inquiring how mother was and whether he had all his papers in order. They clung around their father's neck as if to tell him, "We're still here, we'll miss him, too."

They sat at the table for a simple 'Spartan' lunch. Nobody ate much. They stirred their food in their plates, shifting their eyes from one to another, as if pleading for someone to break the silence, and tried to appear brave.

"I'll probably see you for Easter," Lampis said, not daring to raise his eyes.

"You won't," Nick, the youngest, stated matter-of-factly. "You'll be on the ship."

"I don't have much time. The crowds at the American Consulate applying for the visa are immense, and the processing is detailed and slow work," Lampis continued in an effort to soothe their sadness and in the hope that it may be easier with a "fait accompli."

"We won't see you again," Nick, the spokesman, pronounced with finality. Tears swelled in his eyes and spilled down his cheeks.

Lampis promised to write. "Please answer my letters."

They embraced, kissed each other on the cheeks, and parted, swallowing hard and wiping eyes and noses. Nick and George left for school, and Lampis and his father left for the bus station.

They were late. Their steps were brisk and their words were few. The effort to suppress the sobs was consuming, leaving no energy for the translation of thoughts into words. They purchased the ticket, and he handed his suitcase to the bus driver's assistant, then walked to the entrance of the bus mechanically, passively, like the yellow leaves of the oak tree in the autumn that swirled with the breeze and piled against a bush.

Lampis turned around and embraced his father. "My father," he cried, condensing all his feelings and emotions into that expression. Their tears mixed together as they pressed their cheeks.

"My boy, my boy," his father repeated.

"Departure time," carried the voice of the bus driver.

Their hands joined, gripped firmly to affirm that they were the same flesh and blood, and parted gently to avoid more tearing and bleeding.

Lampis climbed into the bus, took his seat at the window and kept looking intently into his father's eyes who stood motionless like a lone Dorian pillar of an ancient temple, on the sidewalk. He did not move his eyes, turning his head gradually, until the bus turned the corner of St. Basil Square and King George I Street.

He could not see his father anymore.

He was totally oblivious to the other passengers and to the whole world. The signs of the stores along King George Street, the window displays, the wares on the sidewalks, the people, he had seen them all hundreds of times; no new images or impressions, only the realization that the repetition was now being broken and the hope that he will salvage at least some good memories.

The rounding of Kolokotronis Square, with the contrast of the orderly flower patches and walks in the center against the unkempt sidewalks of its borders, studded with coarse truck drivers and peddlers, seemed remote and irrelevant. Only the sight of his school, his Gymnasium, and the faces of the few students he recognized, as the bus drove rather slowly, displaced the image of his father standing on the sidewalk for a last, long look. He wondered briefly, whether these students ever thought of him since he left their ranks only ten months ago; whether his teachers believed in their praises for him; whether those not well disposed toward him would be more objective in his absence.

His gym teacher stood to the side of the entrance at the Annex, appearing firm and austere as ever, looking to his left. He did not seem to notice the bus and receded behind and in the past, as the bus sped on its way. Lampis had received good grades from this teacher but had resented having received only tokens of recognition.

The image of his father returned, luminous and vivid, staying more or less persistently for the next five hours of the bus ride. Lampis recited the names of the villages and cities through which he passed, dwelling slightly longer at the site of the fateful house occupying the northeast corner of St. Peter's Square at Argos, and of the more fateful, gloomy square building on the east side of the square of Agios Theodore (St. Theodore). He recalled the highlights of the history of places and towns: Palamidi, in Nafplio, with the thousand-minus-one steps to the fortress, and the legend of being captured almost bloodlessly by Nikitaras in the revolution of 1821; Dervenakia, where Kolokotronis destroyed the Turkish Army; Corinth, where Philip II united the Greeks and where St Paul preached; Salamina, where Western cavitation was preserved by the annihilation of the Persian fleet.

He inhaled the scent of the spring air and reflected on the beauty and glory of the landscape. He answered questions by the passenger next to him. But he kept his father's image, moist eyes and tight jaw, through and above all of this parade.

CHAPTER 8

LAMPIS HAD BEEN ALONE ON THE DECK FOR HOURS, pacing most of the time and frequently with uneven steps, some short and some long, forward or sideways, because of the quite violent and unanticipated rocking of the ship. He had grown cold and numb with dampness and had ignored the occasional protests of his tired limbs and mind. Finally, unable to maintain a sequence of thought or memory, he looked at his watch: 4:00 A.M., or he managed to calculate, 5:00 A.M. Had the ship remained in yesterday's time zone?

He was now overcome with tiredness. He was spent.

Descending the deserted stairways and traversing the narrow hallways to his cabin in the bowels of the ship, he opened and closed the door slowly in the hope of not waking his cabinmates and pulled himself up to his bunk. Lampis looked out of his porthole and saw the waves receding from the ship, leaving it suspended for a moment only to return after gaining momentum. Mountainous heights smashed with their fury and foam broadside against the ship, tilting it now to the right, then to the left. He listened to the creaking of the hull and the groaning of the engines, now roaring and now muffled, and he let sleep carry him to the shadows of unawareness.

Lampis did not miss breakfast the next morning. He lay still in his bed after awakening with the first bell call and did not talk with his cabinmates before they left. He waited, without thoughts or feelings, for the second call. He shaved without looking at his face as a whole, moving and dressing mechanically, and allowing last night's reminiscing to consume his whole existence.

He did not remember how he arrived at the dining room. He stared at the sad Italians with little emotion and exerted some effort in keeping his eyes from Kalliope. Whether out of respect for his privacy, or because of preoccupation with her own thoughts, she also seemed to avoid him. Their eyes met inadvertently, two or three times They smiled apologetically and retreated to their respective turmoil. He did not talk, other than to exchange the usual courtesies with his table mates; nor did they talk with each other. Every face in the tourist class, Greek and Italian, was familiar to him by now. Most were sad and some were frivolous, with a few standing out.

Lampis's circle had not widened since the first day. It was actually narrowing, with Kostas and one of his cabinmates spinning off to some distance and Kalliope transferring to a different level. He spent time with Demetri and Peter and even more time alone. Walking the decks had not become monotonous, even though he could walk blindfolded and in spite of the unchanging ocean and horizon.

The surface of the ocean rose and dipped interminably. The spray from the waves cooled his face and dampened his will. The ship in the fringes of the southern horizon, bound eastward, gradually decreased in size and disappeared from sight. The realization, as if new, that ships were also going the other way or back made him think and pray that someday he would be on the other ship. He wondered why he could not collect his thoughts this day or why he could not link the flashes of memories either in a time or event sequence.

Lampis lacked the energy and willingness to make the effort to regain control. He passed Kalliope, with her arms folded and shoulders hunched. He smiled, nodded, and continued his aimless walk. Had the rail not blocked his way, he may have walked off the deck and fallen overboard. Most of the time, he walked counterclockwise, but only now he became aware of his habit. He wondered whether he followed the way of the Greek dances or because of the way he walked the first day, boarding the ship and after descending from his "crow's nest." He had walked alongside Kalliope that day. He observed and remembered that when she was alone or with her mother, she nearly always walked clockwise. He felt a skip or two at the thought that she may have chosen this way to come face to face with him. The second thought that she may wish to demonstrate that they were going in opposite directions was followed by a strange feeling of discomfort.

Demetri arrived, looking somewhat pale after last night's storm. "I have been sick," he exclaimed. "I had never imagined that the waves could rise that high."

Even so, he showed no fear.

They watched the waves together, much tamer today, and debated whether the waves were traveling north or south. They talked about the fine innocent ripples climbing to the modest ridges, the ridges rising in succession, like terraces on a hill, up to the crest, and the crest gathering strength to soar, but spreading out and flattening as if only to demonstrate its might. The sun was veiled by a hazy mist and occasionally blocked by a thick cloud. The sporadic collision of two waves, one out of phase with the rest, as if playfully, sent arches of tiny to ping-pong size drops over the cave-in at the side of the weaker wave. There were no rainbows.

Demetri counted the days before reaching Halifax and appeared more sad than excited, in spite of his seasickness. Even at this stage, it seemed that he had not fully comprehended his uprooting. They walked together to the other side of the ship. The waves were darker and more menacing on this side, and the horizon appeared closer. They saw the blond girl at her usual position holding onto the railing and looking through the mist with misty eyes and trying to swallow hard.

She looked pale, but still invited respect for her private torments. Lampis's eyes pleaded with Demetri's, "maybe you could help her."

Instead, they walked in silence to the next deck up.

"How is Kalliope?" Demetri finally asked, blushing slightly as if he had been mustering the courage to ask this questions for a long time. "She seemed tired and preoccupied a while ago."

Lampis thought of her intently for a minute or two, the interval it took to walk the length of the lifeboats, and turned to his younger friend. "Isn't she simply wonderful?"

"She is. She is," Demetri exclaimed, emphatically adding, "and very pretty besides."

They did not talk anymore, and after a few minutes Demetri admitted being cold and went to the lounge.

Lampis walked around each of the three decks one more time, his thoughts scattered and disconnected. He passed the blond girl and wondered whether she remained there all this time. He felt an overwhelming need to return to his cabin. He had seen all his cabinmates in the lounge while searching involuntarily for Kalliope. When he reached the cabin, he did not leap to his bunk in his usual manner. He climbed the ladder slowly as if to the gallows. He lay down with his shoes on and locked his hands behind his head, concentrating on making some designs or shapes from the uneven white paint on the ceiling and pipes. He tried to estimate the height of the waves – smoother and broader than earlier – and was lulled to sleep by the gentle rocking, and the whispers between the breeze and the ocean.

Lampis had not slept long when a steward burst in, yelling, "The porthole! The porthole!" He climbed quickly up the ladder, falling on top of him, shut the porthole tight, jumped down and dashed across the narrow hallway to the other cabin. Lampis heard him yell again, "The porthole! The porthole."

Lampis was perplexed at the steward's alarm. He looked through his porthole and noticed no difference in the waves between now and before falling asleep. He dismissed the thought of the steward playing a joke – he didn't seem the type – and closed his eyes to resume his interrupted sleep.

Suddenly, as if obeying the command of a cruel master, the ship began rocking and pitching furiously. The hull creaked as if it would snap with each nose dive or toss. The wind whistled, the ocean groaned, the waves rose to heights beyond his view, and the foghorn competed against the wind and the roar of the ocean. He held onto the sides of his bunk to keep from being tossed out or slammed against the wall. He breathed deeply to suppress the recurring nausea, wondering how long this storm was going to last and shuddered at the story of a young sailor apprentice perched on a mast trying to lower the sails – before the invention of the steamboat (he had read a few stories of seafarer's adventures and drama in childhood.)

When his porthole submerged, he expected to hear the rush of the waters down the stairways and in the hallways. When the ship was lifted out of the waters, he could not see the surface of the ocean below and wondered whether it had settled on the summit of Mt. Ararat. Did the dolphins ride these waves? How had they learned to deal with the rage of the ocean? Were fish spewed out into the air? He could not hear the familiar sound of the engines; some crashing or slamming sounds punctuated the alternating painful hissing of the wind and the infernal groan of the waves. An occasional shout, presumably from one steward to another, reassured him that there was life on the ship.

He thought of Demetri, Peter, Kalliope, and the blond girl. Did someone pull her inside, on time? How can the ship manage to maintain its course? Where were they now? How far from Europe and how close to the American coasts? The bottles and the furniture in the lounge must be sliding from one wall to the other. The old priest must be supplicating. Where were his cabinmates? Who had offended Poseidon? A new thought with each roll and toss, a new question with each groan. Not of the past, and not of the future, but about now. And the "now" unfolded endlessly.

The moment changed from very finite and eventful to very prolonged and suspenseful, from one wave to the next, from the creaking to the crashing sound. The ship plunged and he was thrust above his bunk, feeling as if he would be suctioned to the ceiling. With the sudden arrest of the fall and the immediate beginning of a new rise, he feared going through the bunk below or to the floor.

The foghorn rented the winds at very short intervals, sounding far away and plaintive. The hinges between the heaving ocean and the dark gray sky, appreciated fleetingly when the ship was lifted on the shoulders of a prodigious wave, appeared just a few meters away. If he had no knowledge of physical sciences, he may have panicked with the thought that the weight of the clouds above and the upward lift from below would crash the ship flat. His reasoning that this ship must have weathered and survived many similar or worse storms kept his fear in check.

The bell call to supper, particularly harmonious and melodic against the background of nature's furor, brought back his lost sense of time. His watch showed eight o'clock. Had there been a first call? The storm had been raging for about five hours. His gentler rolling and bouncing, and the softer creaking of the hull, suggested that Aeolus was running out of breath or that Poseidon decided to take on someone else. His nausea had subsided and the hunger pangs prevailed in his deliberation on whether or not to go to dinner.

His walk to the dining room was quite comical, as he bounced off the walls, and reared back and pitched forward. The dining room was quite empty, except for a few hungry or brave souls swaying this way and that, chasing their sliding plates with their silverware, drenching their shirts with wine or water and missing their mark with the occasionally full spoon or fork. The stewards did not seem very friendly, carrying the tray with stretched arm one way and leaning in the opposite direction, stalking the bowl to empty the ladle of soup in it, and lunging for the wine glass with the left hand – while holding the bottle with the right – at the opportune moment.

Lampis ate as hurriedly as he could and rushed out of the dining room and up the stairway, holding onto the railing and heading for the lounge. Surprisingly, the furniture in the lounge was in its place. The chairs were nearly empty and the shelves totally empty. He figured that the chairs and tables were secured to the floor by screws. The bottles had been taken down from the shelves before the storm and the few occupants of the chairs had been afraid to move. The up and down rocking of the ship was more pronounced in the lounge than in his cabin, the lounge being farther away from the center of the ship and higher up from the hull.

He made a hasty exit and beat an ungraceful retreat to his cabin. His cabinmates were lying in their respective bunks on their stomachs, their faces looking ghostly. They did not open their eyes. They did not greet him and he did not greet them, out of deference to their physical and emotional discomfort. He changed into his pajamas slowly and climbed to his bunk, looking at the ceiling. He could not think when lying in any other position and thinking was his sustenance. He made no effort to link his thoughts of a few hours earlier with the new chain. The new chain was missing some links. He lay motionless, like his cabinmates, and wondered what they were thinking about. How did the one who left his children behind hold up? How can he bear it? Why didn't he talk to anybody, staying alone and aloof? Was he overwhelmed with grief or was the sanctity of his thoughts not expressible? He seemed decent and gentle, and invited respect for his privacy.

The one below Lampis was probably praying or going through the hymns for tonight's services. He probably found strength in his faith. The third one, directly across from him on the upper bunk, was probably wandering aimlessly through the streets and coffee houses, chatting about soccer and pranks or mischiefs he had perpetrated in his childhood and adolescence.

Whenever he looked out, the view from his porthole was a confusion of irregular intervals of gray or pitch-black darkness receding or heaving from foam-crested waves and approaching slopes or rolls or swells. Why had he chosen the bunk next to the porthole? Did he wish to feel less confined, to maintain some contact with the world beyond, to confuse the rage of the waves or the tranquility of a tame sea with his own conflicts? Why was he not afraid of the storms? He knew he was neither brave nor resigned. Was it faith in his mission through life? What mission? To study and practice medicine? To think? To love? To learn all there was to know? To share his existence with worthy friends? To store memories for his return to his home? Was that a mission or a dream? When did the dream become a mission? When did one stop saying, "I would like to," and resolve with, "I will?" That transition took strength. He had the strength; therefore, he must follow his mission.

The rocking of the ship became smoother. The view from the porthole was hardly blocked by a rising swell, and his thoughts were less disconnected. The monotonous groans of the engines seemed like a proper background for making plans, but not for memories; going to school, leaving school to go to work; returning home to study; falling asleep; arising in the morning, and on and on, day after day, year after year, until the first platform was reached, like the grinding of the engines, monotonous and persistent, carrying this ship to the shores of America. In these plans, there were no interludes of romance, entertainment, or relaxation. These "things" would have to wait. He had made a promise that he must keep. Just as the ship kept a westward course to reach the shores of the New World, so must he keep a steady course to reach his destiny. With these thoughts, mostly coherent and frequently returning, he passed into the nonexistence of sleep.

When replenished with energy, he rose to new levels of awareness. His recurrent dream of walking along a ridge, in bright sunshine and with a clear view to infinity came back: a flock of doves passed over his head in an eastward flight; the breeze caressed his face and tilted the top of the cypress tree; the bleating of the ewe called her lamb to her side; the butterfly lifted off a flower and danced in the air; and he, alone, with no other human being in sight, wondered who placed him here and why. Where did he leave his body?

The bell sounds for breakfast transferred him back to the confines of his cabin. He tried to return to his dream, but in vain. He almost began to whistle but thought it inappropriate during Holy Week. He continued his thoughts while shaving and observed that he looked rested, maybe even good looking. He felt light-hearted and wished that Kalliope would be friendlier or that Demetri would be bright-eyed. Why did he think of Kalliope and Demetri at the same time? Was Demetri the link? In a few days, they would go their separate ways. He would never see Kalliope again. She did not appear in his plans or his dreams for the future; Demetri did. She had probably rejected him. He had probably failed her. Demetri would miss him.

Lampis felt strange at breakfast; it was quiet and everyone appeared preoccupied. Not unhappy, not sad, just preoccupied. Greetings were exchanged with nods only; smiles faded halfway; politeness seemed excessive. Awareness of others appeared to surface only with an encounter. Kalliope did not acknowledge his presence. Her mother's glance conveyed a "Wishing you well" – nothing more. The stewards acted and reacted formally. Lampis was infected, and he retreated into his private world. He could think better when pacing the decks. He ate hurriedly and left, not looking in Kalliope's direction. She and her mother seemed strained while talking and were ignoring the little boy.

He walked out of the dining room and the stairways, stopped to look at the position of the ship on the map and was neither disappointed nor relieved. The ship was closer to Europe than to America, almost halfway across the Atlantic, and closer to New York than to Greece. He managed to quickly suppress his apprehensions by recalling last night's resolves and continued to the lounge to find Demetri.

Demetri appeared rested, but his smile betrayed some conflicts and curiosity. They walked outside, even though Demetri suggested that it was cold and damp.

"I just returned from doing calisthenics with Alkis," Demetri explained.

They talked about their parting in a few days, and Demetri choked up, his tears streaming down his broad, early adolescent cheeks.

"We'll meet again in a few years," Lampis promised. "When I finish Medical School, I'll come visit you."

"Maybe we'll go back to Greece together," Demetri said hopefully.

"No matter what, we'll always remain friends."

"Yes, for sure," Demetri said, smiling.

They walked along the decks, forging a stronger bond for their friendship, revealing secrets of their past and of their apprehensions.

"I don't understand why you are keeping a distance from Kalliope," Demetri said. "Especially since you said that that girl back home had existed more in your imagination than in reality. She had never been your girl. You said you were timid, and her ego, among other things, kept you from committing to her."

"I admit that I had been hurt," Lampis said, "but it was more my fault than Demetra's. I should have known better. My friends Kostas and Nassos had warned me about her and had reminded me that I had entered into a covenant with them and that I had to put her out of my mind."

"And did you?"

"I had, but Demetra kept coming back when I compared her to all these other girls: Marigoula, the trusted and understanding friend, and the blue-eyed girl in Naples, whose eyes reflected purity, and Kalliope's character."

"And how did she compare to them?"

Lampis shook his head. "Not very well."

"I agree," Demetri said, nodding emphatically, "and understand your conflicts, my friend, but right now I feel very cold and need to go inside."

Lampis paced the decks alone, defying loneliness with memories, plans, and dreams. He had known love, sleeping between his grandparents, sitting on his father's lap, and waking up to his mother's kisses. He had known security, flanked by parents and grandparents as they sat around the fireplace. He had found strength in his father's example. And he had drawn inspiration from his mother's sacrifices. He was prepared.

The dark gray, heaving ocean fused with the low-hanging, dark gray clouds not far away. No seagulls, no dolphins, and no foghorns. The horizon, the clouds, and time seemed to be standing still. Lampis had to walk to the rear to reason from the churning of the waves and to appreciate that the ship had not stopped moving. He was alone on the deck. He loosened the top three buttons on his shirt, enjoying the cold dampness on his half bare chest, and the numbness that settled in his thighs. He could think more clearly in the cold and was glad he was alone. He had learned to walk in the winters of Tripoli without an overcoat and with his shirt buttoned halfway, imitating his gym teacher. His youngest brother, Nick, tried to imitate him, shivering and goose-pimpled and hunched, insisting that he was not cold.

What a beautiful child Nick had been. "Definitely the most beautiful child," Lampis had proudly announced to his schoolmates in elementary school, "and so clever. He can pronounce his 'r's' and his 'k's' correctly." Lampis would laugh with the rest of them when Nick mispronounced a word that would change its meaning. He remembered when Nick had pleaded with George, the middle brother, to cry with the rest of the family when their uncle was going off to war. George had tried to cry, when he was reminded during his frolicking that their house was burning. Nick would outstare Uncle George in a staring contest, but then he grew defiant and resentful of Lampis's supposed authority, hitting him with a stone on the shin and stating sternly that he did not care if his brother died after developing an infection from a wound. The little rascal had also hit George with a stone, right in the middle of his forehead. He had timed his throw so that the stone would arrive just as George raised his head from behind his cover.

"You both deserve it," Nick insisted, with undisguised pride for his marksmanship.

His two younger brothers must be on their way home today, for the Easter holidays. They would team up with their cousin Tony again; that they had learned to share Tony by doing their duty with the assigned or assumed responsibilities. They'll smother Mother with kisses and laugh at Father's witty one-liners. *How often will they think of me? Would they feel sorry for me or would they envy me? Would they talk of my leaving or of my coming back? Would they cry when alone or together? Would they remember our togetherness, or our spats?*

Lampis felt severed from his past. He stood apart, observing objectively, the flashes of his memories unfolding to remoteness. He looked across a broad, unbridgeable valley, with indistinct figures and shapes in its depths, at illuminated, but unreachable images and faces.

He was alone. Utterly alone, now and forever. That was his fate. He would never read somebody else's eyes, divine anybody else's thoughts, feel someone else's heartbeat. He was alone. Alive, yes. Determined, yes. Hurting, yes. But so totally, almost desperately alone. Not lonely. Not frightened. Not bitter. Just plain alone. No one was near to share his thoughts, his joy, his grief. He would have to hold his forehead in the palms of his hands, instead of leaning it on somebody's shoulder, and he'd have to let his tears wet his lap. Only he would hear his sobs or sighs. He would have to clench his fists when in pain, rather than feel the warm, comforting touch of another's hand, and he would suppress or drown his cry when his heart was torn, praying for strength to sustain him in his aloneness. Mustering his strength to swallow the lump in his throat nearly exhausted him. Stemming the flood of his tears drained him. Allowing his sigh to escape him emptied him. Alone. Alone. Alone.

Carried aimlessly along the decks by his mechanical movements, Lampis lost his awareness of time, place and self, again. He had come unannounced before sunrise or with the sunset. He stood with one foot in the middle of a vast plain and with the other at the edge of the abyss. He was, maybe a shape in the misty air, penetrated by light and cold. He was and he was not. Would he be? What or who would he be?

When awareness returned to stir his consciousness, he retrieved his senses to appreciate the heaving and dipping of the dark gray waves, the clanging of the semi-taut wire against the mast, the saltiness of his tears in the corners of his mouth and the back of his throat, the digging of his nails in his palms, and the faint odor of the diesel in the smoke drifting low above his head. He looked at the huge white letter GL, the abbreviation of the Greek Line, on the broad, blue band around the chimney asserting the Greek presence in the middle of the Atlantic.

He synthesized the whispers of the breeze and the splashing of the waves into a hymn to eternity. He compared the saltiness of his tears with the taste of the spray from the waves. He strained to part the clouds obscuring the sun, and he wondered whether he had retained his ability to identify a flower from its fragrance. He felt cold, damp, numb, fully aware, and all alone.

CHAPTER 9

THE EVENING SERVICES, IN PROFOUND SOLEMNITY, brought new memories. Since the priest of his village would go to the next village for services on Holy Wednesday, Lampis had never attended them. He had read the services, but had never heard them chanted or intoned, and hearing them now, for the first time, moved him. His cabinmate chanted as if transformed and transferred to a celestial meadow. The old priest intoned as if God were only a breath above the congregation. Greeks and Italians sighed and prayed in silence. Christ's passion was approaching its most painful stage, the stage of betrayal, and the congregation agonized. The priest, the chanters, and the congregation remembered from last year, and the year before, the agony of Christ. They knew, just as He knew, and they were praying for strength to carry their own crosses.

Lampis was surprised and disappointed that the services did not last longer. He followed the old priest with his eyes, nodding respectfully and slowly as he passed by him, alone and collected, on his way to his cabin. Lampis remained in the lounge – a chapel only a while ago – to follow Christ's passion in tomorrow's services. He was tangled up in the thought that the pain of betrayal was far more intense and piercing than the flogging, the crown of thorns, the nailing of the wrists and feet, the hanging on the cross, and the derision of the sadistic soldiers. That the corporeal pains were endured because the pain of the betrayal had anesthetized all pain fibers. That the corporeal pains may have even been welcome to divert to the body, even if momentarily, from the agonizing pain of the betrayal by a beloved.

Lampis could not shed the blasphemous thought that his pain of betrayal returned after the Resurrection and persisted after the Ascension, whereas all the physical pains were totally erased. He felt violent rigors with the emergence of the thought of Judas in the throngs of agony and despair, after the awakening of his conscience and his attempt to escape from his pains by hanging himself. And he felt his existence fading, following Mary, behind her Son stooping and stumbling under the weight of the cross.

When the musician brought him back with the benevolent comment, "You're lost in your thoughts again," the need to express his thoughts overcame his initial hesitation. He related his thoughts to the musician, a discreet friend by now, who listened without interruption.

After a long pause, the musician took his hand and looked him in the eyes. "You frighten me. You're twenty years old, you look fifteen, and you're talking as if you're sixty. May the suffering Christ help you. I'll pray for you," he said, stuttering.

They walked along the hallway.

Before parting, the musician took both his hands, looked away, as if summoning help from the strength of the ocean, and haltingly managed to say, "I pray that you sleep tonight. I'll spend the night praying that these thoughts of yours don't come back. At least for a while."

Lampis had no doubt about his friend's sincerity and concern, but he wished that his prayers would be to protect him from betrayal rather than that he'd sleep tonight or that these thoughts be dispelled.

Lampis descended the stairway, counting the steps. He walked the hallway to his cabin, reading the numbers on the cabin doors to keep from thinking. His cabinmates, as usual, showed no sign of acknowledging his entrance. He felt a peculiar comfort in knowing that they were there even though they hardly communicated. For the first time, it occurred to him that the two in the lower bunks may have thought of him as a "young boy" who wouldn't understand them. He did not resent this thought – they didn't know him, and he valued his privacy. He realized that the distance from Kalliope was lengthening and that he spent less time with Peter. Lying on his bunk, he drifted to the past, disconnected images, some vivid and some hazy, appearing and receding to a milky-white amorphous mist into oblivion. The brief or momentary returns of awareness and identity brought a heaving sigh, equal to the heaving ocean out of the porthole, with the prayer, "Oh God, spare me from betrayal."

The next day was occupied, predominantly, with the anticipation of parting with Demetri in Halifax. Just two more days. Lampis wanted to spend as much time with Demetri as possible. Yet, he found talking to him difficult. Repeating his advice and admonitions may reveal his own weakness and apprehension. Declaring his resolution to treasure the memories of Demetri's unadulterated friendship may be superfluous; making small talk or reminiscing may reopen the wounds, in both of them.

"The day after tomorrow, we'll be in Halifax," Demetri offered. "My uncle will meet me there." Then he fell silent.

They walked on deck and went into the lounge for a while, then walked on deck again and finally returned to the lounge in the privacy of a corner. Demetri kept looking away, glancing at Lampis occasionally, with moist eyes, and apparently mustering some strength to say something.

"Tonight, we'll hear the twelve gospels," Demetri blurted out. He talked without stopping for a breath, without much coherence and apparently without regard about making sense.

Lampis listened, looking at him silently and carving the image of this pure, beautiful boy in the inner sanctum of his memories. He was anticipating Demetri breaking into sobs, and he concentrated in summoning his reserves to keep his own sobs in check. The thought that he may never see this boy again pushed him to the edge and forced him to seek reprieve in announcing disconnectedly, "Of course I'll see you again."

Tears streamed down Demetri's face, and his face became distorted in a final supreme effort to suppress his crying before finally convulsing with sobs. "I'll see you again, and you'll see your parents and brothers again," he said.

The second part of Lampis's attempt to comfort Demetri evoked the desired but not hoped for response.

"Oh yes, my brother Takis will join me before long," Demetri responded.

Perusing the room to allow Demetri to dry his eyes, Lampis realized that nearly everybody in the lounge had been infected by Demetri's breaking down. Some people shielded their eyes, elbows resting on the table, some wiped their eyes, and some seemed to lack the strength or initiative to reach for a handkerchief.

Alkis stared through a fixed spot beyond the confines of the ship and the endless ocean. Whether out of deference to the dignity of the other's private grief or out of resourcefulness, Alkis remained aloof, for the moment.

Leaving Demetri in the lounge seemed interminable and turbulent with conflict; Lampis waited for the proper time to retreat to his own thoughts. The spot where he had cried uncontrollably beckoned to him, but he could not leave yet. Demetri may follow him and then know his secret – the secret of occasional despair and more frequent bitter loneliness.

The solution came with Peter's arrival, the light conversation and the gradual widening of the circle with a few other passengers. They talked about how many would disembark in Halifax; about celebrating Easter on ship; about the difference between Canada and the United States. The sadness was dispelled. Possible encounters, traveling across the new continent, plans for a reunion displaced the thoughts of separation and uncertainty. Eventually, jokes were exchanged and laughter began to peal, lifting the spirits of some and arousing some glances of pity or even contempt among others. "They're young, they don't understand."

Lampis walked out on deck and started his usual counterclockwise walk. The ocean kept demonstrating its omnipotence, rising and rolling, spewing and swallowing, spraying the low hanging clouds and pulling the dome of the sky down and the horizon in. Yet, he felt secure in this defiant old ship. There was a truce, it seemed, between the ship and the ocean today, perhaps in observance of Christ's holy passion.

A few other passengers had also walked out on deck, mostly individuals, occasionally in pairs. After a while, Alkis arrived with his entourage of boys. Lampis kept walking, greeting people with an occasional nod, and allowing his thoughts to drift back to his childhood, to his adolescent fantasies, and to his fateful, precipitous resolution to leave Greece in pursuit of a dream that seemed to have vanished only eight months ago. He was deeply in love with Greece. He wanted to give himself totally to it, but he had nothing other than his love and himself to give, and Greece could not give him the opportunity to express his love in his way. Whether he would transfer his love to the land that promised him a chance, he did not know.

Lampis was already deeply grateful to this land that was opening its bosom to him. He understood that the condition for offering the opportunity was honesty and decency. His father's admonition to never allow a blemish on the family name, to safeguard the honor of that name and to pass the legacy to the next generation came back reverberating and filled him with pride and resolve. His grandfather's patriarchal, handsome face, with the sky-blue eyes and neatly trimmed beard, flashed before him and reminded him that he bore his name – a name that was synonymous with honesty, purity of thought, and hard work. His grandfather had become a legend. He, too, had crossed this ocean, in both directions, had spent some years in Chicago and had taken with him some stories from life in the New World. His grandmother's image, clear as an apparition, followed his grandfather's. She had dipped her fingers in a cup of water and with a gentle fling, had sprinkled her blessings on her half-asleep grandchildren, only a few minutes before her death. Her loving action had made him feel that he had been anointed. The phrases, "blessed children" and "Go to Christ's blessings," used by his grandfather in chastisement, and his grandmother caresses and kissed reminded him, once again, of the love he had been nurtured with. It must have been these blessings that had shielded him when an artillery shell exploded only a few feet behind him and knocked him on his face; that had guided the unknown black-clad woman to disguise him as her daughter, when his sponsor-uncle had abandoned him, in order to pass through the German blockade. These same blessings must have kept him from boarding the half-track tank that was blown to smithereens a few minutes later. What could possibly compare with these blessings?

Lampis relished these thoughts, continuing his walk, and felt his faith and strength replenished. He started whistling the martial tune "We, the commando boys, are full of hopes," but finding it somewhat improper for the day, switched to "A new days has dawned." He stopped that too, because the breeze blew directly in his face, muffling it. He smiled at the memory that he used to sing with all his strength, when certain that no one could hear him, out in the country. He knew that he could not sing well but had no other way to express the vigor of his youth when walking along the ravines and ridges alone. He laughed aloud at the memory of his cousin Tony singing at the top of his voice to let him know that the guerrillas had left and he could come out of hiding. Curiously, only now he realized why in the last months of his studies at the Gymnasium, he and his classmates danced in the school yard at every recess, and why he had joined others, impromptu, in singing in the streets, and why he had walked from his house to the end of the village, singing and dancing unobserved. The war was over! The grief from the loss of so many young men dying in the battlefield had been displaced by the need to forget and to build a future.

We had to let the older generation know that we are still here.

But he was not "here" anymore. He had left the others behind to continue with their singing and dancing and promising. He had left "here" to go "there," bringing with him memories of clear blue skies and fragrant breezes for sustenance, of the sound of the church bells and nightingales for inspiration, and of the handshake with gnarled hands for strength in the struggle ahead.

The chimes of the bell, coming faintly through the closed doors, reminded him that he was hungry, but he kept walking, suppressing and erasing hunger with thinking. He did not wish to be disturbed by encounters in the hallways and small talk in the dining room. He felt free on deck. He had not been to the library for days, had not written anything since entering the Atlantic, and had not shared any of his sentiments, except last night, since Kalliope had told him that he "frightened her." The urge to write was not sustained while the drive to keep walking gained momentum.

He walked all day, ignoring tiredness of limb and repetition of thought. When Demetri came out looking for him, he promised he would join him shortly, but he did not look at his watch and lost track of time. He met Kalliope, going in the opposite direction, as usual, wrapped tightly in a shawl, looked into her eyes for a moment

"Are you all right?" she asked.

"Yes." He read in her eyes, "I am here, if you wish to talk or be with me," but he did not wish to talk or be with anybody. He had to learn to be alone, and he might as well start now.

She continued on.

He hoped he had not been rude.

He came to the spot of his secrets but did not stop; he only looked at it intently with the premonition that he would return before disembarking, for another bout of sobbing and tears. Two crewmen moving some loops of rope from the edges to the center looked at him questioningly, then at each other questioningly, and went on with their work. The blond girl with the curls walked to her spot, and as usual, did not acknowledge his presence or existence.

Kostas, minus his cigarette, walked alongside him. "Just a few more days," he said.

Lampis listened to Kostas, though he recognized a need in him for contact and friendship and wondered whether he had been too harsh on him.

Kostas appeared somewhat subdued. "I hope we don't lose contact in Chicago. I am thinking about going to school and hope that we may attend the same school."

They walked together for about one hour, went to the lounge and listened to the band playing Bach.

Kostas appeared hypnotized, and at the end, exclaimed, "Wonderful."

No applause, just exaltation. For a long moment, Lampis felt unburdened. He felt, from looking around, that everybody was unburdened, that the start of a conversation would deposit the burden back on his shoulders and in his soul, that breaking the silence would be a sacrilege. And he waited for the others to commit the sacrilege first.

After a few minutes, some whispers were heard and gradually normal conversation resumed. He was still transfixed. Kostas appeared hesitant.

Eventually, Lampis excused himself from Kostas and went out on deck again. He was frustrated in not being able to remember why the sonata he had just heard was so familiar to him. He had never been to a concert. He had seen a few movies, but not the kind with this type of music in them. Where had he heard it before? Could it be that he had lived before, at the time of Bach or Beethoven? After this last thought, a strange taste caused an involuntary repetition of sucking in his cheeks and abortive swallowing. A supreme futile effort to terminate this taste and swallowing cycle failed, leaving him with a frightening moment of helplessness, and a total loss of awareness.

Lampis found himself against the rails at the stem of the ship. A crewman stood next to him.

"What happened to you?" the crewman asked.

Lampis didn't know. "I am all right," he said, but he was scared. He could have fallen overboard.

The crewman hesitated for a moment. "Please go back inside," he pleaded, and left.

Lampis started walking back, waved to the crewman, and prayed, "Oh God, preserve me, for my parents' sake."

CHAPTER 10

RESUMING HIS STROLL ON THE DECK, Lampis thought of his parents' love for him and for each other. One memory came vividly to him, asserting this love. When he and his father had been given up for dead and had returned home, his parents had embraced tightly, weeping, parting to a half arm's length and looking into each other's eyes. They had embraced tightly again and wet each other's shoulder with their tears, not uttering one word. He watched his parents reunite, waiting patiently for his turn, for his mother's embrace and kisses. He had not seen her for eight months.

When finally realizing that there were others around them to welcome them back from the dead, they parted. His father greeted the others while his mother took Lampis in her arms, saturating his cheeks with kisses and tears. She pushed his hair from his forehead so that she could see all of his face and shook with another bout of joyful sobbing. This memory unfolded back to three days earlier to re-establish a continuity.

Lampis and his father had been stranded in Athens, by the Communist uprising of December, 1944, nearly six and one-half years ago. They had witnessed bombings and massacres and had come face to face with death. Starving, they had finally decided to make a break through the siege and head for home. His father had hesitated, calculating the risks, but he kept pushing with the argument that staying was riskier, with all the fighting and with starvation. They had not eaten anything, except for a few roasted peas per day and about two ounces of bread on Christmas day (where did his aunt find the flour?) for twenty-four days. Lampis had finally prevailed.

They drew the plans and acquired the papers. The permit to exit Athens and travel were procured from the Communist Headquarters (the government had decreed "no exit of civilians from the city and the suburbs of Athens"), and the date was set for December 29. Two other men were ready to go with them. Lampis was up at three o'clock in the morning, prodding his father to get ready and convincing him to let him wake the other two men.

His father would later recall, with conscience pangs and shudders, and with self-recrimination, that he had allowed his boy to go through streets turned into battlefields, about two miles away in the middle of the night. There were no street lights or any lights for Lampis to see, except for an occasional flare drifting down with its miniature parachute to make artillery aiming more accurate. Lampis returned to tell his father that Vasiles was ready and promised to meet them in a half hour.

After Vasiles and the other man arrived, the other man changed his mind just as he reached the door. "Vasiles, it is too dangerous. It's suicide," he said to him.

Lampis's uncle and aunt had come up from the safer basement apartment of his aunt's sister to wish them a safe trip. His uncle said little.

"Why did you let the boy walk (Lampis had run all the way) at this time of night, across Alexandra Boulevard into the crossfires?" his aunt scolded his father. "It was your brother's combat experience that saved us in crossing that broad boulevard."

Lampis sensed that his aunt disguised her fright and apprehensions with uncontrollable anger. His father appeared embarrassed, remorseful and apologetic.

The parting was rather brief and curt. A defense mechanism? But the last embrace squeezed into him all their love, fears, and hopes. Would they ever see each other again?

They had walked as noiselessly as possible, each with a rolled blanket over their shoulders, through the dark streets of Athens. They listened carefully for sounds of footsteps, whispers, commands, and rifle or machine gun fire, avoiding parks and open spaces and heading south toward the Peloponnesus Railroad Station. They had reasoned that following the railroad was much safer, since there was no traffic and therefore, no patrolling. All the bridges had been blown up by the retreating Germans two months ago. The highways would be more dangerous.

The drizzle continued at the same steady rate, but Lampis's spirits were not damp. He was escaping. He was going home. A few kilometers from the outskirts of the city, whether out of fatigue or a sense of accomplishment, he became somewhat careless and had almost blown up everybody, including his father and Vasiles, in pieces, when his foot became tangled in the wire to a mine at the base of the only surviving railroad bridge. Lampis had seen the signs, warning them: KINDYNOS – THANATOS (DANGER – DEATH), in big red letters, in conspicuous places starting fifty meters away, but for some reason, the warning had not registered, until his father and Vasiles called out in unison "Careful."

Lampis did not panic. He inched his foot out of his snagged shoe and untangled the shoe carefully from the wire, managing not to pull at the wire. He put his shoe on again and walked to his father who hugged him.

"Please be careful," his father said.

They were stopped briefly by a communist patrol and were allowed to pass after his father showed him the permit - "the seal of Devil," his father would call it - procured through the offices of a friend of his uncle's.

They walked for thirteen hours, the last nine without any sign of human life, along the railroad tracks, before reaching the outskirts of a farming village. It had rained steadily all day. Their hunger had pushed all other discomforts – tiredness, wetness, fear – out of awareness and gave them enough strength to leap over the fence into a cauliflower field. They each uprooted a cauliflower and devoured it down to its muddy roots. Lampis had stolen once before, a dead bird on a hook, but this time he felt no guilt. After they had eaten, they looked for the gate. They did not have any more strength to leap over the fence.

The rain came down harder and forced them to seek shelter in the first house at the edge of the village. They were made welcome and asked to wait until it stopped raining.

The man of the house kept looking at Lampis and after a while, confessed, "I have only a little bread left for my own children, but I could not bear looking at this child any longer." He went to the next room and returned with a slice of bread.

Lampis took it, thanked the man and offered a bite to his father and Vasiles. He did not remember eating the bread. He must have just swallowed it in one gulp.

When the rain subsided, they resumed their journey. They had a letter from his uncle to a man in this village. They found the man's home without difficulty and before long, they were sitting by a fireplace eating a version of pancakes and olives. Lampis ate seven of the generous-in-size pancakes and emptied a cup of wine in spite of his father's pleas and struggle to take it from him. He had lost his sense of satiety and maybe propriety, letting a very old woman warm his hands and bare knees with a warm towel.

They left hurriedly before darkness set in, returning to the railroad tracks in the hope of hitching a ride on a truck going south from the next town. They walked briskly, silently, without tumbling, in the thickening darkness and thinking only of reaching home. One and one-half hours later, they had reached Elefsina, the next town. The warmed and dried themselves partially by an outdoor fire and climbed on the back of a truck heading south. The dampness, coldness, and aching from fatigue were driven deeper in what was left of his flesh as Lampis bounced in the empty truck as it passed through roads full of potholes. They traveled very slowly, without headlights, along a road that had been churned by tanks and half-tracks hauling heavy and field artillery for the last four years. The pain from bouncing on his seat and against the side of the truck made him wonder whether it would be better to walk.

"It will be much better after we cross the canal into Peloponnesus, when the headlights of the truck could be turned on," his father said.

Three hours later, Lampis sat warming himself by an open fire in an empty warehouse. He listened to empty talk by stranded truck drivers and tried to convince himself that the worst was over. He prayed that his father would find another truck and the ride would be less bumpy. His prayers were answered at about one o'clock in the morning. He had been up for twenty-two hours, walking in the rain for at least sixteen of those hours, and was tired. Earlier, they had crossed the canal with the truck on a raft pulled by pulleys. And, as if secure in the soil of the Peloponnesus or overcome by fatigue, he fell asleep, within minutes after climbing into the truck. He was awakened in a corner of a guardhouse, warm, comfortable and rested across the street from St. Peter's Church in Argos. He didn't know how he arrived there, but he knew that he was much closer to home and far away from the hell of Athens. He stretched out and walked around to limber up. He was stiff but not aching.

Lampis looked around and contrasted the people in Argos, walking and stopping in the middle of the street for a chat, with the people in Athens, dashing from corner to corner and reconnoitering before making the next move in deserted streets. He felt safe and hoped that the short winter day would shrink even faster so that he could start on the next step of his journey home. His father returned with "good news." He had bought some lamb chops and taken them to a tavern, where they were preparing them for them. Lampis hadn't had meat in ages. When they began eating, his anticipation and gratification of the taste were not realized. He had lost his sense of taste! He chewed the meat, making the bite small enough to swallow and washed it down with some wine, following a ritual. He had no taste at all! They talked about starting out on foot if they did not find a ride. Tripolis was sixty kilometers away, or about a fifteen hour walk in the dark. They would make it easily.

The next few hours were interminable. Gazing at the castle atop the hill and counting its outposts, following the winding and crisscrossing of the streets, contrasting the walks and behavior of the shoppers and idlers with each other, and studying the designs on the bell-tower of St. Peter's Church did not make time move faster. Every time Lampis looked at the clock on the belfry, he wondered whether the hands had been stuck. He listened to the Andartes' (guerillas') conversation, but it seemed boring. He wondered whether they were bored and just trying to make conversation or whether they missed their home, like he missed his. He didn't even listen to his father, except when he reported his plans to find a ride or start walking toward Tripolis. His homesickness was overwhelming, and he kept praying to St. Peter, and to the saint whose chapel he could see halfway up the slope of the hill with the castle at its crown – whoever this saint was – and, more fervently, to St. Nicholas who was the protector of the travelers and who had a home in the monastery near his village. In a few days, he'd be walking to the monastery to light a candle and to hear the celestial chanting of the nuns. And with that thought, he pictured himself traveling on the road to the monastery, stopping at every landmark, every turn of the road, recognizing each tree with its particular shape; anticipating the flight and the cries of the birds; and tracing the ridges of the hills cascading and overlapping each other. He'd be talking with cousin Nick about what he had seen and witnessed in Athens, and what the two of them must do together. He had missed Nick in these eight months of preoccupation with survival.

The hands of the big clock on the belfry had been unstuck and made up for lost time while Lampis had daydreamed walking the road to the monastery and talking with Nick.

"Hurry up. We need to board a half-track tank on the way to Tripolis," his father said.

Lampis was slow in transferring back from his chat with Nick to get his gear ready. When he realized what his father had told him, he rushed up the stairs, but an annoying pebble in his shoe made him stop to remove it. In the meantime, the half-track tank took off. His remorse in that the tank did not wait for them, because of his tardiness, was counter-balanced, partly, by the hope that it would be turned back by the detachment of the Andartes (guerillas) at Miloi, just a few kilometers to the south, after a friendly Andarte from their station telephoned his instructions to turn it back.

Dusk descended the slope of the fortress hill, pulling a dark veil behind it. The ramparts of the fortress were shrouded in a dark mist, their connecting walls receding into oblivion. St. Peter's Square and the streets were emptying out and the voices of the remaining pedestrians became more distinct. Darkness and emptiness encroached his thoughts, but he was immune to despair. Faith and determination had taken deep roots in his soul, but he did not forget to pray for another ride.

The roaring of two fighter planes tearing the mantle of dusk did not disturb him or frighten him. He just wondered what they were up to. The answer came a few minutes later with the explosion of their bombs. He wondered what their target was as they flew North, in the opposite direction, and prayed that his father finds another ride. A few minutes later, he heard that the tank that they had missed, because of his tardiness, had been bombed by the airplanes and had been blown to splinters.

The answers to his prayers came quickly. He climbed aboard a truck, sat in a corner for protection against the cold wind of the night, and spent the next five hours half-asleep, half-numb and cold, listening to stories by his father and the other passengers as they traveled slowly in the night, without headlights, across the plain of Argos and then up and down – mostly up - the winding, potholed road. The conversation reflected resignation or defeat. Tales of suffering, descriptions of scenes of destruction and ruins, enumerations of mass executions and of multitudes of hostages were exchanged in a continuous succession without emotion. Not a word about the future, not even about the next day. The story of the young man, about the foiled attempt to blow up the Hotel Grand Bretagne, after walking for interminable hours through the sewers of Athens to come under the Hotel, whether true or not, kept him interested and suppressed his motion sickness. The penetrating cold air of the mountain, coming across and down the denuded slopes, kept him awake and thinking of his return to the bosom of his mother.

They arrived in Tripolis around 1:00 A.M. and went directly to Aunt Katherina's house. He did not remember any distractions from the time when they climbed down from the truck to the moment his father knocked on Aunt Katerina's window, but his father's calling, "Kyra Katerina (Mrs. Catherine)," and her response, "Immediately, Kyr Metso (Mr. Metso)," were as clear now as when he heard them then. The warmth of her greetings, of her trahana soup, heated quickly on the pot belly stove, and of the blankets over him pushed back and far away the memories of starvation and deprivation.

The next morning, refreshed after a sound sleep and replenished with the energy of a hearty breakfast of bread and cheese, he was ready to walk through the snow for six hours to reach his village. His father had hesitated in offering Aunt Katerina some money, lest he insult her sense of hospitality, and she hesitated in taking it, lest her dire need for it be revealed. He understood, from their expressions, that their respect and trust for each other transcended artificial proprieties. His father had been up early, had found a truck that would take them to his mother's village, only a two hours' walk from home, and seemed in high spirits. The encounter with one of his father's acquaintances, a storekeeper in Tripolis, just before boarding the truck, seemed pertinent only in that this well-fed and self-important storekeeper expressed disbelief that they had managed to survive the events of, and escape from within, the boundaries of Athens. Somehow, these comments made him feel superior to this prosperous "merchant," and his father looked like a giant in comparison. Their companion from Athens had remained in the background of his awareness from the time they had devoured the cauliflowers in the field. He had become animated and made his presence rather conspicuous.

The trip to his mother's village was short, in broad daylight, and a joyride in comparison to the long hours of bouncing in the two previous nights. Uncle Nicholas and Aunt Antonia couldn't believe their eyes or suppress their joy when they saw them. It was New Year's Day, the feast of Saint Basil, and a cause for celebration. The meal, lamb with noodles, was delicious and miraculously had returned his sense of taste, to his surprise and enjoyment. The uncle's and aunt's supplications to them to spend the night in their home and leave the next day, after some of the snow had melted during the warm and bright day, fell on deaf ears. Now that Lampis was so close to home, nothing could stop him. The restful sleep of the previous night, the sumptuous and nourishing meal, and more importantly, the anticipation of seeing his mother again had erased all sense of tiredness and fired his determination to overcome any supplications from his uncle and aunt or hesitation in his father. Lampis argued that the people of Vlahokerasia, a neighboring head village, traveled to their wintering sheepfold constantly and that the path from Vlahokerasia must be easy to travel. The response that this would make the journey, on foot, about one hour longer, or three to three-and-one-half hours, was too weak to make a dent in his determination. His father, appreciating his son's logic and desire to return home, agreed without much hesitation.

Lampis walked ahead, feeling cheerful and oblivious to the curious inhabitants of Arvanitokerasia, the first village on their way, until they reached the market place of Vlahokerasia. There, as if by divine providence, Uncle Aristides, one of his father's closest friends in whose home he had spent a summer attending private lessons to prepare himself for Gymnasium, saw them coming and rushed at them. The two friends embraced each other tightly, and Uncle Aristides sobbed uncontrollably. His father, appreciating his friend's love and sensing that he had been thought dead, responded with letting his tears wet his friend's shoulder.

His father regained composure first, pulled slightly back, looked into his friend's eyes and inquired, "My wife and children, are they all right?"

Uncle Aristides nodded, unable to speak. He rushed to Lampis and picked him up in his strong arms and held him firmly and securely. He finally uttered his first words, "My boy. My boy."

They sat at a tavern, temporarily surrounded by a crowd eager to hear about what was happening in Athens, and were treated to hot wine with honey. Uncle Aristides, the good and devoted friend, had visited his friend's wife and children several times to offer his help and support. Lampis had appreciated, in his child's way, goodness personified in Aristides. He had also loved his children, John, Tassia, and George and his wife, Aunt Helen. He had felt love and security in their home, and wished to see them again, but his wish to go home was all-consuming. Uncle Aristides did not insist.

"The path is traveled, the snow has been fairly well packed, but the going would be pretty tough up to the summit of Aghia Kyriake. After that, it should be easy," Uncle Aristides said. He briefly embraced him.

They set out for the last leg of their journey.

Lampis walked ahead, setting the pace, even though his father was a fast walker. The snow did not bother him in the least. The cold breeze on his face and naked knees – he wore short pants with knee-high socks – invigorated him, and the peaked homesickness put wings to his feet. His father pleaded with him on a few occasions to slow down lest he tire out, but accepting the futility of his pleas, gave up. At the chapel of St. Athanasius, they slowed down to say goodbye to their companion, Vasiles, who would follow a different path to his village, Kollinai. The climb along the winding path to the summit of Aghia Kyriake, with a few slips and tumbles in the snow, not only did not tire Lampis, but seemed to increase his momentum, giving him strength. The wind along the ridge was brisk but seemed refreshing – as if refreshment were needed. He started to run, but this time had to obey his father's command to slow down.

The sun was now shining brightly, illuminating the familiar ridges and gorges. The flight of the chirping, disturbed bird across their path, the sound of the bells of a flock of goats and of the coaxing of the goatherd, the scent of the blooming and full of ripe-red berries strawberry trees – the symbol of his village – and the snow covered glistening peaks of Taygetus jutting into the blueness of the skies in the south, brought him back to a life full of joyous awareness. He still walked ahead of his father, light-footed and buoyant, full of anticipation for the moment of encounter with his mother, brothers, sister and the charred, but still comforting ruins of his home. His joy was fanned by the swaying of the branches in the breeze, soaring with the flight of the hawk, shining with the reflection of the sun in the puddles in his path. This was his world, his world of bright sunny days in the winter, of fragrance and song in the spring, of playing in the day and counting the stars at night in the summer, and of watching the swallows fly south in autumn.

Lampis was in the center of this world again, the world with its definitive boundaries by the ridges of the mountains all around; its connection with other worlds through a gorge in the Southwest and an opening in the Northwest; its messages to God with the sound of the church bells, and its perpetual rebirth from the song of the birds and the whispers of the breezes in the quiet of the night. He felt, thought, and exhilarated without words in sequence, without images in array, and without events in order.

Neither he nor his father spoke. Only fleetingly, he wondered what his father may be thinking.

Knowing that his father was happy, he felt licensed to allow his joy to leap from ridge to ridge, to look down on the slopes and ravines, to inflate his lungs with the pure, crisp air, and to connect the landmarks with memories – memories that made him think that he existed from the beginning of time. He did not kick the pebbles in his path. He looked at the thorny shrubs with affection, caressed the branch of heather leaning over the edge of the path, and he knew that they were all happy that he was there. Neither he nor the trees cast any shadows. The crowing of the ravens sounded like a greeting; a patch of cloud grew softer and whiter to announce his coming.

The unfolding of the path before him revealed new marvels of life with the tracks of goats and mules, with the scurrying of a lizard to cover, with the ripe-red berries and bittersweet flowers of a branch of the Strawberry tree. He felt guilty that he had disrupted the tracks in his path with his own, regretted that the lizard hid from him, and looked for more branches with flowers and berries. He was insatiable, but still, the drive to reach home dominated and urged him on, past all these greetings and all these links with existence.

Lampis flew on and on ahead of his father and of his own footsteps, until suddenly, a sound fused the memories with the now, followed by a voice that jarred his heart to pounding hard and detonated his joy with the cry.

"Gheorgo! Nicko!"

This cry echoed a few times from the slopes across ravines, multiplying his joy. His brothers' response came somewhere between his crying out and the return of the echoes. After the last echo, there seemed to be an inestimable interval of total silence and void.

George emerged from the edge of the woods, took one look at Lampis, put wings on his bare feet and flew home, not once turning around to confirm what he had seen.

Lampis' youngest brother and his sister came out of the woods, rushed to them and fell in their father's arms. They hugged Lampis, cried, jumped up and down, and then rounded up the goats and mule to return home with them. Their chatting and chirping together and disconnectedly, added to the mosaic of his emotions from being among them, from anticipating the sights at the next turn of the road, from the realization that he had been resurrected, and from the thought of tomorrow – there was no pattern in this mosaic, only a glow of inexpressible, soul-lifting, beauty illuminating and blinding the universe. He was carried aloft, with his brothers' and sister's voices lifting him up. His father's responses to their joy and curiosity kept him at the end of the leash of security and safety.

George's tiding had brought a crowd out to greet them. Those who loved them the most ran ahead of the others, crying without restraint, beyond the edge of the village. They greeted them, hugged them, and stepped aside to let them pass on their way home. Lampis remembered them all. He loved them all, some more, some less. He felt his knees weaken, not from fatigue, but kept walking home, alongside his father, with his youngest brother in between, and his sister on the other side of his father. His mother stood in front of the house, her arms by her side, the corners of her mouth pulled back in an effort to suppress the sobs, her eyes swelling with tears, her gaze fixed on her family. His father let the hands of his two children drop and walked resolutely to his wife. They looked into each other's eyes for a moment and fell in each other's arms in a tight squeeze that fused their fateful existence into one.

Lampis witnessed this renewal of their covenants, crying softly in his soaring happiness.

CHAPTER 11

LAMPIS STOPPED WALKING, turned to his right, gripped the ship's rails for support in his effort to return from the past, and concluded with the thought, "Yes, I have witnessed and experienced 'pure love' at its strongest expression. I have lived in its confines." Yet he could not leap from the past to this moment without assessing the width and depth of the interval; almost six and one-half years of peaks and valleys, some steep, some gentle, some precipitous, and some rolling. Six and one-half years! So long ago and far away! He had never imagined, until just two months ago, that he would be so removed, in space and time, from his past, that there would be a loss of continuity, except for the memories in his life; that he would accept this gap without tears or resentment.

Lampis looked out into the darkness and the heaving omnipotent ocean. He looked at the chimney and the masts of his ship slowly tearing the heavy settling clouds, and he listened to the repetitious arrhythmic splashing of the waves against the sides of the ship. He estimated that Good Friday services must have begun, but for a few long minutes he was unable to unglue from the rails and start a slow, very slow, walk back to the lounge – converted chapel for the services. The odyssey of six and one-half years ago from Athens to his village, had tired him out. He remembered, on his way to the chapel, his earlier transient loss of awareness and shuddered at the thought of its recurring.

The lounge-chapel was congested by Greek and Italian passengers holding lit candles. They had transfixed their gleaming, sorrowful gazes at and beyond the intoning, solemn priest. Lampis scanned the congregation for Demetri. He found him standing in the front row, holding the candle in his left hand and crossing himself with the right.

The sight of Demetri standing among strangers, the revived memories of the evening out on the deck, the reality of his surroundings in this gently rocking ship and the solemnity of the hymns to the burial of Christ, raised a hard lump in his throat.

Lampis could not raise or swallow this lump to sing with the rest of the congregation the "Kyrie Eleison." He could not hold back his tears when the hymn recounted Mary's dirge at the burial. He remembered his own mother standing with hunched shoulders, cheeks furrowed with tears, and managing to wave slowly as the bus moved into the thin mist of the early morning.

The Italian standing on his left leaned gently against him, with the rocking of the ship, revealed his understanding with a half-smile, and squeezed his left wrist to seal an insoluble bond in fate and faith. Lampis hoped that his own return smile conveyed his appreciation and resolved to retain this gesture – and bond – forever.

The hymns and intonations filled the room and the soul, recounting the events the grief, the despair, and finally, the hope of resurrection. He listened attentively, impressing every word in his intellectual existence and not anticipating, as he used to do in the past, the next verse or movement. He did not look at the fellow passengers, lest he commit a sacrilege against the devout collective grief and the inviolable private response to the most solemn of events.

He followed Joseph and Nicodemus from pleading with Pontius Pilate to their climbing slowly up the slope of Calvary, to their removing the nails from Christ's wrists and feet, to their lowering the limp body from the cross down the ladder, to their stretching His body reverently on the ground and wrapping it gently with the shroud, to their looking into each other's moist eyes, kneeling on either side of Him, with an expression of stunned disbelief at their courage to undertake this enormous task, to their slow, deliberate and resolute walk, with the burden of His body and of their mission, to the gaping tomb, oblivious to the indifferent Roman soldiers and to the resigned Jews. He followed them as they gently deposited His body into the tomb and arranged the fold of the shroud in neat, parallel creases, to their last gaze at His stretched-out body, to their rolling the stone to the entrance of the tomb, to their walking away from Mary and John after a final, supreme and futile effort at expressing their love and grief in words.

He fixed his gaze on Mary, standing fixed to the same spot, stooping from the burden of grief, holding the corner of her kerchief to the corner of her right eye, shaking with the more violent sobs, following Joseph and Nicodemus at their superhuman task, and glancing fleetingly at Mary Magdalene to her right.

Lampis felt the same breeze that made the garments at Calvary cling to their body on one side and flutter in the other direction. He felt their grief weighing heavier with the ingratitude and the injustice from those He came to save, and he remembered or whispered His "Forgive them, Father, for they know not what they're doing."

The concluding "Amen" of the priest hung over him for a few moments. He made no attempt to come back from Calvary, transferring Nicodemus to the priest tidying his shawls and altar. He was finally brought back by the timid "Excuse me," from the Italian on his left who wished to leave. Lampis stepped aside, after exchanging binding glances with the Italian, and looked for Demetri who had left his spot.

A few minutes later, Demetri tugged at his sleeve, his eyes moist and his cheeks pale.

"Remember?" Demetri managed to utter and fell silent.

They walked out of the lounge – no longer a chapel – and out to the deck. The shadows of the lifeboats from the lights in the upper deck, spread and receded; the waves surged and collapsed; the darkness closed in with a heavy mantle; and the distance from life to nothingness seemed frighteningly short. They walked a few paces, stopped, remained silent for a long time, and tried to divine, but not violate each other's thoughts.

"On the way home from church I would stop and listen to the nightingale's song, so clear in the night, with the background of the whispering light breeze and the babbling brook. Did you do that, too? Remember?" Demetri said.

"My home was only about fifty meters from the church, but I'd go to the balcony of my home and listen to the nightingales, and I remember being upset whenever a dog barked and wondering why the owl cried. My mother had to remind me several times that it was time to go to bed."

Demetri was tired and cold. They walked back in, descended the stairways and parted with a firm handshake and a long look into each other's eyes. The stairways and the hallways were deserted. Lampis walked slowly to his cabin and opened the door gently and climbed to his bunk quietly. He listened to his cabinmates' sighs for a few minutes, leaped from hilltop to hilltop around his village and faded into the unawareness of sleep.

The chimes of the call to breakfast stirred Lampis and his cabinmates to life. They exchanged polite "good mornings," dressed and left. Lampis lay in his bunk alone, looking through the porthole at cresting and spreading waves in their ceaseless chase to overtake each other, and waited for the second call. His thoughts surfaced and drowned with the waves; his mind groped aimlessly with the rocking and swaying of the ship; and his emotions, momentarily each time, transferred him to his past and to his dreams. His hunger pangs competed with his mind. His body remained motionless, still. He was suspended in time, and he waited for the chimes to bring him back from the void.

When the chimes rang through the hallways, he rose and dressed routinely, much like his cabinmates had done, and headed mechanically for the dining room. Kalliope was there, exchanging words with her mother and staring at the swaying canary's cage at the far corner.

"Good morning," he said to her.

"Good morning," Kalliope replied, conveying both intimacy and estrangement at the same time, and fixed her eyes on the canary again.

One of the older men at his table kept looking at him, as if inviting a question or hoping for the start of a conversation. "You say you're going to be a doctor?" he asked. The tone of the question suggested benevolent curiosity.

Lampis looked up at him. "Yes."

"Who's going to support you? Relatives?"

"No one is going to support me. My mind and hands will support me. I don't expect anything from my relatives," he answered with the same resolution.

"But all those long years, the competition with American kids. You'll have to eat, pay rent, buy clothes and shoes. How are you going to do it?"

"I'll do it. I'll make it."

"And your health? What if you get sick?"

"I won't get sick. I just won't get sick."

The man looked at him intently, smiled, and concluded, "I think you'll do it. No, I know you'll do it. My prayers go with you."

Kalliope, apparently listening, echoed, "I, too, know you'll make it." She looked at the man, then at Lampis, and finally at her mother. Her mother's expression, without words, was a "Me, too."

Lampis finished his breakfast and started to walk. Someone gripped his arm gently and he turned to look.

Kalliope looked into his eyes. "I am already proud of you." She turned to her mother.

"Thank you." Lampis could not think of anything else to say. He walked out of the dining room. His words and those of the others kept ringing in his ears.

He walked out on the deck. A hazy sun had emerged out of the water to the East. The horizon seemed ovoid, with the ship closer to the western boundary. The mist sprayed the lower decks. The waves rose and dipped, as if gathering strength. The flag fluttered furiously; the cables clanged against the masts. Two crewmen worked silently at the stern. Alkis was strolling alone, broad-chested and erect, like Jason aboard the Argo. The blond girl occupied her usual spot, looking straight ahead with resolution. Had she passed the point of no return? A young couple under the stairway stood silently, hands locked, after exchanging either vows or regrets – she was disembarking at Halifax, he was going on to New York.

Kostas, walking in the opposite direction, stopped to say only, "In a few more days, we'll be there."

Lampis kept his pace. Here the paint was peeling off; there it seemed thicker and fresher; there was a splinter on the railing; the deck was so clean. The mast tilted more to the right; the smoke from the chimney seemed whiter today. Why could he not hear his footsteps? He inflated his lungs with an effort. Saint Nicholas is the patron and protector of the sailors. Did the captain of this ship pray? That extra flag pole! Were the sailors reverent to the Portuguese flag? Who'd want to play shuffle-board now? That door is heavy!

"May I walk with you? What are you thinking?" Kalliope interrupted his wanderings.

"You may. I wasn't thinking anything."

They walked for two to three minutes. He was glad that she was with him but did not know how to say it or whether to ask her why she wished to walk with him. He glanced at her timidly

She was walking lightly, looking straight ahead, her arms folded across her chest, her shoulders pulled forward, her lips lightly blue.

"Aren't you cold?" He was surprised that he had asked the question aloud.

"I am, but I would like to walk with you for a while, if you don't mind."

"I would enjoy it," he said in a somewhat pleading way, especially if she talked.

He was quite certain she would not repeat "You're hopeless." Whatever she said, he would absorb, to recall in the future, the sound of her voice and the ringing of her words.

"I had to tell you how sad I am that you're not staying in New York, that the thought of not ever seeing you again is unbearable. I told my mother this morning after breakfast, that I would like to observe your struggles in pursuing your goal, that I would like to *share* your triumphs, to be there touching your hand when you hurt, to make myself available whenever you needed me. You keep telling yourself, at least since we met – and everybody hears it – that you don't need anybody. I couldn't keep it from my mother, that if you ever needed somebody, I pray that that somebody is me." She stopped talking.

They walked half the length of the deck before he turned to look at her.

She gazed straight ahead, her arms still crossed high on her chest, her jaw tight. A wisp of hair flickered in the breeze across her arching eyebrow and her thick, long eyelashes. Her classical Greek nose, the full, slightly blue lips, the slightly protruding chin, the crease between the lower lip and the chin, the light swarthy complexion, the shallow dimple, the perfect harmony of her features in profile made him wonder how close to perfection her beauty came.

He managed to suppress his desire to answer this question, after an "en face" view, with recalling his timidity and fear of awkwardness. The same fear drowned his wish to tell her she was beautiful.

"My mother cried," she added, obviously with some effort, "and urged me to tell you. So here I am telling you."

He said nothing. They walked in silence again, almost to the "heavy door."

She turned and looked into his eyes, her arms still nailed across her chest. "I know I won't ever see you again after New York. I pray you remember our encounter, even after you reach your goal."

He hoped she could read his answer in his eyes. He could not talk.

She unfolded her arms and offered him her hands, leaning slightly back.

He took her hands gently and shook his head from side to side, not losing eye contact, He tried to smile, feeling a lump expanding in his throat. He drew his hands slowly back. They stepped back, two or three steps.

She turned halfway, still looking at him, and tried to open the door by pushing instead of pulling. When somebody pushed the door from the inside, they were saved from the surge of their emotions. She managed to smile and wave weakly before the door closed and separated them.

Lampis counted his steps, walking away slowly and trying to displace the thought, "What if she opens the door and calls me? What will I do?" He fixed his gaze at the fluttering flag to keep from turning around to see whether she had come out.

Finally, he summoned the strength to quicken his step and walk to the bow of the ship. He stood still, legs apart and hands clasped behind his back, to challenge the strong breeze and deliberate whether the damp coolness in his open-shirted chest was hedonistic or simply numbness.

His tears streamed slowly down his cheeks. The lump in his throat swelled. He could not decide why he was weeping. The memory of climbing the ladder up the ship did not hold. The misty image of his mother through the window of the bus was swept by a gust of the whistling breeze; the comparison with his father standing alone and above the crowd seemed sacrilegious; Kalliope's wisp of hair across her eyelashes kept flickering hypnotically before him.

He leaned slightly forward to maintain his balance against the breeze and his emotions, and he remained transfixed to the same spot for a long time. He could not estimate how long. The intervals between thoughts and memories changed from one to the next – intervals with total void – his own significance shrinking and dissolving in the spray from the waves.

A new thought had formed somewhere in the void, gaining strength and reminding him that he was, that he existed, and that Kalliope was real and not a dream. He had resolved to pursue his destiny and with a final supreme effort, resolved that Kalliope could not, must not, distract him.

He had to hold on to this last thought and hold it up to the returning image of the wisp of hair flickering against the long, thick eyelashes.

Lampis walked slowly toward the stern of the ship. His thoughts, carried with the breeze back to his village, were interrupted now and then by someone asking the question, "Aren't you cold and damp?"

He'd reply, "No, I am not," without loss of continuity.

Back home, they'd be sitting quietly around the dinner table. Everything would have been prepared for Easter Sunday, tomorrow. The goat kid had been butchered, its carcass hanging, head down and dripping, in the cellar, and its mother still bleating in grief. The candles had been cast, filling the entire house with the fragrance of the beeswax. The eggs had been dyed. The shoes had been shined. Uncle George had shaved. In a little while, they'll all be sleeping in anticipation of the tolls of the bells to summon them to celebrate the Resurrection of Christ. Of course, they'll miss him. They love him!

"You'd better come inside, son," the old man who had declared his faith in him earlier implored. "It's cold and damp out there, and you've been walking the decks for a long time."

Lampis felt the firm, yet gentle grip on his wrist, and he obeyed, following the old man to the lounge. The old man's affection, transmitted through his wrist, sent shivers through Lampis's soul.

The old man stood before him, raised his eyes, and after their eyes met, pronounced, "Blessed is the woman who bears a son like you!" After a brief pause, he added, "And you write her often, you hear!" He let go of his wrists and walked slowly away.

"I will write her often," Lampis promised, and added, "Thank you."

He saw only half of the old man's smile, as he turned to acknowledge that he had heard.

Lampis sank in a chair and listened to Bach distractedly. His musician friend, playing the cello today, looked at him intently and inquiringly. He returned a half-smile and shifted his eyes to Alkis who seemed to be totally absorbed. The children around him had been infected and sat still, looking at their hero, but not at each other. Demetri was among them, an expression of bliss, mixed with awe, fixed on his broad face.

The sky hung low. The flecks of gray clouds tangled with the spray from the heaving ocean. The horizon to the South was closing in. Lampis could not imagine all these elements being lifeless.

He gazed out the window and floated with the notes among the clouds, over the swells and dips of the ocean and beyond the confines of the horizon, to a bright mellow expanse of blossoms, swaying in a gentle breeze and kissed by dotted, multicolored butterflies.

He was carried, arms spread out and head turning rhythmically from side to side, over shallow valleys with lazy winding brooks and nightingales flitting from branch to branch and bush to bush; over gentle slopes carpeted with daisies; over low hills rolling to the feet of each other; over broad patches of grass blades in confusion; over tree tops comforting ferns and bunnies in their shade. And he was finally lowered to the roof of a white-washed chapel with its bell ringing in the breeze; he was enticed to swing from cloud to cloud, to nurse on the fragrance of the wildflowers, and to slide down the rays of the mellow spring light to the halo around the peaks of the mountains at the end of his awareness.

He reveled in the weightlessness of his corporeal existence, surrendered to the celestial ascension, and shielded his eyes from his own transfiguration.

He thinned out, spreading high to heaven and across to the limits of his cognizance, but managed to recoil, with pauses between movements, trying to fathom the musician's concentration in transferring the notes from the page before him to the soul-transporting string of the violin or cello. Time, space, and his own existence seemed to have neither beginning or end. The faces and involuntary movements around him receded and faded in the distance or approached and illuminated like comets. The irreverence of the unsuppressed cough of the smokers was cast down in dark crevices.

The slowly, heaving bosom of the young woman leaning on the table sustained the voyage from creation to fulfillment. Lampis circled the horizon steadily, and spiraled with a gradual acceleration to the sky's dome, condensing his awareness into concentric smaller and smaller circles of "Where am I?", "Why am I?", "Who am I?" and finally "Am I?"

When the music stopped and the initially timid motion around him became movements with directions, he had to struggle only with a question, "Why am I?" Perhaps his musician friend, his cello reverently secured in its case, would come to his aid.

They nodded and smiled at each other, walked out on deck, strolled side by side without talking, came to the end of the deck, and… he wondered "What is he thinking about? Does he know that I am not thinking, only wondering what he's thinking about?"

They stood facing opposite directions for an inestimable length of time.

Finally, his musician friend broke the silence. "I wonder how your next Easter is going to be? I hope you remember this Easter for many years; I hope you remember me, too, with kind memories; I hope you keep what you experienced today in a compartment that you can revisit often to see me, wishing you success and happiness."

The pause that followed was much longer than those between the "I hope's." Then he resumed.

"I looked at you a few times. You were in your private world. I hope I had helped transport you there with my music."

The next pause was the longest. It seemed that the musician was waiting for a response.

"I didn't know where, why, or whether I was," Lampis said. "When I found myself, I knew *where* I was because I was watching you go through your devout rituals with your cello. I knew that I *was* because I witnessed, and I prayed that you help me find *why* I was."

"It's cold and damp, let's go back inside," the older man replied.

They walked back slowly, sat in a corner at the lounge and gazed out the window.

"I can tell you only a very small part of why you are," the musician said, not looking at Lampis. "You are to give a few memories of pure pleasure and of a chance to follow you in my imagination, in the pursuit of your dreams; to kindle the hope that I meet someone like you on the next trip from Greece to America; to contemplate what's in you that invites respect, trust and confidence; and to lament my misfortune in not having met you sooner and known you longer."

A very long silence followed. They still did not look at each other. Lampis also lamented not having known this refined and sensitive man longer but thought it improper or difficult to express his sentiments. He stood up, shook his friend's hand firmly and walked away, without turning, wishing to retain these last sentiments and handshake as the final "farewell."

Lampis walked out on the deck again, hoping to meet no one, to be alone. His friend's words were ringing in his ears. Did he really inspire trust and confidence in people? What had this same man and Kalliope meant when they said, "You frighten me?" Did he frighten his parents, who he hoped trusted in him? Why? He had declared to the old man at his table that he "Would not get sick." Where did he find this strength or defiance? No one had praised him for his strength, compared him to any heroes, or cited him as an example of an achiever. He was disciplined, true, but out of conformity to circumstances, not because of a special will-power. He had cried when Poland fell to the Germans; he had rung church bells furiously with the news of the Greek victories against the Italians; he had despaired when the German army invaded Greece; he had looked at the Italian soldiers first with derision and later with pity; he had separated the human tenderness in some German soldiers from the ferocity of the German Army; he was thinking and hurting when the other children of his age, or older, chased butterflies or competed at stone-throwing. Could it be that he was afraid of life while they were enjoying it? Why was his heart rent with the bleating of the ewe who lost sight of her lamb? Why did he transfer the frolicking of the kid at the edge of a terrace to his own heartbeat? Or flitted from branch to branch with every bird in the spring and perched on the telephone lines with the swallows in preparation for the migration in the fall? Could it be that he could not identify his own separate entity when his playmates knew precisely who they were? He knew now what he wanted and set his sights on his goal, but he did not know who he was? Should he be content in concluding that maybe it was enough that the others knew who he was?

Lampis walked and walked returning to the same spot, quickly when thinking and very slowly – or so it seemed – when a void of thought displaced his awareness of place, time, and self. When he started counting the portholes and life boats, he remembered Demetri had done this counting the very first day on the ship, and that tomorrow he will be parting with Demetri. This realization made swallowing painful and his tears hot. He had come to love Demetri who represented the strongest link to his past. He had delighted in Demetri's innocence, trust and lack of inhibition. In about twelve hours, they'll be embracing each other with farewell wishes and hopes for a reunion. Who knows when they'll see each other again. No questions of if, only when.

The ocean began to heave, initially with the assertion of its omnipotence and finally with the menace of its malevolence. Widely scattered white-caps, separated by higher and broader waves, spread to the purple at the end of his vision. As if to remind him of his insignificance, or of the impotence of the ship that carried him, the ocean shouldered the side of the ship, tilting it to one side, then pulled away, making it fall toward the other side. The flag flapped furiously and the cable beat against the mast maniacally, with the sound of metal against metal ripping the hissing of the densely misty wind. He walked at an uneven pace, slanting his body to an angle against the wind to avoid being slammed against the side of the ship. He pulled at the door handle with both hands, anchoring his feet at the corner between the deck and the frame of the door, and squeezed inside through the half-opening. As he heard the thunderous slamming of the door behind him, someone yelled out, "Get in and close that door."

He was embarrassed after he answered, "I'll think about it."

Lampis walked into the slowly emptying-out lounge, sat in the same corner where he had his earlier conversation with the musician and decided to be the last one out, challenging the nausea and dizziness from the ship's giant teeter-tottering and swaying. Fortunately, it seemed that the others succumbed before he did and one by one staggered out. He rose out of the chair, his stomach lifting up to his throat and sinking down to his knees, and staggered from chair to chair to the door of the lounge. He waited for the right moment, anticipating the tilt or the dive, and plunged for the rail of the stairway. Descending the stairs required a steady concentration in planting his foot. When he reached his deck below, he tried to take long strides to avoid hitting the doors of the cabins as he was tossed from side to side.

His cabinmates were silent. He did not greet them, but climbed to his bunk, stretched out, legs apart, and gripped the side rails. Total darkness enveloped everything; his cabin, his ship, his very existence. The whistling of the winds, the deep shallowly undulating roar, the creaking of the hull, the groaning of the engines and propellers sounded like the groans of a departing soul suspended between earth and hell. His muscles involuntarily or instinctively flexed to keep him from being tossed out of his bunk, suggesting that he had a body to protect against pain. He rescued his own suspended soul and swallowed it together with his nausea.

The frivolous cabinmate finally complained aloud to the Fates or to God, "Some Easter Sunday."

In reply, after a long pause, the cabinmate below him supplicated, "Maybe it'll pass by midnight for the Resurrection services."

Nothing more was said. The repetitiousness, though never in the same sequence, made him wonder whether the perpetuity would continue or this rage of the elements would spend itself and expire with a sigh of exhaustion.

Lampis was not sure whether he had slept or not, when a few hours later, his cabinmate asked without addressing anyone in particular, "Are you going to the Resurrection services?"

Everyone dressed without replying or exchanging a single word and left for the lounge. Within a few minutes after their arrival, the lounge, now chapel again, became densely crowded. Darkness outside was still as thick as pitch. Sheets of rain and torn crests of giant waves still beat against the windows. The winds still hissed maniacally and whistled to a piercing pitch, and explosions of thunder followed the repetitive flashes of lightning. The passenger-worshippers braced against furniture and each other in an anticipatory silence for the chant, "Christ has risen from the dead, having vanquished death with death and to those in graves having offered life."

"Come ye, receive the light from the inextinguishable light," the priest summoned them, holding up a lit candle. The passengers approached him, and he lit their candles. They in turn, lit other people's candles.

"Christ has risen," the priest intoned, lifting his candle.

Everyone chanted along, tracing the sign of the cross with their lit candles. The solemn service was totally spiritual and half way between the ultimate human reach for purity and celestial transfiguration. The Italians did not chant but joined in the transport to the heavenly cathedrals or to the flower-fields where the Resurrected Christ stood, apart from and among them, with His divine blessing and smile. When the service ended, they shook hands with the greeting, "Christos Aneste (Christ is Risen)" followed by the reply, "Alethos Aneste" (Truly he has risen). The Italians quickly learned and repeated "Kristos Aneste" or "Aletos Aneste."

They poured out of the chapel toward the dining room. He found Demetri, and Kalliope found him. They shook hands and kissed on the cheek. His hand and Kalliope's remained locked, and they walked, smiling at each other now and then, in front of her mother, brother, and Demetri. They agreed that this was a memorable service and that the storm was subsiding but said little else. After they cracked their red eggs, clinked their glasses and ate their soup, they parted, kissing on the cheeks again, with light, joyful, nostalgic hearts.

Lampis greeted his cabinmates as he entered the cabin. Before falling asleep, he heard the religious one humming, "Christ has risen," and the quiet one sighing, and the frivolous one snoring. His sleep was light, restful and lulled by the steadily softening sound of the wind and splashing waves. No dreams. Perhaps that's why it seemed that the continuity with the previous night was never interrupted by this sleep when he was awakened by the bell call to breakfast.

Lampis saw a seagull glide by his porthole. He dressed quickly and raced to the deck.

CHAPTER 12

NOT TOO FAR OFF TO THE LEFT, Lampis saw green slopes studded with evergreens, the waves rolling gently toward them. A good crowd was already on deck, some more excited than others. Those disembarking in Halifax were smiling.

Demetri was quite excited.

Kalliope walked up to Lampis and squeezed his hand. "There it is, the New World!"

They gazed at the gentle slopes, holding hands tightly and absorbing the sights as the ship traveled north, parallel to the coastline.

"This is a gentle land, a friendly, welcoming land," he concluded. "I could easily fall in love with it; young, like I am young; looking to the future, like I am looking to the future; dynamic promising, generous. Kalliope, do you share my sentiments?"

"Yes, I am happy at the sameness of our feelings," she replied.

They walked along the deck, back and forth along the landward side, mostly in silence, occasionally looking and smiling at each other, and finally descended the stairway to the dining room for breakfast. The excitement was pervasive, universal, but more evident among those disembarking in Halifax; they seemed to enjoy their last meal on the ship. The chatter was incessant, reminiscent of the chirping of so many sparrows at sunset hidden in the thick branches of the cypress tree.

Kalliope sat with her mother. He returned to his table, after pushing her chair in under her and receiving a "Thank you."

The conversation at his table was lively, mostly conjectural about the differences between Canada and the United States, and punctuated frequently with mixed wishes of "Christos Aneste," and "Good luck." The feeling that the Resurrected Christ had offered them life, along with "those in the graves," was cherished and shared freely. They had suffered through many years, living from day to day, had become accustomed to struggling for survival, and had prayed for deliverance. But now, with the sighting of the coast of the New World, they could look beyond tomorrow into the distant future; they could plan, dream, shed the fears and superstitions – each in his or her own way – and fortify or brace themselves for the challenges in building the new life that the Resurrected Christ had offered them.

Lampis turned to look at Kalliope frequently, and their eyes met with understanding, trust and respect. With their "reconciliation" they had lost some of their inhibitions. Her mother smiled with a mixture of sweetness and serenity, conveying a feeling of satisfaction and gratitude for the encounter. Occasionally, his thoughts drifted off to home, oblivious to the conversation and activities around him, to watch the priest leading the dance around the old plane-tree, after the services of Love in the afternoon, to scan the mountain tops in the horizon, to follow the hawk in its lazy flight.

He would be brought back by the clinking of the glasses and would automatically respond to "Christos Aneste," with "Alethos Aneste" or to "Good Luck," with "Epises" (likewise). He ate voraciously and was eager to return on deck to feast his eyes with the sight of the shoreline of the New World, but he waited for Kalliope to rise first.

When she did, they joined hands and walked out leaving her mother and little brother behind. The first words they exchanged, after assimilating all they could see from the deck, was about the majestic evergreens, the firm foundations of the shoreline, and the smoothness of the green slopes. Their conversation was fragmentary, the continuity provided only with their entwined fingers. His thoughts were incoherent, fleeting, confused with memories and sentiment.

Canada, his friend George's birthplace and the land he loved from early childhood without knowing why, was smiling at him. The whitecaps between the ship and the shore looked like many handkerchiefs waving welcome and bon voyage. The entourage of the seagulls seemed like a welcoming party or the envoy of the divinity of the New World.

The tenderness of Kalliope's touch and smile promised the realization of hopes and dreams. The surfacing of an earlier observation that her legs were "not so pretty" was drowned by the sense of guilt for succumbing to irreverence.

"Are you thinking again?" she asked, with her disarming smile.

The guilt surged to his face with blushing. "I am panting after my thoughts. Many of them escaped me and some of them overwhelm me."

She smiled and squeezed his hand. After a long pause and looking away, she turned to ask him "Have I really met you or am I dreaming? Are you really the way I see you or do I see only what I need?"

He hesitated for a moment before answering, "We have met. Whether you see in me what's good or make me into something that conforms to your needs, I cannot divine. What I know is that I'll be looking for Kalliope in every girl I meet from now on." He wished to say more but fearing he had already muffed what he wished to say and that he may make a worse mess, he kept silent, and so did she.

They paced the deck, glancing and smiling at each other occasionally. He gave up trying to amend what he had said earlier or to start a new conversation, and he rationalized that "maybe she does not wish to talk, anyhow!"

He didn't know what to do with his right hand after they parted. Ahead and to his left, he could see the silhouette of buildings in the mist. He did not pace in the opposite direction anymore. He had observed nature's works in the New World. He wished to blend the wonder of nature to the works of men – Western men, he corrected himself.

The city of Halifax moved gradually out and in front of the mist. The multitude and the noise of the seagulls increased. The ship slowed down. The Canadian flag fluttered in the breeze. The evergreens on the slopes and ridges, the rocks on the shore, and the buildings of the city grew larger and larger. He thought of Demetri who was busy with the final inspection of his Visa and collecting his gear. He would miss Demetri, who in about two hours, would leave the ship and start on his journey to Toronto. Who could not love Demetri? One broad smile and one look from those moist brown eyes is all it took to adopt him. He followed Demetri, in his thoughts, chatting and winning over his uncle, asking what else he could do after he concluded his assigned task, and brightening the confines of his uncle's store or the souls of his coworkers.

His thoughts were interrupted by Demetri's voice. "We arrived! Look! I am ready." His voice full of innocence, excitement, and anticipation. Kalliope excused herself to return to her mother and brother. They turned around, watched and waved back when she, sensing they were following her with their eyes, turned around, smiled, and waved at them.

"You'll be together for two more days; then you part. You'll miss her, won't you?" Demetri asked. "Maybe you can go visit her in New York. Is Chicago far?"

"Yes, Chicago is far away from New York. I'll miss her company!"

They watched the Canadian motor boat escorting their ship and marveled at the tranquility of the land, the city, and the crew of the motorboat. They exchanged vows to never forget their friendship and waited until the ship docked before they turned to look at each other. They embraced tightly and felt each other's chest heave, and parted with choking words, "Good luck. Don't forget." The tears were running freely, silently.

Demetri left to collect his precious luggage of a single, small cardboard suitcase.

Lampis followed him with his eyes to the door, and after a few minutes, moved to the side of the deck to watch him emerge on the pier for one last look.

Alkis was leaning against the rails, conversing with a customs official on the pier. He couldn't decide whether the conversation was in English or in German. He didn't know enough of either. He had tried to study English in the last few weeks, before leaving Greece, but couldn't concentrate and hadn't retained much.

Demetri appeared on the pier, stopped, turned around, scanned the deck, and waved furiously when their eyes met. Alkis interrupted his conversation to join in the waving. Demetri was beaming and continued to turn around, for one more look, as he moved with the small crowd. Lampis watched Demetri and the crowd enter the Customs House and was struck by the resolve and dignity of each individual and collectively.

When Alkis observed, "Look at them, a sample of a great nation going out to conquer," Lampis thought of his remote ancestors disembarking on the coasts of Sicily, Italy, Southern France, North Africa and the Black Sea, to establish cities like Syracuse, Tarans, Naples, Marseilles, etc. He thought of correcting Alkis by substituting, "Making their useful and constructive presence felt" for "conquering," but decided that the interval between Alkis' observation and his appreciation of the difference with his own concept was too long. Besides, this may start a conversation, and he'd rather think than talk, even with Alkis. He remained at the same spot long after the last of the newest immigrants to Canada moved inside the Customs House, imagining them standing in line and moving solemnly to the window where their Visas were inspected and stamped just as they would move in church to partake of Holy Communion – now to start a new life, then to maintain or regain purity of life.

Lampis wondered how the young married woman, who danced and clung amorously with one of the passengers throughout the voyage and whom he had seen in a tearful embrace under the stairway last night, would face her husband; whether she had already made her choice. The blond girl with the thick curls had walked into the Customs House with head held high, looking straight ahead and far away; no trace of sadness or smile on her face. When did she make her resolve?

Kalliope walked slowly toward him. He saw her out of the corner of his eye, but didn't turn to look until she was next to him. She looked sad and preoccupied.

"Are you going to the city?" she asked.

"Yes, I am. I did tell you, didn't I, that I've been in love with Canada since I was a little boy?" he answered.

"I can't," she added. "Mother is not feeling well. I'm not sure whether it's from last night's storm or the anticipation of seeing her sons again. I have to stay with her."

"We're sailing again in about three hours," he said, touching her hands. "If I am to see anything, I better go now."

They walked to the exit holding hands, just like he walked home from church with his sister when he was a little child, and they parted with his wishing that her mother feel better.

The experience of stepping on Canadian soil was not fully anticipated. The physical sensation of goose bumps, the lump in the throat, and the tears streaming down his cheeks were born from and replaced by the emotions from realizing a cherished dream, the attainment of the ultimate fulfillment in the embrace of the strongest love, and the abandon of one's own very existence to a nurtured passion.

"This is Canada. This is the New World. I am in it and a part of it now," he kept repeating as he roamed aimlessly in the streets of Halifax.

He was impressed with the solid, austere buildings, with the broad peaceful streets and with the confident people he observed. But these impressions swelled and spilled to flood his whole world of awareness, identity and intellect. He floated in this flood, now in total abandon, now with his sights on a distant goal, and now flexing his muscles with a grip at the oars of his destiny. He walked for about two hours, keeping the landmarks of the harbor in sight, absorbing all he could when not occupied with thinking and dreaming.

It seemed strange that darkness fell so early and so quickly. The quietness made him feel that he was left behind in a retreat. He looked at his watch, and started walking toward the harbor, turning around to look at the empty street and measuring its length to the borders of darkness. His steps were uneven at times, as if he were still on the rocking ship. Before reaching the ship, he mailed a postcard to his parents. He was one of the last to board the ship.

The lights of the city faded gradually. A hazy yellow light spread across the northern curve of the horizon, shrinking and compressed by darkness to a faint glow before sinking behind the waves. The familiar sounds of waves splashing and tearing, the forever traveling breezes, and the groans of the engines returned in a cacophonic competition that could neither lull or stimulate. He lingered on deck, recalling and rearranging in sequence his memories of the day. Some of his emotions returned with the same intensity, some became magnified with re-emerging images, and some were dulled with the arguments of logic. The bell call to supper seemed distant and faint, but his hunger was quite strong.

When he descended to the dining room, he was almost overcome with the oppressiveness of silence. Half empty, subdued, ritualistic. Kalliope sat next to her brother with only one other man at the table, reminding her distracted brother to eat. Her mother was still not feeling well. His table was half empty, even though only the man sitting on his left disembarked at Halifax. The man who had shown him his faith, managed to toast "Christos Aneste," and "Kale Patrida" (happy return to the fatherland); after a while, he toasted those who disembarked for Canada with a simple "Good luck to them."

Kalliope left with a nod and a half smile. He wondered if they were all sad because of the separation in Halifax, the loss of short but intense friendships, or were they mustering strength for the challenges ahead with a last call on their reserves? They had made contact with the New World! Had that strengthened their resolve or drained some of their determination? For his part, that contact had sealed his Fate, the Fate that he was pursuing. He felt stronger than ever.

The ship began to roll and pitch more violently. The dishes slid from side to side and some over the edges, breaking or sliding across the floor. Lampis rose, concentrating on the lessons he had learned in the past fifteen days, and walked out of the dining room to his cabin without any mishaps. He was quite proud of this accomplishment.

After he climbed to his bunk and braced himself against the rolling and tossing, he decided to concentrate on assessing the furor of the storm and comparing it with his past experiences. Before long, he found it more expedient to concentrate on holding onto the rails and to keep from being flung across the cabin or against the ceiling. The winds hissed with diabolical intention; the waves rose as if to tear a hole in the dome of the sky; the horn bellowed every minute with long warnings or defiance; the engines roared and drowned intermittently; and the hull creaked to a chilling pitch with every toss rise, or dive. The cabinmate across from him on the upper bunk said, "This storm can blow itself with all its might and all the furor of all the battalions of its devil allies. God, the risen from the dead Christ, will protect this ship."

This comment amused and reassured Lampis. He thought of Kalliope's mother and little brother, of the captain and the pilot on the bridge, of the old priest who had disappeared again after the Service of Resurrection – he had not seen him disembark in Halifax. The tossing and pitching began to decrease at 4:00 A.M., when he looked at his watch. He drifted off to sleep until about 10:00 A.M., missing breakfast.

The ocean looked tired and defeated, but not accepting defeat very graciously. It still rose and dipped threateningly and sprayed him a few times when he walked out on deck. He could not see land, but the haze, shredded at its circumference, with the sun to the left of the broadside of the ship, told him that they were traveling south-southwest. He climbed to the upper deck, to keep from being sprayed and walked slowly round and around. The memory of last night's storm, the gray low sky, and the unpredictable rolling of the ship were not conducive to thinking – not even to deciding whether to stay on deck and keep walking or return to the lounge. When he finally returned to the lounge, he found the same oppressive silence he had witnessed the previous night. Even those playing cards were silent.

Lampis sat with Peter and his sister Maria, who looked very pale and tired.

"Did you hear that the waves kept going over the bridge last night, that this was one of the worst storms this ship has encountered?" Peter asked.

"I had not heard," Lampis answered. He had not talked with anyone, but he was not surprised. He scanned the lounge again, looking for Kalliope. She was not there.

The musician joined them.

"No music today?" Lampis asked him.

"No. It'd be a waste of effort, can't you see? It's always like this on the last day. Even without a storm."

They sat there, silent like the rest, until the bell-call for dinner – one sitting today and one tomorrow. They went to dinner together. They could sit anywhere and with whomever they wished. They sat with Kalliope, her mother and her little brother. Dinner was slow, quiet, and punctuated only with occasional laconic remarks out of politeness. Both Kalliope and her mother appeared tired and pale. The little boy seemed to be studying everybody new at his table. The few, awkward attempts at starting a conversation were followed by an uncomfortable silence after either a blank stare or a half-smile. Knives were used when not needed; spoons and forks were suspended halfway between plate and mouth and deposited back on the plate, laden, most of the time; mouths were wiped again, two-three times, between swallows, and glasses were placed back on the exact spot with their contents at the same level, even after reaching the lips.

With a supreme effort, Lampis raised his glass, looked at and past everyone, and managed to toast without choking. "May we start on the right foot to a future of success and happiness."

All glasses, including the little boy's, were raised and met over the center of the table. The sound of the clinking was followed by a uniform "Amen."

Kalliope's mother looked at everyone successively, her large dark eyes full of tears and benevolence, before pronouncing with sweetness and sincerity, "You have all become a part of me, in these last two weeks or so; I will miss you and pray for you. I know you're good, and that you'll stay pure. I hope you'll remember me as someone who loved you."

Kalliope leaned over and kissed her. The rest looked at each other and at her and answered in unison, with a simple, "Thank you." Then, as if frightened at the prospect of another prolonged silence, they started talking at the same time, apologized, started again and finally laughed and joined hands as if to affirm an indissoluble bond. The spell of sadness had been exorcised by this pronouncement and demonstration of love.

Lampis turned to Kalliope, his knee touching hers accidentally – she did not pull her knee away, probably to spare him the embarrassment for not begging her pardon – and invited her, by looking into her eyes, to start the conversation.

She obliged. "I told Mother about your poems and about some of our conversations; that I was flattered in your sharing your thoughts with me; that I hope you turn to writing whenever your emotions threaten to overwhelm you; that some of the greatest writers were physicians…"

She halted between each "that," but after the last sentence, she looked at her mother for her response.

Her mother continued. "And that you're very sensitive and easy to hurt. She does not keep much, if anything, from me."

"Why didn't you show any of those poems to me?" Peter protested to Lampis. "Were you afraid I would not understand?" This comment suggested that no response was needed and was followed by teasing. "Maybe you think girls are more sensitive to poetry."

Maria thrust her elbow at Peter's rib and made Peter and everybody else laugh, to Maria's bashful embarrassment.

They talked about those who disembarked at Halifax, about their journey to their final destination, about their own anticipated encounters, and about their return to Greece – whenever that may be. Their spirits were up again, and when they left the table to return to the lounge, they seemed to infect their fellow passengers with a "cheer up, better things are coming," attitude.

Lampis walked with Kalliope, behind Peter and Maria, full of self-confidence and resolution again. Now and then, Peter would turn around to make some clever remark and laugh at Maria's embarrassment, the laughing echoed by Kalliope's brother who was bringing up the rear. Although careful not to bump against Kalliope, with the rocking of the ship, Lampis was half-hoping that she would lose her balance and fall against him. It didn't happen.

They found a table in the crowded lounge and sat in silence, listening to music. His musician friend was playing the cello, totally absorbed in his music and looking only at his notes and to where his left fingers touched, pressed and quivered on the fingerboard.

For a while, Lampis displaced all thoughts and emotions of the day with the soul-purifying messages from the cello and piano, floating above his corporeal existence and traveling to the ends of the universe with no hindrance from obstacles or time. He shrank back to awareness of his surroundings when joining in the applause for the musicians. His eyes met with his musician friend's.

Lampis assured Kalliope and Peter that he was all right, excused himself and walked out on deck for his last farewell stroll along the intimate-by-now decks. Every lifeboat, every porthole, every clank of the cable against the mast reminded him of thoughts and doubts that he had hoped to suppress or conceal. Surrendering to the realization that he could not escape, he allowed these same thoughts to surface, to pull him in all directions, to scatter, to return, to take new forms, and to drain him.

The wind hissed and howled. The ship rose and fell, rolling from side to side. His limbs were numbed from the cold. He descended to his cabin and after putting on his pajamas, climbed to his bunk to spend his last night on ship.

A chapter of his life closed with the menacing of a whistling wind, the battering of the waves against the porthole, and the groaning of the tireless engines.

The mist thickened in the distance and shrouded what lay beyond, allowing only the imagination to penetrate and reach the sites from the memories of pictures in books or movies: the Statue of Liberty raising its torch toward the heavens and the skyscrapers piercing the clouds; Broadway and Fifth Avenue crowded with slow moving cars and street-cars in the middle and with people along the sidewalks; neon lights flashing, and flowing titles and advertisements in bright colors; and the present pitting its vitality against both the splendors of the past and the lull of eternity.

Lampis strolled from deck to deck, from one site to the other, eager for the moment when his memories would collide and fuse with a reality for the beginning of his new, fertile existence. His acquaintances moved across his gaze and into the past, changed imperceptibly into memories and surprised him with their return to his present at the next encounter in his dream-walk. He acknowledged and exchanged greetings, echoed the announcement "We've arrived" to strengthen it into a conviction, and gathered the forming and changing images from the activities around him to forge one more link between his past and his future.

The burst of activity, spontaneous and unpredictable, disrupted the prolonged, expectant silence and pulled his thoughts from beyond the gray mist of the almost touchable horizon and from the folding-unfolding past to the expressions in the faces of his fellow passengers. Condensing all his emotions, dreams, and apprehension into "I've arrived at my destination, at the foot of the mountain to climb," he tried to divine the messages from the depths of emotional turmoil to the tight jaws, hard swallows and moist eyes. Was the silence a tribute to the strength of the determination to reach this moment? Was it in reverence to the union of past and future? Was it in deference to the privacy of whomever stood next to him or was it plain awe before the unknown? Some walked straight with chest puffed out and chin up; others retreated with hunched shoulders and a gaze fixed to their toes; some invited support with their glancing at whomever happened to be next to them; and still others, the majority, seemed distracted.

Lampis felt detached! From his past; from fellow passengers; from any fears or apprehension. He observed, divined, retrieved a memory for comparison, allowed a rush of thoughts from all direction to fill an unmeasurable blankness, and chased after silhouettes of dream-memories in the twilight. He stood still from time to time to reassert his existence, apart from his surrounding and from his past, to pull the shores of this destination closer, to weld his will with his promise.

The mist still enveloped the ship, mixing with the spray from the waves, changing from monotonous to patchy and playful with the breeze and concealing the tip of the mast.

"Attention, please!" the loudspeaker announced, "All passengers are requested to pick up their passports and the Permit to enter the United States at the Purser's office. All of those whose last name starts from A to K must present between nine and ten."

Lampis did not listen to the rest of the message. He had heard all he needed to hear. He observed a stir among those on deck, even the Italians, and wondered whether they understood the message or knew instinctively. He smiled with the observation that everybody moved and with the reasoning that it was not possible that only passengers whose names started with A to K were on deck. He saw the stars and stripes raised on the mast, stared at the white and blue stripes with the cross in the right upper corner, and wondered whether the refrain from the Greek National Anthem, "Hail, oh Hail, Liberty!" had escaped him to be heard by those near him.

He descended the stairways almost running, rushed to his cabin, stuffed his belongings in his cardboard suitcase, tipped the steward on the way out, and hurried to the Purser's office. He wanted to return on deck, to not miss the sight of the Statue of Liberty.

The line and the clerks behind the Purser's window moved slowly. The stacks of suitcases were increasing in breadth and height, and his patience was thinning out. Others must have anticipated the announcement and had arrived before him.

When he returned on deck, he saw two small boats from the Port Authorities escorting the ship. A tugboat guided the ship, rising and dipping as if in an assertive gesture of "Welcome to the land whose flag we fly." He watched the fluttering flags snapping in the breeze and saw "duty" on the faces of the officers of the escorting boats and concluded that the understanding of duty under this flag must be uniform and direct, in contrast to the individual and "loose" among those serving under the Greek flag.

He felt frustrated at having missed the sight of the Statue of Liberty - it had appeared briefly and disappeared in the mist and fog while he was down below claiming his passport.

He looked for Kalliope to ask her to share her emotions from her experience. He met Kostas but did not ask him, not trusting the sincerity of either his experience or sentiments. He found Kalliope strolling with her mother. She was moved by the coveted sights and by his request to share her experience with him. Her descriptions, adorned with her sentiments, transformed the statue into a transcendental, celestial power, emanating life and promises from its torch. Her eyes were moist; her face was flushed with happiness and awe. Her mother looked at her as if trying to remember whether she had ever seen her daughter in this state in the past, or she'll every witness it again.

They talked about the greatness of the country they were about to adopt, of the sacred heritage from their ancestors, and of the embodiment of some of this heritage into the life and destiny of this new nation. They knew that they were not enlightening each other. They were just sharing their last moments together with a conversation that identified more of their identical views and shielded their vulnerable attachment to each other.

Her mother walked behind them for a while, probably to understand more than they were expressing in words, then lagged further behind and turned around as they crossed from one side of the ship to the other.

When the loudspeaker announced, "Those whose names start from K to Z or "Omega" must now present at the Purser's," they stopped and faced each other, joined and gripped both hands, looked into each other's moist eyes for an all-too-brief moment and parted with the sterile promise, "I'll see you later."

Kalliope walked away.

He did not follow her and did not dare look to see whether she turned around.

He wandered aimlessly from deck to deck, straining only for brief intervals to estimate the height and the bulk of the building along the shore or the size of other ships moving slowly and majestically in and out of the harbor. At equally fleeting intervals, his thoughts escaped in search of memories or were concentrated in the scattered clusters of his fellow passengers. Even the thought that he would soon be setting foot on the soil of the promised land escaped and returned, leaving him an empty, walking, smiling, greeting, or responding form. He had exhausted his quota of emotional and sentimental excursions for the moment and fell into a mental repose with a hazy awareness of his last sixteen days of life on this ship.

The long resonant sound of the fog horn echoed from the shore, traveled along the Hudson River, and was answered by the brief crescendo horns of the tugboats. A few more of these sounds, at unequal intervals, and then the quiet before the final approach to the expecting and inviting dock. The ship turned slowly, gently and approached the dock as if to caress it. The crew at the stern exchanged signals with the workers standing at the dock. The mooring ropes were hurled, grabbed and secured. The ship touched and clung to the dock, cheek to cheek, and rocked gently in the bosom of the quay to rest after its struggle and encounter with the mighty ocean. The great moment had arrived. His heart responded with a forceful, assertive beat; his throat tightened and made swallowing painful; the tears burned his eyes before spilling a salty taste to his lips; and his hands squeezed a last "goodbye, forever" to the railings of the deck.

CHAPTER 13
The Deliverance

THE BRIDGE FROM THE PAST TO THE FUTURE was lowered steadily, with sturdy chains, onto the deck where Lampis stood. The gates opened on both side. The crowd moved forward resolutely. He stood for a moment, staring at the Greek flag, scanning the length and breadth of the ship for a last farewell. He picked up his suitcase and walked slowly across the bridge to his future. He was oblivious to those in front and behind him. He was alone in the crowd. He did not walk down from the ship. He had climbed it, but now he just walked across.

For seventeen days, he had nurtured and forged the courage to deliver himself to the future, but that final step, off the suspended bridge onto the firmness of the new land, seemed to require all his strength and all his reserves. He did not turn around.

Lampis followed the signs and the crowd, inside the Customs House, regaining his strength with each step, to a spot under a giant letter "A" and waited for the inspection. His fellow passengers, detached from their past and each other, stood silently in wait for the final divine seal to their fate.

The Customs and Immigration officers moved among them equally detached, checking luggage, passports, and Visas – all participants in a ritual. No emotional display; no gestures other than those prescribed by duty and obedience to higher authorities or powers; no remonstrations and no enforcements. He waited to be plucked and moved, devoid of self-determination, to a new position.

The officials stood before him, glanced at his open suitcase, inspected his papers, and responded to his invitational stare with a half-smile that may have meant "prove yourself worthy of our hospitality."

Lampis closed his suitcase, secured his papers and looked around for Kalliope. He saw her, some fifty meters away, in the arms of a young man, her head resting on his shoulders, crying; her mother was in the arms of another young man, the other son; while the young boy was looking from one embraced couple to the other.

After a brief deliberation, he chose not to intrude, to not spoil the joy of their reunion, to just retain a vicarious pleasure of their embraces. Did the pain in the loss of the Patriarch of their family or the pride of his sacrifice return with all their intensity to strengthen their bonds and resolve? When would Kalliope and her mother think of me, he thought. What would they say about me? Would they feel remorse in forgetting about me when they were all together and I was alone?

Peter and Maria came back from a distant, long-ago, interval of two hours, excitement and sadness shining in their smiles and weighing their eyelids, respectively.

"We'll never forget you," they declared in the squeeze of their embraces;

"We'll get together in Chicago, for sure," Peter said. "Our uncle is waiting for us. How are you going to Chicago? Is anyone waiting for you?

"I do not know," Lampis replied.

"Goodbye! Goodbye!"

Kostas strutted toward the exit, turning around to motion with authority to two men following behind. In one of those turns, he waved to Lampis and tossed an empty, "I'll see you in Chicago." Lampis's curiosity of how Kostas behaved in the presence of the Customs and Immigration officers tilted to the side of submissiveness or self-effacement.

"Good luck, Kostas," he remembered to call out.

Kostas acknowledged him, waving his left hand over his head, without turning around.

Many of the waiting relatives were allowed in the Customs House. Some stayed outside. No one was waiting for him. Did they know that he was coming? Had his parents sent a letter by Air-mail or a telegram to inform his uncles?

He inquired at the desk of a young Greek-speaking woman. He was informed that she had a train ticket for him, that he should board the train at 8:00 PM, but that he must stay at the Customs House until about six o'clock.

Lampis did not look at his watch. He had lost concept of and interest in time, again. He made small talk with some of his fellow immigrants, distractedly, as if he had never seen them before. Strangely, he felt no bonds with his fellow travelers, with the Greek-speaking young woman, or with anyone.

Kalliope's image had receded and faded in a distant mist. The farewells and the encounters on deck and in the Customs House blurred like a dream in a restless sleep. The light through the windows and doors, closed or opened, dimmed, as if filtered through uneven layers of a coarse cloth – in contrast to the endlessly clear light through the open windows of his home. The traffic moved in spurts, with a direction or purpose, as if controlled by a remote all-governing power. The few pedestrians seemed to be thinking of where they were going and totally unaware of the activity or structures around them. He wondered how many, or whether any, had noticed that large pothole in the middle of the street, the clusters of new immigrants stuffed into taxicabs, and him delivered among them from a different world.

Lampis wandered, without knowing it, out of the Customs House, feeling frustrated in his attempt to make the guard understand that he had just come off the ship and must be allowed to return to retrieve his luggage. He did not panic.

"Could you go inside to find my nephew?" an old Greek asked Lampis without telling the nephew's name or explaining to the guard what the problem was.

Eventually the guard understood, without the help of the old Greek, and Lampis was allowed back to retrieve his luggage and the "nephew."

The gray daylight began to thicken into hazy darkness and was soon compressed in narrow semipermeable walls, halfway between the equidistant street lights, to support the canopy shielding the stars above. Pedestrians and taxicabs became scarce.

The Customs House grew quieter, then very quiet. The occasional footsteps of some official on duty seemed in discord with a faraway dull hum. A rare "what" or "yes" was diluted in the emptiness of the Customs House and died out before reaching the far wall to bounce back as an echo.

When the young Greek-speaking woman reappeared to tell him and the others that the taxi was coming to take them to the train station, he wondered about the emptiness of the ship, whether the crew was sad or relieved, or if the ocean had spent its fury. He counted the lamp posts to the end of his vision, estimated the distance between them, and forgot the numbers. Did that woman say that he'd travel all night? He'd miss the opportunity to see so much of the country!

Lampis did not try to imagine what he'd miss, except the people would be sleeping comfortably in their homes while the train carrying him to his new home sped by, and that they, these people, would be unaware of his existence. He still stood apart from time and waited for the next move of his fate. Somewhere in this vast city there was a taxi, preordained from the time he was born, headed his way for this part of his transport in his journey. He followed it, not waiting for it, through the broad streets he had seen in the movies, to the port, and he announced to the others, "Here it is. Let's go."

Three of the others joined him, silently. Whether the taxi driver said anything, he did not hear. They traveled through the city, marveling at its splendor and vitality. The neon signs, sweeping sideways or flowing down, conveyed the message of man's conquests louder than the words they spelled. The surge of the traffic with each start, when the light changed from red to green, was translated into the pulse of the city's life. They crossed the famed Broadway. He remembered it from the movies, but it had grown in dimensions. Its image followed him to the train station, displacing or pushing back lesser impressions. The New World, with all it vigor and promises, was announced by Broadway.

The taxi left them on the sidewalk. Did the taxi driver say anything?

They carried their suitcases into an immense waiting room, bustling with orderly life, and were told to wait for the departure call. The very high ceilings, the mural paintings, the deferential encounters, all revolved in sequence or out of turn with each new distraction. His pulse changed when he listened to a young, attractive woman relating how she was working and studying at the University. She was seeing someone off, heard them talk in Greek and approached them. He was impressed as much by her good looks as by her serenity. If she could do it, he could do it.

The call for departure to Chicago put an abrupt end to his conversation and encounter with the young student. She offered her hand and good wishes. He took both, the hand for a first pleasurable touch with a member of the New World and the wishes for a remedy to sadness or pain. The forever parting handshake with his fellow-travelers transferred, in both directions, a message of goodwill and identification.

He followed the uniformed man who picked up his ticket and suitcase, turning around for one more look and a wave at those he was leaving behind. Waiting for this last gesture of separation of their paths, they waved back smiling. Thousands of miles away from deprivation and uncertainty, across a vengeful ocean, he measured his steps on firm grounds of promise and expectations. He saw the milestone in his journey in the chain of the train-cars as he walked behind the porter. The bright images of Costas and Nassos, the other two members of "The First Triumvirate," flashed before him with the Confidence and Faith, in that star-lit evening of their Covenant to become physicians.

"On my way," he thought, as he walked and walked, beginning to wonder: "Is the porter going to walk me all the way to Chicago or is he going to throw me in with the cargo?"

Lampis was not tired. Nor was he hungry, even though he had not eaten all day. He waved at the porter, shook his hand and walked to his seat wondering whether he was traveling first class. The coach was spacious; the seats were comfortable and reclining. He helped an older lady put her heavy luggage in the compartment above her, understood her "thank you," appreciated her smile and sank in his seat speculating about what else she said. The train was not even out of the station when he fell into a deep sleep.

The conductor's announcements, presumably of the stops, echoed from far away and were submerged beneath the surging waves of the left-behind ocean, interrupting his sleep only momentarily.

When he awoke, the light of the day unraveled, behind the speeding train, flat fertile lands, gently sloping low hills, neatly arranged houses with cars in their driveways, small towns or larger cities, tree lines approaching and receding and repetitions. He absorbed everything greedily, mostly to return for memories he could not share, but also to abstract for his first letter to his parents. He struggled with the impulse to leave his seat, to do something actively, such as walk around, wash his face, cut himself while shaving, in an attempt to dispel the returning thought that all this may be just a dream. He did not wish this to end abruptly like a dream.

He had to force himself to eat the sandwich he ordered; it tasted rotten or worse, but he drank the juice and the milk with pleasure. He had slept well, but he was aching and his throat felt raw and scratchy. He remembered his promise to the old man on the ship that he would "not ever get sick" and resolved that it was all because of the sandwich and that he would feel better by the time he reached Chicago.

Lampis tried to fight off sleep, but the quiet in the coach and the rhythmic repetition of the sound of wheels on the joints of the rails were not on his side. He continued to hear the clanking of the wheels in his sleep and was somehow aware of the movements of the passengers and the conductors. He even knew, without waking up, that the conductor checked the stub of his ticket stuck in the back of the seat in front of him. No dreams! Some disconnected images, maybe with each clanking: his mother calling the chickens to feed; a flock of doves circling above a freshly plowed field; an old goat-herd standing on the edge of a rocky cliff calling his son who was washing his face in the river some three hundred meters below; his father among the beehives; the mother-swallow hesitating for a moment before inserting its filled beak inside one of the five gaping mouths in front of her; his father, again, walking behind the mule loaded with two coffers full of grapes; the lonely crow flying silently into the sunset, flying, gliding, diminishing, vanishing. Total darkness! Unawareness.

"We must be approaching Chicago," he reasoned when he awakened by a brief, soft conversation of the lady across the aisle with the conductor. Lampis looked at the land stretching and receding to a horizon with undulations along ridges of hills or mountain peaks. He followed cars traveling in opposite directions from his train until they vanished. He started to count the number of houses next to red rectangular buildings and erect cylindrical structures. And he contrasted this tranquil land with the defiant, ragged mountains, the skeletons of the castles and fortresses, and the groans from the gaping windows or roofless burned-up villages of his homeland. The rare war or alarm cries of the natives had been silenced by the call to the future on this continent; while the clashes between invaders and defenders or oppressors and liberators gained in volume with the echoes in history and folklore in the old world. For centuries, armies of pillagers and marauders had plundered and devastated the land of his birth, when herds of Buffalo roamed this land fertilizing the fields they grazed and steering away from the clusters of Indian huts.

The receding landscape behind the train decreased gradually and the intervals between the clanking of the wheels increased inversely. He turned to look at the other passengers in their seats, motionless and quiet. Whether returning home or visiting, he thought, someone was waiting for them. Would anyone be waiting for him? If not, he would take a taxi. He had his uncle's address and enough money for the taxi.

The train slid slowly into Dearborn Station and came smoothly to a stop. Lampis stood up, stretched, as politely as possible – he did not wish that the other passengers would think of him as uncouth – and lowered his luggage from the compartment above his seat. The last stretch of his long journey had come to an end. Thousands of miles across a furious ocean and a vast land, from his step on the bus in his village; a lifetime since the last image of his father, standing like a pillar, as the bus rounded the corner of St. Basil Square onto King George Street in Tripolis; now the New Life.

The lady across the aisle stood up and stretched to lower her luggage.

"May I?" he asked, stepping next to her. That much English he knew.

She lowered her arms with a smile. "Thank you."

Her luggage was much heavier and elegant than his. She walked ahead of him, after another "Thank you" followed by "Welcome, good luck."

Lampis arrived at the door of his coach and saw two of his uncles waiting for him. He recognized the older, who was also his godfather, from their encounter in Greece two years ago. The younger man, Uncle John, he recognized from pictures. Uncle John had left Greece about ten years before he was born, yet his embrace was warmer, longer, and reassuring.

Lampis assured them that his journey was problem-free, that his parents and all the relatives were well when he left, and that he was not tired. Uncle John insisted that he carry the suitcase and commented that it was lighter than his own about thirty years ago.

The sky was overcast and the day-light was gray, even though the big clock on the wall showed three o'clock. The noise from the elevated trains, while waiting for a taxicab, drowned his voice and even the voice of his uncles who talked much louder than he, forcing them to interrupt the conversation. The beams and columns of the elevated train tracks seemed rusty but sturdy – just what he expected in a giant industrial city like Chicago. The massive buildings lining the streets did not look man-made. Maybe Zeus had resurrected and transferred the Titans to this land. He wondered what kind of life, if any, moved inside of them and whether his uncles knew.

A yellow taxi stopped in front of them, answering his uncle's whistles. They entered and Uncle John gave the address, 3900 Archer Avenue, and the directions. Lampis continued answering his uncle's inquiries while trying not to miss anything they passed. All the buildings looked dark brown, the trees dull-green, the streets wide and uninhabited, except by cars and busses. He concluded that he would live with Uncle John, since Uncle John had sponsored him, and they were going to his home.

Uncle John's store, a combination of restaurant, confectionery, ice cream parlor and bar, was drab, dim-lit, triangular, rather quiet, and totally different from the large, square, brightly lit, orderly business establishment that he had expected. He was treated to a "malted milk" and he liked it.

A friendly Greek friend of his uncle welcomed him and assured him that his Aunt Sophia, Uncle John's wife, would teach him English "in no time at all," adding, "she was a teacher, and she's very nice."

Lampis strained to understand the conversation, or at least pick up some of the words he had learned in his furious study of the "Greek-English Method," until 2:00 or 3:00 A.M. night after night, after his decision to emigrate to the United States about three months ago. He picked up a few words, most being garbled or unfamiliar, yet could not guess the meaning of the conversation. He would have to work hard.

He welcomed the suggestion to walk to Uncle John's home, about five blocks away. He wondered how frequently the people that lived on this street walked into the neighbor's house by mistake, since all the houses looked the same – two storied, six steps up to the first floor, a narrow-paved walk to the left, the same scrawny tree between the sidewalk and the street, the same bushes separating the sidewalk from a patch of a front yard.

Aunt Sophia greeted them at the top of the stairway, on the second floor. She had a sweet, but somewhat reserved smile; she was thin and slightly hunched; she addressed Uncle Gus with deference and somewhat formally. The tone of her voice became quickly predictable. He did not feel entirely comfortable in this neat, polished apartment. It seemed more like a hotel and lacked the warmth of a home. The chat, rather than conversation, was deliberate and reserved or framed, not spontaneous and probing. He remembered his father's admonitions to be discreet and attentive. He answered questions without elaborating and wondered what they thought of him.

Uncle Gus excused himself after a while. "I will return tomorrow to take you," he told Lampis.

After he left, Uncle John appeared more relaxed and volunteered, "Gus is *too* hung up on religion." He seemed to be amazed, as well as amused as he looked at Lampis. "Your mother was just a young girl when I left!"

Lampis remembered that his mother had idolized Uncle John, never missing an opportunity to sing his praises and his popularity, his love of fun and excitement, and his righteousness. Perhaps he had mellowed or had been humbled. He was not as tall, self-assured or outgoing as Lampis had imagined him. His eyes did not smile; a not-so-subtle sadness never left him, and his gestures were somewhat restrained and awkward.

"Now I have to go back to the store," Uncle John said. He seemed to have repeated a preprogrammed phrase, without either enthusiasm or resentment. "You go to bed and rest," he suggested.

"No, I'll go with you to the store," Lampis said.

"All right," Uncle John said, in a simple, emotionless manner.

Lampis was uncomfortable at the thought of being alone with Aunt Sophia. She may ask impertinent questions about his past and his plans, and he wished to postpone the confrontational discovery that his plans may be in conflict with theirs. The first half of the walk to the store was silent.

Uncle John, without looking at him, announced, "I am told you were a good student and a prudent young man. If you wish to continue with school, I'll help you. If you choose to go into business, I'll help you."

Lampis was pleased with Uncle John's offer and lost no time in declaring his resolve or in thanking Uncle John for his intended support.

"As you wish," Uncle John replied laconically and sincerely, marking the end of the conversation.

Lampis wondered whether the "I" instead of "We" was deliberate and final, and whether it was spontaneous or after an agreement with his brothers. "Time will tell," they used to say back home. He did not try to divine what Uncle John was thinking.

Lampis could not understand how this store could be called a "gold mine." Uncle John, with his apron around his waist, moved rather slowly behind the counter, his slight limp to the right more apparent from a distance. Bill, the bartender, acted as if he owned the place and his handshake conveyed a little condescending attitude, in contrast to the firm handshake, sometimes with both hands, or a pat on the shoulder and the warm "Welcome," by the customers.

Uncle John, who had no children, introduced him to everyone in the store, repeating with some pride, "My nephew, he just came from the old country!"

Lampis declined the offered drinks politely and heard the proud "Good boy!" He offered to help, but his uncle declined with the answer, "There's plenty of time for that, don't worry!"

Observing and studying the customers and his uncle's reactions did not allow for boredom. The continuous inflow and outflow of customers suggested that Uncle John was doing pretty well. He wondered how this man made the transition from herding sheep and plowing the fields to running a business.

Aunt Sophia's arrival brought a little cheerfulness to the place. The men tipped their hats and the ladies acknowledged her warmly. She greeted every one of them by their names. Bill, the bartender, seemed to resent her in a subtle but poorly concealed way. Lampis did not care for Bill. The soreness in his throat had returned and his aches intensified. He could not suppress his cough during dinner, and at the booth with Aunt Sophia. He didn't talk much. He thought of dinner at home, always a cherished experience with a stimulating conversation and the sense of belonging together. Uncle John related a couple of stories about his first encounters with his brothers, as if to prepare his listener, and finally suggested, "You'd better go home and go to bed."

He walked with Aunt Sophia back to the apartment, totally preoccupied with the thought that he had arrived at his destination and that he must now start on working toward making the transition from dream to reality memorable and fruitful. He answered his aunt's questions simply and politely. She spoke Greek fluently, with a generous hint of an accent and with a sprinkling of words he did not recognize, but he quickly concluded that they were 'Hellenized' English words. He paced his steps to stay even with his aunt, who was a good walker. He thought it improper to ask any questions of her, but decided it was both proper and appropriate to express his gratitude and appreciation to her, privately, for their sponsoring him.

She responded graciously, but her adding, "Let's hope it works out well," kept returning whenever there was a pause. He heard it again, clearly, before sleep overtook his thoughts and awareness.

Unable to suppress a coarse cough, he admitted, "I feel aching, but I will feel much better in the morning."

They exchanged very few pleasantries once inside the apartment. She showed him his room and retreated to the living room. He tried to be as discreet and as quiet as possible. His last thought, "My first night in Chicago," was suspended until his uncle awakened him at about 2:00 A.M. to give him a back rub.

"Your aunt told me you were coughing and aching. This should help. Sleep late in the morning."

Lampis read gentle affection in Uncle John's concern – definitely a good sign.

The deep restful sleep in a comfortable bed and the back rub helped Lampis to feel much better in the morning. Breakfast was plentiful as well as prolonged and full of questions. How was it for them, who had only had each other for so many years, to have a stranger in their home? What did they talk about? Whose future were they contemplating? And what was the meaning of, "You're going to Bill's today, then we'll decide where you're going to stay?" Were his three uncles so close that all decisions were made collectively, or was Uncle John deferring all decisions to Uncle Bill? What was Uncle Bill like? Why did he not call yesterday to welcome him? Lampis did not voice these questions, nor was he impatient for the answers. But the sadness in Uncle John's eyes, even when he smiled or laughed, bothered him. It seemed so permanent.

The conversation was fragmented or perhaps exploratory. After the inquiries about his parents and the other children, came the questions about the war, the years of occupation and the civil war. Uncle John seemed more touched with his answers. Yes, he was just a little boy when the war broke out; he may not have understood the magnitude of the horror and destruction but was frightened nevertheless. He had suffered from the hunger pangs as much as or more than the adults; he had exerted just as much effort as any grown-up in trying to chew and swallow bread made out of roasted and ground acorns; his despair must have been deeper than that of his parents when they were left homeless, since he had not had a chance to develop any strength. He grew quickly, accustomed to death around him and to a mixture of cruelty and barbarism. He had grown to accept poverty and deprivation. He had learned to counterbalance the material advantages of some of his classmates with the love in his home. And he had participated as a young man now, in the celebration of the end of the war, with singing, dancing, reveling, and planning for the future. Uncle John and Aunt Sophia admitted that they had not appreciated, from the newspaper reports, how much suffering the

Greeks had endured, and that it was hard for them to imagine how they survived. But enough of that for now.

"Uncle Gus will be here shortly, so you'd better get your things together."

His aches and soreness had disappeared. He had kept his promise to not get sick, but an uncomfortable feeling that he was not in control of his moves could not be suppressed. Instead, it generated new apprehensions about his relationship with his uncles, the possibilities of conflicts and confrontation, and his preparedness for these challenges. The pace was accelerating.

The doorbell interrupted his thinking. Aunt Sophia commented, before answering, "This is the second time that Gus has come to our home, the first time being yesterday!"

Lampis was not surprised. In fact, this conformed with his assessment of Uncle Gus during their encounters in Greece, almost two years ago. The greetings were formal and restrained. The offer for coffee was declined. The visit was brief. The taxi was waiting.

"Goodbye, we'll see you soon!" Uncle John and Aunt Sophia said.

"Goodbye, thank you!" Lampis said.

The sadness in Uncle John's eyes weighed heavier, and Lampis thought: "I'll never sleep in this apartment again." As they drove by Uncle John's store, he had a sequel to his last thought: "I won't work in this place, either."

The drive was not long. The broad streets were lined with dark brown brick buildings. The river appeared sluggish and murky, the traffic orderly, the trolley buses half-empty, and the pedestrians not looking at anything or talking to each other. Uncle Gus did not talk very much, except for pointing out some obvious landmarks, such as barges in the river, the bridge they crossed, or a cluster of chimney stacks spewing out thick gray smoke, and for explaining the difference between street cars and trolley buses. He showed a polite appreciation, tried to think of a pertinent and proper question, but was not distracted from the preoccupation of "What is it going to be like?"

"Left, on twenty-sixth," Uncle Gus instructed the taxi-driver.

Twenty-sixth street was rather crowded. The street cars were noisy. The taxi moved very slowly.

"It's more crowded in the evening. Today is Thursday, and the stores are open for business," Uncle Gus informed him, and without waiting for an answer, added, "We've been here at the same store for forty years."

"Forty years is a long time," Lampis responded. "You must feel comfortable here."

"The Bohemian and the Polish ladies like chocolate and ice cream. Their men like beer and whiskey," Uncle Gus pontificated, then announced, "Here we are, in front of the store at the Northwest corner."

The taxi came to a stop, before Uncle Gus remembered: "Go down to Drake Avenue, three blocks west, then turn right. It's just three buildings this side of twenty-fifth street, on your left."

His understanding of Uncle Gus' slow clear, instructions boosted his self-confidence.

"You're going to stay at your Uncle Bill's home. He has a family. Then we'll see."

CHAPTER 14

THE GREETING FROM UNCLE BILL, "Welcome to the Kalteziotes," with a pointedly deliberate or condescending emphasis to Kalteziotes (dwelling in or originally from Kaltezai) provided a taste of what he would have to swallow. The insincere smile and limp handshake from Aunt Helen, Uncle Bill's wife, seemed to lay the foundation of barriers between them.

Lampis carried his light suitcase inside and waited to be told where to put it down. The wait seemed long, not because of the weight of the suitcase, allowing enough time to begin to wonder whether he was to stay or move on.

Uncle Gus excused himself and left.

Lampis was led to a bedroom and told, "This is where you sleep."

The modest-in-size room was crowded with polished, shining, neatly arranged furniture, but it looked sterile and inhospitable. He was uncomfortable with his observation of pretentiousness, but did not forget to say "Thank you," and chose to not ask questions or initiate conversation.

He did not feel any bonds to them and wondered whether their concept of blood relationship resembled his. He could not push back the memory of a story of a young peasant girl delivered by her impoverished father to be a maid to a wealthy family. Uncle Bill behaved with a mixture of arrogance and no-nonsense. His wife assumed the airs of a grand lady. Pretentiousness pervaded every corner of their house.

Lampis followed Uncle Bill to his garden, among his flower patches, and wondered whether he found pleasure in his flowers or was striving to measure up to his wife's expectations, and finally decided to withhold his conclusions. Sensitized by the condescending greeting, his discomfort increased with his inability to stem the flow of all these judgmental thoughts.

After the display of his talents and opulence, Uncle Bill announced: "I am going to the store now. You get acquainted with your aunt and you come to the store later."

When Lampis inquired about their children, she volunteered to take him to their school to meet them, only two blocks away. He accepted the offer gladly to escape from the oppressive atmosphere of this artificial environment.

Robert Burns School was a large, sturdy building with a spacious yard and playground. They walked to the children's classrooms. The teachers were accommodating and appeared perfectly civilized. The children looked lovable and well behaved, both expressing the wish, Sophia in Greek and George in English, that he would live with them. They were nine and seven years old, respectively. He felt that he could easily establish a bond of love with the children. His steps down the stairs, across the school yard and back to his uncle's home, were lighter after his brief encounter with his cousins.

The stay at his uncle's home, after returning from the visit to the school, was brief, but long enough for his aunt to inform him about her patrician origins and background, her cultural superiority and her ability to "See through anyone." He wondered whether she had forgotten that he had known her mother and two sisters quite well, having lived in their house as a tenant for about three years, or whether her delusions had swelled with time, and his predominant reaction was one of pity – with a close second, "I better brace myself and watch my step."

He listened politely and agreeably, concealing his true feelings of contempt for the behavior and conduct of her family that he had personally observed and heard more about. When asked for the confirmation of her assertions, he answered that his limited exposure, because of his position, young age, and commitment to his studies, did not allow for such assessments, but that he accepted her word. He also avoided the bait with the suggestion that her sisters, accustomed to comfort or opulence, may have had to resort to compromising means and associations, such as consorting with the occupying forces, for survival. He wondered whether she "Saw through" him in his responses and whether her enumeration of the virtues of her family, all the way to the store, was an attempt to enlighten him and set the record straight, right now, or to convince herself of their veracity.

Lampis was not distracted from observing the stores and buildings lining 26th Street or the mood of the people walking in the opposite direction or in the opposite sidewalk. Had he been asked what he saw and heard on the way to the store, he could have recited both without hesitation and accurately.

His uncles greeted him from behind the counter. The atmosphere was antique but without aesthetic appeal. Gaudy mirrors, with bold semi-calligraphic writing in chalk of offerings and prices on the east and north sides; small round marble-top tables and chairs in the back half; a washroom in the northwest corner; two telephone booths on the west wall in the back half; a jukebox against the middle of the north wall; two pinball machines between the telephone booths and the glass partition, halfway up to the ceiling, of the two halves of the store; a series of glass cases, with boxes of chocolate candies in and on top of them, on the right, with some space between them and the east wall, and an old bar, bout twenty-five feet long, without stools, on the left, with shelves stacked with bottles and glasses behind. The windows displayed open and wrapped boxes of chocolate candies and signs of "Homemade ice Cream – Vanilla, Strawberry, Chocolate." The patrons appeared indifferent, detached, at least to and from his uncles – different from what he had seen at Uncle John's.

Lampis was guided to the top of the stairway to the basement, through a narrow passage between the north end of the bar and the ice boxes for the ice cream, this side of the glass partition, and asked to take off his jacket to hang against the wall. He was asked to roll up his sleeves and was given a white apron to wrap around his waist. Then he was told to take some cases of empty beer bottles down to the basement.

"Your aunt will show you where to put them."

She led the way. The lighting was dim and the passage narrow; the steps worn; the odor damp and moldy. He almost stepped on the cat, as he turned to the left at the bottom of the stairway, before his aunt pulled a string and turned the light on, a naked bulb dangling from the ceiling. Old benches, crates, boxes, a gas stove in the far-left corner before the exit door, a small table with a worn and faded plastic cover at the north wall; no sense of orderliness and no cobwebs. "This is what must be called a dungeon," he thought.

He returned to the top of the stairway, put one box on top of another to carry down

"One at a time. No showing-off here!" Uncle Bill shouted at him.

The initiation was full force. He complied, but heard another shout when he ran up the stairs.

"No running or jumping. One step at a time. No showing-off here. The girls can't see you."

His aunt faded in the background. Uncle Gus just left. People moved in and out. Some bought candy, others bought cigarettes or cigars. Some girls and older women were served ice cream at the tables by Ted, an old man with large, straight-out ears, bald head and pinched face.

Uncle Bill moved swiftly, repeating, "Yes, sir," even when no one had asked or said anything, and laughing when no one else was laughing.

"People work here," Ted pontificated," Not like in the old country."

No need to answer that remark. Lampis was shown by the masters, how to clean tables, rearrange chairs, washing glasses, and even scoop out ice cream, one step at a time. He expected that soon he would be taught the art of carrying out the garbage, mopping the floor, washing the windows, and cleaning the toilet. He had prepared himself adequately. He would not be humiliated or intimidated.

The routine was established early: up at about 8:00 A.M., he would walk to his uncle's store about 10:00 or 10:30 A.M. after a quick breakfast and some work in the front or the back yard, and work until 10:30 P.M. with a brief lunch break in the basement, alone, at about 2:30 P.M.

He learned his duties and what was expected of him quickly. Whenever there was a lull, he would try and write letters to his parents or other close relatives and friends, or he would retrieve his books and concentrate on improving his vocabulary and diction of English. He realized, soon enough, that Uncle Bill did not approve of his "extracurricular activities," when he was interrupted with requests for entirely unnecessary tasks, such as inspecting the glasses to make sure they had no water marks or cleaning the windows for the second time, while Ted leaned against the wall and stared into space. Lampis carried out his assignments quickly and efficiently to return to his letter writing or his studies, until Uncle Bill told him that this was not allowed at work. His polite or timid remonstration that he was studying or writing only when there was no work involved, evoked an angry answer with a transfixed stare, "You do as you are told!" Lampis did not do it again. His resentment was neutralized by his reasoning that he would be appreciated after they had a good chance to know him.

He did not discuss wages, assuming that they would compensate him fairly and equitably. After all, they were his relatives and declared loudly and fervently that they were devout Christians. He did not feel comfortable staying at Uncle Bill's home. He was neither a guest nor a member of the family, but he also did not wish to offend them. Aunt Helen's pleasantries, including her repeated remarks to him and to Aunt Sophia about his "extraordinary good looks and polite manners, both unusual and unexpected of a village boy," veiled her resentment thinly.

He began to wonder whether he was oversensitive and unfair, and he spent more and more time rationalizing her attitude and remarks. He wondered also, about her motives, in all her inquiries, and decided to respond with simple honest answers and behavior. He ignored her gloating when he answered her sarcastic questions, "What did you learn in school today?" or "Did the girls in your class flirt with you?" with "I didn't understand much," or "I didn't notice."

Perhaps she had enrolled him in school with the old Czechoslovakian immigrants in the 50s and 60s, just to humiliate him. He was the youngest in the class of about twenty "students." The only other young "student" was a pregnant woman, with a sweet timid smile and auburn hair, in her thirties. He was going to show his aunt that he could not be humiliated. If she wanted to test him, he'd accept the challenge. The contest grew steadily, though for the most part subtly, and he began to count the points scored. Uncle Bill either pretended he did not notice or decided to enjoy it – or keep score himself – until she finally decided that he could not remain neutral.

One day, when he returned from classes, she asked the usual question. "What did you learn in school today?"

"I told the teacher what the Monroe Doctrine was about and I named a few American inventors: Alexander Graham Bell, Thomas Edison, Benjamin Franklin."

"And just how did you know that?" she asked.

"I had read about them," he replied.

From his room, he could hear both his uncle and aunt. They had loud voices, maybe louder on this occasion to make certain that he heard.

"Your nephew is a 'know-it-all smart aleck," she blurted in frustration. "You had better to talk with him."

"I'll put him in his place, don't you worry about it," Uncle Bill responded, pacifying her for the moment.

At the next session, his teacher told him that his aunt had questioned her about what he had related and added, quite emphatically, "I also told your aunt that you belong in college."

The challenges seemed to multiply. Uncle John was completely removed from the picture. He saw him only rarely and very briefly, about once every two weeks, when he stopped at the store after his business transactions at the bank, about one-half block down across the street.

The old man, Ted, apparently in an attempt to discover his employer's intentions, suggested, "Now that you have your young nephew who learns and moves quickly, perhaps you won't need me."

"But he plans to go to college," Uncle John said sarcastically, and they both laughed. "Without knowing English!"

Lampis looked at both of them straight in the eye. They both looked away. "I *am* going to college," he announced simply and resolutely.

The attempts to put him in his place intensified. He washed the windows, mopped the floor, scrubbed the washroom, cleaned and mopped the basement after the flood from the sewer. He replaced the deliverer in carrying the barrels and cases of beer to the basement. He painted the store and Uncle Bill's house (including the stairway to the second floor and the basement), and mowed the lawn, and tilled the garden. He should be ever ready to carry out whatever menial tasks popped into their heads.

In addition, Aunt Helen "reminded" him frequently that he came of peasant stock; that his having learned how to wear a tie, which she had provided, did not change his status; that his sufferings during the occupation and the civil war were pure fabrications (the burning of a shack or hovel and the deprivation of things he never knew existed didn't mean very much); that he should stop looking for sympathy and 'get to work;' and that "America has plenty of young people to fill its schools – it doesn't need the likes of you!"

Lampis was determined to protect his self-respect and dignity and fortify his determination. He did not respond to the insults and derisions. He found some solace in the purity of his little cousin's affection. Only once he was unable to bottle up a mournful song while cleaning up the remnants of a sewer flood in the store's basement and sang with tears burning his cheeks: "Come out, Mother, to behold your son and take pride in him, how he is led by the Albanians and the gendarme; they're going to hang me, Mother." The song may have been, except for the first verse, inappropriate, but it was the first verse that brought it to mind. When he realized that he may have sung a little too loudly from the way his uncle looked at him, he brushed it off with the thought, "Maybe he can take pride in his behavior."

The distance between his uncle and him was not decreasing. His attempts to paint a rosy picture in his letters to his parents became more and more draining. He abhorred lying, in whatever form or for whatever reason, but he also wished fervently to spare his parents, especially his mother, of a bitter disappointment in her brothers. Uncle Bill helped a little, with his rare or occasional hint of a suggestion of understanding and even of remorse. He decided that he would wait for such an occasion to write his letters. Uncle Bill observed that he wrote "too many letters, too often," but did not press the point.

The letters from his parents, his sister, his brothers, his Uncle Vasiles (Basil) and his friends became his sustenance. They kept coming at regular intervals – full of love, memories and expectations. He answered them promptly in the hope that they also would respond promptly. He wrote about the people he met, about the way his uncles were, or seemed to be, transacting business, about his determination to master the English language, and about his unshakable resolve to study medicine. He never mentioned his work assignments or labor. He was careful to conceal from them that he was an indentured servant.

The sight of the Greek flag alongside the American and the French flags, symbolizing the birth and rebirth of Freedom and Democracy, at the head of the parade on the "Fourth of July," filled him with pride. He felt a new surge of strength. His day at Brookfield Zoo, where he climbed the vines to harvest tender leaves for his Aunt's dolmades (is that why she took him with her?) was a rejuvenating interlude. The attention and smiles from the young women and the friendly approach of the young men lifted his spirits. Uncle Bill's inadvertent comment to his wife, "The patronage by the young crowd has tripled since the D.P. came." (Lampis had a new name now, the D.P. It was an acronym for Displaced Person. Lampis was also called "the Greenhorn.")

The regular customers at the bar seemed to be partial to him, and offered to help him, frequently correcting him, always politely, in English. Business-minded Uncle Bill did not mind at all, in fact, he exploited every opportunity, introducing Lampis to everybody, particularly the new or infrequent customers, not with, "Meet the D.P." or "This is a Greenhorn," - that would not have been good for business – but as "Harry, my nephew just come from the old Country."

Lampis rejected the name "Harry," after a little research showed that there was no connection between his name and Harry, just as there was no connection between Basil and William or Demetrios and James.

The period of adjustment gradually entered into the second stage. Their respective identities became better defined. Seemingly minor incidents, for which neither side was prepared, contributed significantly to the assessment of each other's characters or personalities. The prerogatives of his youth and his uncles' submission to old habits or prejudices caused some conflicts but also revealed weaknesses and strengths. Confrontations were avoided or aborted. Communication improved, but subjects such as his obsession with going to school or where he was going to live were not discussed. His cousins' affection grew to the point that he was not addressed or referred to as the "D.P.," or the "Greenhorn," in their presence.

Still, in the first few weeks he found examples of genuine interest, and perhaps even affection, to fan his hopes for mutual understanding and appreciation. Breakfast was a good time. During this brief interlude, every morning, he answered questions about the agonies and the sufferings of his family and relatives during the war, the occupation, and the Civil strife. He sang the newest songs for his aunt, aroused his uncle's interest in modern Greek history, and entertained the children with stories of pranks by the street urchins at the expense of the occupying forces. He almost threw caution to the winds when he heard that the children had never been happier and saw them cry when told that he was going to move to "Uncle Gus's place." He even felt guilty in not being able to suppress the suspicion that "this honeymoon will not last," from surfacing from time to time.

When his aunt suggested that she and her husband sponsor his sister to immigrate to the United States to join him, his initial impulse and enthusiasm almost drove him to write her and implore her to exploit this opportunity to join him. He had enjoyed and cherished the time he had spent in the company of his sister, in the last few months, and he had loved her more than he had ever loved her before. They had been separated by the civil war for about four years, and when brought together again, had clung to each other. She had become his confidante and advisor, and held his arm tightly when going for walks, trusting him, and learning to read his thoughts. He was proud to walk alongside her, and talked about her to his friends, and missed her when they were separated for more than a day. And now, there was a chance for them to be together again.

They would support and confide in each other, and laugh together, and share dreams. But would they? Would they be allowed? Would he be able to stand the pain of seeing his sister exploited and treated as a maid? Would he be able to convince her, early enough, that she must not give them a chance to hurt her, to move into an apartment with him and take a job at a Department store or a factory? And what if he were drafted into the Army? What would become of her then? He deliberated intently and finally decided to write to her about the proposal and his thoughts. Her response, read to his aunt, brought relief to him and to his aunt, apparently, who had second thoughts.

When alone with Uncle Bill for two weeks – Aunt Helen and the children had gone to Kansas City to visit her sister – Lampis felt a bond developing. He listened to his uncle's frustrations about his wife's pretentiousness and condescending behavior toward his relatives, her unrealistic demands and her "extortion tactics." He heard about Uncle John's pure-heartedness and gullibility, and Aunt Sophia's cleverness and Uncle Gus's fanaticism with religion. There was no covenant about confidentiality. The conclusion that his uncle had never confided in anyone before was followed by the hope that a bond of trust and mutual respect would develop, that the barriers of suspicion and cautiousness would finally break down.

He was happier at work and looked for more things to do. He wrote long, light-hearted letters to his parents and sister. He felt buoyant. He was not lonely! And when he danced at a Name day party, he enjoyed the moment, feeling oblivious to past and future.

Uncle Bill seemed to be aglow with vicarious pleasure and pride. "You can have your choice among the girls, with your looks and the way you dance," he announced with conviction.

Lampis did not let the opportunity escape to tell his uncle, "My top priority is going to school. Girls would have to wait."

"You can have everything!" Uncle Bill said with enthusiasm.

He began to laugh again with Uncle Bill, at home, walking to the store, and at work.

Uncle Gus seemed undecided about approving or disapproving of this laughing at the store, and then he joined them. For the first time, Lampis realized that Uncle Gus, when relaxed, had a sweet charming smile, a springy step and no frown. Even big-ears Ted began to laugh, his ears almost flapping with the more uninhibited laughs.

"What the exuberance of youth won't do," the philosopher-drunk John, one of the steady patrons, commented one evening.

"Including making us feel young again!" Uncle Bill concluded.

Uncle Bill missed his children. He talked about them and longed for their return. Lampis had missed them, too. But when they returned, they appeared different; distant, aloof, and reserved. Lampis held back, waiting for the readjustment. There were some overtures, from time to time, but the recoil was always back to the recently established distance. He could not help but wonder and be sad.

The not-so-sudden change in Uncle Bill, conveying a message of regret or remorse for his overtures and confessions in the last two weeks, suggested that something had happened in Kansas City. Aunt Helen was rather openly resentful. His suspicions that she and her sister had decided on a course of action remained unanswered. He decided against a confrontation in the hope that the closeness with Uncle Bill and his patience will neutralize whatever was hatched and plotted in Kansas City.

CHAPTER 15

THE COMMENT OF THE OFFICIAL at the Local Board of the Selective Service system, where he had to register within two months after his arrival, that he may be drafted, "any day," was no less shocking to Uncle Bill than to him. But he already knew of the benefits of the G.I. Bill from one of his friends and decided that being drafted may be a good solution. He did not know how to interpret his uncle's reaction. Somehow, he felt that his uncle still liked him, but was cautious. It was Uncle Bill who first brought up the subject of his going to school.

"If you want to go to college, go to college, but first you have to know enough English. That means in a year or two," Uncle Bill said.

"It's not going to take me that long to learn English," Lampis replied.

Uncle Bill gave him a prolonged stare. "You think you're that smart?"

"I am determined and I think I am smart enough!" Lampis said, ending the conversation.

The advantages of business over a profession were enumerated and rehashed on a daily basis: earning a good living and investing, right from the start, instead of wasting precious and long years in going to school; starting and supporting a family while young, instead of waiting until getting a diploma; the opportunity to branch or diversify instead of committing to a single pursuit; the overabundance – "a dime a dozen' – of professionals and the fierce competition or humbling compromises, instead of a wide open field in business; etc., etc.

Yet Uncle Bill, the main advocate of the advantages in business, repeatedly expressed the wish or hope that his own son become a physician. What was the substance of these arguments, then? That he, an immigrant of peasant stock, a D.P., a Greenhorn, was not good enough and should not aspire to become a physician? Instead of wasting his energy in venting his indignation, Lampis chose to strengthen his resolve with a simple, "I'll show them!"

On rare occasions, his resentment overwhelmed him and he countered with antagonistic remarks, exemplified by his response to the story that a certain Greek immigrant who had arrived penniless in this country "left ten million dollars" at his death. "He was an idiot. Had he been smart, he would have taken it all with him," he retorted.

The deprivation of intellectual contacts and conversations began to depress him to the point that he made some overtures to his uncles – he could not converse in English yet. The usual cut-off remark was, "That's not going to put bread on your table," added to his frustrations. When he tried to appease Uncle Gus and satisfy his own needs with a philosophical discussion of religion, he was sternly addressed with "Are you questioning the Holy Scriptures?"

His only exposure to intellectual challenges was the sermon at church on Sundays. The Priest was learned, eloquent, clear, and stimulating. After church every Sunday, when business was slow, Lampis repeated and analyzed the whole sermon in his mind (on Sundays he worked from 1:00 P.M. to midnight).

An interesting friend of Uncle Gus, who was a liquor salesman, came every two weeks and had a tendency to speak ex cathedra. Lampis looked forward to listening to this articulate, intelligent man, probably not as much for his dissertations as for the words of encouragement. "If the Good Lord placed you on this earth to become a physician, nobody can change that!" he repeated almost every time before he left.

Lampis found words of encouragement from unexpected sources, and it seemed whenever he was beginning to weaken, Morry, the manager of the clothing store next door, who came over frequently for a Coke and a chat, became one of his staunchest supporters. His uncle's apparent resentment of Morry's interference was neutralized by their business interest and they eventually gave up trying to find different jobs to keep him away from Morry. Louis, the young man just recently out of the Marines, who stopped every day after work, lamented that he lacked the "smarts and the will to go to school," and was told to "mind his own business."

The dignified new liquor salesman who was insulted rudely by both Uncle Gus and Uncle Bill – they seemed to compete in hurling insults – but whose dignity did not suffer in the least, appreciated Lampis' embarrassment and fear of being identified with his uncles and commented, "You must have arrived from Greece recently. I hope your goals are noble and your principles uncompromising. Be prepared for sacrifices and even suffering, but never lose sight of your goals."

He thanked this perfect gentleman and prayed that they meet again.

"What nonsense was that charlatan talking about?" Uncle Bill asked.

His embarrassment turned into indignation and disgust. "That's what is called a man of dignity," Lampis replied. He reasoned, but did not express it, "You don't know what dignity is."

"Men of dignity don't sell liquor," Uncle Bill, who had to have the last word, said.

Lampis could not suppress the comeback, "Would one that serves it know?"

The strongest support came from Nick, an old acquaintance in High School or the Gymnasium as it was called in Greece. Lampis saw this young man in church, but did not recognize him at first, and did not talk with him. After he remembered who he was, he insisted on going to church every Sunday in the hope of seeing him again, and his "devoutly religious" uncles did not object.

When Lampis eventually met Nick again, he found out that he was a freshman at Northwestern University Medical School. Lampis told him of his aspirations and goals.

Nick advised him resolutely, "You start college in September and you improve your English in college. You don't put it off. Here is the telephone number of Dr. Argoe. You call him and talk with him."

Lampis could have spread his wings to soar before descending to his uncle's place. He lost no time in calling Dr. Argoe, who repeated Nick's encouragement. He also announced to his uncles, "I am enrolling at Wright Junior College in September."

His uncles seemed dumbfounded, looked at him intently, conferred briefly – one of the few times he had seen them confer – and announced, "All right. We can arrange your schedule of work and better tell Ted to stay for a while."

Uncle Gus's attitude remained unchanged, in resignation. Uncle Bill vacillated between enthusiastic support and rather overt hostility. Aunt Helen's furor was expressed in many forms, from refusing to talk with him, to lengthy derisions, to keeping the children away from him. His definitive reaction to this wide spectrum of treatment was "So be it." His new friends, Louie and Joe, commented that he had a brighter smile now.

Lampis began counting the days until registration. He did this work with more enthusiasm than ever before and talked more excitedly and stayed up later at night trying to enrich his vocabulary. Aunt Helen began talking to him in English, not so much to help him or to show off, but rather to frustrate him with the realization that if he could not understand her simple talk, how could he expect to understand the professors at school? He called Nick frequently and before long, realized that Aunt Helen's wrath had spread in different directions – his way, Dr. Argoe's way, and Nick's way. Dr. Argoe was a "Well-known, no-good communist." Nick was "A liar and nothing more than a bus-boy." Nick's relatives were uncouth and pretentious peasants.

Lampis found his patience challenged and draining, with her repeated references to his ingratitude. He had survived only because of their support – her support in particular, who constantly reminded his uncles that they had an obligation to their sister and her family – and now that his uncle was sick with diabetes, "Nobody would help him." He felt that he had not transgressed his resolve to not argue with her, when he simply reminded her that he and his family had survived during the five years of war and occupation without any contact with her or his uncles, that the clothes they had received from them in packages, immediately after the war, were fit only for the scarecrows in the vineyard, and that the two hundred dollars, in five years, while welcome and appreciated, were hardly enough to rebuild their home.

Lampis appreciated that he had not scored a knock-out but had scored some points.

Uncle Bill compromised with the suggestion, in private – he had said nothing, though present during this exchange – that "Women get carried away, don't know what they're talking about, and sometimes should be ignored."

The controlled indignation about her comments was partly diffused by his pity for Uncle Bill. They all appreciated that the die has been cast, that the battle lines had been drawn. His strategy was simple: determination, perseverance, sacrifices, unalterable goals. He may have to maneuver, to change positions, but he would not retreat. And after assessing his opponent's position and weapons, he felt invincible. Consequently, he lost no sleep preparing his defenses.

The end of summer seemed to be sealed by the festivities of Labor Day. High school students invaded and occupied the back half of the store, the shifts changing with a break in the music from the jukebox. The bar was crowded every evening, with everybody back from vacation. And work, or waves at work, seemed more predictable.

Uncle Gus protected him against temptations from the girls by insisting that he himself serve at the tables, though he did not refuse the girls' offer to clean the tables and wash the dishes to help the "good-looking nephew." Another way to protect him from "young females in heat" – that was Uncle Bill's expression – was to find work for him in the basement. Girls were simply not allowed in the basement in the evening. When the ranks of the girls thinned out and the wall of the men crowding the bar consolidated, there was no need for additional protection. The tempo did not change on Sundays. He continued to go to church with or without his uncle's family. Aside from anticipating the new, stimulating sermon, he hoped to see Nick again, or perhaps, make new friends.

Lampis met Kostas once, the old acquaintance from the ship, who had bragged about making "Fifty dollars a week," and was planning to go to school "sometime soon."

The message of his resolve had finally made its impact. The objections echoed only arguments from the past. The distance from his uncles appeared to be decreasing. A truce evolved out of the silence, but his natural or inborn optimism was not enough to convince him that his uncles, and especially Aunt Helen, had surrendered or even conceded a temporary defeat. They had just retrenched, he concluded, to reassess their position and plan a new approach or attack. He continued to work the long hours, and did not object to any assigned tasks, even when obviously meant to either provoke him or humiliate him and maintained his defenses against insults in readiness. He had licked his wounds, the scars eased the pain, and his strength had not been diminished.

His excitement grew. Though he knew, or suspected, that talking about school irritated his uncles, he could not bottle-up this excitement.

Uncle Bill's responses were unpredictable: sometimes a neutral comment, more frequently an encouraging or even enthusiastic remark, and occasionally a hostile glance. In contrast, the attitudes of Uncle Gus and Aunt Helen remained accurately predictable: resentful resignation in Uncle Gus and bitter hostility in Aunt Helen. Uncle Gus frequently expressed his worry that his nephew did not possess the strength to resist the temptation of sin, that he was not prepared for this world of lust and worship of the flesh, and that he must pray for salvation. Aunt Helen never missed a chance to repeat that he was transgressing, that she had washed her hands for the inevitable and deserved punishment that was coming to him, and that he "must not look to us," for help or comfort when he was hurt. Lampis was not sure who was included in the "us."

He continued in this new state of euphoria. He thought less and less of the past and was mesmerized by the calls of the future. The postcard from his father's closest friend, a priest, who had sensed his frustrations in his letters about two months ago, flashed repetitively and vividly before his eyes – an old, twisted, strong trunk of a pine tree issuing out of a crag near the top of a vertical cliff, with branches bent by the forceful wind over the top and away from the cliff. The verse of the poem by Ioannis Polemes in the back of the card reverberated in his ears – he had read it aloud after the third or fourth time - "Do not fear for him who has built his hope in faith; I have watched him struggle, but I have always seen him invincible."

Lampis had an unshakable faith in his mission, and he had more than "hope." He had a pact with his destiny. The glow behind the mountain of Aghios Christophoros (St. Christopher) to the east of his village was growing in brightness; the clouds, packed in horizontal layers, were losing their purple-gold gild; the half-moon hung alone on the other side of the sky below the gray-blue mantle that covered the stars. He was always transferred back to the home of his birth and childhood, where his visions lifted him high above the peaks of the mountains.

He rode with Uncle Bill on the bus, the trolley-bus and another bus, on the way to Wright Junior College. It was a ride in ecstasy. The people in and outside of the buses appeared happy and handsome; the streets were broad and welcoming; the buildings looked warm and majestic; the Indian at the top of the waterfall, in front of a large building, in the northwest corner of an expansive lawn, with arms stretched over his head and face turned to the sky, seemed to convey his own gratitude to heavens for this beginning of another journey from dreams to reality. Fleetingly, he thought of the contrast between this journey and the last one from his village to Tripolis; the familiarity or identification with everything and everybody that his eyes encountered then, versus the total strangeness of his new impressions now. He was saying "Goodbyes" then; he was hearing "Welcomes," now. Lampis did not ask Uncle Bill many questions. He wished to form and store images without comments. When his thoughts were disrupted by a remark from Uncle Bill, he sensed some satisfaction or excitement in Uncle Bill's voice and face.

The walk from the last bus to Wright Junior College was brisk. Uncle Bill's face was radiant. The first view of the building of Wright Junior College was moving: austere, academic, challenging. He accepted the challenge as an invitation and walked through the open, massive door. He listened to the sounds of his steps in the long hallway on the way to the gym where registration was held. Dr. Argoe's face lacked the halo, but his sainthood was obvious. The handshake was the seal of irrevocable covenant, with the transfer of strength and expectations for the fulfillment of the commitment.

Registration was orderly, with Dr. Argoe having prearranged the courses, explaining his reasons: English 100 was essential for a foreign high school graduate before taking the required English 101 course; Speech 99 would help his diction; History, the courses he taught, Ancient History and History of England, would help him understand "the meaning of words," by following a story without resorting to a dictionary; Gym was required. The schedule seemed somewhat light, but Dr. Argoe argued that "It is just right for a beginner from a foreign country."

Lampis could not argue, and his uncle must have had at least two reasons for not objecting: one, that he did not know much about higher education and the other, that there may be more time to work at the store.

Dr. Argoe's parting words were warm and reassuring: "I'll see you in my class. You'll do well. I know!"

Uncle Bill's comments, concluding with a "Nice old man," were puzzling. Dr. Argoe seemed much younger than Uncle Bill and totally different from the "Degenerate High School teacher," that Aunt Helen had described – she had insisted that she, "Knew an awful lot about him."

They met other students, some serious and some frivolous, in the hallway, on the way out, and in the walks leading to the entrance. Uncle Bill's remark, "This is what makes America great!" suggested that he was impressed.

They bought some books and supplies at the bookstore and boarded the bus. Uncle Bill was quite talkative, with advice, warnings, and even encouragement. Whether it was courage or curiosity for a response that made Uncle Bill say, "Pay no attention to your aunt, my wife, when she talks about your going to school," Lampis could not decide, but wondered what kind of a reception they would have on their return. He made no response. The trip back was much longer. Uncle Bill had decided to follow a different route, with apparently faulty reasoning about bus connections.

The reception from Aunt Helen was a mixture of strong resentment and almost explosive hostility. "Go to the store right away," she ordered, "where you are needed while Uncle Bill has to do a few things at home."

He left for work feeling light-hearted, in spite of Aunt Helen's vehemence, hardly dwelling on what kind of an attack she may have launched at his uncle or what exchanges may be going on. He plunged into his work with total disregard for time, hunger, or tiredness. Uncle Bill came about one hour later, but did not exchange a word with anyone, put on his apron and began to wash some dishes. His "Yes, sir," escaped him only once, just as a customer turned to walk away with his just bought cigarettes. Uncle Gus walked out without a word or even a glance.

The store was quite empty of customers – the usual lull between lunch-time and the invasion of the swarm of high-school students. Uncle Bill suggested that he go to the basement to eat something, "Whatever Konstantes (Uncle Gus) had prepared." He suspected that Uncle Bill's suggestion served more his own wish to avoid conversation and less his concern that his nephew may be hungry. He ate rather hurriedly. The damp darkness in a low-ceiling basement, with frequent visits from long-tailed, scurrying or squealing rodents, was not exactly conducive to contemplating when eating alone! He returned upstairs. Uncle Bill retreated out of sight behind the tall glass cases across the bar without a comment, obviously very disturbed and strikingly different in mood in comparison to the morning's.

The hands on the wall-clock seemed to have stuck. His prayers that some customer walk in were not answered. He rearranged the bottles, the glasses and the dishes, slowly, deliberately, to kill time. He couldn't find anything else to do. He retraced the experiences of the morning and remembered objects and faces, displaced, earlier, by stronger impressions. He glided back to his last days in high school and recalled events and faces from his subconscious stores. He wondered, fleetingly, what influence these seemingly unimportant encounters may have in his future developments; whether the "what now?" that he read on some faces on the new graduates had changed and to what; whether the bullies were lost and wandering aimlessly; whether those who had compromised their aspirations by lack of financial means or strength of resolve would be content or plagued by regrets. He was surprised that he remembered so much about so many of those whom he thought he hardly knew. He leaped to his memories of his favorite uncle, his father's only brother, and prayed that the infectiousness of Uncle Vasiles' perennial and sweet smile may have infected him incurably; that the reflection of purity and love in his clear blue eyes would guide him in the darkness of despair or depression; that his habit of giving for the joy of giving may spread to all the recipients of his goodness.

"Your goal and mission must always be to contribute to the welfare and betterment of the society," frequently changing "humanity" for "society," Uncle Vasiles would repeat or admonish practically every day. "Society" and "humanity" were synonymous to Uncle Vasiles, with no prejudices or discrimination, and included the whole human race. He transferred to his first encounter with his uncles in Chicago and was embarrassed in his rash initial judgment. Inescapably, he wondered whether his present assessment is correct, whether he may have misjudged his uncles, even Aunt Helen, or whether the real confrontation was yet to come.

Uncle Bill emerged from his hiding place, looked at him rather intently for a moment as if to make some declaration, but retreated once more without a word. He had no doubt that Aunt Helen had taken an uncompromising stand and demanded that the presumptuous 'peasant nephew' be put in his place once and for all. Uncle Bill must have been told that this clarification and separation of responsibilities must be made today! Uncle Bill's predicament or dilemma seemed obvious as well as unenviable. Had he been given an ultimatum? She had threatened suicide a couple of months ago, Uncle Bill had inadvertently related. He now wondered whether he was the cause of all this strife, but he quickly decided that he would not dwell in explaining or understanding their conflicts. He could not dismiss his pity for Uncle Bill, nor remain unscathed from Aunt Helen's barbs, but he would not be deterred from his defined path.

Whatever he did in this unusually quiet span, pacing behind the bar from one end to the other, he did mechanically and without disturbing his thoughts. He transferred himself to the classrooms; he followed the professor from the door to the podium; he studied the faces of his classmates and experienced the comfort of security.

He was brought back by old Ted's entrance. He returned the condescending greeting deferentially. His attempts to retrieve the images that he had just created flashed only some blurs. His effort to divine his parents' reaction rewarded him with only a dry "That's what you traveled to America for." And he concluded with the conviction that Mr. Ted's comment, "A lot of young people register in college," implied that "Only some graduate," and that he would not be among those that succeeded. The sarcastic laugh to his answer, "I'll graduate," brought Uncle Bill out of his retreat.

"Check on those tables in the back," Uncle Bill told Ted.

Lampis knew there was nothing to check, and he was told to go in the basement to see how many cases of Budweiser and Schlitz were there. Uncle Bill could not have forgotten that he had just taken an inventory. It was obvious that he was irritated by Ted's laugh.

He had more time to reflect before the high school girls would start coming in. Watching Ted's shuffle among the tables made him try to imagine what Ted would think of himself when seeing his own shadow in front of him – without a hat; ovoid bald head, on a thin long neck stemming out of sloping shoulders; large ears straight out! Would a breeze against those ears set the cantaloupe-like head spinning on the neck? Would the dangling arms flap against the empty trousers? Would he still laugh at him, after seeing his own shadow? And was his son's graduation from the University of Chicago Medical School enough to give him the prerogative to disparage a young man's dream?

His mood vacillated from mirth to indignation, but he neither smiled nor frowned. He just felt buoyant. He had tested his wings since early adolescence, he had gained the confidence that he could fly, and now he was ready to soar. The awareness of predators and of storms, the appreciation of the rockiness of the harbors and of the thorns in his lairs, and the anticipation of loneliness not only did not frighten him but served to buttress his resolve. He had already decided that he would learn to avoid and fight the predators; he would find a way to rest in the damp caves or in the shade of scrawny bushes; and he would not allow his loneliness to carry him into lonesomeness.

The giggles and gaiety of the high school girls transformed the whole atmosphere, in an instant, from thoughtful reflections in him and presumably frustration in Big-Ears Mr. Ted and Uncle Bill, to lively exchanges of compliments, smiles, and money for ice cream or sodas. The less inhibited girls would reach for his hand or say something like "I tried to look pretty today, just for you." He read innocence and playfulness in their behavior. He did not recognize the lust or the mischief that his uncles and Mr. Ted were describing as obvious. He enjoyed the attention but maintained a respectful distance. His ventures into advising against smoking were rewarded with either a blushing downcast of the eyes or an immediate crush of the cigarette in the ashtray, rarely with, "I like it." Their stay did not exceed fifteen or twenty minutes. They came in waves, but only a few were left when the steady "Shot-and-a-beer," customers lined up along the bar.

The men greeted each other with a nod, less frequently with a "hello" or a "hi" and rarely with "A nice day today." They all saw a difference in him. He answered, or repeated, that he had registered in college and they drank to it. Louie and Joe, who came and stayed later, were overjoyed. Morry made his appearance, as if only to congratulate him and express his confidence in him. Uncle Bill's eyes sparkled with every "yes sir," and his laughing seemed both appropriate and genuine. The pace continued, after the men at the bar gradually filed out, and a steady stream of mature women shoppers kept everybody busy – it was Monday night and the stores stayed open until 9:00 P.M.

In sharp contrast to the high school girls, these women seemed to have spent their energy and their money; they had shopping bags but no smiles and no chatter. He did not indulge in a psychological excursion, but he was amused in recalling the differences between the young girls, the men, and the serious women.

Aunt Helen, who didn't even talk with him when she came in at about 10:00 P.M., didn't share any of the qualities he had observed in the three groups. Her glances, her stomping steps, and the rigid sweeps or swings of her arms revealed a stockpile of hostility ready to explode. He had no intention of providing the ignition! He enjoyed his euphoria. He wondered later, after she and her husband left at about 10:30, whether the explosion took place on the way home or in their home. He knew it was inevitable.

When he arrived at their home after midnight, all was quiet. He went directly to his room to write to his parents about the great events of the day, in great detail, and share his joy and excitement with them. He paused at irregular intervals, spreading and stretching each image his memory brought back to life, and raced with his pen in his hurry to record his emotions before they evolved into regimented thoughts or plans. He closed his letter, but not the doors or windows of his animated mind. He lay in bed with his hands locked behind his head and leaped five days ahead, to the time his parent would open this letter and across the vast waters of the Atlantic and the Mediterranean, to witness the tears of joy streaming down their cheeks; to hear them sharing their glad tidings with trusted friends; to hear Theia Christitsa's (Aunt Christitsa), his father's older sister, declaration of her unshakable faith in him; and to watch them light a candle of gratitude in front of the icon of St. Nicholas at the Monastery. Sleep left him wandering among the olive groves of his village, transported him with the breezes from hilltop to hilltop, and purified him with the waters of the fountain carved by his father at the spring of Panaghia (all-Holy Virgin Mary). He was alone, in all these vivid dreams in silence, without a shadow in a mellow light, rediscovering the joy in following a lone white cloud moving slowly from east to west, and in anticipating the view from the ridge of the next hill.

He kept returning to these dreams throughout the next day, not to divine their meaning, but to recapture his rapture when fully awake and to force the unpleasant memories of yesterday into retreat.

His anticipation of starting school began to foster impatience, and this impatience grew steadily. The atmosphere at his uncle's home and at work did not change. He realized gradually, that his homesickness began to fade before his preoccupation with his immediate future and his concentration on the paths to his goal. He was aware that he was day-dreaming and was conscious of a permanent smile on his face.

Strangely and gratifyingly, he found Louie's and Joe's and Morry's smiles more spontaneous and warm. He knew intuitively, and he read in the sparkles of their eyes, that they were sharing his excitement; their greetings and their handshakes told him clearly, "We have faith in you."

CHAPTER 16

THE DAYS SUCCEEDED ONE ANOTHER, without a change in the routine, with no distractions, and with frequent repetitions of his thoughts springing out of his most recent encounters: Nick's encouragement; Dr. Argoe's support; the registration; the revelation of another side of Uncle Bill; Aunt Helen's rage; big-ears ted's resentment. Lampis sorted all these thoughts out, in their frequent returns, into strengthening and deterring, illuminating and unexplainable, memorable and petty. His whole existence seemed condensed now, between the day of his registration and the first day of classes.

The hot, humid days of the summer and the anxiety of frustrations of adjusting to his new environment were receding in the past and into memories. His strength was growing at a steady rate. And his self-confidence reached a higher level. He was on his way.

The first day in school was introductory. Dr. Argoe and Mr. Anderson, his History and English-100 professors, respectively, simply stated the objectives of their respective courses, their expectations, and their criteria in evaluating their students' performance. He realized, painfully, that he understood less than he had hoped, but he was not embarrassed to approach some American-born students of Greek descent to ask for amplification. The introductions among the students was rather formal, the handshakes hesitant or reserved, and the encounters barely exploratory. He was not discouraged by his impaired comprehensions and interpreted the students' reactions as a sign of maturity and of purpose.

He met two other new students, newly arrived from Greece: one a very tall young man, Mike, with a mixture of congenial and superficial airs about him, and the other, George, with some traits of a spoiled brat. He concluded, rather hastily, that he would outdistance them in grades and performance. They both appeared secure in their relatives' commitment for financial and moral support. Mike, like him, had decided to go into medicine. George didn't know – "Maybe law or business."

A third young man approached them in the hallway, having heard them talk in Greek, and offered to help, since he knew his way around, this being his second year, or to show off by greeting some girls and introducing himself as Jim. Lampis reminded Jim that he knew him in Tripolis, and of the rivalry of their schools (he was in the 1st Gymnasium and Jim was in the 2nd), and of the competitions between their respective Boy Scout Troops (they were both squad leaders) to check the boasting about academic and athletic records.

They spent about one hour in the cafeteria, exchanging notes, after Jim excused himself to go to practice with the football team. They would be together in all their classes. He could not decide whether that was good or bad but was hoping to make more friends.

The ride to his uncle's store – he did not stop at Uncle Bill's home – was made very brief by his reflections and thoughts of anticipation of future encounters. He leafed through one of his textbooks, registering only some chapter headings and the number of pages. His reflections changed directions, with the bus-driver calling the stops or the changes in the passenger sitting next to him but kept revolving around the challenges ahead. Politeness dictated that he acknowledged whomever sat next to him with a smile and a nod of the head, but he quickly retreated to his private world. He did not dwell on his encounter with Dr. Argoe in the classroom. He concentrated more on Mr. Anderson, the English professor, with the throaty voice and deliberate pronouncements. He had not met Professor Anderson's eyes, but did not hesitate in concluding that he felt more comfortable in his classroom. He hoped that the Speech-99 professor would be like Mr. Anderson. He planned his routine commuting to and from school, transferring from one bus to another, and he wondered how it'd be waiting for the bus in the cold or rain. He hardly looked out of the window, and when he did, the images just flashed and faded quickly.

"Charalam," Uncle Bill greeted him, mispronouncing his full name that would make all those who knew him wonder who this Charalam was. He looked at him over his glasses and hid behind the candy counter.

Lampis deposited his books reverently on a counter, tied his apron around his waist and checked the mail. No letter from Greece today. He tried to find things to do and redo, and to avoid talking.

Uncle Gus walked in and went directly to the basement to prepare his meal. Sometime later, he walked right by him again, without a word – he was accustomed to this routine by now – and straight up to his apartment above the store. He had been here for nearly four months now and still had not seen Uncle Gus's apartment.

The rest of the day was a repetition of the day before and every day, ever since vacation season ended after Labor Day and the high school students had returned to classes.

His encounter with Mr. Link the speech professor, the following day, left him strangely and inexplicably uneasy. He could not decide on the proportions of a condescending attitude, invitation for a closer contact, and self-aggrandizement. He detected a similar bewilderment in the expressions of his classmates. But he was cautious to not jump to conclusions from his observations of the effeminate mannerisms and intonations in the voice.

The Gym teacher, or coach, seemed like one of the students, only more physically fit in a mature, disciplined display of his position and responsibilities, not unlike his gym teacher in the Gymnasium. Their exercises, they were told, would include swimming, judo, and team games such as baseball, football, basketball, and volleyball, twice a week. He declined the invitation to join the wrestling team when he realized that he would have to practice a few extra hours a week, and he read disappointment in the coach's remark, "That's too bad."

His circle of acquaintances remained small for about two weeks. He had regimented his life in the confines of work, school, homework, and correspondence with his family and close friends or relative back home. His entertainment would have to be extracted from or fit in these activities. He became more observing and learned to laugh at himself. His ignorance of baseball to the point that he thought all he had to do was hit the ball hard and far, when his turn at bat came, brought chuckles almost daily, when he recalled that he held the bat slanting down and away from his body; that his playmates laughed when he missed the ball with his first two swings; that he decided he was going to have the last laugh; he readjusted his hold on the bat and hit a homerun with the third swing; that he dropped the bat and walked away thinking he had met his challenge; and that one of his teammates took him by the hand and ran the bases with him. He laughed at his mistakes in English, and louder than his listeners. And he decided to shave his mustache just when some other students were starting to grow a beard for Homecoming.

Mr. Anderson and Dr. Argoe offered to tutor him and the other three Greek students – the third one, Kostas, had registered a few days later – twice a week. They met in the cafeteria, for about one hour, and went over their compositions. His knowledge of Ancient Greek syntax and his appreciation that sentence construction in English was very similar to that of ancient Greek helped him immensely. Before long, he was the first to raise his hand in class, to identify the subject, the predicate, the object, etc. in a sentence. He was always right and made Mr. Anderson smile, and drew glances of astonishment from his classmates. He saw no envy or resentment in those glances or in the remarks, "You must be a genius."

Male and female classmates offered to help him enrich his vocabulary in the cafeteria, in the hallways, and in their homes, if he "Would just come for a while." Lampis began to experience and enjoy a kind of happiness he had never known before – he was learning in an atmosphere surrounded by pure-hearted, benevolent human beings. He was happy at work, also, and did not mind sleeping on an old spring bed in the same room with Uncle Gus, with coarse blankets brought by his uncles and made by his maternal grandmother fifty years ago. (He had moved in with Uncle Gus, after Aunt Helen's sister, Elpida, and her three children stopped for an extended visit on the way back to St. Joseph, Missouri, from their vacation in Greece. Both he and Aunt Helen were relieved when Elpida arrived and provided the right excuse, though jumping from the frying pan into the fire did not resemble a deliverance.)

Uncle Gus insisted that they pray together in the morning and at bedtime, taxing God's patience with their lengthy repetitions of Psalms, hymns, and "Kyrie Eleisons." He was not going to antagonize his uncles in any way, still hoping that eventually they would come around to his way of thinking.

The punctuations in the monotony of the first few months, from new encounters and acquaintances, became progressively more frequent to the point of not perceiving monotony at all. The compromises were now understood as expedience, and the deprivations were simply ignored. His sadness in declining invitations by his new acquaintances was rationalized and neutralized by the hope that his position was appreciated for now and would change in time.

However, he did find the strength to ask his uncles' permission to accept an invitation for a Sunday dinner in the home of Pete, a young man he had met right after his "famous" home-run.

Pete had laughed as he extended his hand to congratulate him. "What a hit. You really showed them."

In their brief conversation, Lampis detected maturity, sincerity and sensitivity in Pete, qualities promising a lasting true friendship. They sought each other out in the cafeteria, in their precious free time; they talked about their studies and plans and parted always with a handshake. The invitation to Pete's home for dinner was the crowning of their new friendship.

Uncle Bill hesitated for a moment before giving his permission, but the tone of his voice conveyed the unpronounced follow-up of, "Just this once."

The anticipation of spending a few hours with a friend, away from his environment, infused Lampis with a euphoria approaching that of the day of his registration. Mr. Big-ears Ted must have thought he had flipped or something else, but he was not going to waste any time divining.

Uncle Gus chastised his brother sternly, and Aunt Helen remonstrated that Sundays were busy days and, "Your sick uncle needs some help!"

Uncle Bill did not go back on his word.

Lampis had no trouble finding Pete's home even though he had to change buses twice. The anticipation and the concentration on his "homework," riding the bus, made the time seem shorter than what his watch showed – one hour and fifteen minutes.

Pete and his mother greeted him at the door. Pete's genuine friendliness and his mother's serene and gracious beauty were displaced for quite some time by the imposing, aristocratic and Olympian figure of Pete's father. Lampis was stunned, grateful, and somewhat disarticulate in shaking the hand of the man who had been insulted so coarsely by his uncles; who had deflected the insults with his dignity and who had counseled him to keep his sights on his goal no matter what the obstacles and challenges. His wish that he could meet this man again had been granted, and his happiness was doubled in that this man was his friend's father.

In the few hours that he spent in his new friend's home, in an environment of genuine interest in him, of respect for each other's individuality, of total honesty and openness, and of ignoring the base of vulgar existences (not condemning, just ignoring), he felt replenished with the essential elements to continue on his road to his destiny. The parting handshakes, the buoyancy from the expressed wishes that they see him again soon, and his euphoria were marred by the foreboding thought that his uncles would try to make another visit difficult or impossible.

Waiting for the bus allowed Lampis time to retrieve some of the impressions of the evening. He had some difficulty in arranging them in order of sequence, and he flitted from one to another. The intervals were filled with exclamations such as, "How wonderful," "admirable," "ideal," "enviable," etc. He had not been shown such affection and respect since he had disembarked in New York. He had been totally absorbed that he had not once thought of his problems in his uncles' environment – after his initial apology to Mr. Liakakos, Pete's father, for his uncle's behavior. The response was a gratifying demonstration of the dignity he had witnessed a few months ago and made further comments superfluous.

Lampis boarded the near-empty bus, opened his book and tried, in vain, to read. The images of Mrs. Liakakos' serene beauty and grace, of Mr. Liakakos' gentleness and understanding, of Pete's deference to and affection for his parents kept revolving and spinning off flashes of exchanges of stories and expressions about their past experiences and future aspirations. He had learned that Mr. Liakakos had met Mrs. Liakakos while a graduate student at the University of Chicago; that she had been born and raised in Indiana, where she had been crowned Miss Indiana; that they had moved to Greece before the war; and that they had returned to America after they "had lost everything" during the war. They had not elaborated on what "everything" was. He had managed to clarify "everything material, that is" and was rewarded with a smile from everyone, after they looked and smiled at each other. He had told them about his goal and dreams beyond, and was fortified by the sincerity in their unanimous expression, "You'll do it!"

Uncle Bill greeted him by simply pronouncing his name, and without another word, retreated behind the glass cases for a good hour. Two old ladies had finished their ice cream and were chatting across the table. The old Bulgarian, a frequent patron, was caressing the thigh, under the skirt of one of his many "girlfriends" without looking at her, and a young woman in blue-jeans walked into and out of the washroom with only a half-smile for a greeting. One young man bought a box of candy and another a pack of "Lucky Strike" cigarettes. Time was moving slowly, even with his frequent returns to the evening at his friend's home, mainly because of the suspense of hearing his uncle's decree. Eventually, Uncle Bill came out of his lair and without looking at him, decreed, "This is the last time you went anywhere," took a few steps toward the washroom, half-turned and added, "Without us."

Lampis read finality in those pronouncements, concluded that any response would be futile, and suppressed his indignation with the decision, "This arrangement cannot last long."

Aunt Helen broke her silence five days later, with the accusation that he had abandoned his sick uncle for the sake of a visit with a "bum." Lampis protested firmly that he did not associate with bums. The children stopped talking with him, but his affection for them did not decrease. He had developed the habit of falling back on his promises to "pay no attention" – he had borrowed this phrase from Uncle Bill – to these provocations and was able to fence them off without effort.

He fortified his defenses for assaults from all angles: Uncle Gus' redoubled preaching about the traps set by Satan; Aunt Helen's insults about his humble origin and his insolence; Uncle Bill's mixture of sarcastic remarks and assertions of authority; and even big-ears Ted's derisive laughter. Lampis concentrated on his studies with an even greater intensity; he stood before the mirror pronouncing difficult words aloud, until his hearing was satisfied; and he finished assigned or even expected tasks at work before Uncle Bill had a chance to complain. He suspected that they were anticipating "something is going to give," "he's going to burn out," but he'd show them. Strangely, he felt no resentment.

He transferred, or took with him, his new attitudes to school. He preferred solitude to concentrate harder. He discriminated in choosing acquaintances and was not insulted by the Greek-American students referring to him as a "DP." His patience and forbearance, however, were taxed by Mr. Link's mixed overtures for closer contact, of provocation and humiliation. And he decided to show him, also, by preparing and standing up to recite a paragraph from Shakespeare's *Julius Caesar*.

He stood before the mirror and practiced, after memorizing the paragraph, not only for the correct pronunciation and deliverance, but also the appropriate gestures for the maximum affect.

The next day, Mr. Link asked the question, "Who's going to deliver Marc Anthony's address today?"

Lampis raised his hand.

Mr. Link appeared stunned when he saw his hand raised. His eyes scanned the room. "Who else?" he asked. He acted as if he had sensed a conspiracy and stared at a few of the students in succession. "We'll do it next week, then, since nobody is prepared."

One of the students remonstrated, "Well, Mr. Link, Mr. Anagnostopoulos raised his hand and is prepared."

The rest of the class clamored, "yes, yes, yes."

"Well, you asked for it," Mr. Link said, conceding.

Lampis strutted to the podium even before Mr. Link's comment, and without looking at anyone. He stood at the podium, waited for a long moment, raised his arms and began: "Romans, countrymen, and lovers! Hear me for my cause and be silent, so that you may hear!" He went on, looking at his audience of Romans, not recognizing any faces, and not even glancing to his right, at Mr. Link. But when his eyes met with those of a girl with glasses, who was looking intently at him, he forgot the next line.

In the pause that followed, he tried to transfer to the page he had memorized.

Mr. Link seized the opportunity to pronounce, "That's enough."

"No, that's not enough. I am not finished. I'll start from the beginning," Lampis retorted.

And before Mr. Link had taken a step away from his chair, he had started again, louder and more assertively, "Romans, countrymen..."

Not a sound from the audience.

When Lampis forgot the line preceding the one that alluded him before, he simply walked to the desk in front of him, took the book of his classmate, and after a quick look, resumed and completed the address. The audience broke out in a loud applause, and the girl with the glasses stood up and clapped more enthusiastically.

"Sir, have you ever heard a better Mark Anthony?" a student in the back asked aloud.

"Not bad, not bad at all," Mr. Link replied.

Lampis returned to his seat with a sense of "mission accomplished." He felt a gentle approving tap on his shoulder and heard nothing during the rest of the hour. When the class was over, Mr. Link stared at him with a half-smile in which he read: "You scored. You showed me this time."

A number of his classmates came up to shake his hand. His Greek classmates seemed prouder of him. Two of them came spontaneously and the third joined somewhat hesitantly.

The girl with the glasses took his hand. "I can't wait to go home to tell my parents about you and what happened today; you're simply wonderful!" she announced.

"Thank you. I had to do it."

"I bet you can do anything you want to do!"

Mr. Anderson expressed his satisfaction with his progress and encouraged him to "stay on track." His vocabulary, diction, and familiarization with some idiomatic expressions approached the point where he did not shun engaging in conversation. He began to feel more "at home" in school and looked at his uncle's environment as "just a place of work." He did not talk with his uncles about school, and they did not ask. They must have listened, however, when he talked to Louie and Joe who seemed to enjoy his experiences. He swallowed his resentment when ordered to stay at the store and work fifteen hours a day for the two days preceding Thanksgiving Day.

"We need you here. School is not important!" Uncle Bill had decreed aloud, in his wife's presence, to impress her and maybe himself.

Thanksgiving Day at Uncle Bill's house was a day of boredom, alienation, restraints, deliberation about answering simple questions, and an overwhelming awareness that he was among people with whom he shared practically nothing. He had no trouble being polite and deferential, but he did have to exert some effort to appear attentive and part of the group. The congenialities and amenities exchanged between his Uncles' wives amused Lampis, when pitted against the venomous remarks and stories he had heard about Aunt Sophia. Uncle john's intimidation by Uncle Bill was apparent and sad, but his sympathy for Uncle John was more than counterbalanced by the angry question, "Why can't he stand up to them?"

Walking out of that house was not just a relief; it was deliverance! He had heard from his friends and read in a magazine article about the meaning of Thanksgiving. He had not witnessed even a semblance of that meaning in the gathering. He recalled the evening at his friend Pete's home and knew that he would have experienced the true meaning of the day, had he been with them. The cool breeze on his face as he walked back to his "Monastic cell," – that's what he called Uncle Gus' one bedroom apartment – blew away all memories of the evening and carried him back to the bosom of his family where he could enjoy his parents' affectionate teasing of each other, his brothers' and sister's antics, and the comfort of belonging to those that belonged to him. He walked around the block once more until the retrieved memories of the past totally displaced the remnants of today's lingering impressions – at least for now!

The next three days seemed interminably long. The mornings, from 7:00 to 10:00, spent in studying and thinking, went quickly, but the next fourteen hours at the store dragged. During the lulls, he thought of what he had read earlier, repeated phrases that had impressed him, and anticipated questions that may be asked in class Monday.

Saturday and Sunday, with far fewer customers coming in, were more taxing in that he had to try harder to avoid or minimize his exchanges with his uncles. Lampis may have been rude to Mr. Ted when he cut him short in his attempt to inform him about the meaning of Thanksgiving, by stating that Dr. Argoe explained it all. He mused about the young girls' behavior, in general, and their greetings to him in particular, being so different in the presence of their mothers. Some acted as if they didn't even know him. He did not cherish the thought that after three weeks he would have to spend two full weeks of this routine away from school. Still he did his work, cheerfully and efficiently. He mopped the floors, waited on tables, served behind the bar, made fresh ice cream, filled boxes with candies late at night, and he prayed with Uncle Gus in the morning and at bedtime.

There were times that Lampis had to concentrate in re-establishing his identity and re-asserting the thought that he lived for a lofty goal. In gathering strength, he tried to identify his weaknesses, to measures his inadequacies, and to take inventories of his reserves. He reassessed the height and breadth of the obstacles, the width and depth of the pits, and the deadliness of the traps arrayed or hidden before him; and he planned his battles to ensure victory. He could see

Victory beckoning to him, with the shining crown raised high, a gold ribbon with the inscription, "Yours, if you earn it," fluttering in the breeze.

Aunt Helen's frustration at his stamina was mounting. He did not underestimate her resourcefulness. He treaded carefully and even found some satisfaction in her frustrations. Uncle Bill's vacillations fell into a more predictable and explainable pattern. Uncle Gus' expectations had already been carved in stone, and Uncle John's dissociation was receding into a blur.

<hr />

The Christmas holidays came and went with an assortment of memories dominated by commercialism and superficiality. The loads of shopping bags, the ornaments and colored lights in storefronts and homes, the slurred "Merry Christmas" wishes repeated at the bar, the shirt and tie he received for a present, and the "Business as usual" at the store served more as a contrast with the past than as an inspiration. His imagination was shackled by the strains of servitude to his uncles and by the demands on his physical and emotional reserves. He could not lift his soul up to the stars simply by gazing in search of the one that guided the Magi; he could not transfer the chant, "Christ is born, glorify..." to a chorus of angels; and he could not find comfort in the warmth of the radiators after having enjoyed the warmth of the love of his family.

Lampis had been sustained by that warmth, without a fire from fear of the patrolling enemy, on Christmas Day of 1943; he had leaned on his father in his distress when a flare to light-up targets for artillery had displaced the star announcing Christ's birth on Christmas night in 1944; and he had reveled in Aunt Katerina's chastisement for spending Christmas day in 1948, alone, instead of joining her. He tried to fill the void with the memories of Louie's handshake, Joe's smile, John the drunkard's, "All the best to you," and Morry's admonition, "Stay on course."

On New Year's Eve, the store was unusually quiet. Lampis could count the customers on the fingers of one hand after 5:00 P.M. he paced from one end of the bar to the other, looked out on the deserted street, wondered whether the clanking of the streetcars was to break the conductor's boredom, and appreciated his solitude after scanning the emptiness of Woolworth's and Kresge's stores across the street. Uncle Bill was secluded behind the glass cases. Aunt Helen was preparing, with Aunt Sophia's help, for St. Basil's feast day, Uncle Bill's name day, tomorrow. Lampis chuckled at the thought that they should celebrate on St. William's day, if there were a St. William, and decided to ask Uncle Bill when he came out of his retreat. But his questions took a different form when Uncle Bill came out.

"Is it always like this on New Year's Eve?" Lampis asked.

"Yes, it's always like this."

"Why don't you close the shop, then, and go home to be with your children?"

Uncle Bill hesitated for a long moment. "Who knows, someone may realize he forgot to buy a box of candy. We should be here to help," he replied, without raising his eyes.

Lampis did not answer, but thought of a different explanation, "This is their way of life, a habit acquired long ago, maybe even an escape from his wife."

In the long silence that followed, Lampis recalled the momentous events of the year: the dashing of his rekindled hopes about entering the Military Medical School, after his appeal to Queen Frederica; the despair in finding a job; the pain in accepting money from his Uncle Vasiles for minor chores; his decision to try for a career in the army; the whirlwind after the unexpected opportunity to emigrate to the United States; his experiences on the ship; and his starting on the road to his destiny. An eventful year, he concluded, this year of 1951.

He heard his names, "The D.P." and "The Greenhorn" repeatedly at his uncle's party on New Year's Eve. He indeed felt displaced in this environment and did not resent it. Nor did he protest that his name was not "Greenhorn." Uncle John discreetly asked him about his parents and school, and complimented him about his dancing, and offered some advice against aggressive women. The conversations revolved mostly around business. The young women shunned him. He never had a chance to answer the questions, "How do you like this country?" even though he heard it repeatedly through the evening, sometimes twice from the same person, since the answer, "Great country," was offered in the same breath by the questioner.

Lampis was civil and deferential, but did not wonder what they thought of him since he had decided that D.P. and Greenhorn must have a special or unique definition and status in their thinking. The anticipation of meeting some of these people again, at Uncle John's party in about one week was not particularly exciting. Still, he would like to verify that touch of tenderness he detected in Uncle John and try, once again, to approach Nick, the young man with the soft eyes and genuine smile, for a closer, if exploratory, contact.

CHAPTER 17

THE WINTER WAS HARSH, bitterly cold, with hissing and whistling winds, even on sunny days; snowfalls with the mounds of snow turning dirty; heavy frost on the windows; frozen pipes; long waits at the streetcar or bus stops; and frequent returns, for an escape to the mellow winters of his hometown, where the warm sun of the day melted the snow of the night, where birds sang and chirped, chasing each other playfully, and where he could hear the song of the olive harvesters or the shepherds. He had taken pride in walking with an open shirt and not overcoat during the winters, even in Tripolis, but found it necessary to "bundle up" against the harshness of the Chicago winter. He remained healthy, just as he had promised the old man on the ship. He knew he was losing weight without weighing himself, but that mattered very little.

His confidence did not waiver, but when the notice from the local Selective Service Board Office came that he may be called soon, he wondered whether this may be a good way out of his predicament. He deliberated at length, talked with Louie and Joe, and finally decided to apply for a deferment to finish the academic year. Lampis took a qualifying college deferment test but scored seventy-three points, two points below the required seventy-five. The possibility that he may be drafted any day now, aroused a spectrum of emotions from a realistic acceptance of the inevitable to the fear of fighting in Korea. The comfort from the thought of extracting from his hardships and of the G.I. benefits made the day of his draft less disturbing and more promising. He prepared his parents in his letters and appealed to the Board in person for a postponement until he could finish the academic year.

The ambivalence in Uncle Bill was all too apparent and probably reflected only a blurred image of his wife's strong reactions. Lampis knew that he was a thorn in her side, but on the other hand, she knew they'd have to pay three times as much for somebody else to do the amount of work that he was doing. Uncle Gus responded with, "God's will be done," and never discussed the subject again.

They were not surprised that he did not qualify for the deferment, but they could not suppress their disappointment when they read he had missed the qualification by two points.

"He must have cheated, but not enough," Aunt Helen pronounced, squirting her venom.

"Maybe you can tell me what cheating is since that's a new concept for me," Lampis responded indignantly.

"I know your kind," she replied.

He did not pursue it farther. He remembered his father's frequent quotation of Socrates, "If a donkey kicks you, are you going to kick the donkey back? If a dog bites you, are you going to bite the dog back?"

When Dr. Argoe had taken him out for lunch, he had amused him with this quotation. Lampis was flattered that he was singled out of all the students for this treat and found the conversation enlightening and inspiring.

He returned to his tasks even stronger and more confident.

Dr. Argoe allowed him to take the test home and work at it without the pressure of time limitations. He had performed well, Dr. Argoe assured him, but he still had "a lot of work to do."

The semester came to a close. Lampis had B's for his two history courses, Ancient History and History of England, and an A in gym. He had no grades for English 100 and Speech 99 that he had audited. He registered for two more history courses with Dr. Argoe, History of the Middle Ages and History of the United States from the Civil War to the Present, for Math 101 and English 100 again. He had no desire to see Mr. Link again.

The break between semesters was not a break from work. He was at the store from 10:00 A.M. to 1:00 A.M. The preparations for Valentine's Day were just as demanding as the preparations for Christmas. He did not expect any type of compensation either in salary or in expressions of gratitude. In his stubborn, naïve character, however, he still hoped that his selflessness and sincerity would be appreciated in the end.

The nights were short and his sleep was deep. The old dreams kept returning: flying over the apple orchard; standing alone among the wild flowers on a hill; wondering why he had no shadow. He avoided conversations with his uncles, returned to the past to summon some reserves for his struggles, and looked to Dr. Argoe and Mr. Anderson for inspiration. He appreciated that his weight was going down but did not wish to know by how much. He was learning to think and reflect quickly, to fill the intervals between work and study with plans and with dreams, and to redirect his frustrations after abstract philosophy or the epics of history. Still, he could not suppress resentment or self-pity entirely, especially when witnessing the mirth and carefree behavior of some of his peers, or when some young women expressed the desire – and sometimes quite directly – to be with him.

Time seemed to advance with leaping strides or to slow to a snail's pace. The young crowd continued to flock to the shore, but the girls were no longer attentive to him: sometimes they hardly acknowledged his existence. His friendships with Louie and Joe were strengthening. He anticipated Morry's visits with growing eagerness. Uncle Bill stared at him with the same question in his eyes, the question that he could not express in words, "When are you going to give up your foolish dreams?"

"Your English has improved extremely rapidly," Mr. Anderson assured Lampis, looking at him with pride and even affection.

Lampis' confidence grew to the point that he requested of Dr. Argoe to take the test along with the rest of the class. A shadow of reservation formed on Dr. Argoe's face but was replaced with a glow of pride. Dr. Argoe agreed and offered to let him continue for ten minutes after the rest of the students in the class turned in their papers.

"No," Lampis responded resolutely. "I'll turn my paper in with everybody else."

Skepticism and hope were obvious in Dr. Argoe's final answer, "As you wish."

This was not just an academic test for Lampis. It was a test of his efforts.

Lampis did not finish the test. He left the last ten questions unanswered.

Dr. Argoe's prolonged stare, as he turned the paper in, told him with conviction, "I believe in you."

Lampis waited for the return of his graded paper with its comments without apprehension. He would not desecrate his anticipation with Aunt Helen's comments, if he told his uncles.

A few days later, Dr. Argoe smiled at him in the hallway without greeting him. He read a reward in that smile. Finally, the day of truth arrived. Dr. Argoe read the grades aloud, as he was returning the papers, all but his. Lampis began to wonder why his paper was not returned; it should have been among the first, since his name started with "A."

"What was the highest grade?" Dr. Argoe asked the class.

"Eighty-three," someone answered.

"Up to now," Dr. Argoe announced with a serene voice, fixing his gaze on Lampis. "The highest grade is eighty-seven, and it belongs to someone who just came from Greece."

Lampis felt all eyes riveted on him. A warm kiss on his cheek made him turn around. It was from the young woman who sat behind him. He knew he was blushing.

"There are dividends from a good grade, like a kiss from a pretty young lady," Dr. Argoe pronounced, and added after a moment's pause, "Of course, being handsome and Greek helps, too."

Lampis had passed the test. He was surrounded by his classmates who expressed congratulations and admiration.

Dr. Argoe walked to him, took his hand in both of his own and declared: "I am so proud of you. I am positive your score would have been ninety-seven if you had time to answer all the questions."

Within two days, it seemed that everyone in school knew about him. He was stopped in the hallways, he was surrounded in the cafeteria, and he felt that his acceptance was complete.

The "A's" followed one another, in Math, in English, in History and according to Mr. Anderson, "In an example to imitate." Lampis felt he could soar, but he was still tethered to the galleys of his uncles' prejudices and weighed down by the cruel reality. Aunt Helen found out somehow and accused him of false modesty and haughtiness. "He wouldn't condescend to tell us, who are sending him to school, what his grades are."

Uncle Bill's ambivalence seemed more obvious.

Uncle Gus expressed remorse for having initiated the process for his immigration. "Satan himself had devised a scheme to fill his head with pride and lead him astray, away from God's paths."

And Aunt Helen expressed the wish, "The Army would straighten him out, and the sooner the better, for his own good."

The prospect of being drafted kept Lampis in readiness. The men in the local Draft Board assured him that he'd be allowed to finish the semester, or maybe even summer school. If he were allowed to complete summer school, he'd have a full year of college credit behind him, to make a new start, after returning from the Army.

He had begun to anticipate his two years in the Army with some eagerness. The possibility of being sent to the front lines in Korea did not frighten him. His exposure to the horrors of two wars, and his survival through them, had instilled in him a mixture of courage and invincibility, with a good measure of fatalism. He went as far as to plan in detail, his pursuits after his return from the tour in the Army, during the quieter periods at work. Still following his resolve to not challenge or provoke his uncles, he refrained from doing any homework in the store during the lulls, and to stave off boredom, continued to travel in the past and in the future to fill time with memories and dreams. He may have romanticized some of his memories, but he kept his dreams within the bounds of reality or his capabilities, never underestimating the obstacles of the hard work lying ahead, in the pursuit of those dreams.

He celebrated his first anniversary in America with a long letter to his parents, elaborating on his plans rather than on his accomplishments. The year had gone quickly; a year of re-adjustments, surprises, heartbreaks, hardships, more resolutions, and further buttressing his determination. He could tell his parents that he was "holding his head high," an expression that his father and Uncle Vasiles used frequently. He did not care much about what these uncles thought; he had placed himself above their mundane preoccupations.

Lampis studied even harder, sleeping and eating less, and braced for the approaching final examinations. He had to maintain his momentum in academic achievements and in the quest of rewards of praise from Dr. Argoe, Mr. Anderson, and his classmates. He could see, while shaving or grooming in the mirror, that his face was becoming thinner – and his newly regrown mustache accentuated his thinness, but he still shied from recording his weight.

The gap between him and his uncles was steadily widening. He insisted on speaking English with his classmates of Greek origin, and he realized that he would have a better chance at success if he initiated the conversation.

His interest in the political campaigns was aroused by reading the newspapers, fleetingly, and by observing some rallies by the student body. He was disappointed in Truman's withdrawal, was not satisfied with the answers to his questions why Eisenhower chose the Republican party and wondered whether the students that paraded behind the banners "I LIKE IKE" knew much about Ike and his political philosophy. He began to shorten his sleep even more by reading all he could about Adlai Stevenson, Kefauver, and Taft. He followed the primary elections through the non-committal Sun-Times and the new pro-Taft, now pro-Eisenhower Chicago Tribune. His idealization of F.D.R. and his admiration for Truman's stand for the Constitution and against personal ambitions or personality cults, transferred to Adlai Stevenson, weighed heavily against his concept of elitism in the Republican Party and strengthened his belief that military men were transgressors into political realms from the narrow military regimentation and mind.

He expressed his views uninhibitedly, and only Uncle Bill and Aunt Helen, though staunch Democrats, argued with an overdose of sarcasm, that he had no business discussing politics, not being a citizen or worse yet, being "Just a Greenhorn and a D.P. to boot."

Lampis was unable to resist challenging them both in a debate about American History and American politics.

"You haven't even hatched out of the egg," was their scornful reply. The insult was obviously intended to sidetrack him and to avoid the challenge.

"The yolk of the egg I grew in was made of knowledge that made me explode out of the egg," he bounced back.

The semester was over. Louie and Morry requested, separately, that they be the first to know about his grades. He was not embarrassed to tell them that he had three "A's" and one "B." The firmness of their handshake impressed their genuine sentiments deeper in his appreciation of their friendship.

One week later, he started summer school, taking Chemistry and History, a heavy load of eight credit hours for a short eight-week period. He was happy in school, especially when helping and laughing with the pretty, sweet girl next to him in the laboratory. He "pulled" A's in every test, but was crushed when the final grade in Chemistry was a "B." He tried to be polite in his protest, reminding his Professor that he had had "an A" in every test, including the final, while the pretty girl next to him had consistently had "B's" and still received an "A" for the final grade.

"It's my discretion, and you get out of here," Mr. Slotky retorted.

159

Lampis could not suppress his indignation. He had not expected this injustice in this society. He managed to convert his anger into contempt for this Mr. Slotky who never learned the difference between "than" and "then." His "A" in History helped a little, too.

The notice from the Local Board came the day after his last day in school. "Greetings," it read, "from the President of the United States of America...you must appear at the Selective Service Station, 600 West Van Buren St., on September 3, 1952, at 6:00 A.M. for induction into the United States Armed Forces."

The next two weeks passed quickly. His uncles, in their ambivalence, seemed at a loss in expressing their feelings. Louie would miss their chats in the late afternoons. Morry advised him to "Make the best of it no matter what happens." The girls were sad, some even cried. He began to long for the rigors of basic training, for new acquaintances and friendships. Some of the patrons recounted their experience in the war, probably magnifying them after a few drinks. He did not know how to interpret his uncles' never mentioning "When you come back."

Lampis worked until the last day.

"You have three hundred dollars in the bank, after deductions for your tuition and some other expenses," Uncle Bill informed Lampis.

After working for sixteen months, sixty hours per week during school, and a hundred hours per week off school, he had amassed the fortune of three hundred dollars. He found some consolation in Uncle Bill's crying when he said goodbye to him. He chose to interpret these tears as a sign of affection and remorse.

Uncle Gus's parting words, "May God protect you and guide you," were anticipated.

Aunt Helen's frigid, "Good bye," taxed him in suppressing his contempt or disgust.

Uncle John's indifference puzzled him, until he concluded that he had been maligned to this simple man. He felt neither bitterness nor excitement. He would follow Morry's advice.

Lampis had his parents' blessings and the best wishes of his friends to sustain him.

CHAPTER 18
The Emancipation

LAMPIS WAS WELL RESTED AND RESOLUTE after a sound, dreamless sleep. He boarded the East-bound, nearly empty, streetcar, with his little bag, glanced at the half-asleep passengers and sat alone in the back. Once again, he felt totally and utterly alone. He thought of the time that he was totally alone without a permit to travel, in a truck on the way to Athens; of the time that he fled from his village through the night, by foot; of the time that he spent Christmas alone. He was going to the unknown, like the time that he left his home to go to Athens and the time that he left for America. He was not a novice or neophyte in the ventures to the unknown, but it had always been by choice or necessity in the past. Now he was commanded, and he had no choice.

He must find a way to guard his individuality, to compromise insofar as his integrity would not suffer, and preserve or fortify his values from degradation or dehumanization with regimentation. He must survive and remain intact or even stronger. Had he not gained strength from every adverse experience in the past? Had he not rebounded higher from every setback? Had he not emerged more determined from every encounter against overwhelming odds?

The clang-clang of the streetcar, at regular intervals, faded in his thoughts; the filing in and out of passengers moved like shadows across a distant slope; the occasional cough or sneeze stirred his awareness of other human beings in narrow confines. These people, the ones in and out of the streetcar, will be back home in the evening. Where was he going to be? He had no home. Not for well over a year now. They had someone waiting for them. Who'd be waiting for him? They had a continuity in their lives. His life was fragmented.

He walked, after stepping off the bus, to 600 West Van Buren Street, a square, gray, drab building. He ascended the stairs, as he was told, with a herd of other detached young men, each carrying small bags and talking to themselves.

"I hope they put me in the Marines."

"I hope they assign me to the Navy, I like traveling."

"The infantry is the worst."

"If I'm lucky, they'll send me to O.C.S."

161

Lampis did not conform, knowing or suspecting that he had no control.

He stood naked in line, by chance, next to George, another young man from Greece who spoke little English. The doctors came in succession; one listening to their hearts and lungs – did they really? – another to look at their mouths; another to size up their bodies; another to look at their feet and make them squat. Some were taken off the line and told to stand aside; one who couldn't squat was told to go home. The rest, he among them, were herded to another room, weighed, measured, and told to wait. No explanation.

"Please stay next to me to interpret. I do not understand them," George, the Greek man told Lampis.

They dressed, when told, facing in opposite directions, and resumed their questions about each other: "Where are you from?" Where did you go to school?" Why did you come to America?" "What are your plans after you get out of the Army?"

They were from the same Province, and even had a few mutual acquaintances.

Lampis liked George, who seemed honest, straight, and of a similar background.

They were loaded, on command, on buses, and were transferred to the train for Fort Sheridan. Tall buildings, rows of smaller uniform buildings, isolated houses surrounded by green yards and shaded by trees, all receded rapidly. He talked with George briefly, intermittently.

"I weigh one hundred and seventeen pounds," Lampis offered. *Was that correct? Had I lost thirty-one pounds?* He was lucky that his mother hadn't seen him like this.

"You do look skinny and tired," George said. "How did that happen?"

"I had to work and go to school."

George shook his head. "Maybe they'll send us to the same unit, then we'll stay friends."

They descended the train and gathered on the platform, facing in every direction. A whistle blew. Everybody turned.

"This way, men!" a sergeant half-pleaded, half-ordered. "Follow me. No talking in the ranks."

What ranks? He should have said, "The herd."

"You're in the Army now. Look sharp! I am not taking you to the gallows. Don't forget to write Mom tonight, you hear?"

The herd followed, silently listening and straining to hear the next verse about what was requested of them.

The barracks looked uninviting. The few soldiers, in small groups or apart policing the grounds, looked at them, speared the litter, and transferred it to bags hanging from a strap on the left shoulder.

"These are not soldiers," Lampis thought, "These must be convicts, or maybe soldier-convicts."

Some others seemed to walk aimlessly.

They were turned over to a Master Sergeant who barked out his name and followed with a stream of obscenities. Lampis put the words between the obscenities together and came up with something like, "First, you're going to have your hair cropped off, then you're going to get your underwear, boots, uniforms and all a soldier needs, then you report to me."

Lampis hoped they would be turned over to someone who didn't curse that much. They poured in and out of the shearing chamber, with the clippers cutting two and pulling one hair in between. A corporal stood at the exit and grabbed his hair above the ear between thumb and index finger. He was among those unlucky ones whose hair was "grabbable" and was sent back for another clip-pull treatment.

The next barking session of obscenities was translated into, "You so and so's, go in your assigned barracks - they were assigned alphabetically and he was separated from George – and put your khaki uniforms on, and come out looking like soldiers, we have work to do."

Lampis went to his barrack. Rudy, the man in the bunk next to his, introduced himself.

After dressing, Lampis hardly recognized himself in the mirror, with his cropped hair and cap.

"You're so damned good looking," Rudy remarked.

He was learning new expressions!

The foul-mouthed sergeant led them to a large room where they were greeted, after sitting down, with, "Afternoon, men!"

Lampis knew he meant "Good afternoon," but why didn't he say it in full?

"The next two days," the sergeant continued, "you'll be taking written tests to determine your assignment. Those who score higher than 125 will qualify for O.C.S. – Officer's Candidate School." He gave them a brief history of the Army, a detailed account of the hierarchy, and the admonition to salute an officer, or else.

Lampis looked around; everyone was listening attentively. This was not so bad.

After the sergeant finished his speech, the captain spoke. "I am aware that you have not eaten all day," he said, and apologized.

This captain is a gentleman, Lampis thought, in a glaring contrast with the coarse sergeant.

"After chow, you are free for the day," the captain said, "you could go to the P.X. (Post Exchange) to buy stationary to write home, and whatever else is needed."

Lampis quickly learned what the new word, "chow," meant. The food was a royal treat. "It won't take me long to regain those thirty-one pounds back," Lampis thought.

Afterwards, he walked around and to the shore of Lake Michigan with George and Rudy. They talked about their pasts, their families, their plans, and tomorrow's tests.

"I know I would score low, and I'll be sent to the Infantry," George said.

"With three years of college, I'm sure that I'll be going to O.C.S." Rudy said.

"I don't particularly care where I go, and I'm not afraid to go to Korea," Lampis offered. He thought of his uncles, only fleetingly, behind the bar with their dirtied white aprons and their rolled-up white shirt sleeves. He didn't miss them one bit.

After sunset, they went to the Day Room, even though it was night – strange names! – and wrote letters to their parents.

"You have to be in bed before twenty-two hundred hours," the orderly reminded them.

"Nothing orderly about this guy," Lampis thought and was amused that he had used the word "guy." "Who, in God's name, would last twenty-two hundred hours without sleep?"

"Don't play dumb, smart-aleck," the disorderly orderly snapped. "You heard what the sergeant said about what twenty-two hundred hours meant!"

The orderly had no sense of humor.

"Quiet!" the corporal with the flashlight ordered Rudy and Lampis when carrying out bed check at 10:00 P.M. (or twenty-two hundred hours). "The bugles blow at 5:30."

They exchanged "good-nights."

Lampis fell asleep promptly, as if he had no care in the world. He did not remember dreaming, when the bugles blew. He was up and in the latrine among the first, reasoning that lingering may cause a delay, and a delay may lead to punishment. He was out and in line for breakfast, also among the first. And what a breakfast. Cereal, eggs, ham, bacon, milk, juice. He'd never seen anything like it. He filled his tray and devoured the lot, as if it were his last meal. He recalled the times when he was stirring the pot, filled with sand, for the few peas in it;

when he had lost his taste after starving for nearly a month; when bread would be rationed to a small, thin slice for each member of the family.

The tests ranged from History to Mathematics to Government to Languages. His overall score was 137, two points lower than Rudy's, but he could not qualify for O.C.S., not being an American citizen.

"Maybe we could send you to Military Intelligence," he was advised, "with your knowledge of foreign languages."

Lampis was tired at the end of the day, at about 4:30 P.M., but a leisurely walk with Rudy and George revived him. They walked to the shore again, watched the waves splashing in the sunlight and the seagulls gliding in the breeze, talked about their first full day in uniform, and promised to stay in touch. How quickly friendships form, he mused.

There were more stars out here at Fort Sheridan. He had not been caressed by this evening breeze for so long. His senses awakened and revitalized some dormant awareness of existence and appreciation of life, rekindled the vigor of his youth and pushed his inhibitions below the surface. The Army, suddenly, appeared as if unfolding new opportunities before him, affording new sources for tapping energy and strength, and presenting new challenges for enhancement of self-esteem. He'd "make the best of it," like Morry had advised.

The next day was vaccination day, but after they had their individual pictures taken with the flag spread in the background. His smile in the picture was genuine. His groans, when stuck in both upper arms as he walked down the aisle lined with medics, with T-shirt sleeves rolled up, were suppressed. He did not count the shots, but he estimated about twenty. The soreness progressed steadily, to the point that he could not raise his arms to a horizontal level. The boring "Processing" in the afternoon seemed to intensify the soreness and, at the end of the day, he did not really care where he was going for basic training. The walk along the shore, in the breeze, with Rudy, George, and Brad, another new-found friend, cooled his burning forehead. Rudy's and Brad's lightheadedness erased the resurfacing memories of his shivers from malaria and paratyphoid fever. When they admitted that their muscles ached, they went to bed.

Lampis was awakened by a corporal at 5:00 A.M.

"Get ready for K.P.," the corporal said.

"My name is not on the list," Lampis protested.

The corporal apologized and left but returned. "Your name is on the list, and you'd better get ready," he told him.

Since he was the last to arrive, Lampis was assigned the hardest job: scrubbing the pots and pans and mopping the floor of the mess hall. He was still feverish and aching, and after finishing his assignment and eating his breakfast, he crawled and stretched under the counter, among the pots and pans and fell asleep. He was discovered after lunch, cursed soundly, and put back to work, "On the double!"

Still, in spite of his tiredness and soreness, he joined the others for the walk along the shore, enjoying their company and shared their suspense about their "shipping out."

The next day, Lampis felt almost as well as ever. He enjoyed his breakfast and joked with the corporal who had aroused him twice and with the cook that had discovered him asleep under the counter. The parade, in mid-afternoon, left him quite unimpressed. The marching band, the precise strutting and turning of the platoons and companies, and the erect, saluting officers on the stands contrasted sharply with the still disoriented recruit on one side of the field and the milling crowd of civilians on the other side.

The "shipping out" and the goodbyes started in midmorning. George was sent to Armour, in Arkansas. Brad was sent to Fort Ord, California. Rudy and he had to wait. In the meantime, they had the day off, after policing the area. They worked hard to finish early, so that they may have more leisure time. They talked all afternoon and late into the evening. Strange, he thought at bedtime, how he hardly thought about his uncles – so quickly they had faded into a distant not-so-pleasant dream.

His suspense, such as it was, was not prolonged. He was assigned to Infantry and had to pack his duffel bag. He had to leave for Camp Breckenridge, Kentucky, in the afternoon. Rudy was going there, too. They were among the last to be shipped out. The mess hall was nearly empty; no rush. He talked with Rudy, forging and strengthening their bond, oblivious to all other activity around them. They took turns in talking and listening, unfolding memories and dreams before each other, until they were interrupted with the threat, "We'll put you to work if you don't get out of here." They continued their conversation in the Day Room, waiting for the time to leave.

Having stuffed their duffel bags as neatly as they could, they boarded the bus and bid goodbye to Fort Sheridan. The ride to the train was short, too short to either recall memories or start a conversation. He saw no point in counting the rows of barracks they passed, in trying to guess what the civilians were doing there, or in anticipating his encounters in Camp Breckenridge.

He was surprised and pleased that they were loaded into a regular civilian passenger train with all the comforts he had experienced in his ride from New York to Chicago. The sun was sinking and blotted in the industrial haze in the west when they boarded the train. Hypnotized by the gradual decreases in the brightness of the sun, he was transported again to his home where it hardly lost its brightness before rolling behind Mountain Tsemberou (the kerchiefed mountain with a cloud always hiding or circling its summit) and fanned out its rays to gild the tufts of clouds settling in for the evening. Here it seemed that the sun retracted all its rays and wrapped itself in the haze before bidding good-night.

"Another journey," he thought again, after the sun's farewell with a violet spread across the west to the unknown. Still, no fear, resentment or regrets; just acceptance of what was pre-ordained – two years of taking orders, carrying out duties, and looking forward to new challenges and anticipating the day of yet another journey. The train sped and clanked softly through the night, wedging and slicing through an occasional small town, reflecting a flash by the scattered lights in the distance, and blowing a whistle now and then to announce its speeding presence. He pitted his existence against the strength of the engine, the vastness of the land that he was crossing, the lives that he had and had not encountered, and the eons that passed since the appearance of life; but he was not overwhelmed. He still found a significance in his life, separate from all else, a significance in that he had a mission to follow.

Lampis was a soldier now. Soon, he'd be trained how to kill the enemy, of course – whoever the enemy may be – to neutralize and prevail. He prayed that he would never have to kill, that he would neutralize what was bad, and the he would know when and over what or whom to prevail. He had come close to being killed, many times, and a couple of times to killing. He had witnessed the terror and grief of killing, the aftermath of "neutralizing," and the devastation following the glory of prevailing. He turned to Rudy for deliverance from these thoughts, but Rudy was sound asleep. He looked across the aisle; they were asleep, too. He must find another escape. The old faithful standby memories and dreams were easily accessible. In them he could change directions from any point. And so now, starting with the memories of exuberance of youth in his cousin Christos and friend, Panagiotis, who had been killed in the war, he recalled the dances in the village square, the young women's songs as they harvested grapes or olives, the foot races on St. George's Day, and his convictions that he would remain forever young in the pursuit of his dreams. Recalling the details in these memories and chasing after a chain of dreams carried him to the train station of Evansville, Indiana before he knew it.

He had not slept but was not tired. Rudy seemed disoriented: "We can't be in Evansville! I just fell asleep for a few minutes." Should he envy Rudy?

The duffel bag grew heavier as he carried it on his shoulder to the bus. The corporal and the bus driver greeted them with "Get in; move it; hubba-hubba." "Hubba-hubba?" That's not English. Or is it a curse word he had not heard before? Hardly a word was exchanged in the thirty-mile ride to Camp Breckenridge. The night was dark, overcast. No bumps on the road, and the absence of any type of stimulation made his eyelids heavier. Memories were carried into dreams of the night rides escaping from Athens and further back leaving his village after the burning of his home; the transition from memories to dreams was made easier by the absence of bumps.

Half-asleep, he and the others were herded and goaded into the "processing" barracks: "Move it, men; snap to it." His dream of the ride after escaping from Athens returned, briefly, then faded. Some whispers, far away, receded farther into oblivion.

He could not decide, in the morning, whether it was the sound of the bugle or the coarse call, "Up and at it," that awakened him – just like he could not decide whether he washed, shaved, and dressed deliberately or mechanically. He devoured his breakfast, went back for seconds and wondered for how long Dave – he had just met Dave – would continue to pick and choose what he ate. He also wondered whether the others accepted this turn in their lives with resignation, resentment, or anticipation. He found only anticipation full of challenges, not apprehension, in his own thoughts. He already had a friend in Rudy. He'd make some more friends. He'd meet others from other parts of the country, learn about their homes, their lives, and their plans. He had no doubts about his endurance or his fortitude.

The "briefing," after breakfast, was brief. They were given their assignments, and he and Rudy were sent off to Company C (C for Charley) of the 3rd Battalion, 6th Regiment. They were issued their insignia and their Screaming Eagle, the emblem of the glorious 101st Airborne Infantry Division, ordered to have them sewn on the sleeves "no later than tonight," and reminded that their rank was Private-1 or Pvt. 1. Then they were loaded into buses and transported to their respective companies where, after another briefing by a gentlemanly and articulate sergeant, they "lined up" – his vocabulary was being enriched rapidly – in front of the supply room to receive their M-1 rifles, bayonets, and field packs. Now they were real soldiers. He had enjoyed the briefing by the gentlemanly sergeant – quite a contrast with the sergeant at Fort Sheridan. He'd like to make friends with this sergeant. He already knew, from day one, that "fall in" was synonymous with "get in formation," and "stand in formation" meant stand shoulder to shoulder, three men deep, in a straight line facing the sergeant – "fall in" did not mean to fall in a hole or a pit. He memorized his serial number on his dog tags – now he was a tagged dog! – U.S. 55293860, and his rifle number. Those who didn't, had to "drop down and give me twenty," which meant doing twenty push-ups. He also heard "Never volunteer for anything!" from some invisible seer or oracle. He was learning so much, so quickly – like when you're the last one to fall in, you'd have to drop down and give twenty;" answer with "yes, sir," or "no, sir;" the "army way" superseded the right and wrong way; and "first you do as you're told and then complain." He'd show them. If they can dish it, he can take it.

Lampis was amused with his thinking in army jargon already and laughed at the others' and his own mishaps or clumsiness, recited Bowman's rifle number to Bowman's frustration and kept count of Bowman's push-ups, the punishment for not remembering his rifle number. The drilling, the lectures, the K.P. detail – what's the connection between K.P. and detail? – gnawed at his individuality, bored him to yawning and tired him out. The rush to fall-in at the sound of the sergeant's whistle with the crowding at the doors in anticipation and the pile-ups in the steps, humiliated them to the level of cattle even though he was able to leap over the pile-up. And he ran for the mail call, knowing full well that there would be no mail for him for about three weeks, experiencing some vicarious pleasure in watching the others jump to catch the letters tossed in their direction after responding "here" when the names were called. While everyone else sat on his food locker to read the letter from home, he read a book. Rudy seemed to understand, interrupted him to read the part of his mother's letter about how glad she was that he had a friend in "the nice Greek boy" and shared the candy and cookies that she sent.

The friendship with Bill was short-lived after Bill's display of arrogance and contempt toward those less privileged than he, a squad leader now; friendship with Brad blossomed and with Rudy, it matured. Lampis was shocked at the number of men, black and white, mostly from the "Deep South," who could not read or write and had to be excused from all night-duty to attend classes every evening.

Having accepted "reality" and resolved to follow Morry's advice to "make the best of it," he did not sulk or remonstrate. He accepted his assignments and challenges, followed orders, reminded himself that he was in the Army now, and guarded his individuality and self-respect. He shunned confrontation even at the risk of being labeled a coward – fortunately, it did not happen – but responded assertively when his choices narrowed. Reconciling his obsessions with being a distinct or separate entity and not a number identified by his dog-tag with his desire to being liked by everybody created conflict and caused some wide mood swings, from seeking isolation to participating in or even starting some mischievous pranks. His steadfast refusal to curse, his challenging Corporal Dunlop about his platoon's assignments to carry the weapons for three days in a row (Dunlop was getting even with the platoon-sergeant), and his flipping big, burly Brown over his shoulder when pushed too far, earned him some respect. Learning quickly the "Rules and Regulations" of the Army and challenging the NCO's (Non-Commissioned Officers) in their application of them earned him the nicknames of "Sharp" and "Genius."

The exposure to his uncles' environment must have stimulated some entrepreneurial trait in him to buy boxes of candy bars at the PX and sell them to his fellow soldiers in the field or even in the barracks. But the fear of losing the respect he had gained, or worse yet, of being branded a profiteer made him quit in about two weeks, after confessing his fear, with a crying spell, to his trusted friend Brad.

He was disappointed but not discouraged in discovering that Corporal Dunlop disliked him, Corporal Hooker resented him, and Corporal Mason, the supply-sergeant, hated him. Dunlop was determined to put "those college boys," in their places. Hooker resented all foreigners or all with a non-English name. And Mason hated Greeks in particular. Lampis pitted Dunlop, ignored Hooker, but stood up to Mason, even before he found an ally in Sergeant Burgess whose life, he found out later, was saved by a Greek soldier in Korea (Sergeant Burgess had been left behind, badly wounded, in a mine-field in a retreat, but a Greek soldier ran back and carried him out, "in his arms, like a baby or a bride, with the Chinese firing from all directions.") And he became an accomplice, unknowingly, in the brutal beating of Corporal Mason, by Jim Dionissiotes, and his subsequent court martial, conviction, and sentencing to twenty-five years at hard labor.

In his hatred for the Greeks, Corporal Mason had gone too far. Every second or third night, week after week, he'd return to camp drunk at 1:00 to 2:00 A.M., wake up Jim Dionissiotes, order him to "put on a full field-pack and run with his rifle at port-arms" until he dropped from exhaustion.

Jim had conceived a plan. Knowing the night that Mason was going to Evansville, Indiana, he asked Lampis, "Could you be in my bed for bed-check so I could call home about my sick mother, from the Main Post, after 9:00 P.M.?"

Lampis agreed. As planned, he lay in his own bunk under the blankets, fully dressed and in his boots. After bed-check, he ran from his bed in the 1st Platoon barrack while the Officer of the Day with the First Sergeant were in the 2nd Platoon barrack and jumped in Dionissiotes' bunk in the 3rd Platoon, pulling the blankets over him.

The next morning, Lampis was told that "Corporal Mason was in the hospital, beaten to a pulp," at about 9:00 P.M. and would stay there for two months.

Jim Dionissiotes, whom Mason had accused as the perpetrator after regaining consciousness, claimed he was in his bed when all that happened – the Company Commander, the Officer of the Day, and the First Sergeant testified to that. Masons' replacement as the Supply Sergeant found in his inventory missing bazookas, machine guns, blankets, etc. The subsequent investigation revealed that Mason had been selling weapons and supplies to the rebel Fidel Castro in Cuba.

Lampis even began to enjoy his Army life. Marching to cadence, or singing "I left my girl way west, I thought this Army life was best," and drills, were easy and frequently entertaining. The compulsory gym and marching at parades throughout High School not only had prepared him but also served as a source of distraction and contrasted with revived memories. The drill sergeant's frustration with some of the recruits reached its climax in the shouting, "Not that left, damn it, the other left."

Having regained all the weight which he had lost in the last year, Lampis felt reinvigorated and welcomed all challenges to his stamina or endurance, outlasting or outperforming most of his fellow-soldiers and hardly ever falling behind anybody.

The firing range aroused a strong ambivalence. The sounds of the firing weapons revived in him the terror and horrors of the war, yet his high scores filled him with a sense of pride. The chain of his sharpshooter medals grew longer as he finished his training with the M-1 rifle, the Carbine, the BAR (Browning Automatic Rifle), the 30-millimeter machine gun, the 50-milliliter machine gun, the Bazooka, the hand grenade, the rifle-grenade, and the Mortar.

"You're buying your ticket to Korea," some of his friends warned him, but that did not make a dent in his compulsiveness to excel.

The dreaded and unavoidable K.P., welcome on cold, rainy or snowy days, provided a different challenge: to be the first to report for duty, so he could choose the easiest jobs. And paying Harrington five dollars to do K.P. was not bad, until Harrington, being in demand, doubled the price. His remonstrations with the mess-sergeant about his being the first to arrive for K.P. and his consequent assignment to the hardest job of scrubbing the stoves and the pots-and-pans aroused his indignation for this gross injustice and forced him to resort to pretending that he became violently sick with stomach cramps, after the lady-guests arrived for Thanksgiving dinner.

The rumors that his company may have to guard prisoners charged the atmosphere with a mixture of apprehension, bravado, and silent prayers. Reactions were expressed in petty arguments, boasting and withdrawal. He looked for Rudy and Brad to share his apprehensions and to find some reassurance. *What if a prisoner tried to escape, or God forbid, attacked me? Would I shoot, try to reason, or plead for mercy?* He tossed and turned all night, repeating his three-word prayer, "God help me."

The day arrived, dark, overcast and chilly.

"I have four hundred and eighty-seven bodies in this compound this morning. I want four hundred and eight-seven bodies in it tonight. I don't care if they're upright or horizontal; if it's not them, it's going to be you," the Stockade Commanding Officer barked.

Lampis shuddered and did not dare look at his friends, lest he revealed his fright or magnified his helplessness by finding no support. His desperate attempts to summon memories of desperation to raise some courage from them were aborted by a simple sneeze, a cloud shredding down from the dark-gray canopy, or the smell of burning wood.

"Yes, sir!" Lampis responded when hearing his assignment and orders. He waited for his two prisoners, lowered his carbine, and with his index trigger-finger at the trigger, marched thirty paces behind the prisoners, to the Court Martial Building.

The five judges in uniform appeared serene, detached, and expressionless. They, and he, heard the accusations and the defense; they deliberated briefly; he waited a long time. The defendants seemed suspended in a void without any signs of self-awareness – no emotion, even after the sentences; two years for AWOL (Absence Without Leave) and five years at hard labor for theft.

His prayers became more fervent on his way back to the Stockade. *Do they know what they're in for? Are they resigned or are they plotting? What about their mothers and fathers? Don't they care?*

At last, he was relieved, with a deep sigh, of this nightmare. "Thank the Lord."

The next day's rigor training was a picnic in comparison. Crawling through the mud under barbed wire with mines exploding just a few feet away and machine-gun fire just three feet above ground – that's what they were told – rolling down-hill with the butt of his rifle between his knees and the muzzle on his nose, charging up the next hill and thrusting his bayonet through the popping-up dummies, and riding the truck fully-encased in mud erased all of yesterday's memories and displaced the dreadful thought of a repeat.

The repeat did come, two weeks later, after visiting a new friend from another company in the Hospital. He heard how his friend was beaten up, after offering cigarettes and candy to his prisoners, and was now awaiting Court Martial. He would not let this happen to him. Still, he was polite in pointing the NO SMOKING signs to one of his prisoners, when assembled at the Motor Pool. The barrage of obscenities and insults from the prisoner, and the vivid image of his friend's black-and-blue body ignited rage in him that was diffused only partly after the cigarette was put out and stripped at his command: "Put it out *now*, and not a word, or I'll blast you – all thirty bullets in this cartridge."

Lampis was still boiling when, on the way to the mountains, he heard this same prisoner whispering to another prisoner: "I have five years to serve, and I ain't going back tonight."

All Lampis needed was an excuse. The other soldiers, huddling against the hub of the truck, with the hoods over their heads, seemed to have heard nothing.

"What are you going to do, man?" the other prisoner asked.

"When the truck slows down, at the next turn, I am going to jump."

This answer raised Lampis' carbine. He pointed to the prospective escapee and detonated his rage: "Jump, you bastard, jump! I got the highest score on the firing range! I won't miss." His yelling aroused the other guards who instinctively raised their carbines.

"I aint' jumpin'. I ain't going nowhere. I'm sittin' right here. Don't shoot!" the prisoner pleaded, trembling and cowering close to the other prisoner next to him.

They climbed down from the truck, prisoners first, and lined-up on the opposite side of the road, facing the prisoners. Fortunately, the three prisoners assigned to him did not include the troublemaker. Still, sensitized and alarmed, Lampis leaned against the trunk of a large oak with his left shoulder, protecting all of his body, and the butt of his carbine on his right shoulder at the ready while the prisoners split wood with heavy axes and warmed themselves at an open fire.

Later at night, lying awake in his bunk, he shivered at the recurring reflection of how close he had come to killing a human being, how rage had extinguished reason and his reverence for life, and how the witnesses of his confrontations had been repeating and embellishing his dealings with the prisoners while waiting for the Mail-call or in line at the Mess-Hall. He felt uncomfortable with his new label of "tough guy."

He kept thanking God and praying for being spared a fourth close-call.

The first "close-call" had come years ago, when Vasileles, the man who had vowed to present the head of his father on a platter to his mother, after joining the

Communist guerrillas, returned to the village with the apparent intent of keeping his vows. Aunt Christitsa had appealed to her cousin, Captain Ladas, a leader of the guerillas, to spare her brother's life, and he had promised her that he would, at all costs. But Vasileles was determined. The war between the Nationalists and the Democratic Army was still in balance. Children were taken from their parents, mostly in the Northern Provinces, and shipped behind the Iron Curtain.

Lampis had been targeted by Vasileles and was instructed by his parents to not come home for the Easter Holidays. Lonesome and homesick, he jumped at a rumor that the National Army was in his village and went home. The rumor proved to be false. Whether Vasileles had been informed of his arrival or just came to show his armed manhood was anybody's guess.

Lampis was working in the family's small General Store, when Vasileles walked in, in all his fearsomeness, ordered wine for everyone and toasted to the victory of the proletariat. The response was restrained and suspenseful, just "To health."

Then the fearless warrior smashed a couple of glasses on the floor and fired his rifle through the window, staring now at Lampis' father, now at Lampis, with a provoking expression.

Lampis stared back in defiance and reminded the palikaras (bully) that barefoot children may walk in the store, that they did not have any glasses to spare, and that people may be walking by the window.

Vasileles turned to the father, angrily. "Make your son behave!"

"My son has come to manhood. He knows when and how to behave," his father replied, stirring the coffee for two of his patrons.

"Then I'll make him behave," Vasileles threatened, pointing his gun to Lampis' feet.

In an instant, Lampis leapt with the meat-cleaver, having snatched it from behind the counter, and held it over Vasileles' head. "One move," he bellowed, "and I'll cleave you in two, one half to the right, the other to the left!"

"Kyr Metsos (Mr. Metsos)," Vasileles screamed, frozen with fright.

No response. Absolute silence.

Lampis glanced to his right at his father, and to the left at the patrons, storing a still image of motionless men, one with his glass of wine halfway to his lips and another with his left hand turned up as if to plea or pray.

"Unload your rifle," Lampis ordered, then yelled: "Now!" He counted the clicks aloud. "One, two three, four, five!" The "Mauzer" a German rifle, was empty. "Now step back and get out of here! I can still cut you in half with a throw of the cleaver!"

At the top of the stairs, five steps up, starting about ten feet from the door, Vasileles, feeling somewhat safe, threatened: "I'll be back!'

"I'll be waiting for you, with a loaded shot-gun," Lampis barked back.

One by one, the men filed out of the store. His father squeezed him in his strong arms and assured him, without words, "We're not afraid of the likes of him."

A few minutes later, they heard a shot. Vasileles stood over his sister's dead donkey, and within a few more minutes, took to his heels after hearing a rumor that the Army was approaching.

"The Stench will have to answer to Captain Ladas," Lampis assured his father.

"I had been frightened. Too frightened to pray," his father admitted.

The second "close call," not so close, but more deliberate, came about two years later, when the remnants of the "Democratic Army" roamed the countryside in small bands. The men of the village had all gone out, in three separate groups to ambush these bands, when rumors spread through the village that a large band was headed toward them from the East – the ambushes were west and south of the village.

Those left behind in the village decided, in a brief whispered conference, that going out, in the middle of the night, to alert the scared and probably trigger-happy men at the ambushes would be suicidal and that each family would have to defend its own home in its own way.

Lampis and his mother drafted and rehashed their plan: He would sit at the window with the shot-gun facing the outside of the door; his mother would stand behind the door with the axe; she would hack the men entering, after opening the door, and he would blast the other or others – there would be no more than two or three – then, they and his two younger brothers would escape through the hatch door to the stables and out on the other side to the darkness to hide in a ditch at the foot of the hill. He had not slept all night, listening to the barking of the dogs and keeping in readiness. When the men from the ambushes returned at sun-rise, Lampis surrendered in relief to a deep, dreamless sleep.

Lampis sat at the edge of his bed, perspiring lightly and pondering. *Who was worse, Vasileles or this nameless prisoner? Which Conscience Furies would have been the most relentless? Those of Vasileles' cleavage, the others from the shooting in defense of his home, or those released by the prisoner's riddled body?* Vasileles was the worst, for he had it all planned, whereas he had reacted without thinking to the nameless prisoner. He could not withstand the furor of any of the Conscience Furies. He could hear the fluttering of their wings and their piercing shrills even now. He tried to escape in soaring with a hawk, in scurrying in a crevice after a lizard, in hiding behind the curtains of a waterfall.

He ended up praying: "Please, God, no more – three times is enough!"

CHAPTER 19

LAMPIS BECAME ASSERTIVE, resourceful, and even selfish. Sergeant Burgess called him a "survivor." He marched, he ran, he shouted, and he met all challenges. The weeks passed into months; winter and snow came; discipline grew to near a robot level; fights decreased; and anxieties about "shipping out" began to surface.

Two weeks in bivouac and two weeks in the trenches were cut short by the holidays. For four days, during their training in the trenches or the fox holes, he was totally alone, guarding the supplies. He had it all planned, and it worked out perfectly, volunteering to load, and figuring he had to unload the trucks after riding to the "battle grounds," while the rest marched with a full-field pack for six hours.

He built a hut with logs and cardboard from boxes, dug a trench around it, covered the ground with dried grass, exercised to keep warm and from being bored, ran up and down the slopes among the oaks, and in the comfort of his hut, reminisced about sleeping in a hut with his father and brothers, hiding from the Germans. Five thousand miles away from home, all alone in a hut in the mountains of Kentucky – in such a short time. In about three weeks, he may be heading further away, to the mountains of Korea. The gunfire he listened to now may be directed at him, and with real bullets, not blanks. This last thought came back every night. Some other thoughts, fused with memories, were disconnected, fleeting: An Italian battalion coming to his village, turning the square into a mud field, raiding the chicken coops and uprooting the vegetables in the gardens; the squadrons of German bombers overhead and against the horizon; the rattling of the machine guns and the thundering of artillery in Athens; the piles of dead Communist guerrillas; the funeral processions of the ambushed soldiers; the mournful tolling of the bells. The return of the contrasting memories of the symphony of the goat bells, dispersed on the slopes across the deep ravines, and of the goat herdsman's flute, were aborted by a burst of gunfire. Tranquility was brief, elusive. Still, he enjoyed being alone, not taking commands, letting his thoughts displace each other and playing games with his intellectual self.

His pleas with Sergeant Burgess to not burn his hut proved futile. His argument to leave it for "the next guy" was neutralized with the counter, "The previous guy didn't leave anything like this for you. Let him build one for himself, if he can think of it!"

Lampis watched the flames consume it, but did not relate his memories of his burning home to Burgess. He saw vividly, once again, the flames curving out of the windows of his home, the thick smoke swirling over the roof, the darkness descending between the houses and engulfing the despair of wailing children.

"Too bad you're not a citizen; you'd make a damn good officer," Sergeant Burgess said, on the way back. "I wasn't supposed to tell you that, yet," he added, "but you haven't heard it." He knew that.

The dental and medical checks intensified anxieties, increased the number of fights, once again, and spread a mixture of bravado and retrenchment throughout the company. In a few days, they'd part, most likely never to see each other again. Rudy, Bill, and Brad went to O.C.S.; Lampis was assigned to Military Intelligence; most from A to K went to Germany, and most from L to Z went to Korea. He was lucky – for now.

The theft of his money, the night after payday, put a damper on his joy. He had wrongly figured that his money was safe under his pillow, trusting in his light sleep. But Rudy, Billy Ball, and Charles Burnette each gave him five dollars to buy a ticket to go to Chicago for a week before going to Fort Jackson, South Carolina. Sergeant Burgess had left a few days earlier without saying goodbye.

Lampis looked at his bunk for a last farewell, slung his duffel bag over his shoulder and strode to the truck waiting on the street. The severance from a brief span of his life, an interlude, left him only with the questions: "What am I taking with me, other than what's in the duffel bag? How long will the memories last?" He had not concentrated in storing or sorting memories. His observations had been limited to practicalities: look out for the Dunlops, the Hookers, the Masons: be skeptical of the Dionissiotes, the Bill Callahans; shun the Ecks and the Harringtons; and appreciate the Billy Balls with the stinking feet and innocent hearts; treasure the gratitude for remote kin, extended to you by the Burgess.

Lampis read the sign across the median of the divided highway LEAVING CAMP BRECKENRIDGE. Leaving to memories only, he hoped. The ride to Evansville, Indiana, seemed longer than from it – he was awake. His thoughts were in disarray again. Why did girls carry their books across their bosoms and throw their heads back when they laughed? The farms, the school buses full of children, the little town of Huntington, Kentucky, so far removed from the marching, the fist fights, the cursing and the gunfire. He was Private 2, Pvt. 2 now. Big deal. He might be a corporal before being discharged. Bigger pay, one hundred twenty dollars a month, and no K.P. That's as much as he made working for his uncles. And the food and the hours were so much better. All those steaks behind the barbed wire fences, and the pork chops at the feeding trough. Back home, oh yeah, back home they'd fatten one pig for the slaughter just before Lent began, or at Christmas, sometimes. He'd get the bladder, blow it up, roll it in ashes, put some corn kernels in it and run with it on a string. The simple primitive joys!

The Ohio River, winding to the belly of Evansville, grew larger as the bus approached. He remembered the wooded island in it, from his only visit on a Saturday, during his basic training. It seemed stagnant; maybe tired or dizzy from all that winding. Wonder where Dionissiotes beat Mason so savagely. It must have been in an alley since nobody stopped him.

The wait at the train station was not long. He was not hungry and did not want a beer. People were so indifferent to soldiers. They didn't even notice them. Didn't they appreciate that they were fighting to preserve their "American way of life?" Ingratitude! That's what it was.

The train station was much, much nicer than that of Tripolis.

He paced back and forth, kept an eye on his duffel bag, returned a smile to a couple of whispering girls, ignored the MP's strutting along, full of self-importance and finally picked up his duffel bag and made his way to the softly hissing, occasionally sighing train.

Fields, farm houses, barns, cows grazing, all faced in the same direction, approaching, focusing, receding: tufts of trees and low hills glittering before the setting sun; daylight changing to mellow, dim, before rolling up to a violet carpet to cover the last rays of the sun. All that and more, such as the unpredictable flash of the headlights of a car or the steeple of a church in a cluster of houses, conspired with the quiet in the train to lull him to sleep until the conductor announced: "Chicago, Chicago."

He picked up his duffel bag after the train came to a gentle stop.

"Careful now," the porter said.

Lampis responded with a smile – was it becoming for a soldier to smile? - and headed for the exit, aware that he was hardly or barely a curiosity. He gave his instructions to the taxi driver, reminded him that he was going the wrong way, and decided that he was not going to pay a penny more than what his uncle had paid in one of his two visits downtown. The city looked different, warmer, more welcoming, even suggesting home. He thought more of the people he saw in the streets, the cars, the shops, whether Louie may be at his uncle's place, and less of his encounters with his relatives.

It was cold outside. Louie saw him, as the taxi stopped in front of his uncle's shop and came to greet him. The taxi driver argued about his fare, but outnumbered and wrong, he drove away cursing.

Louie chatted like a schoolboy: "I knew you were coming tonight; I was waiting for you."

What a shame, Lampis thought, that customs or hang-ups stopped him from embracing someone who was waiting for him. He'll just "get the most" with a handshake. Uncle Gus was beaming! Uncle Bill's eyes and smile sparked for a moment, then carried him to the telephone booth for the "surprise" to his children. Much more than he had expected.

He answered questions, toasted with Louie and Uncle Bill, laughed at John's half-intoxicated witty remarks, was touched by Joe's "rushing over" to see him, and climaxed his joy by picking up and swirling his little cousins, Sophia and George, when they burst through the door. He could not suppress his skepticism about Aunt Helen's remarks, "I just couldn't hold them down!" Was she glad or resentful?

The week of his leave passed slowly. He helped out at his uncle's store, wrote some letters, visited Uncle John, had a brief encounter with Arlene across the street, just enough to write down her address, and was bored. He was accustomed to a different regimentation by now. He was eager to move to his next assignment. The possibility of going to Korea seemed quite unlikely. He imagined Military Intelligence duties being going through and deciphering a lot of reports, moving among a lot of brass, and keeping regular hours in an office. He had learned so much in these four and one-half months. Amazing! He did not feel quite equal to those Veterans of World War II, or even to Louie who had spent three years in the Marines, but he was "getting there."

The goodbyes when leaving for Fort Jackson, South Carolina, were rather unemotional. The severance had taken place at least four and one-half months ago. He had changed the pace on his circuitous path to his destiny, and his path now circumvented his uncles. He was an experienced traveler by now, but his curiosity was insatiable. He observed as much as he could, and when dark and quiet, he thought, planned, and dreamed. The murals at the Cincinnati train station were magnificent! Could Uncle Gus divine that he was sitting next to an attractive, attentive young woman? Were these broad streets of Atlanta wide like this before General Sherman burned the city? He walked the deserted streets of Atlanta for about two hours, between 1:00 A.M. and 3:00 A.M., looking at the buildings, the street signs, and the traffic lights. He could not well compare it to Chicago, since he had not seen much of Chicago's downtown, but it seemed like a city of confidence and secure future.

WELCOME TO FORT JACKSON. Tall pine trees among the uninviting, austere barracks, swaying gently in the breeze; gentle, low hills behind each other to a distant mist; A platoon marching down the road – all welcoming.

"Here you are, guys. Good luck to you." The driver smiled and waved.

Nice guy! Lampis went through another check-up.

"Breathe in-and-out. Cough. Cough again. Skin back. You can go."

He had to wait for the others. He was tired and abandoned. Nobody smiled, talked, or smoked. He waited to be transferred to the transfer unit. The large square surrounded by the barracks atop a gentle hill, the volleyball nets, the quiet surroundings made him hope that the transfer to his next assignments be delayed. It would be a long time before he'd be bored here. No K.P. or details while awaiting transfer; and they were issued passes to go out. Columbia, the capital city, was only about ten miles away. The buses ran regularly.

Lampis wrote letters to his parents, his sister, Marigoula, and Arlene. He played volleyball, went for long walks among the pines, lay on a thick layer of dry pine needles and slept in the sun, after concluding that lazy interludes were not bad. He made friends with Nicholas, an American-born Greek young man, and Zimmer, a German who had served with the German Army on the Eastern front. Zimmer was talkative and interesting while Nicholas was private and polite. They spent a lot of time together, playing, talking, or lying in the sun. He went to Columbia, on Sunday, longing to establish some contact, however temporary, with the Greek element. He had not been to church for about eight months. Curiosity about the Greek community in Columbia and his need to recover the part of himself that had been submerged in the rigors of summer school and work, before the army, and by the emphasis in basic training to discipline for martial survival, stimulated an irrepressible desire to go to church. Finding the church would be easy. He'd find a restaurant, and if that, by chance, was not Greek-owned, he'd go to another. He was already acting like a military intelligence agent. It worked. The first restaurant he went to, right across from the capital, was Greek-owned. He was treated to breakfast, directed to church, and invited to dinner, all because he was Greek, a soldier, and away from home.

Two young men, about his age, approached him after the services, spent the rest of the day with him, and offered their hospitality for the next evening, if he had not shipped out. They showed him around, talked about their aspirations, and aroused a desire to see them again, nearly as overwhelming as that of going to church earlier in the morning. Not a hint of indecency, frivolousness, or lack of self-respect – quite a contrast to the two shapely WACS that he had quickened his steps to approach on his way to the PX, whose coarse or obscene language aroused disgust and contempt.

The following day, his pass was pulled. He could not leave the post because he was to ship out in the morning. He resolved, after some deliberation, to chance it and go out without a pass. He'd think of something, if caught. His heart sank and pounded when two MPs walked in the bus at the gate and asked everybody to show their passes. His college ID card had the same shape, color, and size as the pass. He held it out, nonchalantly, and was ready to laugh, apologize, and pay for his mistake by going back. It worked. They did not inspect it. And he had a nice evening with his new friends. They'd keep in touch.

The highlight of the ride to Fort Bragg, on a Southern Trailways bus, was stopping at a restaurant in a small town. The lady at the counter was proud of herself and excited when her intuition that he was Greek proved correct. Some of the other soldiers showed annoyance at the special treat for him and at the foreign language. But he became aware of that much later. His luck was definitely changing.

WELCOME TO FORT BRAGG, HOME OF THE 82ND AIRBORNE DIVISION AND THE XXIII AIRBORNE CORPS, the sign read. That's nice. From one airborne outfit to another. More processing, more exclamations at his long name, and more of "How do you pronounce that?" He wasn't annoyed anymore by their rudeness and insensitivity. He dealt with it by assigning those who made that type of remark to the class of the ignorant and uncouth. But this particular ugly sergeant's evident irritation in pronouncing "525 Military Intelligence Group," suggested outright resentment, or even more, frustration that he couldn't change it. Maybe he should brace himself for more encounters of this sort.

The first day moved slowly, boringly. Lampis was eager to move to 525 MIS and settle down. He and the rest were warned to protect their money and that if they were caught stealing, punishment would be at least five years in the stockade at hard labor. He put his wallet in his shorts, folded the sheet over him and tucked it under the mattress on the other side to prevent access of a search or marauding hand to his body. He was awakened by something, like a hand, moving under and over him. He made a move to grab this something, felt something rolling under his bunk and lay still, reasoning that this guy under his bunk may have a bayonet in his hand – if he could only manage to move all the air in his large bowel to its exit, in one bolus! He felt some movement again, like crawling but he did not move. He was safe, and eventually went to sleep again.

The next morning, he could not decide whether it was the guy that stared at him, or the guy that looked away, every time he scanned the mess hall in an effort to pick out the unsuccessful thief. He was hardly aware of the taste of what he was eating in his preoccupation in trying to identify the thief. Finally, he was satisfied in his conviction that the would-be thief, whoever he was, got the message: "Maybe next time you'll get a bayonet in your chest and/or five years at hard labor." Living or moving among animals and thinking like them was demeaning, dehumanizing.

Captain Leggett, who had assigned him to Platoon 32, and Colonel Horstmann, who greeted him, were real gentlemen. The first greeted him with a "You-do-your-best-and-we'll-get-along-fine," attitude, and the second with a fatherly, reassuring smile. His platoon had the total strength of five men: Lieutenant Byrd, Sergeant Yamamoto, Sergeant Yoshio, Sergeant Lutkowski who was to be discharged in two weeks, and Corporal Claude Ganz. All the rest had been sent to Korea one week ago. That meant he could still be sent to Korea. Sergeant Lutkowski and Corporal Ganz had been lucky. The other two sergeants, both twenty-year men, had been to Korea and back. How lucky would he be? He'd have a lot of K.P., trash-detail and latrine duty, that's for sure, since he was at the bottom of the totem pole. Two more enlisted men joined them in the next few days.

The platoon above them, on the second floor, the 20th, was almost full strength, with handsome, tough Jim Hasapis keeping everyone in check and the tall Yermakov singing in his beautiful bass voice. Hasapis assumed the role of the big brother, introduced him to happy-go-lucky Tom Edgos, and warned him against the "Communist" Gus Lekkas. Gus was a sergeant and pulled rank. Tom was a corporal and made fun of it; and Jim resented being "just a PFC with three months to go." Again, he was at the bottom of the totem pole. No change after Jerry returned from his leave; Jerry was a PFC also, but didn't care less if he were a general and had no friction with anyone.

Lampis quickly fell in Gus' disfavor and was labeled a Fascist after questioning Gus' claims of EAMS (United Liberation Front) patriotic objectives, during the occupation, and suggesting that towing the Moscow Line may have been its overwhelming obsession. He prepared for a major confrontation, maybe even a fist fight. He was drawn to Jerry who had been in and was going back to college.

Tom and Jim vied for his company. Tom, because of his own gregariousness, and Jim because he needed him, he said, to attract the girls. But it seemed as though these budding friendships or conflicts were not destined to grow. There was a new "levy" for Korea and he was second on the list from his platoon. He had his picture taken to send to his parents, before going to Korea in case he didn't come back.

Jim's prayers – and his own, of course- were answered. This time, they took only one out of his platoon and twenty from Jim's platoon. And the new friendships grew. After an uneasy "armistice," during whose period he was made the instructor in translating and deciphering Greek Military Intelligence documents, the collision course with Gus was re-established, the momentum gathered, and the impact was more shattering than anticipated. After relating a story of his father's in which a three-thousand EAM force took to its heels before a force of only two German battalions, Gus responded with, "Your father is a liar and now I understand what kind of a family you come from."

Dead silence in the mess hall.

Lampis stood up, choking. "Step outside, sergeant," he bellowed, before he could deliberate, in a rage.

Gus did not raise or turn his eyes.

"He'll apologize," Jim said firmly.

"No, I won't," Gus answered, his hands shaking.

Lampis stood motionless, staring at Gus' trembling hands, all muscles flexed to keep from exploding. Just one fear: that Gus would go down with one punch and cheat him from letting all his rage loose.

Sergeant Bauer, the Headquarter Company's Master Sergeant, strode resolutely from the first table, stood, stretched to his full height, and barked at Lampis: "Sit down! That's an order!" He turned to Gus without waiting for the execution of the order and commanded him to come along.

Gus un-nailed himself from his seat and walked out in front of Sergeant Bauer, who turned around at the door. "You, soldier, sit down and eat, and no talking!" he ordered.

The silence was punctuated only by the sounds of the silverware against the trays.

"That was something," somebody whispered.

"Quiet!" Jim yelled.

Sergeant Bauer returned, scanned the hall for a moment and sat down to finish his meal.

Lampis could not eat or talk. Jim took the initiative. "Let's go. I'll keep an eye on you. I don't know what I'd do in your place, but I'll stay close to you."

The afternoon was interminable. Jim stuck to him until he had to report for guard duty. Then Tom took over; but Tom was not vigilant, and Gus was careless. They met in the day room.

Lampis challenged Gus again, "to step outside."

"I am not going anywhere. I am a sergeant and you're just a PFC."

"You're a coward, hiding under those stripes." Lampis grabbed Gus by the tie with the left hand and began to drag him, the other fist cocked.

"Let him go," Tom yelled from his pool table, then added: "He'll apologize, publicly."

All eyes riveted on them. Lampis kept his left hand half-twisted, with Gus' tie in his grip, and his right fist cocked, just in case Gus had any notions.

"Apologize!" Tom screamed.

"I apologize," Gus enunciated meekly.

"We didn't hear you," Tom yelled again.

"I apologize. I am sorry for what I said," Gus responded loud enough.

"Now get out of here," Tom ordered him. "You, Sergeant, stay here and watch me win this game." The corporal was ordering the sergeant.

Just then, the Officer of the Day walked in the still hushed room. "What's going on here?"

"Nothing, sir," Tom responded. "We just had a misunderstanding. It's all right now."

The officer walked out, and Lampis followed. He went to his deserted barrack, sat on his foot locker and cried. He could not understand why he was crying. Jim came by later, free to do as he pleased, having been chosen "The Colonel's orderly" (the sharpest soldier of the guard detail). Lampis told Jim what happened in the Day Room, and after some hesitation, told him that he had cried and didn't know why – at which point Jim cried, too. Crying together added a new dimension to their friendship, one of trust and understanding. He listened to Jim's story.

Jim's father had been executed during the occupation of Greece. He was taken hostage and shot, by lot, in retaliation for some sabotage by the underground. All Jim remembered about him was his love, and that he had been the handsomest and most wonderful father in the world. Jim's affection and concern for his sister were touching. His reverence for his mother, moving.

Lampis smiled at the thought that he had considered Jim as a tough guy. Had he ever met a more sensitive son and brother? What an eventful day that turned out to be, he reflected, lying on his bunk with his fingers interlocked behind his head. Gus, Jim, Sergeant Bauer, Gus again, Tom, the Officer of the Day, Jim again. Maybe he can write about it someday.

The platoon and the group, the 525th, came to full strength within about a month after the Day Room show-down. Lampis had about twelve soldiers in his session, was exempt from all details during the week, began to forget what K.P. was like, was given credit for helping to make his platoon the best in the Group, was cited for running the most disciplined and efficient session, and was frequently told that he was "The most popular guy in the Group." He formed many strong friendships, but Jim remained the strongest friend and most diversely challenging personally, cutting the tough guys down to size, making everybody mind his manners in his presence, humanizing the brutes, raising the officers to their ranks, and putting the pretentious in "their right place" – and having fun doing all that.

Tom, in his turn, may have been rascally in some ways, but made everyone laugh in telling stories about himself as if someone else had been the author or perpetrator – or even the victim – laughing at himself more than at anybody else, and even put Jim in his place. Gus remained outside of the circle and isolated for a brief while, walking and looking past everyone, until Jim's stern, but not offensive admonition that he "come down from your high horse and out of those stripes to join the human race." A handshake erased all that took place in the Mess Hall and in the Day Room to start on a new course of respect for each other's opinion.

Among the newcomers, Steve stood out for the purity of soul; Leo Mitsas for his sensitivity and beautiful singing; Jim Mohas for shallowness and disparity between his wonderful voice and the rest of him; Leo Mihas for his entertaining rascality; Dean Vasitis for his unique spoiled-bratness and noble declarations; George Pamphiles for his unconditional surrender to love; George Bardanis for his chain-smoking and "keep-them-guessing" games; Harry for his total unawareness of scruples; Andy for his uncompromising fair deals. The others were just a part of the crowd.

The evenings, with the coming of the spring, were filled with a succession of singing, dancing, pranks, discussions, or exchanging stories in a combination – or total lack – of order. The exuberance of youth found many expressions. Still, they kept the Leo Mihas', the Jim Mohas', the Harry Georgiou's and the Argyris' in the orbit of decency. Steve Stavrianoudakes' arrival added a new dimension and outlet of energy with his performance on the pitching mound as the star of the 525th's baseball team.

The excursions to White Lake in the summer, kept them roaring with repeating the stories of games they played on gullible girls, each other, and their officers. Back on camp, Lampis ran a tight ship, staying ahead of schedule in his sessions, getting his platoon off weekend after weekend for outstanding performance, and making the rounds of the towns from Fayetteville, 30 miles away, to as far as Charlotte and Wilmington, about 150 miles away – after the paratroopers ran out of money about two weekends following payday. When embarrassed by Georgiou, he and his friends disowned him collectively and individually. They rallied around George Pamphiles when he decided to marry Bertha, against his parents' wishes and against common sense; they showed "the Greeks of Fayetteville" that they had self-respect; and they took pride in hearing from their commanding officer that they had been the answer to his prayers for the morale of the troops.

Lampis had hardly finished sewing on his PFC stripes on all his sleeves when he was promoted to Corporal after a waiver of the service-in-rank requirement "for outstanding performance in the line of duty." His pay now, after the deduction for his contribution to his parents, was eighty-five dollars a month. (He had declared himself as the main supporter of his family when he was inducted, and forty dollars of his monthly pay went to his parents, the government adding seventy for a total of one hundred and ten dollars). His pride in helping his parents to rebuild their house was uncontainable. Before leaving, he started helping to build the partitions of the rooms from the hallways – pounding nails (and thumbs), mixing and applying the mortar, and carrying planks and buckets of mortar on his shoulders. How rewarding to experience this tiredness, after a day's hard labor.

His reaction to the information that he could be given an emergency leave of absence and free Military transportation to Greece, in case of serious illness in the family, stirred a strong conflict between his passionate desire for an excuse to see his family again and his ardent prayer that all in his family remain healthy. The conflict reached its sleepless end when a letter from his uncle informed him that his mother was hurt seriously by a kick from a mule. Should he exploit this opportunity? What if Uncle Vasiles used the word "seriously" inappropriately? He hadn't said "critically."

He sent a telegram stating, "Please advise Mother's condition."

The reply was alarming. "Mother's condition is critical."

Lampis took the telegram to his Commanding Officer and then to the Red Cross. The next day, he was on his way to Greece, via Baltimore where he had to obtain a re-entry permit, and Springfield, Massachusetts, where he would be boarding a MATS (Military Air Transportation Service) airplane. Luck and aggressiveness, combined, helped him acquire his permit within an hour after arriving in Baltimore, by train, the next morning, and be on the plane after spending only one night in the barracks in Springfield. He knew his rights and the Army Regulations, when he stood up to the sergeant who was going to put him on K.P. for the night and when he demanded that a Major be taken off the plane to make room for him who was on Emergency Leave.

The first leg of the flight, via Casablanca to Tripoli, Libya, was long and full of anguish. Was his mother critically hurt? What was his reception going to be like? Was his stay going to be joyous or sorrowful? He had missed his family in these two and one-half years, and he had so much to tell them. He felt he loved all of them more now than ever in the past. He did not talk with anyone on the plane, exploiting the opportunity to retrace his memories, reflect on their formation, and speculate on their impact on his personality.

The stop-over in Casablanca was not long enough to visit the town – just long enough to refuel, inspect the airplane, and… stretch. In the flight from Casablanca to Tripoli, the occasional, isolated fire or cluster of fires awakened his imagination to watch the Arabs squatting around the open fire and telling stories, after a long day's journey across the desert with the Caravan of Camels, while the camels chewed their cud, and a sentry or two guarded the load against marauders or thieves from their own band.

The memories of his lying on the freshly-harvested wheat field next to his older and much-loved friend Louie and talking until dawn while marveling at the multitude and brightness of the stars reemerged vividly and nostalgically.

The second leg, the next day, after a good night's rest at the Air Force base, from Tripoli to Athens was short and anticipatory, and made shorter by his chatting with other soldiers. He was overcome when he stepped on the soil of Greece, the glorious land of his birth

CHAPTER 20

LAMPIS TOOK THE PUBLIC TRANSPORTATION to his uncle's home. He gave a dollar to a little boy after getting off the last bus, to run ahead and announce his coming.

Aunt Violetta ran out to meet him. He shed his first tears on her shoulders.

"I thought the boy was playing a painful joke on me," Aunt Violetta said, "and scolded him for it, but I knew it was true when he said, 'How would I know that you have a nephew in the American Army?'"

Uncle Vasiles embraced him in his strong, gentle arms and held him while his little cousins hugged his legs and tugged at his 'Ike' jacket. He was assured that his mother was better, was well, and they deliberately exaggerated in their letter and telegram, not without conscience pangs, in the hope that he could be given a leave of absence to come home. His leaving so abruptly, two and one-half years ago, had left an open, draining wound in his parents' hearts. "It was Divine Providence," Uncle Vasiles concluded, "that guided us in writing that letter and wording the telegram in the way we did."

His cousins listened to his stories wide-eyed and were allowed to stay up past their bedtime. They pleaded to sleep with him. His uncle and aunt kept expressing their belief and confidence in him, their looking forward to the celebration of his receiving his Doctor's degree, and their convictions that he would devote his efforts to serving humanity. The comfort and joy in their love made him feel privileged and blessed. The spontaneous, uninhibited, warm embraces and kisses of his aunt, the messages in his uncle's smiling eyes, his cousins' outbursts of giggles and hopping around him, transferred him back to the world he'd known until two and one-half years ago, the world he'd like to carry wherever he went.

His uncle saw him to the train, to be with him a little longer. Love flowed in both directions, transferred and embodied with a squeeze of the hand. The happy memories displaced those of suffering and dulled the pain from the wounds of malice or ignorance. He shared a little bit of his past and was admonished to change the directions of his energies.

"Remember, they know not what they're doing," his uncle admonished.

No one has ever had an uncle as good at his.

The landscape from Athens to Eleusis, ingrained in his memory from his escape, along the railroad tracks, almost nine years ago, brought back flashes of the hunger, the cold, the despair – flashes that were left behind, as the train clanked and hissed softly along the ragged mountain or curving seashore, through olive orchards, and past white-washed villages.

More memory flashes returned with each crossing or the side-by-side journey of the railroad tracks and the highway. Veering away from the highway unfolded new revelations of forested slopes, aging mountain ridges, freshly plowed fields or creeks twisting among orderly groves with lemon and orange trees. He had never traveled south of Athens by train before, and he concentrated in absorbing all he could to interweave with his imagination, clashes between defenders and invaders, celebrations after triumphs, revivals from calamities, defying odds or even mortality. His concentration was not interrupted by his considerate and deferential seatmate. Even his anticipation of the embraces and kisses of his family and relatives was placed on hold, after the sudden resurfacing of "Mother is well. Efstathia is home, and George has graduated from Gymnasium."

The "excuse me" plea faded in a distant twilight, returned with a new resonance, and aroused him from his dream-like excursions.

"Excuse me." The conductor stood in the aisle, facing him. "There are two young men, xenoi (guests from a foreign land, foreigners would have a condescending or even hubristic connotation to a Greek); I think they're Englishmen. Would you please talk with them, so they don't feel unwelcome?"

Lampis obliged gladly, and was led to two young men who turned out to be German, but spoke English. They were friends and studied in the same University, one in Architecture and the other in Archeology. They had stimulated each other's love of Greece and were now fulfilling a mutual dream. Starting from Athens, they had visited Delphi, Sounion, Olympia, Corinth and Marathon. They were on their way to Argos, Mycenae, and Sparta. He enjoyed their company, listening to their description of what they had seen and felt. They listened to his plans after his release from the Army and showed no sign of questioning whether he would realize his dream.

The conversation came to an abrupt end when, at Andritsa, he answered their inquiry, "What are those?" pointing to ropes and cables hanging from tree limbs.

"The Germans hung thirty-two men, ten years ago, during the occupation, in retaliation for the Resistance Fighters' blowing up a railroad bridge."

After a long silence, the student of Architecture, without turning his head and still looking out of the window commented: "You must really hate Germans!"

Lampis had felt remorse at having answered their question truthfully, without thinking, and in violation of the dictates of Greek hospitality. He tried to apologize for his rudeness and assured them that he and most Greek people divorced the cruelties of the war by the Nazis from the German noble culture, and that the traditional mutual respect between the German and Greek people was far, far, too strong to be neutralized by the base and cruel acts of war. He hoped they believed him.

The firm handshake and warm smiles, when parting at the station in Mycenae, convinced him that they had believed him. His total preoccupation with this encounter veiled memories and landscapes.

The slowing of the train in approaching Tripolis switched off the retracing of his exchanges with the German youths and unfolded the countryside with all its familiar details. Hissing and whistling, the train slid to a stop in front of the main building of the Station. He scanned the area between the train and the building, in search of his father and/or his brothers and found them, shifting their gaze from one exit to the next.

He ran to them as they rushed to him.

"My son, my boy!" his father cried, squeezing him in his strong arms. He tasted the saltiness of his father's tears, kissing his weathered cheeks. He absorbed and assimilated as much love as he could from his father before turning to look into his brother Nikos' glistening, moist blue eyes. Sobbing was squeezed out of him with the tightness of their embrace. Words were overlapped with or fragmented by the sobs. Looking into each other's eyes pulled them into another embrace to start the flow of the strange mixture of laughter and sobs.

"How's Mother?" his first words were.

"She's well," his brother replied laconically. His reply told Lampis "She loves you and can't wait to see you…we must not keep her waiting or she may start out on foot for Tripolis," and a lot more.

They walked with their arms around each other. He in the middle and Nikos proudly carrying his duffel bag. They talked rather incoherently or all at the same time, with so much to tell, that they were unable to control the urge to tell it all in one breath.

They stopped in Nikos' room to drop off the duffel bag and hurried to Theia (Aunt) Katerina's.

She rushed to him, arms spread, crying. "My boy, my pride, my life." Her love lifted and spun him in a spiral of heavenly happiness, seeing all that was good and purely beautiful, forgetting all that may have contaminated the sanctity of their memories, and glowing in the radiance of her smile and soul. How can the world, the universe, exist without a Theia Katerina? She treated them with sweets and the sweetness of her essence, spread her goodness out to warm all future deliberations, and took his hand to guide him in a luminous path to the end of his life. He stored, in a special compartment of his mind, her every word and her every gesture or expression to raise against temptation from the calls of fanciful promises and to renew his resolve "to never fail her." He could never say "Goodbye" to her – he'd always carry her with him.

Nikos went home with him, assuring their father that there would be no classes for the next three days because of the National Oxi (No) day of October 28. The bus ride, in the opposite direction of two and one-half years ago, displayed familiar landscape, strewn with memories, and carried him to the fountain of his beginning and of his dreams. He confided his dreams to his father and drew more strength from his father's faith in him. Nikos listened without asking questions, showing respect for his father and for the momentous occasion. Afraid that Nikos may feel left out, he asked him about school, who his teachers were, about his plans. The answers were brief, deliberate, and sometimes incomplete, as always.

The bus moved slowly, bouncing in the uneven rocky road and prolonging his anticipation of seeing his mother, sister, and his brother George. He scanned the ridges of the hills and the peaks of the mountains; followed a flock of pigeons; contemplated the thoughts of the mules pulling the plow; and wondered whether he'd see the blackbird darting out of a bush across the road at the next bend – maybe in the opposite direction it had flown two and one-half years ago. The chatting and the silence were punctuated by a smoker's dry cough. His thought returned with the more jolting bounces of the bus. Memories displaced awareness of his immediate surroundings – happy moments, suspenseful anticipations, brushes with danger or death, despair, renewal of strength for survival – all in disarray and chasing each other flashed and faded.

A man in the back started singing; another joined him: "As I started my journey downhill, along the bank of a river…"

The bus descended to the river and traveled, smoother now, parallel to and in the same direction as the flow of the water.

"And the river is muddy, muddy and darkened," they sang, "It carries the heavy boulders and uprooted trees. It carries two brothers in tight embrace…"

The lump in his throat swelled to choking. He let his tears run down his cheeks – wiping them would have attracted his father's and brother's attention.

"Who was the mother of the two boys? Go tell her not to wait for them, the current of the river has swept them."

The song ended. Silence followed. The groans of the bus echoed in their souls. The muddy dark current of the Civil War had swept and drowned Mother Greece's sons of the Right or the Left. Can Greece save herself from drowning in grief? he thought. She's done it before. She must! Her mission was not finished. It'll keep pulling Her to Eternity.

"Your Aunt Christitsa has probably put up some roadblocks," his father said, smiling and pulling him back from his revolving thoughts. He saw Aunt Christitsa's moist and smiling sky-blue eyes, was engulfed in the love of her embrace, and floated in her unfathomable tenderness. Her resonant, joyous, youthful voice contrasted with the raspy, firm voice of her daughter's Motho's, who had inherited the blue eyes and deeper dimples, the latter at some expense of the sparkle and warmth in her mother's eyes and smile. The repetitions of the same questions and answers, hugs and kisses, smiles and sighs of exhilaration intensified his thirst for more of the same. Nikos, and even his father, had receded in the background, echoing, at irregular intervals, the laughter and the merry sighs.

Lampis swung from the summit of love from his aunt and cousin to the outstretched arms of his mother, back again, remained suspended on a white cloud rimmed with memories of belonging, and leaped back into the center of his childhood world. His mother's tears flowed, saturated with love, anguish, resignation, faith. The mixture of restrained happiness and the stamp of a suffering soul contrasted with his aunt's uninhibited demonstrativeness and stirred his hopes to erase all her suffering with pride in him. He returned her embraces and affection with at least equal fervor; he gazed into her eyes to displace the sadness with joy; and he kept repeating: "Don't cry, I came back to you, I am here, look at me!"

His brother Georgos and his sister lost their patience, pulled him away and squeezed him in between them, forming a triangle – with him at the apex. Cousins Nikos and Antonis waited their turn discreetly. Aunt Antonia, their mother, wiped her eyes and nose with her apron; Uncle Georges just beamed. Was this enough atonement, he wondered, for the grief that his sudden departure, two and one-half years ago, had caused?

The stream of visitors – relatives, neighbors, friends – delayed their dinner and increased his hunger. His cheeks began to itch from being scratched by the whiskers of his "uncles" and neighbors who rushed to welcome him, hearing the news of his arrival, as they returned from their fields or their flocks.

Had he ever had a more delicious meal? His mother kept placing more and more in front of him, including a portion from her own plate. They toasted, clinking their glasses of wine, each time before a sip, to more reunions like this one, to the joy and happiness of all, to the "rightful progress" of all the children, even to the "blessed memories" of the grandparents. Chatting was uncontainable and sometimes even irrelevant or disconnected in the unrestrainable excitement. He answered questions and elaborated, for a better understanding, and occasionally embellished his answers in the hope of entertaining them.

His brothers' voices had deepened. His sister's laughter rang in a higher pitch. His father's unanticipated "one liners," made them roar. Their mother's inviting a tease from their father made them all anticipate her leaning away from him and laughing with appreciation. Uncle Georges returned without knocking on the door. "Did you see your Uncle Meetsos, my brother? Have you eaten?" Uncle Georges could see, of course, that they had finished their dinner, and he knew that Lampis had never seen his Uncle Meetsos, but he obviously couldn't think of another excuse.

Soon, his cousins and Aunt Antonia arrived.

"Here you are," Aunt Antonia said, instead of a greeting and as if she had finally found them.

Lampis tried to summarize his life in America, to contrast his new preoccupations with their struggle for survival in the past, and to strengthen their faith in his resolve to return to them when he completed his studies. The intervals between Uncle George's nods, with closed eyes, became shorter and shorter, to the point that he hardly finished his anticipated, after each nod, "What did you say?"

"It's time to go to bed."

The weightlessness of sleep carried Lampis to a blissful unawareness. The crowing of the rooster hurled him back to his childhood, when he won a bet that he could start all roosters crowing in the evening, by imitating them. He stayed in his childhood, half-remembering, half-dreaming, until Aunt Ghianoula, next door, started her dialogue with her chickens. She talked while the chickens cackled back, and then she clanked her pots – a long ago established habit.

He scanned the familiar part of the horizon through the window, following the gentle swinging fall of the oak leaves, ascending to the peak of Aghios Christophoros, riding along the ridges of the overlapping hills, and returning with the whispers of the breeze among the olive branches. Uncle Gregores prodded his mule, laden with plow and yoke on one side and sacks of seed and the noon meal on the other and pulled on the lead rope to the balking donkey with Theia Gheorgia astride.

"Big-teeth" Georges whistled and coaxed his sheep, cursing the horned devil instead of invoking a Saint's assistance, aimed his stone-throw in front of the roaming ram, and relived his frustrations by taunting his brother. A crow, perched on the lone oak tree by the threshing floor, stretched its neck and summoned its relatives for a feast on the corn spread out on the threshing floor to dry in the sun. A flock of sparrows was flushed out of a stack of wheat-shaft by Vasiles' dog, and Vasiles strode in his manhood with his shotgun slung on his right shoulder. The world he knew and was now visiting surrounded him. He was part of it. Yet, he was viewing it or enjoying it as a spectator from a distance. He had stretched the cord, but it recoiled and brought him back. He rebuked, with contempt, the thought that it may snap.

His mother hung on his neck and waited until her eyes dried before asking him whether he was ready for breakfast – bread, cheese, and water. The repetition of this sequence every morning, until the day he left, served to fill part of the void, left from his hasty departure two and one-half years ago, and to be used for sustenance until his return, whenever that may be. His pilgrimage to the Monastery and to the ruins of the castle, his hunting excursions with his brother Gheorgos, his visits to relatives in other villages, his confiding his unrequited and unnamed loves to his cousins, Symeon and Nikos, his discovery of nobility in the lives of his old acquaintances Gheorgos Kyriazopoulos and Euripides, and his new acquaintance with the much-talked about Theios Nikos, all combined to fill his days and lift his spirits higher. His sister's soft singing, while knitting in the balcony, his mother's dusting the blankets, his father's whistling a light tune or chanting a hymn, his brother's aiming with a stone throw at a dead tree trunk, the shyness of his sweet Godchild, the bleating of their goat, all entwined into a Gordian knot and tethered him securely to the mulberry tree in front of the family house. The exchanges of glances and smiles, at meal time, conveyed the message, back and forth, "We're part of each other and of one unity – forever."

His sister talked back to his mother, and he considered that disrespectful. Not wishing to magnify an incidental or thoughtless remark into a major confrontation, he withdrew to his room and cried. He admired his father for asking forgiveness of his daughter when she remonstrated at length for something minor and inconsequential. He was saddened by the realization that the closeness that he had felt for his sister, for a few months before he left, had changed to a respectful distance, with formalities displacing spontaneity, and he felt frustrated in his inability to identify, or even guess, the cause.

Lampis became more reserved and almost withdrawn as the days passed, torn between his need to wander alone in the countryside, in search of some missing links in his memories, and his sacred duty to spend as much time as possible with his family. The painful proportions of this conflict ignited an explosion of shaking sobs at the thought of "leaving in a few days will extricated me from this dilemma." His guilt was not relieved by his weeping; instead, it made the grip on his heart tighter and the burden of his remorse heavier.

His encounter with Demetra, a few days later, though inspirational for a novel – she was watering her chrysanthemums and singing in her balcony, when he called her name from the street, then she rushed to him aglow with surprise and joy – had revived memories that had been covered up in some dark recesses. The ascent of the sun from behind Aghios Christophoros illuminated his future paths to his goals. And the swaying of the olive tree branches in the gentle breeze fanned his hopes for a meeting with his destiny. He had reaped more affection and belief in his unique mission from practically everyone he encountered, and he was saturated with so much faith in his invincibility that doubt faded before it surfaced.

The distance between the faraway land, where he directed his Fates to carry him, and the hearth where these same Fates were summoned at the time of his birth, had shortened to almost visible, if not touchable, ends. He could and would return to find his parents and siblings just as they were now, before the sounds of the church bells faded or changed in his memory, and in time to challenge his younger cousins to a race uphill or to target shooting.

His father's and even his mother's countenance and parting embraces revealed the same optimism. His brothers' goodbyes' he interpreted as "the links will hold us," and in his sister's eyes he read, "Our paths will be diverging, let's hold on to some cherished memories."

He kept saying, "So long," to the unfolding landscapes; engraved the crags of the cliffs in his memories; measured the height of the wild olive tree for comparison at the next return and tried to divine the secrets in the depths of the ravines. The muffled voices of his fellow passengers in the bus were incoherent and faded into whispers by the intensity of his thoughts, an intensity that almost severed him from self-awareness.

His futile attempt to convince the principal of Nickos and his own old Gymnasium to rescind Nikos' suspension from classes for three days distracted him briefly from his preoccupation with the storing of his recent mental excursions. The introduction to the new Principal by his old French teacher, after wrapping her arm around his waist, with "He was one of the best students and finest young men to attend this school," surprised him. He had never been aware of any special attention to him from this attractive lady. The disciplined half-smile of his old gym teacher suggested an expression of pride and high expectations. And his math teacher's squint spelled, "You still have to prove me wrong."

Lampis bounced, with the bumps of the bus, from old to new memories; the winding road unwound emotions and uncertainties. The succession of contrasting landscapes reflected the conflicts between his needs for a return to the security of familiar boundaries and his following the call in the songs of the sirens to the unknown future. The blasphemy of this insignificant bus and the vulgarity of the asphalt road winding through orange groves, spewing foul odors against the eternal messages from the verses in the ancient theater and from the defiance in the medieval castle across the bay, aroused a contempt for the loss of reverence to true beauty and fostered despair in the thought that his fellow passengers were oblivious to this irreverence.

He pulled in and condensed the images from the collision of the wave with the cliff, from the goat's silhouette against the precipice, from the twisted trunk of a pine wedged among the rocks, from the peak of the mountain piercing the clouds, from the lone traveler with a sack on his back, from the city of Megara reclining on the gentle slopes among olive trees. He condensed these images to leave space for more and to not displace others rushing in.

The emergence of the Acropolis, as the bus followed the curve to the right coming up the slope to Daphni, appeared more glorious than the last time – just as it appeared more glorious the last time than the time before. The sun seemed reluctant to descend, glorying in reflecting its rays from the Columns of the Parthenon and the Propylaea. Mount Hymettus reposed in the background with a few tufts of white clouds crowning its summit. And the sea of the Saronic Gulf spread its tranquility to the distant horizon. The immortal city of Athens glistened in the sun, contemplating the next turn in the destiny of the human race or the depths and the dimensions of human dignity.

The six-hour travel from Tripolis to Athens had come to an end quickly. He wondered how much had escaped his senses. He had not slept, nor had he been distracted, except for flashes of memories from his past and of the deeds of his ancestors. Yet, he feared that he came away with only a sample of the display before him. To soothe his frustration, he rationalized that some images were recorded in his subconscious stores and that they will emerge relevantly, in future reflections.

In his brief visits with his Uncle Vasiles and his Aunt Nikki, he reestablished continuity of his sentiments, bridging the gap of the two and one-half years and strengthening his bonds by their unselfish love. Uncle Vasiles' goodness still transcended ordinary human understanding to divine awe; Aunt Nikki's declarations of faith in his pre-ordained "Pride of the Family" neutralized the memories of Aunt Helen's insults; Uncle George's, Aunt Nikki's husband's, uninhibited demonstrations of affection lifted him to new heights of self-esteem; and his cousins' display of pride in being with or talking about him inspired him to more solid earnings for respect. "I belong among them," he pronounced aloud, and swore to take them also with him, wherever he may be.

The city of Athens seemed to have cast the horrors and devastations of the war to the depths of a pit in the remote past. It gazed up, smiling at the clear blue skies and at the future, to hum the echoes of the Panathenan processions, to listen to the messages from the Agora and the Pnyx, to caress the multitudes milling in its streets. The humble homes of Plaka, clustered at the feet of the rock of the Acropolis, translated: "We start from here and we end up there." The Columns of Olympian Zeus hoisted and suspended hope and ambition above the soil. Regas Pherraios' aphorism, "Better an hour's free life than forty years of slavery and confinement," emanated from the statue and echoed from age to age. Athena and Apollo, Wisdom and Poetry, high up on their pedestals, inspired and challenged those who chanced their countenance.

He roamed the streets of Athens in his American soldier's uniform, absorbing, reflecting and even amusing himself with some of his encounters – like the shoe-shine boy who solicited his "business" in English and responded with a wide-eyed question, "Are you Greek?"; or the young man who accosted him with the promise of "A good time."

He did not identify with the Marine at the U.S. military Attaché's office, where he stopped for the inspection of his papers and for the arrangements to fly back to the States. This marine looked and behaved more like a petty clerk than a soldier. But the sight of the Stars and Stripes flag stirred an emotion of pride and security. He dwelt on these feelings until distracted at Constitution Square by the precise, manly, and reverent strutting of the Honor Guards, in front of the Monument to the Unknown Soldier, and by the Greek flag flapping in the wind above the Parliament building. His pride doubled. Both flags, of the country of his birth and of his adopted country, symbolized freedom and human dignity. The verse "From the heart the land Washington rejoiced," from the Hymn to Liberty by Greece's National poet Solomos, linked his two countries, one resurrected after centuries of oblivion and the other born only fifty years earlier, with a cry that changed the world.

The encounter with another soldier, Jim Mohas, from his unit, who was also on leave, evoked more negative than comfortable feelings. He declined the offer of the "Native Athenian" to be shown "around the interesting parts of the city," preferring not to share any memories with a stranger. He had an aversion to boasting and to exaggerations, both of which Jim never lost an opportunity to display. And he was not looking forward to traveling all the way back to Fort Bragg with Jim, the "guy from Philadelphia" – that was how he had introduced himself, to demonstrate his "Americanization," when he arrived at 525 MIS.

The farewells at the airport resembled those at the Seaport, two and one-half year ago, only superficially, in that he was leaving Greece to go to America. The return to Greece and the return to America seemed to have diminished distances and fears of separation, to at least measurable and controllable dimensions. Would he have laughed, two and one-half years ago, at his four-year-old cousins' authoritative remark, "See those children? They're American made."

The atmosphere was almost festive, as if he were just going away for a visit. The demonstrations of love for and faith in him were the same as before boarding *Nea Hellas* but expressed differently. The flow of tears was inevitable, but tempered with wishes such as "Until we meet again."

After the final embraces, he walked to and up the stairs of the airplane light-footed and lighthearted. He turned at the top of the stairs and waved his last goodbye. He collected their smiles, snatched the kisses blown to him, entered the airplane, and looked for a comfortable seat.

During the two-hour trip to Tripoli, Libya, Jim elaborated on his encounters, adventures, and conquests without a break. The rest of the passengers, all servicemen, seemed preoccupied, looking out the window, staring in space, or perusing a magazine. Lampis wondered fleetingly how Jim's stories would change when repeated at Fort Bragg. He could not imagine Jim in a true love embrace with his mother or father, capable of tender expression, or moved by another's pain. In contrast, he divined anticipation and eagerness, for a reunion in the faces of the other fellow-travelers. They must be returning home for good or on leave, he concluded. Home! They had a home. The bird had a home. He was like a snail. He carried his home with him, foraging far and wide. Jim's constant chatter did not allow for sequential thinking. Contrasting Jim's egocentric revelations or pontifications with the inspirations from Uncle Vasiles' disregard of his own needs to comfort or support others, with the rooted strength from his father's commitment to honesty and truth, with his brother's excitement about the bud from his graft on the wild pear tree, tapped another store of memories. These memories flashed brightly, ironically illuminated by Jim's confabulations, in disarray, reminding him again that he was different.

"Are you listening to me?" Jim asked repeatedly, and probably feeling offended.

"Oh, yes, I am," Lampis replied.

He was listening, but not interested in what he was hearing. He found the memories of Uncle Vasiles' sharing his rationed slice of bread with their dog (he tried to hide it, too), his grandmother's version of the birth of Jesus, his father's defiance to the decrees of the Communist Guerrillas, and his sister's ignorance of the meaning of certain obscenities far more interesting or rewarding than Jim's bragging.

The ride from the airport to the barracks, with the unfolding of new or even exotic images before him, pushed Jim back to oblivion. The sturdy olive trees, probably there since the third day of Creation; the clusters of Arabs, with dusty headdresses and garbs, squatting in the shade of the tuft of a palm tree – they'd have to move soon as the sun shifted; a dark boy goading his sheep and followed by his dog; a minaret in the distance; the roar of a jet, all crowded in his memory closet for storage. He prayed that his flight to the States would be delayed for a few days. He wanted to see and learn more of this land. As long as he was in a military base, he was secure with his military obligations.

Lampis experienced three days of unexpected or even unimaginable events. The meals at Mess Hall were varied, abundant, and delicious. A dollar to the Arab orderly ensured a made bed, washed laundry, and his gratitude. The white-washed buildings in the city reflected the sun and their mysticism. The veiled women – only the left eye was seen as the right hand twisted the veil over the rest of the face – stirred the imagination. Were they pretty and therefore resentful, or plain and consequently indifferent, or ugly and naturally appreciative? The white-robed large man walking in the middle of the street, ignoring and disturbing traffic suggested either arrogance from his social position, or defiance against European customs and rules. The lined-up, uniformed, silent group of young girls following a solemn nun transferred him back to the Middle Ages.

Lampis wandered away from the European section and into the narrow, crowded alleys of the Arab quarter, where a barber shaved men's heads in the middle of the alley, and a butcher brandished a large cleaver with the left hand and brushed the flies from the hanging carcasses with a horse tail with the right. The stares of the barber and the butcher chilled his heart. The barber, he thought, could sever the head with one move of his straight razor; the butcher could cleave one of the passersby, any one, with one swing – and nobody would stop to notice.

Lampis searched for the shortest way out of this nightmarish maze.

The laughter of a young, unveiled woman in the European quarter, when Jim made some smart-aleck response to an Airman's warning about being "careful how you look at or talk to an Arab girl, or your head would be rolling away from your body," seemed to come from a different planet, a remote age. And when she addressed them in Greek, in this out-of-the-way place, he expected to see Greeks in their ancient garb and outlook (this used to be a Greek Colony, after all).

The Greek girl took them to the Greek Club, where they met a number of hospitable, polite people eager to know more about them and to entertain them. After the polite and accommodating exchanges with the priest and the elders, they drifted to the end of the room where the young crowd was perfectly relaxed, fraternal, and effortlessly civil. Jim's display of superiority with his Athenian origin and American uniform neither offended nor impressed these apparently cosmopolitan and self-confident young people. Consequently, he felt neither the need to apologize nor felt any apprehension about being identified with Jim.

He was eager to learn more about them and found out that they recovered only the ruins of what Mussolini confiscated from them during the war; that they were all interned in concentration camps from the beginning of the war between Italy and Greece until the Italian Armistice; and that they had to start from nothing – just like their ancestors did so many times in the last two and one-half millennia. He did not sense any bitterness or enmity toward the Italians, until the next day.

The pleasant surprise and interlude ended with the realization that he and Jim had to be back in the "Post" before 9:00 P.M. They planned to meet with three young men the following day. The strong images and personalities of the people he met blurred his vision for all that unfolded or spread before him. Jim's constant chat did not distract him. The laughter of the young woman, the serenity of the priest, the clasp of the handshake of the older man, the dignity of the ladies, the confidence of the young men convinced him that they must be direct, true descendants of the Ancient Colonists.

The bus ride back to the city, shortly after the noon meal the next day, puzzled him. Everything looked so familiar. He wondered whether the cluster of Arabs squatting in the shade of the palm tree was the same that he saw two days ago, whether they never left. He did not see the uniformed school-girls with the nun, but he was sure they'd be coming out any moment.

The coffee-house where they were to meet their new acquaintances was large, dimly-lit and with a broad aisle stretching from the door to the back wall. Not recognizing their friends, after walking in this dark room from the bright sunshine, they headed for an empty table to the left. A firm grip on his right shoulder startled him.

"Not on this side," a voice as firm as the grip commanded.

"Why not?" he asked his new friend, who had recognized them and came to meet them.

"This side is for the Italians. We Greeks sit on the right of the aisle."

"And if we sit here?" he asked.

"Then these things will be flying," his new friend responded, pulling a straight razor out of his pocket.

They sat on the right side for about fifteen minutes.

They walked around the city center, the French and Greek quarters of the European section, and stayed away from the Italian quarter.

"They know us here," their friends reassured them. "They did not resist moving into our homes and taking over our businesses when Mussolini rounded us up, and three years later when we were freed, they acted as if they were the rightful owners."

The bitterness surfaced and surged. Apparently, nine years were not enough to erase the memories and to cultivate forgiveness. Had they not concluded with

"We'll prove to them, once again, that we're better," he may have left wondering whether they would survive. He was assured that they'd prevail.

CHAPTER 21

THE NEXT DAY, THEY WERE PUT ON A PLANE for the Azores Islands. Stretches of sea coast, expanses of desert, and the mountain range of Atlas served only for a comparison with the town-studded northern coast of the Mediterranean, the fertile plains of the American Midwest, and the snowy peaks of Taygetus. He did not remember how Atlas, the Titan who supported the firmament on his shoulders, was turned into a mountain. And if he didn't remember, how could Jim know? Would they have a book on Greek Mythology at Fort Bragg?

The stay at the Azores was brief. These "Air Force guys" were treated better than the "Army guys." Their food was better, their mess halls more impressive, their sleeping quarters more spacious. That didn't seem fair. Who wins the wars? The foot soldiers, of course. And yet, these sissies…Oh well, who cares?

Going to town, gazing at the vastness of the Atlantic Ocean, meeting new people was more interesting. The heavy mist, the cobblestone streets, the oxcarts, the distracted people in the streets, the two girls they picked up at the waterfront, the ride up the mountain slopes to a hay stack, his self-recrimination for having followed Jim in this misadventure, his subsequent embarrassment, and finally managing to "shake Jim off" had to be counter-balanced by at least one strong positive experience.

The view from the summit of a hill, shared with a nice young Airman, who had been stationed there for about a year, displaced the memories of the previous day. No spouts of whales to stimulate his imagination, but his companion's repetition of stories he had heard carried him to the sea among the whalers, excited him at the sight of insignificant bipeds cutting up, on ladders, these gentle giants. What seemed like ripples in the ocean, from where he stood, may be mountainous waves, like those that tossed the ship *Nea Hellas* like a walnut shell two and one-half years ago. Talking and listening to his companion, straining to follow the travel of the waves, and inhaling the breeze from the shores of the island, diluted time to his almost missing his plane.

He ran down the slopes, leaving his friend-of-the-day behind and made it to the airplane just as the door was being closed – they had to lower a ladder for him to climb aboard.

Being at the airplane on time gave Jim, somehow, an air of superiority and the right to chastise him loud enough, of course, for everyone to hear and recognize him as their spokesman. Lampis did not retain a single word of Jim's ten-minute tirade, and he resisted the temptation to pull rank and order him to be quiet. It may have been amusing, but it was not worth it.

The plane rose through the mist over the Atlantic, then over the tufts of gray and white clouds, swayed and dipped from time to time, and stayed with the chase of the setting sun. The fan of rays, from a point on the ocean's surface, illuminated the clouds in the horizon, and was gradually extinguished by the overlapping folds of light gray, gray, light yellow, deep yellow, rusty, purple, deep purple, and finally, a glistening dark mantle.

Eventually, darkness caught up with them from behind, and covered them. The flashing light at the tip of the wing, the occasional dip or tilt, and the monotonous hum of the engines created the feeling that they were suspended halfway between the ocean and the sky – to eternity. Jim talked for a while, something about girls fighting over him, and then started to snore – a snore that was as interesting and as stimulating as his talking.

Lampis retrieved the memories of his hunting trips in the village; the disturbing stories he had heard about one of his through-marriage uncles; the pilgrimage to the monastery; and the resignation on the pale face of his childhood friend. This last memory swelled a hard lump in his throat and raised a prayer. "God, please help her, preserve her." He repeated the prayer, maybe aloud. *If God were merciful, if He were just, He would cure her of her tuberculosis; He'll restore her to health and to joy for all who knew and loved her.* Her laugher and giggles when at play as a child, her radiance at picking wild flowers as a young teenager, her smile when singing softly with her head tilted slightly to the left as a self-conscious young woman, her attentiveness and bewilderment at his reading his poems to her, her expression of faith in him in supporting his decision to emigrate to the United States, and finally, her pain in her answer to his request that they stop writing to each other dissolved the lump with tears. The tears burned his eyes.

How much pain had he inflicted on her?

"How are you?" he had greeted her.

"I am much sicker than you think," she had responded, making his guilt more oppressive.

He had chosen not to express his belief that he had tried to spare her from a deeper hurt, in requesting that they stop corresponding, and he had prayed that she understood. She had always been understanding and trustworthy. He had confided in her with little, if any reservations, and her chastisements had increased his love for her. Even in her anger, rarely witnessed, she was gentle. When his hope of catching a glimpse of her at the window, walking the streets at siesta time was realized, he was elated; when not, it was rekindled for "Next time – tomorrow." Yet he had hurt her. He could not curse the Fates; not yet. They were still at work weaving, after casting him in a far-away land, in hostile surroundings, to chase after the dreams that they created for him – maybe they'll be kinder in the future – better not tempt them.

Half-convinced that he had no alternative, Lampis leaned back, reappraised the hum of the engines, checked his impulse to give Jim the elbow to stop snoring with the thought that he may wake up and start talking. He contemplated the depth of the darkness to and below the surface of the ocean, climbed up the path to the ridge with his lantern in his right hand, listened to the calls of the owl in the emptiness of the night, and woke up with a plunge of the airplane about four hours later. Still dark. "I am much sicker than you think;" the pale sad, smile; "God, please help her;" He had hurt her! He'd left her behind, thousands of miles. They parted forever. The melancholic smile, the glistening in her eyes, the limp handshake, the melancholic smile…

The weight of the duffel bag on his shoulder was much lighter than the weight of his thoughts. The distance from the airplane to the train station was longer than the distance from the bosom of his family to his New World. No distractions. Jim's meaningless and occasionally annoying chatter faded and receded into nothingness. Jim was stopping at Philadelphia for a few days.

Lampis traveled alone, with a sigh of relief, to Fayetteville, North Carolina, and then to Fort Bragg. He slept all the way to Fayetteville.

He marveled at the comfort and security from the familiarity of the land, even in Fayetteville. Only ten months at Fort Bragg and it felt like home. For two years in Chicago, he felt displaced, not belonging there. He had come to America as a Displaced person, and he indeed felt displaced in Chicago; not here. Not because nobody called him "D.P." or "The Greenhorn," with a condescending and derogatory tone, not because the uniform bestowed an identity identical to everybody else in the same uniform, but because he was accepted as an equal and because his individuality was respected. He had made friends in Chicago and had earned the respect of some of his teachers and fellow students, but here in the army, the friendships and respect that he had cultivated and received were not counterbalanced by the discrimination from his uncles and their circle.

The initial joy of reunion was soon marred by the news that some of his closest friends were being shipped overseas. Jim Hasapis and Tom Edgos were discharged already; Jerry Metaxatos would be discharged in a few days. Leo Mitsas and Steve Kondos were going to Germany. Dean Vasitis was going to Korea. He was troubled by Dean's assertion that he requested to extend his duty so that he could go to Korea. The "spoiled brat couldn't resist the chance for adventure," he reasoned. He'd even miss Leo Mihas and Argiris, the rascals.

In just a few days, the unit was down to skeleton strength. His section was closed, and he was moved to the Headquarters Company; and he was promoted to Staff Sergeant. This time, he had a tailor sew his new stripes on his sleeves. His promotion, his obtaining his U.S. citizenship and his award of the "Good Conduct" and "Exemplary Service" medals, coming in short succession, made the loss of his friends more tolerable. His discovery that Dean Vasitis had volunteered to go to Korea, extending his tour of duty, in place of George Pamphilis, raised Dean to the highest degree of esteem, especially after his request of the adjutant and the Commanding Officer, that they, "Make sure that George Pamphilis never finds out. George has a wife and a three-month-old baby. It's not fair that he goes to Korea. I'll go in his place, but he must never know." (Major Leggett, the adjutant, confided this information to Lampis, after his vows and behind closed doors, to keep it a secret for the next ten years). How could he have not recognized such nobility in Dean's character? His recalling some of their exchanges made it clear that there were other expressions of noble behavior, camouflaged by an apparently deliberate display of being bratty.

The day of his taking the oath to citizenship of the United States would remain engraved deeply in his memory – a bright, cloudless day with a soft breeze fluttering the Stars and Stripes at an angle of about sixty degrees from the pole, tipping the top of the pine trees gently, and carrying the voice of the judge administering the oath directly to the stands where he stood with about three hundred other soldiers. The response, in so many different accents – Greek, Italian, German, Polish, Czech – was sonorous and moving. The bond he had felt with all those in the same uniform, serving under the same flag, strengthened. He shook hands right and left, front and back, as far as he could reach. The brief, inspiring speech from the judge, after they were pronounced "Citizens of the United States of America," was followed by prolonged applauding – from the new citizens with relief and gratitude, and from the spectators with pride.

Lampis looked at the flag, feeling hypnotized with the merging and parting of the stars and with the overlapping of the stripes caressed by the breeze, recalled his reverence for the Greek flag, and contrasted his surging emotions with his intense hatred for the Swastika fluttering at the end of the Acropolis – the ultimate sacrilege! The parade that followed in their honor with the bands of the 82nd Airborne Division and the XVIIIth Airborne Corps, stirred emotions, strength, and confidence. Doubts and fears were scattered beyond retrieval.

Later at night, lying in his bunk, he classified his experience from solemn to exhilarating to magnificent. He knew his family would be proud of him. He had written his parents as soon as he returned to the barracks. Dean, Leo, Steve and the others had been shipped overseas to fight, if called upon, without being citizens. Now that he thought about it, it did not seem right. He had not thought about it before. His commanding officer expressed the same sentiment when congratulating him. He had thought of changing his name, like so many others did, but he procrastinated and finally decided it was too late – and he had to sign his name all around his picture on the certificate.

He learned his new duties quickly. Next, he learned to pace his work so that he looked busy, even after he took over the job of two "guys." He had plenty of time to review and reexamine the records of all those who had been exempt from duties, such as K.P., trash detail, and guard. The depletion of the ranks below the grade of sergeant, after the recent levies to Korea and Germany, had left the remaining few men grumpy, cursing, fighting, and exhausted. Lampis proposed to remove the "assistants to the assistants," the platoon clerks, and the corporals from the "exempt list." The adjutant and his commanding officer (Major Leggett and Colonel Hostermann, respectively) applauded him, those removed from the list cursed him, and all who experienced some reprieve made him their champion. In one stroke, he had become a hero and a villain; he had made dozens of friends and a host of enemies. His convictions that he was fair made all this easy to take.

His walking the hills and ridges around his village, hunting, or just reveling in his childhood surroundings, and his traveling on foot to the villages of his uncles and close family friends in his visit to Greece, had prepared him for an easy transition from the leisurely office routine to the vigorous morning exercises, P.T. (Physical Training) that had been awaiting him on his return.

"Is this the army or a girl scout camp?" General Leland, the new commanding officer, was quoted as exclaiming when he had inspected the 525th MIS group. His out-of-shape friends had a tougher time, but started to enjoy it also, before long. He was placed at the head of the column, when running, to set the pace, and incurred the wrath of those who thought his pace was too fast. He did not think that he was showing off or punishing the likes of Captain Klepper and Major Potaki, as some of the rumors inferred. He just could not control his youth.

He gave up guessing why Captain Klepper had vowed "To get" him but continued to cleverly defy him – like when he whispered softly so no one could hear, "You'll never get me, never; I'll never give you that chance!" His belief that Colonel Vernon and Colonel Hostermann approved of his performance and character was strengthened daily with their comments and smiles. He was having fun. Having seen his parents again, having lightened the guilt of having left two and one-half years ago without saying "goodbye," and having dispelled the fear that he may never return to them had removed a dark cloud threatening despair. Laughing and playing came easier. The days seemed brighter and the nights shorter. His future and the future of his friends, even those who left for Korea and Germany, appeared secure, until Senator Joseph McCarthy's calculated exploitation of international confusion about Communism versus Democracy or about Monolithic dominance by the self-appointed champions of the Proletariat versus the Capitalistic Lords, with his demagogue charges of Communist infiltrations in Government, the State Department and the Military, was followed by a mass near-hysteria.

The Military, in its pre-occupation with its mission to safeguard the "American Way of Life," reacted quite defensively and deferred quite appropriately to the Government – all three branches. The inevitable hysteria and paranoia proved difficult to contain.

The 525 MIS Group with its high proportion of foreign-born members and its unique assignments, appeared particularly vulnerable. The extensive News-Media coverage, with big headlines vying for public attention commentaries and dramatic (or polemic) articles or accounts in magazines such as *Time,* were followed attentively and discussed animatedly or gravely. Soon, the atmosphere became tense and oppressive. Laughter, merriment, and even goodwill was subdued or silenced. Friendships were strained. Conversation was transformed to measured or laconic exchanges of facts – as defined by, or conceived as, conforming to Military regulations.

The background of everyone was to be scrutinized again and the "Clearance for Top Secret" information was to be suspended, pending closer reviews. Those whose origin was from countries behind the Iron Curtain felt particularly insecure and almost defenseless. The dimensions of caution spread to overlap with paranoia, and paranoia infected ranks and brass, sparing no one. Rumors were repeated and magnified to the anticipation of imminent disbanding of the 525th.

His initial withdrawal and defensiveness was followed by a surge of anger and indignation. He marched to the Commanding Officer's office to declare his readiness to take another "Lie-Detector-Test" – he had taken it twice before, once for "Clearance for Top Secret" information and again when some documents were forwarded to the Pentagon without the stamp of "Top Secret." Colonel Hostermann's standing up and saluting smartly, followed by a tight handgrip, conveyed a message of appreciation and promise. Within two days, every member of the 525th, about six hundred and fifty men, volunteered to take the Lie-Detector-Test. The colonel sent his report to General Leland, the Commanding General of the post who in turn forwarded it to the Pentagon.

The mood throughout the compound changed from a pervasive submissiveness to a courageously festive exuberance. Confidence courted with defiance, and pride was displayed in the brisk Military strutting even to the mess hall. The nightmare was over in the 525th long before it began to fade across the Nation.

Still, time moved slowly, and the closer to his anticipated day of discharge, the slower. The excursions to Raleigh, Durham, Greensboro, Charlotte, and Wilmington became almost weekly events. He made friends in every town, except Wilmington, and experienced a range of emotions from frivolous and amusing to serious and reflecting. The Korean War had come to an end, but a state of readiness was maintained. As the cease-fire continued to hold, drastic changes began to sweep through the army. In just a few days, a sizable number of officers, from captain to major, were demoted to their permanent ranks of sergeant and shipped out. And some of the new arrivals in the 525th, with the rank of sergeant, had been captains and majors.

Lampis felt quite uneasy when his old Commanding Officer (CO), stopping his car to say "hello" in an accidental encounter, corrected him with, "Don't sir me, fellow sergeant."

He found some comfort when Captain, now Sergeant, Goodman informed him that his pay at retirement would be that of his highest rank. He had liked Captain Goodman, even after the threat of court martial for not keeping his carbine clean.

The confidence that he had gained from the trust and respect of his superiors emboldened him to the point of playing games with his Master Sergeant, Sergeant Bauer, or challenging the military minds with the appeal to the appreciation for feminine beauty – like the time when, against strict orders, he pasted the centerfold of the Playboy Magazine on the inside of his footlocker, before general inspection, and the time when he told General Leland that he had reared his jeep into the general's car while looking at a WAC's legs. Sergeant Bauer never forgave him for the display of that centerfold, even though the generals had appreciated it. General Leland had just laughed when told about the cause of the accident, and ordered him to "Just get out of here before I get angry."

Time did not stand still but seemed to lag behind a snail's pace. Boredom was neutralized by plans for the next day, decisions on impulse, and challenges to the established order. His efficiency at his duties left ample time for adventure. Rules were bent or even broken. Regulations were circumvented, and ebullience surged beyond the boundaries of prudence – not often, but often enough to raise the necessary clever precautions and devices. The close calls evoked a strange pride and frequently led to an irrepressible bragging. Luck was not given its due credit, even though its generosity outweighed the cunning and the manipulations in his plans. Nor did the Guardian Angel ever receive any thanks – not even when the jealous husband checked his fury and backed off at the White Lake confrontation (he was supposed to be on duty at Fort Bragg), or when his friend sped at 120 miles per hour from Greensboro to "make reveille" at 6:00 A.M.

In contrast, these escapes bred a hybrid attitude of compliance and defiance, of obedience and subtle insubordination. He could exploit the weaknesses of his superiors without discomforting them, and he used the leverage of his popularity to keep his adversaries at bay. He enjoyed his outwitting and exposing the fabrications of the Georgiou's and the Hamphers, frustrating Captain Klepper or Major Potaki in their determination to "teach him a lesson he won't forget," and profiting from the goodwill of Colonel Vernon or Colonel Hostermann. He "could get away with murder," his friends mused and his enemies complained: "With Major Legett and Colonel Vernon on his side, he's untouchable." Not quite. Major Legett did agree with Captain Klepper that he needed a haircut, compromising to wait until the weekend, and Colonel Vernon did remind him that he should "Walk through, not jump over, the gate."

The trips to Charlotte became more frequent – a new territory to exploit - and to Raleigh-Durham, rare. He appreciated the virtues of Agape from Durham and admired the stately beauty of Mary from Charlotte, but having fixed his sights on his road to Medical School, he guarded against the evolution of the relationship from casual to serious.

He was touched by an old gentleman's offer, barely conditional, "To help to establish you in business, or send you through school – and a bonus of a wonderful girl for a wife."

Had he become aware of his attention to Mary?

Lampis declined politely. "I have to go back to Chicago, but I'll never forget your kindness." He hoped to gather some good memories and leave the same of him behind.

The last trip to Charlotte, when the old gentleman offered his help, brought him closer to his past and to a new chapter in his life. The landscaping, the woods, the pavilions, and the services commemorating the Transfiguration of Christ, in the Chapel of Gastonia Park, transferred him to his childhood days and forged a new link with his new country. He managed to lose Jim and roam in the woods, pushing the sounds of the festivities to the background and bracing for the likely new confrontations with his uncles. He dwelt on his predicament that he needed their help in his application to bring his brothers to America, and he had no illusions about their motives in binding him and his brothers to work, or more accurately, servitude for them. Still, he did not wish to extinguish the glimmer of hope in that "maybe they've changed."

Maybe his rushing to Chicago last year, to help keep the business going, when Uncle Bill became sick, made him appreciate him. Besides, he would specify the hours and days of work, if not the salary, in the beginning. In four more weeks, he would be out of the army and headed back to Chicago. Colonel Vernon had apologized the other day for "Giving the re-enlistment talk," and wished him, "Best of luck."

His envy for the children swinging and sliding was interrupted by Mary's wave from across the shallow ravine. He couldn't possibly ask her to wait for him all those years, and it may be too late to start something now. He wasn't returning to Charlotte. He'll go join the dance; maybe Mary will dance with him. She was so graceful. Jim had been looking for him and found him.

The flirting blue-eyed blond from Greensville, South Carolina, mischievous and alluring, competed with Mary's serenity for a brief moment. He'd spend the next day in Charlotte, also. Maybe he could see her one more time. He knew where she worked. He danced the Tsamiko to the applause of the spectators and to the relief of his conflicting emotions. He checked his impulse to wander into the woods with the blue-eyed blond and tried to suppress his annoyance at Jim's, the Athenian's, condescending remarks about, "The peasants and their unsophisticated offspring."

Lampis read in Mary's eyes, in a fleeting message, "I wish you were staying."

The goodbyes came later, after a party in the home of a gracious family, singing and dancing to the virtuoso piano tunes of a student from Duke University.

Some of the girls acted surprised that a Greek from Greece could play the piano so well and expressed their regrets about "Good things coming to an end."

His disappointment, the following day, in not seeing Mary at the department store where she worked, was soothed when she waved at him from the Delmonico Restaurant, across the street from the bus station. Had she, too, longed for one more encounter and come there with a friend, for the last farewell? His impulse to run to her was checked by the excuse of "I may miss the bus." The realization that he would never see her again saddened and fortified him at the same time.

Processing for the separation – not discharge, he was reminded – from active duty began a few days later. Expressionless looks, or hardly any looks at the Main Post contrasted with the warmth and camaraderie of the 525th M.I. and fired the anticipation of returning to civilian life. His curiosity about the change, from a remembered friendly and warm smile to a distracted, if not cold, stare in a fellow soldier from basic training was answered with the story of how his unit was annihilated in an ambush on the first day in Korea. He knew almost every one of those killed, but he knew best Charles Burnette, whose bravery saved the rest of the unit.

"You'll never know how lucky you were," his old friend concluded, staring away and probably reliving the horrors of that ambush.

Lampis returned to his unit from the Processing Center, slept in his bunk, ate with his friends, but he felt he did not belong there any longer. He was just a guest now. He walked around his old unit, measured the length and breadth of the parade ground, tried to divine the thoughts of those working in the Motor Pool or picking the garbage, saluted the officer smartly, and smiled when he realized that he was counting cadence crossing from the Personnel office to the Headquarters Building. He'd miss those majestic pines, the crispness of the bugles in the early morning, the fist-fights of the paratroopers across the street, the spire of the lonely chapel in a far corner.

He shook hands. "Maybe we'll meet again, you never know," he repeated. He finally slung his duffel bag over his shoulder to walk out of this "home" for the last time. He could not resist turning around for one more look before driving away with his friends, George and Steve, for the train station in Fayetteville. George was going back to school to become an engineer. Steve had received a contract offer from the Chicago Cubs, but turned it down to go back to the family farm in California.

After some repetitions of their plans for the immediate future, his going back to college and then on to medical school, Steve's returning to the farm, and George's becoming an engineer, they seemed to wait for someone else to start the conversation. He looked out of the windows. Some landmarks brought back vivid memories, shared with either or both of his friends. He was amazed at the return of forgotten experiences, pushed aside as insignificant or barely registered at the time of their occurrence. He dwelt in some of these memories before expressing his emotions connected with them. His friends seemed distracted, serene.

"Remember those guys carrying their own silverware in their pockets on Wednesdays, the 'all-the-spaghetti-you-can-eat-for-one-dollar' days," he said, "then finding a booth out of sight and all of them eating from the plate that only one guy ordered?"

They all laughed.

"Can't really blame them; Wednesdays were coincidental. C-ration days!"

They laughed again and stopped, then chuckled and fell silent once more. They chuckled again, muffled this time.

"Remember this drive-in, Steve? Tell me again," George, who knew the story well, requested.

Steve blushed. "We were lucky, real lucky."

George laughed. "Do you think that guy will ever forget? One punch. Wow! Flat on his back. Out. Deflated. Did the carhops drop their trays? Hah, hah, hah! Were you scared when the MP's stopped you at the gate? Hah, hah, hah."

Steve blushed again. "I was."

"Irving must have turned white!" George laughed again. "Did you take him with you when you went back with the MP's? I forgot that part."

"No, we didn't. Give us some credit, George. We dropped him off at the Group, on the way back."

"You were heroes. You know, especially among black friends."

"Believe it or not, we were surprised when that big guy told us, 'take that Nigger and drop him off at the road, if you two want to be served!' Weren't we? We had totally forgotten that Irwin was black. You should have seen the expression of that pretty carhop when her hero lay spread-eagled after one punch!"

"Are you going to stay in touch with Agape?" George asked Lampis, starting the conversation again. "Or has Mary displaced her?"

"I don't know. Maybe. I never started anything with Mary. I don't even have her address."

"Agape is terrific. She's got everything. If I were you, I'd stay in touch – you just can't go wrong!"

"Are you in love with her, George?"

"Maybe, but you got to her first, and she's stuck on you. My mother would go crazy over her. What a marvelous girl!"

It was time to change the subject.

"What about you and Diane, Steve? There is another pearl. Pure gold!"

"It hurts," Steve replied. "I am going back to California. If I pluck her away, she may wither. I don't think I'll ever find another one like her, Diane."

"I'm glad I'm not vulnerable like you guys, with your looks and charms. No heartbreaks. No regrets! Are you sure you're not coming back for Agape?" George went on.

"Quite sure," Lampis replied.

In the silence that followed, Lampis remembered Agape at the piano, smiling at her father; walking to the kitchen to bring soft drinks for him and his friends; looking into his eyes, fleetingly, with those coal-black, moist, secretive eyes; standing at the door and waving goodbye.

George interrupted the silence and the memories. "I am going to hold some grudges against you, you know. Sometimes, you didn't think of your friends. You played the role of the noble knight, in our presence, and then we didn't even exist."

"What are you talking about, George? Be specific!" Lampis said.

"Remember Loulou? You remember her too, Steve, don't you? You met her on the beach, six months after you slammed Bob's knuckles on the table – ouch, that hurt – when he reached out to grab her and you scolded him. You told him, 'When you're with me you behave.' When she stopped you on the way out to thank you, you told her, 'What in God's name were you doing here? Go home.' I remember how she looked at you and shrugged her shoulders, and what did you do? You just figured that you're leaving in a couple of months, without ever thinking of getting her telephone number for your friends who're staying."

"I remember her," Steve butted in. "She was more beautiful than Ava Gardner and so innocent. I wish I had crushed Bob's knuckles. Why did we take that guy with us? I remember how she looked at you. You should have gone back to see her. You said her mother thanked you with a kiss and invited you to dinner. You should have accepted and taken George with you, with one grudge less."

The laugh that followed ended with a choke and groping for words.

Loulou's image flashed back, the way George and Steve remembered her, standing before him with a bewildered expression of gratitude and begging for help or understanding.

Lampis heard her footsteps on the beach, running after him. He felt her touch his left arm again and listened to her timid voice, "Remember me? Remember Loulou, at the bar?" He held her hand while she took him to meet her mother; her mother was beautiful, too!

George started to laugh, slapping his thighs. "What's wrong with him?"

Steve shrugged his shoulders.

George wiped his eyes. "Did you sleep after you pushed the chest-of-drawers behind the door? Did you hear Hilda trying to open the door? You were scared, weren't you? I bet you could see her father with a shotgun, right behind her. Just think, you could have married her, become a prosperous tobacco-farmer, and supplied me with cigarettes for the rest of my life."

Steve must have felt it was his turn. "Postman, postman! Make it like a bunny and take this quick, to my Fort Bragg honey," he recited Hilda's writing on the back of the envelope of her letter, then apologized and added: "Remember all the teasing from that? It wasn't fair making fun of the love of a pure farm-girl."

Hilda's image flashed, pure, innocent, pretty, frustrating. *Wrong time, wrong place, wrong move, wrong end.*

"Here we are. Shut up, Steve! Don't say it! Even if it's true, don't say it, damn it."

"Don't say what, George?" Steve asked.

"You know damn well what I mean, Steve!" George stuttered.

"If you don't want to hear it, you don't say it, either."

Nobody said it, but all three knew what it was. It was the "forever" or "maybe forever" that would follow the "goodbye."

Lampis got out of the car, flung his duffel bag on his shoulder and walked away. They got back in the car but didn't start it. He knew they were waiting for him to turn and wave. He did, and he waved with the hand that they had just squeezed. "Take care, you two," he called out.

"Agape!" George answered with a raised fist.

Was he calling out her name, or was he expanding from friendship, the sentiment that had bound them for over a year, to Agape, the Greek word for the all-inclusive eternal love.

He bought his ticket and walked out on the platform. They were still in the parked car.

"Go," he ordered them with a gesture, pointed to his sergeant's stripes, and ordered them again. "Go."

They waved and laughed. He could not pull rank on them anymore. He was a civilian. Tough! They'd leave when they pleased. A few more gestures, some more laughs, and he pulled his handkerchief out. His eyes were burning. "Go, you guys, go!" he yelled, and added, "Please."

They laughed and left. He laughed and cried at the same time.

He strolled on the platform, waiting for the train.

A young woman, caught looking at him, asked, "Are you going home for good? I've been watching you and your buddies. You'll miss them, won't you?"

He didn't talk but nodded repetitively.

She smiled and started to read her book. He sat at the end of her bench, held his face in both hands and wondered whether she was looking at him. When his curiosity gave him enough courage to look, their eyes met.

"Has your girl been waiting for you?" she asked smiling.

"I don't have a girl," he replied. Did she read regret or relief in his answer?

CHAPTER 22
A New Beginning

THE TRAIN RIDE TO DETROIT, to spend a week with his old friend George, did not take him away from Fort Bragg. Darkness kept distractions to a minimum while the excitement of having passed another milestone kept him awake. Steve and George returned to the barracks for three more months. Steve had been easy to read. George had been secretive, chain-smoking, and moody but trustworthy. Steve had been sensitive to the weaknesses of others and fair in his dealings. George could be generous but occasionally cruel. Steve's smile was reassuring while George's smile puzzled.

Lampis would like to meet Steve, Leo, and Dean again. Now he was going to meet another George, the one who declared falling in love a weakness, who was happy when his tears flowed for the first time in seven years at hearing that his younger friend was leaving for America, who seemed ready to sacrifice everything to preserve a friendship.

The reunion was joyful and fulfilling. Thousands of miles away from the birthplace of their friendship, they embraced in disbelief and cried without restraint. When they parted, almost three and one-half year ago, George was in uniform. Now it was reversed (he could wear the uniform for a full month, he was told, and he was proud to wear it!). They stayed up late, night after night, reminiscing, planning, and joking. The old label of "lazy," stuck to George in the past, was definitely peeled off. He worked hard or furiously to save enough for a start at his own business. They went to see Jim Londos wrestle and visited old relatives and new friends. Lampis felt welcomed. He enjoyed this interlude, in spite of repetitive sneezing, itching eyes, and congested nose. He just couldn't get rid of this "cold" for a month now. No goodbyes now, when they parted, only "so-longs." They'd see each other again, they promised.

His resolve to stay and work with his uncles, at least temporarily, had freed him from the anxieties of looking for a job and a place to live and had galvanized him with the determination to dictate some terms. There would be no compromise about going to school full-time and limiting his hours of work to five hours on weekdays and eight hours on weekends. The salary was negotiable.

Lampis slept soundly all the way from Detroit to Chicago. He did not expect, nor did he find anybody waiting for him at the station. The city looked brighter, more welcoming than when he came to Greece. The then gray sterile buildings now looked pregnant with promise and hope. The then monotonous broad streets now looked like avenues to new horizons. The skyscrapers were new bridges to the skies, not modern versions of the Tower of Babel.

He hailed a taxi and gave specific directions. "I know the way," he emphasized.

There was no need to repeat the instructions. The Greek signs on Halsted Street and Blue island stirred a mixture of emotions, ranging from unbridled pride to pity and included nostalgia, purpose and contempt. He had been there a few times and witnessed pomposity, idealism, and decadence – the last accentuated by Aunt Helen's remarks of contempt. The sight of Uncle Pete's building, quite impressive and an eyesore for Uncle Bill, aroused his eagerness to meet again with Uncle Nick, now reunited with his family after a long separation, and to start a new close relationship. He smiled at the memory of Uncle Nick's witty humor and wondered about Uncle Pete's serious, no-nonsense expressions. Did Uncle Nick's presence help to patch up or to intensify the differences between Uncle Pete and Uncle Nick's wife, Artemis? The next smile came with the memory of an older lady flirting with him rather crudely, with a mixture of innocence and street-walking, when he was serving ice cream at a party in Pilsen Park, about three years ago. Every storefront looked familiar now. He even recognized some people on the sidewalks. Reality was rising higher and higher, above the surface to meet him. Will he cling to it and wrestle with it to turn it to serve his goals? No doubt.

He paid the taxi driver and walked to his Uncle's store. Louie and Joe rushed to him. He dropped his duffel bag and squeezed their hands. Then John and Rudy came. They were glad to see him. Uncle Bill and Uncle Gus grinned. He shook their hands last. No hugging. That would be both improper and embarrassing. A few inquiries about the train ride, army life, and the girls he left behind.

"What girls?" Lampis answered.

Uncle Bill and Uncle Gus looked at him uneasily.

"Back to school now?" John asked him bluntly.

"Going back next week," Lampis declared.

Both uncles appeared stunned. They must have nourished the hope that the army cured him of this dreadful "going to school disease" or that he had his "fill of sin."

"What about your parents? Who's going to help them?" Uncle Bill asked, in an insulting manner, losing no time.

"I am going to help them realize their dreams about me. I won't let them down," he responded firmly.

"Good boy. That's the spirit," John added, raising his glass and then appreciating the pun.

Everybody laughed, but Uncle Bill, not connecting, couldn't see what was so funny.

By the time Aunt Helen arrived, the boundaries of the gap separating him from "them" had been drawn.

"He's going to be a schoolboy again," Uncle Bill announced.

She must have anticipated this would be the case and affirmed her or their position with finality by saying, "He's on his own. We have nothing to do with it."

Her brother, whom she introduced with hyper-inflated pride as "The doctor" (he had come from Greece a year ago) joined their camp. "If I were you, I'd go into business," he told Lampis.

Remembering Alexander's answer to Parmenio's advice to accept Darius' offers after the battle of Issus, and before considering the possibility of offending "the doctor," he replied with a smile, "So would I, if I were you."

After a moment's reflection and without apologizing, he concluded that not only the boundaries, but also the battle lines had been drawn – all within a couple of hours after his return – and the skirmishes had begun. He was glad and confident of victory.

The children checked their excitement when their mother warned them that, "He's not going to work here. He's going to school."

"I'll start looking for a job and a place to live right away. I'll go to the YMCA tonight."

Aunt Helen reared and looked at her husband with mushrooming resentment.

Uncle Bill stopped drying the glass in his hand, returned her look and turned to him. "We need you here. I already told Ted not to come back Monday."

"You can ask him to stay, or you can find somebody else."

"I want you, not Ted, not anybody else."

"All right. I'll work Ted's hours. We'll talk about the salary later."

"All right. And you're not going to the "Y" tonight. You're staying with Kostandes (Uncle Gus). We'll see after tomorrow."

Without a word, Aunt Helen took the children and left with "the doctor."

"Brace yourself, Uncle Bill," he thought. "She has an ally now."

Uncle Bill looked at him and half-ordered, half-pleased, "Go upstairs and get some rest. Write a letter to your mother and give her my greetings." Was it – and – now? We'll see. Time will tell.

Lampis met Uncle Gus on the stairway. "Your bed is by the window," Uncle Gus said.

"Good night," he responded.

"We'll pray in the morning, then," Uncle Gus commanded.

"I'll do my own praying, my way," he asserted irrevocably and close the door.

He took some clothes out of the duffel bag and arranged them neatly, as if expecting an inspection. And he did write a letter to his parents, not omitting Uncle Bill's greetings. He was confident and ready to do battle. He was seasoned.

"Quite a day," he thought as he lay on the hard bed with the rough-hewn covers brought from Greece by Uncle Gus some forty years ago. "I've got to buy some sheets, a couple of blankets, and some towels."

He got up and made a list. He had saved some money, plus he had his separation pay of $300.00. He dreamed about Myrtle Beach and struggling up the hill to the mess hall. The wooden stairs had been torn down, and he sank in the mud going around them. His legs were so heavy! And the flag fluttering atop the steeple of the chapel was off to the left. Steve was now driving in first gear, so serious. Should he salute Sergeant Chapralis? He used to be a captain and the color-bearer.

"Wake up, it's time to pray," Uncle Gus' voice came from the door. He'd rather wake up to the sound of the bugle. He turned the other way.

"Are you going to get up?" Uncle Gus asked, sounding annoyed.

Lampis did not move. Uncle Gus was not giving up. Nor was he. Finally, his message got across. He waited until Uncle Gus left, before leaving his bed, washed, shaved, and went out to breakfast and shopping. He wondered whether he was counting cadence aloud while walking to Goldblatt's. He enjoyed the attentiveness from the sales girls and reasoned, "It must be the uniform."

Uncle Gus expressed his disapproval of his eating at restaurants and remonstrated, "There was enough of sheets, pillows, and blankets."

"Those are yours. I want my own," he replied firmly.

There was more testing.

"When are you going to do your laundry?"

"I am not. I'm going to take it to the Chinaman."

"You're lost!"

"So, I am!"

Lampis spent the next few days preparing for school, checking with the 5th Army Headquarters about his reserve status and renewing old acquaintances. He registered for a rather heavy schedule at school and started working the hours that he would keep after school began.

His "hay fever" – Aunt Helen made the diagnosis – was quite annoying. And "the doctor" recommended calcium shots, bragging, "They don't know about this type of treatment in this country."

It didn't work, in spite of reassurances about the "successes at the prison."

After "showing them," according to Aunt Helen, during his internship at Columbus Hospital, "the doctor" got a part-time job at the prison First-Aid station and prepared for his State Board exams – he, an established authority should be taking boards. So unfair, according to Aunt Helen.

His hopes in communicating with this "educated" man, were dashed rather quickly. He related his thoughts of buying a used car, in the hopes of cutting down on travel time to and from school, after compromising on giving up the idea of finding a room or small apartment near the school. "The doctor" promptly offered to sell him his car at the same price that he had paid one year ago, in spite of the fact that Steve, his new friend, had to jump it or haul it three or four times in just one month. Disappointed? Kind of.

He'd ride the bus, the trolley, the elevated train, and the bus again, just like he did before, and save his money. Next year at the University of Illinois he would not need a car.

The letters from his parents, brother, now married sister and new brother-in-law, Uncle Vasiles, and Aunt Nikki were coming at regular intervals. Uncle Bill seemed to have won the round in sparring with Aunt Helen. He was polite and respectful, but he also kept a respectful distance. Uncle John had barely shown a trace of emotion at their meeting.

Lampis was enjoying school. His circle of friends widened. He traveled by train to Galesburg to meet and thank Uncle Jim, his father's cousin, for the cards and packages that he sent him in the last two years while in the army. He met Uncle Nick, with his reunited family, and he found ample moral support from all of them. Uncle Jim's saintly smile and Uncle Nick's wit, more than counterbalanced Aunt Helen's venom or "the doctor's" sarcasm.

He could fence off the poisoned darts and block the blows from every direction, but one unexpected blow from Uncle Gus left a lasting bruise.

"You never paid me for the expenses I incurred in bringing you from the old country, with all the papers and your ticket. It amounts to $300.00. I need it now."

Lampis reminded Uncle Gus that he had worked without pay for four months to compensate for these expenses, according to Uncle Bill's calculations.

"You settle with your Uncle Bill. I paid the money and you must pay me back."

Lampis paid it.

Uncle Bill promised to give him the money, expressing a little surprise that Gus would do anything like that.

Lampis was not invited to Uncle Bill's house, except to get his calcium shot after insulting Aunt Helen's intelligence by insisting that North Carolina was in the south.

"How could "North" be in the South?"

His popularity at school exploded with his grades after the first tests. He didn't exactly have to fence off the girls, but he collected a generous share of smiles and blushed at being called "the genius." He had no pangs of conscience in refusing to take off from school to work in preparation for Thanksgiving or Christmas. He did not apply for the G.I. Bill, having decided to go back to Wright Junior college, where tuition was nominal for a year, saving his G.I. benefits for later. His confidence and self-assurance had become unshakable and his course was unwavering. He did not work on Wednesdays – he had an evening class – but worked ten hours on Saturdays and Sundays for a total of forty hours for the week.

Lampis never thought of going out. The regimentation and discipline in the army was continued by self-imposed rules and constraints. He was satisfied with the vicarious pleasures in listening to Joe and Louie talk about their dates, especially in the respect and tenderness they showed for the girls (he was becoming their confidant). They brought their girls so he could meet them – decent, genuine, unpretentious, considerate, and honest young people and relationships.

The unexpected call, followed by a visit from his army friend, Steve Kondos, brought some more excitement to his life. The uncles and Aunt Helen – were all there when Steve came – were as polite as their uncouthness would allow. Comments such as, "Nice, serious young man," by the patrons at the bar, were answered by simple stares and silence from Uncle Bill and Aunt Helen. Steve was a threat! Cicero, where Steve would live with his uncle, was not far, and he might start coming around. By coincidence, Uncle Bill or Aunt Helen were not within earshot when he made plans with Steve to go out the following Saturday; they seemed stunned with Steve's last words, when leaving, "I'll see you Saturday."

After a hard look from his wife, Uncle Bill started at Lampis. "You're working Saturday, aren't you?"

"I'll go out with Steve after work," Lampis responded simply but resolutely.

"Maybe this one time," Uncle Bill conceded.

"I'll go out whenever I please," Lampis answered matter-of-factly and added, after a moment's conciliatory reflection, "on my own time, when I'm not in school or working."

"I told you!" Aunt Helen fumed, after a vengeful glare at her husband.

Lampis wondered, fleetingly, what she had told Uncle Bill. "I have to go study now." He opened the door to leave.

"You should hire someone who's reliable," Aunt Helen told her husband.

Lampis turned around, looked directly at her and responded, "He should!"

"Enough! I'll see you tomorrow. Go to your studies," Uncle Bill commanded.

Lampis was not upset. He returned to his books and, during breaks, anticipated going out with Steve next Saturday.

Uncle Bill seemed to be in a lighter mood the next day. Maybe he had won a major victory. "Steve is a nice boy. You should go out with him. You should have other friends, too. You're young. You need to go out and meet some nice girls, too. Don't listen to Kostandes. I wish I had your youth." He moved behind the shelves, in his reclusive little chamber, without waiting for an answer, for the next hour.

"Must be hard on Uncle Bill," Lampis concluded, boarding his brother-in-law and dealing with never-ending demands from his sisters-in-law, plus facing remonstrations and nagging and whining from his nephew whose only fault was his determination to go to school and who never asked for anything. Still, he'd never talk to Uncle Bill about his feelings, and the gap remained unbridged.

The Saturday night outings with Steve became a routine, usually to a movie, followed by a meager snack and a protracted stay at Lucy's Restaurant downtown, before returning to their respective abodes by bus. They reminisced a great deal, exchanged jokes, shared each other's dreams, but never commiserated. Girls were out of the "order-of-the-day." They used army jargon a lot – and mused that "they were going steady."

They wore their army overcoats and marched on State and Randolph Streets, if the crowds were thin enough, not to break their stride. He would go to church alone or with Steve, and now and then stop at the Three-Corners Restaurant if Helene had indicated that she'd be working as a waitress for her father. He liked her walk, her giggles, and the mixture of flirt with innocence in her eyes. He still hadn't decided whether the "What?" after answering her questions about his grade in the first Biology 101 test – the highest in the class – expressed disbelief, disappointment, or admiration. All the students she mingled with scored much lower than he did. Her visit to his uncle's place to see him, while working, once again displayed spontaneity stemming from innocence and openness devoid of hints of ulterior motives. In Aunt Helen's eyes, however, who could "see through everybody," she was wicked and "pretty dumb" – besides, "what could she see in a peasant D.P.?"

His circle of friends widened gradually. Steve introduced him to another friend, Nick, from the army in Germany, and Nick, to his friend, Ted; and with the other Steve, the five of them would go dancing on an occasional Saturday night or for "chicken-in-the-basket" lunch in a country restaurant on Sundays. These excursions made him relax and become more productive with his work at school.

They all celebrated when, at the end of the semester, his name headed the "Dean's Honor List." The other Steve brought the local newspaper to show the uncles the front-page article, "Local Boy Makes Good." The uncles didn't know how to react. Aunt Helen's remarks were caustic: "He put him up to it, to show off, but I'm not impressed in the least."

The D.P. was now a "local boy" – and the uncles' store was crowded with people walking in to offer their congratulations. Of course, business picked up, too, that should have offered some compensation for Aunt Helen.

The new semester appeared more challenging, with a heavier schedule and French late in the evening two nights per week. Surprisingly, Aunt Helen did not remonstrate – and he did not inquire why. He "was in the groove" now, attending classes, working, studying, and relaxing with his friends.

One of the girls, Tassia, from Greece, impressed with his grades, suggested that he go to Northwestern, where her boyfriend was, to apply for a scholarship. He had not thought about this possibility, having decided to go to the University of Illinois, at Urbana, where tuition was affordable. But Tassia's suggestion was tempting. He was impressed with the campus and with Jim Lekkas – Jim and Tassia seemed so different.

His interviewer was impressed with his grades, but indicated since he had the G.I. Bill, he would not be eligible for a scholarship.

I have no other means of support," Lampis countered.

"You can get a job."

Since he had already decided he would go to the University of Illinois, he was not disappointed. He thanked his interviewer, adding, "Maybe I'll come back to your medical school after Illinois."

The serenity and atmosphere of the campus stayed with him, until a few days later, when Mrs. Helen Karanikas, from the Dean's office, recommended that he apply for a scholarship at the University of Chicago. She appeared confident, and he was getting excited.

Two weeks after the submission of his application, he was advised that a man from the University of Chicago would come to interview him next Monday.

A warm, introductory handshake was followed by sitting across each other with only a brief or momentary interruption during the exchange of questions and answers for about one-half hour. The parting, warm handshake ended the interview with the conclusion, "We like students like you on our campus."

His interviewer's parting words kept mixing with his teacher's lecture in the next class. Mrs. Karanikas congratulated him, as if he had already been awarded the scholarship. Mr. Savoy, the chemistry professor, was a little more cautious. Dr. Argoe assured him that he "had a good chance." (Mr. Savoy and Dr. Argoe were University of Chicago Alumni).

The suspense did not interfere with his studies, seemed greater in his friends, and did not last long. A week later, a simple congratulatory letter from the Office of Admissions, the University of Chicago, advised him that he was awarded a full tuition scholarship. Louie, Joe, John and Richard reached for his hand all at the same time (he read the letter at his uncle's store). He was aloft, and they shared his exhilaration.

John, the philosopher, raised the toast. "May you be yet another University of Chicago Nobel Prize winner – that is what that school turns out, you know."

"It's full of communists. Don't you read the *Tribune?*" Uncle Bills said.

"it's full of Masons and atheists," Uncle Gus added.

Neither of his uncles congratulated him.

"It's a great school," John declared.

"The greatest," Joe emphasized.

"Nowhere near as good as Northwestern," Aunt Helen hissed, "and they didn't want him."

"If they were better, they'd be smarter and if they were smarter, they'd fight for him. There!" John had the last word and bought drinks for everybody.

Lampis summoned all his disciplines to keep from shouting with joy but could not suppress his surging ebullience. The young girls looked prettier; the ladies looked more beautiful; all the men grew handsome; and everybody was aglow in a halo. He glided between the tables; he flew up the stairs from the basement; and he soared with the laughter of witty comments from John's direction. After Aunt Helen left, without another word, Uncle Bill looked at him intently for a moment, then looked away and half-pleaded, "We're not busy now. Go write your parents. Make them happy."

Another round of handshakes, and he left to do Uncle Bill's bidding.

Uncle Gus did look up from his writing. The shades were drawn. He was used to the humming of the traffic and the occasional honking from the cars. Halfway through his letter to his parents, Uncle Gus fixed his gaze at him, wrapping his apron around his waist.

"I wrote your mother and father. May God have mercy on your soul. Masons, atheists, communists! Uncle Gus said, then walked away, slamming the door behind him.

Lampis rose from his chair, stretched his arms skyward, looked at himself in the mirror and yelled, "Whoopee!" He looked at his uncle's icons and expressed all that had swelled in him, with a mixture of pride and humility in one sentence, "Thank you, God."

He finished his letter to his parents, wrote a briefer one to his Uncle Vasiles, and stretched out in bed with his hands locked behind his head. "Another step up the ladder, closer to my goal!" he thought. He looked back to gather strength from his humble beginnings and from the blessings of his family, to meet the challenge ahead. The stores of the sunshine and breezes from his village, of his grandparents' caresses with their eyes and touch, of his teachers' confidence in him, of Aunt Katerina's faith in his mission, were recounted to strengthen his reserves.

He could not rest on his laurels. He must plan carefully and deliberately. He must not waste time. He had no difficulty making decisions. He would go to summer school, take a course in Physics at the Navy Pier, the University of Illinois extension in Chicago, and work longer hours. He would move to the dormitories of the University of Chicago in September.

He did not delay conveying his decisions to his uncles. Uncle Bill's response was a simple, "All right."

Uncle Gus made an attempt at bargaining. "You can buy a car, live here, work at the store part-time, and save some money." This was one more attempt to save the soul of his prodigal nephew.

"Buying a car would cost me about as much as room and board at the dormitories; gas and repairs would cost more, and I am *sure* I can find a part-time job on campus."

Uncle Gus was not interested in logic and was not persuaded. He tried again, resorting to a plea, "I'll miss you. I'll be lonely without you."

Taken aback, but careful to avoid extrapolations from any conciliatory remarks, Lampis responded, "I'll come visit you as often as I can."

He had never thought of Uncle Gus' loneliness before this time. He had accepted somebody else's, or maybe everybody else's conclusion that Uncle Gus did not want, did not need, anybody else, that he was perfectly content with the lot he had chosen. His occasional awkward attempts at rapprochement had – must have – been shrugged off as crude attempts at casual conversation. He felt sorry - for the first time? – for Uncle Gus. It was all the others, also, and especially Aunt Helen for whose sake, or because of, Uncle Gus must have suffered a lot of grief and humiliation. He still felt grateful for his opportunity to come to America, but he must always keep his sights on his goal, and the expression of his gratitude can be directed only by his conscience.

Lampis shared his joys and dreams with his friends, indulged in an occasional joyous interlude at a party and retreated from romantic adventures after the first timid or playful step forward.

Easter, awaited with some excitement after his plans for an excursion to the countryside, brought instead of joyous frivolity, a mixture of anger, resentment, and contempt. His little cousins cried when their father, Uncle Bill, announced that after church service, he was going to work at the store. They had expected to spend the day with their father. Torn, briefly, between his desire to keep his plans and his wish to make the children happy, he told the children, "Your father will spend the day with you. I'll take care of the store."

The children hugged and kissed him. Not a word from their parents, until he was dropped off at the store when Aunt Helen asked, "Are you coming to the house later, after Gus comes to the store?"

"No," he replied with finality. "I have work to do."

He was alone at the store and tried to dissipate his frustrations in rearranging bottles and glasses, dismissing the thought of writing his parents, planning responses to Uncle Gus' greetings or Uncle Bill's inquiries, and trying to engage the occasional customer in a conversation. The memory of last Easter's picnic a few miles from Raleigh, North Carolina, was not amusing (he and Steve tricked Harry into going with them to Raleigh to bring the feta that one of their hosts had forgotten, only to dump him there to spare themselves from further embarrassment by his behavior).

The striking contrast between the community spirit and collective merriment at Raleigh, of last year, and the apparent dedication to or worship of Mammon of this year, fueled his anger. He pushed back the surging memories of his childhood Easters, with the bright blue skies, the bird songs, the frolicking lambs on the hillside, the reverberating tolls of the church bells, the fragrance of the wildflowers, and the swaying of the olive-tree branches with the breeze. He almost forgot to call Steve to tell him that he could not join him and the other friends for their excursion to the country. Steve promised that he would come late in the evening for a cup of coffee.

Lampis read some guilt in Uncle Gus' greeting, "Christ has risen," and almost failed to check himself from replying, "But you're crucifying him again. What's the difference between Judas' thirty dinars and your dollars?" Instead, he managed to counter with the customary, "Truly he has."

After an unusually lengthy stay in the basement, Uncle Gus came back, moved around silently for a while, and finally suggested, "You can go, if you want to. It's quiet now."

Having apparently run out of reserves in checking his impulses, he answered, "It's been quiet all day, and it's going to stay quiet. It's Easter, you know. You could have closed the shop!"

Uncle Gus stared at him before responding. "Bill insists. I have to go along. I have no choice!"

Lampis pitied them. If they only talked with each other. He could not concentrate in studying, and after crumbling a few sheets of paper, in trying to start a letter, he pulled out all the letters from the last two months and transferred across the separating distance and time to the warmth and security of his memories. The sentiments in those letters, from his recent scholastic accomplishments and rewards, finally erased the bitterness of the day.

Steve's and Tom's visit, at the right time, enhanced the resurgence of happiness from these enduring sentiments and helped to submerge the occasionally resurfacing resentments from this dark, up to now, day.

Thanks to his new friends, to the moral support of his teachers (Dr. Argoe, Mr. Savoy, Dr. Rietz, Mr. Anderson) and to his popularity at school, he planned and moved without allowing any "ifs" to undermine his confidence. The news of his scholarship from the University of Chicago made the first page of the school paper. The invitation to parties multiplied and his recognition at school functions was crowned by a special invitation to dinner, with a few other "exceptional students" by the Dean.

His unexplainable uneasiness with Dr. Weingarten's attitudes, in spite of the consistently A or A+ grades in all his papers, changed into bewilderment when he received a B for his final grade while a girl who never received a grade higher than B+ was given an A.

"Why did I receive a B, after nothing but A's or A+'s in all my papers and your calling on me more than on all the rest of the class combined for the challenging questions?"

"That's what you deserve, sir, get out of my office," Dr. Weingarten replied sternly.

His disappointment in the Dean's professed impotence to do anything was not counter-balanced by Mr. Anderson's indignation or even by Dr. Rietz's elation that his "favored student" had turned in "the only perfect final exam in my thirty years of teaching Organic Chemistry."

Lampis eventually managed to suppress his anger with his old resolve, "I'll show him." That was the only B for the semester.

He bid farewell to his friends and to his school of two years and gathered momentum for his next challenges at the University of Chicago. The summer session at "the Pier" would serve to keep him "in tune" for the big show. And the party at Dr. Argoe's home, for "all his boys and girls" will be flashing, with Dr. Argoe's glow, memories of gratitude and promises.

"Where," Lampis wondered, "did this man gather all his goodness, all these virtues, having never known a father and having lost his widowed mother at the age of eight? Did Darwin ever write or think of the 'Survival of the fittest to the attainment of sainthood?' Most of Dr. Argoe's students would scatter among various universities. Some would stay at Wright for another year, but they all nurtured an affection for him rivaling that for their respective fathers.

Lampis worked longer hours in the summer, added another "A" and some more inspirations from his teacher at "the Pier" and postponed his visit to the University of Chicago for one "all-or-none" encounter. He would miss his friends, he assured them. They kept wishing him "good luck," reminding him to call on them if he "ever needed anything," and asking him to not forget them. He was touched and moved, especially when Morry offered financial help, "Anytime, whatever amount."

CHAPTER 23

THE LONG-AWAITED DAY DAWNED. Steve No. 2 helped Lampis move his possessions, all fitting in his old cardboard suitcase from Greece and his army duffel bag, to B-J (Burton Judson) Dormitory, Dodd House, third floor of the University of Chicago.

The campus, with its austere Gothic architecture, seemed demanding, uncompromising. The spires of the towers, the massive masonry, the ivy, the carillon bells, the wide gates, the preoccupied men and women walking in the Quadrangles or along the Midway. . . a new world, totally separated from the outside world, with the promises of wider horizons and of unfathomable heights.

He took the room without the direct entrance from the hallway, for a little more privacy, leaving the larger room for his prospective roommate. He wondered whether he'd like his roommate. He wished his parents could visit him in this great university, to reward them for all – or in part – of their sacrifices in their pursuit of their mutual dream. He felt secure in this fortress of learning and a sense of independence or individuality he had never known before.

He walked around the campus to foster a feeling of belonging, to assimilate the physical aura before plunging into the fountains of learning in search of his ultimate destiny. The carillon bells of Mitchell Tower, chiming at noon, carried him airborne to aspirations distinctly his own but probably resembling those of the girl with the knapsack, lost in thought as she contemplated the lilies in the Botany Pond. The Rockefeller Chapel did not seem large, until he walked around it. Would the dining room remain orderly and quiet, with attentiveness and deliberate exchanges, after the students were well acquainted?

"Girls are not allowed beyond the lounge," the lady at the office advised him matter-of-factly, "Except on Sundays, when they may be invited to the dining room, or on special occasions for concerts or lectures in the recreation room."

He had no problem with that. Max, the housemaster, a Ph.D. candidate in German literature, inspired trust with his smile, showing genuine concern in the welfare of his residents, and left no doubt about the sincerity in his invitation to come to him with "any problems, whatever."

His advisor, Dr. Dorothea Miller, advised him that "Everybody here is special. The competition is stiff. Don't be discouraged if you don't get A's in your first few tests."

His confidence was not shaken, but he braced himself anyhow. He liked Dr. Miller, but he was going to show her that he could pull A's anywhere. He did not follow her advice and registered for Humanities, Biology 201, Quantitative Analysis, and OMP (Organization Methods and Principles of Sciences) – she had suggested that "four courses in one quarter is a heavy load," – but he promised he would not hesitate to see her as often as he "needed to."

He visited "the tree," the trunk of a tree cut down about ten feet above the ground, on 57th Street, and the basement at Mandel Hall, where notices about used books for sale, "Wanted" announcements, etc. were pinned. He bought used books and Syllabi (he couldn't make the mistake of saying "syllabuses," around here!) to save money, and made a few acquaintances – undergraduates, graduate students, law students, medical students, divinity students, post-graduate students and "professional students." He was elated but also bewildered in his new environment.

His roommate, John, came three days later. They became instant friends – the first eye- contact, the exchange of smiles after they pronounced their respective names, and a prolonged handshake sealed the friendship. His luck was holding up. John came from the University of Toronto, via Harvard, to study Philosophy, with more reasons than he to be confident, not arrogant (he had graduated Summa Cum Laude from Toronto and come to the "U of C" with a Woodrow Wilson Fellowship).

His reaction to the policy that attendance at lectures and discussions was not required, that grades during the quarter did not count, that the examinations were "open books," and that the grade was determined by the comprehensive examination at the end of the year was somewhat bewildering, with a good measure of skepticism about its soundness.

"How can anybody not turn in a perfect paper if he or she has the books there to check the answers?" he thought.

John had not heard of this policy, anywhere, either and agreed that they "had some adjustment to do."

The heavy load of assignments on day one, the presence of two thirteen-year-olds in his Humanities class and of a fourteen-year-old in his OMP round-table discussions, and the round-table sessions themselves, unsettled him not a little. How could "Miss Houston" and "Mr. Cass," the thirteen-year-olds, understand and discuss Plato, Aristotle, St. Augustine, Kant, etc.? They were just children! And there was Mr. Caplan, a fifty-some-year-old man with gray hair, in the same session, taking the course for credit. Some adjustment! His shaken confidence was partly restored after placing out of Biology 201, having done "very well," according to his instructor. Dr. Miller was pleased with both his performance and his lighter – but not light – load.

Lampis studied long hours, staying up late at night, but he had a great deal of difficulty in overcoming his timidity in speaking up at the round-table discussions. He felt more comfortable in the Chemistry classroom and laboratory, even though the stunning beauty of Millicent Rupp proved a difficult distraction to resist (She did not look at him or at anybody, after only a couple of glances and fleeting smiles in their first encounter). The assistants, always available to answer or to invite questions, seemed to be at perfect ease with their assignments, helpful and never condescending or patronizing, and stimulating with their own questioning. He walked out of the classroom with the urge to rush to his books and review his notes for more answers and even more questions.

In the first quiz in Chemistry, he received a B- and was quite disturbed about it: A C in OMP and a D in Humanities devastated him. He lost his appetite and his sleep, developed stomachaches, avoided his friends, and was grateful that John was not around much. He did not blame his professors – he knew he had failed – and took them at their word to go to them to ask for guidance. They were fair, honest, and encouraging. And he resolved to never again take his books with him and waste time looking for the answers that he could not find in them. He went to the Student Health Service where Dr. Nicholes, the mother of one of his classmates in OMP, performed a number of tests, including a gastric aspiration and some counseling. Memorization and regurgitation or rumination, having served him so well in the past, seemed detrimental now.

John confided first that he was depressed. "Never in my life had I had a C."

They commiserated from about 11:30 P.M. 'til 1:30 A.M. in the Recreation Room that night, shaking hands and promising each other that they would do better. They had to. He, at least, must look to his professors not for answers only, but more importantly, for questions to his own answers. It was not easy. He did not wonder about his classmates; they seemed to have an easier time – both thirteen-year-olds got A's – except for one fellow who complained bitterly about "this terrible way of testing," and swore, "To get out of this place and go back to the University of Illinois."

While still recovering from these setbacks, Lampis suffered another staggering blow. His MCAT (Medical College Admission Test) was marked when he inadvertently held a page of the preceding section while waiting for the next section, and flipped the pages absent-mindedly. His protests to the proctor, that he was not looking, were to no avail, and his concentration was disturbed. He appealed to his advisor, who helped him draft a letter to the Princeton Examination Center explaining his position. The answer came a few days later, that the marking of his paper would be disregarded. The high scores a few days later stopped the pain – but the scar would remain forever.

His job as a part-time waiter at Alexander's Restaurant did not help in distracting him from his misfortunes or improving his finances. George, the proprietor, introduced him to his patrons as "A poor student who's working his way through school." The response from the patrons was the opposite of what he expected. He remonstrated to George, about six weeks later, that in spite of his better than anybody else's services, his tips were the most meager. George and the head waiter agreed, but George could not increase his nominal salary. Lampis quit. The attentiveness and seductiveness of the young waitress would not be missed. He did not despair.

The visits to the Recreation Room with John became more frequent and, gratefully, more comforting. Max's suggestions, never presumptuous and usually subtle, and Dr. Dorothea Miller's parental, more than counseling, guidance, began to restore his diminishing self-esteem and stop the sliding of his self-confidence. The B's in the next tests, in all three courses, propelled him into euphoria (He had been so indignant about his B from Dr. Weingarten!). John got a B, too, and they celebrated. His stomachaches vanished, his efficiency at studying improved, and he rediscovered Millicent – not Millicent the beautiful, but Millicent the brilliant and charming. His professor's remarks, one echoing another, "We knew you could do it, or you wouldn't be here," gave him an additional boost. The steady, unfailing arrivals of his G.I. Bill checks relieved him of some anxiety that he had not identified in the last few months.

His inquiries about Medical Schools were not encouraging. He would not have enough credit hours for the University of Chicago, was not particularly interested in Loyola, was somewhat turned-off by Northwestern, and would not consider Chicago Medical School. He finally applied to Illinois, Northwestern, and the University of Chicago.

His Letters of Recommendation came from his teachers at Wright Junior College since his professors at University of Chicago did not know him well enough. His hopes were not high, since the vast majority of the applicants, he was advised, had had three or more years of college and were expecting to have – or already had – Bachelor's degrees. But, he might as well try, even though he could hardly spare the application fees totaling thirty dollars.

The first quarter ended in an upswing. He had regained his confidence, strengthened his determination, and licked his wounds. The loss of his illusions did not leave a vacuum – it was replaced by a more realistic appreciation of his weaknesses and by the concentration in search of ways to overcome his shortcomings.

Lampis was pleased when Uncle Bill advised him, with some reluctance, that he did not need his help during the holidays. The hardly concealed message of resentment from their "being in a bind," from Aunt Helen's malignant stare, removed any seeds of potential feelings of guilt about the turn in this relationship. He went straight to the post office and found a job as a mail sorter for two weeks, two shifts every day.

Working next to a witty, relaxed, attractive black girl made him look forward to going to work; a student at Williams College, she was going to be a teacher. The only thought about her that bothered him was that he was not going to see her again after the new quarter started. Adding almost two hours of traveling to the hours of work did not leave enough time to miss John, who had gone home to Rochester, New York, for the holidays. He was sure that his desk missed him. The dormitories were empty. Being the only one in the common bathrooms, hearing only the sound of his footsteps, crossing the deserted Midway, accentuated his loneliness.

"Why aren't you home?" the lady at the front desk asked.

"I *am* home. This is my home, until I am kicked out," he answered jokingly.

Apparently not knowing what to say, she looked at his mail box and hesitated some more. "No mail today, like yesterday or the day before. I am sorry. Good night."

His visits to his Uncle Bill's house on Christmas and New Year's Day were brief and quite unpleasant. On Christmas Day, Uncle Gus never looked at him. Uncle Bill was entertained by his brother-in-law's (the doctor's) stories; Aunt Helen tolerated his peasantness' presence with displayed magnanimity. Uncle John appeared guilty in asking him about school; the children stayed away; and Aunt Sophia faded in the kitchen. He kept waiting for Uncle Gus, who was not exactly welcome, either, to leave so he could leave also. New Year's Day, Uncle Bill's name day, was different in that there were more people to ignore him. When Joanne, Uncle John's goddaughter and a Northwestern student, approached him, she was asked by vigilant Aunt Helen to help her with the drinks. Everybody was drinking "seven-and-seven." Uncle Bill seemed quite uneasy about his brother-in-law's attentiveness to his eighteen-year-old goddaughter.

When he finally decided that they'd enjoy themselves more without him, he left. Why had he come? He wanted to show that he was above their pettiness, to keep a glimmer of hope that they may finally respect his aspirations, and to postpone his own acceptance of the inevitable final severance of the ties until his anticipated youngest brother's arrival. One more try at Uncle John's name day, one week later, and that may be the last time.

He did have better luck the next time. He even felt buoyant after spending much time talking with Nick Katris, who had also just come out of the army, returned to school at Northwestern, aspiring to be a dentist, had a genuinely friendly disposition, and introduced him to his sweet mother and lovely sister, Anna. When Anna and Joanne joined them, he even became animated, attracting more attention and was shown some, unaccustomed in this circle, deference. He heard Nick's mother comment, "What a nice, young man your nephew is," to Uncle John.

"He wants to become a doctor," Uncle John said.

"He wants to look at and wipe people's bare rear ends," Uncle Bill remarked caustically. Only he laughed and looked around. "It was only a joke," he added, as if to make amends for his offensive remark. Had it backfired?

Nick touched Lampis' hand. "It was only a joke."

Somehow, he perceived that no one thought of him as "the D.P" or "Greenhorn" anymore – after all, he, "the D.P." had served in the Army of this country; had any of them? And Joanne's announcing quite firmly, that "He has a full tuition scholarship at the University of Chicago," drew more than a few glances at his direction – some as if in disbelief. He and Nick promised to "stay in touch."

The new quarter started with no time for readjustment. Organic Chemistry, Humanities, OMP, Comparative Anatomy; heavy load! He tried not to discomfort John with his formaldehyde smell, showering immediately after returning from his dissections of his shark (frogs and cats would follow). His new circle of friends widened with some classmates from the previous quarters staying in the same sessions of Humanities and OMP, and he made several new acquaintances in Organic Chemistry and Comparative Anatomy. His final grade of A in Quantitative Analysis had boosted his morale.

His contact with his old friends was limited. Only Steve Panos, who had a car, came to visit him occasionally. He had not distractions – from his room to the classroom, to the library to his room – that was his circuit. He began to speak up more at the round-table discussions, to relax in the laboratory, and to even play pranks, like the time he offered a bottle of Nitric Acid to his classmate, who got a mouthful of ammonia while pipetting "an aliquot" to "neutralize" the ammonia. But the hole in his pants from sitting on the spilled Sulfuric Acid on the desk top was no laughing matter. Luckily, he did not have a hole in his buttock! Also, his jacket was long enough to cover the hole in his pants, provided he did not bend over.

He appealed to the Comparative Anatomy professor after a disastrous grade of D in a quiz by arguing that his response to the way he understood the question was correct.

"Too bad, be careful next time," the professor replied laconically.

He had better be careful next time. This was no place for sympathy.

The interview at the university of Illinois Medical School went well. He felt quite optimistic and encouraged. He made sure that the Admissions Office had his new address by tearing up the card with his uncle's address and completing a new one. He uncles had never bothered to call him to tell him about the letter from the University of Illinois. Had he not found the letter in an impromptu visit, he would have missed this appointment. The parting words, "You'll hear from us soon," from one of the interviewers, muffled the clanking sounds of the elevated train and the chatting of the other passengers, reverberating without a break, all the way back to the dormitories.

John was ecstatic, also, more about the news that he placed first in a nationwide competition for a two-year Fulbright Fellowship at Strassburg. The answer for John was final; for him, it was promising. He would miss this place, and John. Waiting another year for a chance at the University of Chicago seemed like a big gamble. One bird in hand…

The suspense for the final answer was diluted by the demands of his assignments. There was no room for complacency or daydreaming and no time for a respite. He made his contingent or alternate plans in studying hard and waiting.

The news of the forthcoming arrival of his brother necessitated some quick changes in his plans. Since he wanted his brother with him, and Nick could not stay in the Dormitories, he had to find a new place to live, and he had to find a job for him until starting school in the fall. A semi-dilapidated Hotel with kitchenette apartments near campus offered an acceptable temporary solution.

Nick was private, not demanding, and quite independent. He knew a bit of English, traveled around the city without difficulty, looked for jobs by himself when necessary and before long, found assembly-line work at Hot Point.

Emotions swung for both of them, from the initial excitement through stages of frustration, anger, indignation, and depression. The points that he scored in reminding the Western Electric interviewer, after the rejection of Nick's application on the basis of not being an American Citizen, were countered by a simple, "I am just following the rules."

The reeling blow came in the evening of March 25th, a Friday, when Uncle Bill called him about a letter from the University of Illinois. Lampis learned that "This is the third notice, and unless we hear from you by March 25, 1956, the position held for you will be offered to another candidate."

Lampis could not contact anyone on Saturday or Sunday. On Monday, he was told "Unfortunately for you, it's too late."

"The two previous letters had been tossed into the garbage by Kostandes (Uncle Gus), and I just forgot to call you sooner after this third letter arrived," Uncle Bill admitted.

Lampis had no recourse, just bitterness. This was the final straw! He had even pushed aside the slander about him, to his brother Nick, that "Your brother is a bum, a liar, and a frequent visitor to the whorehouses."

"My brother is studying hard at the University of Chicago," Nick had protested.

"What University of Chicago? He hasn't even graduated from High School. He's lying to you."

All this vehemence because Nick was prevented by Lampis, the whorehouse patron, from conforming to their designs. Lampis hoped that Nick understood and would not doubt his sincerity. With all that going on, he was not terribly disappointed with the B's in Chemistry and in Comparative Anatomy. The grades in Humanities and OMP did not count but were encouraging with the range of B to A in every test.

Dr. Miller was quite pleased. "Considering the transition, the slow start, and the heavy schedule, you did well."

The expensive Hotel forced them to look elsewhere for lodging. They rented a room with kitchen privileges from an old Jewish lady, two blocks from campus, and moved during the break between the winter and spring quarters. They shared the only double bed, their deprivations, and a lot of laughs with the old lady's antics – she and her brother would chase each other in the hallway, screeching; she would open their door without ever knocking and would bring the food, even ham, from their compartment of the refrigerator, asking, "Is this yours?" She would demand a dime for every telephone call made or received and complain about the telephone bill. She would use them as bait for prospective female roomers with remarks such as, "I have the nicest, handsomest young men living here," and she would threaten to throw them out when Lampis told her he'd be moving at the end of the quarter, unless he agreed to pay her for the next three months. They mused about whether she'd go to the police if they stole the globe with the sickle-and-hammer over it – she had brought it out for a gathering, mostly of older women on May Day.

He carried a heavy course load for the spring quarter – Humanities, OMP, Organic Chemistry, and Embryology – leaving no time for the "whorehouses" and hardly any time for a couple of "friends" from Wright Junior College who remembered him when they needed help with their "term papers." He accommodated his "friends," wondering what kind of example he was setting for his brother. He enjoyed Embryology the most, settled into the routine of the Chemistry schedule and participated more actively in the round-table discussions of his Humanities and OMP classes. He had planned to take Embryology in the summer but was able to change from Physics to Embryology after concluding, in two sessions, that he may not pass the Physics course – it was over his head. (He'd go back to the University of Illinois extension at the Navy Pier in the summer and get his A). Nick volunteered for overtime work every day, traveling one hour each way to and from work and coming "home" feeling tired. They were content in each other's company, anticipating spending part of Saturday and all-day Sunday together. They invited John for dinner a couple of times, went for walks, planned, and even relaxed.

The inevitable apprehension about the approaching finals, particularly the Comprehensives in Humanities and OMP, began to interfere with sleep and appetite, with the consequence of the "what ifs" and the weight loss. The deepening recession, with the scarcity of jobs, intensified his anxiety about his financial needs. What would he do if his grades were not good enough for a renewal of his scholarship? Was Nick aware or suspicious of his anxieties? Should he confide in Nick? Would that be fair? He did not know how to interpret Nick's apparent aloofness. Was it discretion, timidity, or insensitivity? He found some comfort in concluding that Nick's preoccupation with readjustment and the inevitable insecurity may be so consuming that his perceptions or awareness of his brother's struggles were dulled. He also had to remind himself that Nick was only nineteen years old.

The distractions by the young black woman in the building across the street, walking around her room naked, with the windows wide open and the light on, or of the charming English young lady stretching her hand out for a gentle handshake before walking up to her apartment, every time they met and chatted in the stairway, were easily displaced by the all-consuming thoughts of his studies and of his immediate needs for survival.

The decision that Nick should start school at Wright Junior College, for a flexible schedule and to save money on tuition, entailed moving to an area from where the traveling distance should be approximately equal for both of them. They shared the expenses of rent and groceries, some of the anxieties and grievances, and for an interlude or for revitalization, memories from their childhood and from the love in their humble home. Rarely did the combination of frustration, physical fatigue, and homesickness overwhelm Nick into prolonged withdrawal and only on one occasion to an outburst of accusations.

"It's all your fault that I have to live like this, work like this, and travel all these distances. I could have worked and stayed at the Uncles!"

Lampis was hurt but kept his composure. "Is it my fault, Nick, that I was asked to pay for my fare from Greece, after working like a slave without pay, for four months? That I was paid the same salary for twice as many hours as the seventy-eight-year-old Ted? That lies and slanders they told you about me were invented? What makes you think they'd treat you any better?"

Nick was not persuaded, but neither said more.

The demands for the preparation for the final examinations in Organic Chemistry and Embryology paled in comparison to his apprehensions from the challenges in the comprehensive examinations in Humanities and OMP. The latter, lasting for seven hours each, covered the entire year's curriculum and determined solely the final grade. Though firmly resolved to not refer to his books – the open book policy applied – he carried them with him. He was quite proud and grateful in having resisted the temptation and not once opened them. His hope that he be infected by beautiful Millicent R.'s composure and self-assurance, during their brief break, did not materialize. He had to resort to prayer again. His confidence about Chemistry and Embryology was much stronger.

The vacillation between relief and uncertainty, the toll of the physical exhaustion, and the fear that he may not find employment during the summer combined to serve, mysteriously, as a spring-board for new leaps over whatever obstacles may block his way.

The search for a job and a place to live offered a welcome escape, temporarily, from his worries about his academic roller-coasters, failures and future, but this escape took him to a tunnel with only dim lights at the end of the day. He checked the most promising ads in the newspapers – the *Tribune, Sun-Times*, and the *Chicago Daily News*, and went to each place in person. The standard question, "Are you going back to school in the fall?" raised a conflict between dire need and honesty, the latter winning every time, in spite of his vows "next time I'll lie."

"Sorry, we can't use you."

Bitterness, desperation, and near-hopelessness fortified his resolution to "lie next time," yet next time he would hesitate, swallow hard and answer, "Yes, I am going back to school in the fall."

A Greek restaurant owner who needed a dishwasher for the summer wouldn't hire him. "Because some day, after you finish your studies, you'll be cursing me for making you wash dishes."

Perseverance finally paid off. He was hired as an orderly at Henrotin Hospital, and he found a small efficiency apartment at 1323 North Dearborn Street. He could walk to work about six blocks away and to the Navy Pier, about two miles away from The University of Illinois Extension in Chicago where he planned to register for a summer course in Physics.

The small kitchenette apartment was quite an improvement from the single room at the old lady's apartment. His new landlady, quite young, attractive, and seductive, did not distract or disturb him. Nor did the young woman next door, who came frequently, in a short see-through nightgown to borrow sugar, milk, or something. He was too preoccupied with work, school, and worries about his future, and he had secured his blinders against distractions from his goal a long time ago. He guarded his privacy and hoped that neither of these women was offended or embittered.

Nick reacted with a nod only, when Lampis shared first the news of his grades, "A's in Embryology and Chemistry, and B's in Humanities and OMP," – and later, of his failure to qualify for a renewal of his scholarship. The second blow was cushioned somewhat by his qualification for a "Grant-in-Aid" half-tuition. He appreciated, more and more, that he would have to divine Nick's thoughts and not expect much openness. Besides, the barrage of the accusations that he was responsible for Nick's present predicament still hung like a dark cloud over his head. He went to school, worked, and studied. No time for anything else.

The eight weeks of summer-school came to an end pretty quickly. His enjoying his work at the Hospital, from 3:00P.P. to 11:00 P.M. and his consistently high grades in all the tests, contributed a great deal to lifting his spirits. He sensed that he was liked at work, was comfortable with his supervisors and the nursing staff, and blushed with anticipation when a couple of patients referred to him as "The Intern." He was flattered by the attention from the young student nurses – and some older nurses, too – never felt any bitterness for constraints to respond, and he hoped that Judy, the brightest of the young women in his class, was not offended when he had to decline her invitation to go to a play with her. The final grade "A" in Physics gave him a little boost, too.

Starting classes for the Fall quarter, at the University of Chicago, was still about seven weeks away. He needed a second job. Who would hire him for six or seven weeks? He remembered his indignation from the encounter at Western Electric, six months ago, when he took his brother Nick there in answer to a "Help Wanted" ad in the *Tribune*. ("We hire only American citizens," he was told briskly; and the answer, "I am only doing my job," to his questions, "Why don't you clarify that in your ad?" and "Would you rather hire someone like your employee who's accused of having murdered the three Grimes sisters?" had left him in disgust).

Lampis resolved to apply to Western Electric and lie about going back to school in the fall. He did not hesitate a moment to answer "No" when asked as to whether he planned to go back to school, adding, for good measure, "I can't afford to." He had no conscience pangs. He was hired, assembly-line work, 7:00 A.M. to 3:00 P.M. Monday through Friday and was accommodated at Henrotin Hospital to work from 4:00 P.M. to 2:00 A.M. Monday through Saturday. He saw Nick only on Sundays, condensing all they had to talk about in just a few hours. He kept putting off "the boss" at Western Electric, about joining the union, with all sorts of excuses; "Is there a rush?" he would ask with a smile and make some comment about his belief in the union causes. He must buy time until school started.

A letter from his Aunt Nikki, his father's sister, followed by a call from her son, Takis, about six weeks later, disrupted his routine. He could not refuse her request to go to Newport News, Virginia, to see Takis, whose ship was going to be there for a couple of days.

Lampis left in such a hurry on a Friday afternoon, that he did not notify Henrotin Hospital. When he returned Sunday, he was told he was terminated. His appeals to the Nursing supervisor were of no avail. This heartless woman just walked away from him, but he felt no resentment for her, knowing that he was at fault. He could have asked Nick to call and explain. He had to keep reminding himself repeatedly, that he could not have said "No" to his aunt whenever the anger about the loss of his job – and the money from it – overwhelmed him.

His amusement in relating his adventure, following his meeting with Takis, soothed his pains only temporarily.

"I had fallen asleep in a movie and my ship had sailed," Takis had told him. "But I have a permit to remain in the country for thirty days."

Lampis had some reservations about Takis' story, but he decided the decent thing to do was to take Takis with him to Chicago. He had enough money for a bus but not for a plane fare. Takis was arrested at the bus station and taken away. As if the frustration from having been deceived, having incurred all these expenses and losing a day's wages – he wouldn't make it back to Chicago to work at Henrotin – was not enough, he had to suffer the indignity of being followed by a Secret Service agent. He became aware that the man sitting three seats in front of him in the bus, by the aisle on the other side, would look at him frequently in the mirror next to the bus-driver and quickly lower his eyes when he looked up. Noticing the gun-holster, when this "curious" man bent over to scratch his ankle, he decided on a confrontation. He pretended he had to ask the driver whether they would be on time for a connection to the bus for Chicago, and on the way back to his seat, he tripped deliberately, falling on this man. Apologizing, he asked, "By the way, do I remind you of somebody? You keep looking at me in the mirror."

Caught off guard and looking embarrassed, the man answered, "I am not looking at you."

"I am sorry, but every time I looked up, you were looking at me."

Lampis returned to his seat, waved at the "spy" every time their eyes met in the mirror, and wished him a "safe trip" when climbing down from the bus.

His being watched at the bus station in Pittsburgh was not difficult to detect. Nor was the plan to shake this guy off difficult to conceive. The Departures Board showed that the bus to New York was leaving five minutes before the bus to Chicago; the telephone booth without a light and with a good view of the boarding of the bus made a perfect hiding place, and asking loudly, after the lady at the Information desk asked him to speak a little louder (he had deliberately kept his voice low).

"What time is the bus for New York leaving?" he asked loudly so that his "shadow" could hear. His plan was to lure this man to the toilet, hopefully in the booth next to his, then run off and hide in the dark telephone booth about ten minutes before the departure of the bus to New York. He could now relax, but he must not betray his plan.

It worked perfectly. He stood at the mirror near the entrance, combing his hair and when the "shadow" committed himself opening the door, he greeted him with a smile and walked in the first booth, sitting on the toilet seat and watching under the partition from the next booth, ready to run. The "spy" entered the next booth, just as he had hoped, the pants folding over the shoes. "Perfect," he thought, "the idiot lowered his pants," and he ran off quickly to hide in the empty, dark, telephone booth. The "spy" came running – he had a good view – trying to zip up his pants, pinching his finger in the process and scurrying around the bus station before jumping on the bus to New York, with the "last call, bus to New York, all aboard."

"Have a safe trip," Lampis called out from his hiding place.

***

Lampis had more time now, with only one job, but summer was over and school would start in two weeks. He had to look for an apartment, somewhere around Wrigley Field from where Nick would have to take only one bus to go to Wright Junior College, and he could take the elevated train and one bus to go to the University of Chicago. He kept checking the ads in the newspapers. He reestablished contact with some of his old friends and even decided to drown his sorrows after an unceremonious rejection by a girl at a bar – just like they do in the movies. He felt even more – or utterly – humiliated after a couple of sips and left with a heap of self-recriminations. Meeting with Steve, his old Army buddy may help, he decided. Nick agreed that it was a good idea; to mark the occasion, they would have steak. Steve would return the books he had borrowed, also.

Little did they know how this planned meeting and respite would turn out – with Nick eating all three steaks. They had forgotten to check their horoscopes! Two hillbillies, sitting behind Steve and him on the elevated train, took offense at their talking in a foreign language and determined to teach them a lesson. The attempts to avoid them and even to apologize seemed to provoke them even more. The fist-fight that ensued in the stairway down to the subway was brief, with the hillbillies knocked out at the bottom of the stairway, one on top of the other, blood and teeth scattered on the steps, and with Steve and him staring at each other in disbelief.

Steve sat on them while Lampis ran to find his watch, which had flown off with all that swinging, and the police. He found his watch in the circle of dirt surrounding the sapling tree on the sidewalk a few feet from the top of the stairway but not the police. When he came back, Steve was alone.

"Where are they?" he asked.

"I let them go. They paid a good price, with teeth and blood."

They boarded the subway train and did not exchange another word until they arrived home and told Nick what happened.

Nick ate all the steaks. They were so upset. He had escaped totally unscathed. Steve had reeled back to avoid a blow, with his adversary barely reaching him and losing his balance to fall flat on his face on the step and to receive a swift soccer style kick on the jaw.

Nick became a little animated after eating three steaks and started asking questions. "Were you hurt? Couldn't you just go across the street to avoid them? How did you managed to knock them out so quickly? Lucky that you didn't kill them!"

In answering Nick's questions, they concluded that the Army training must have helped in their thinking and acting quickly. And they prayed that "nothing like this would ever happen again."

It almost happened again, two days later, in the elevated train on his way to look at some new apartments. His Guardian Angel, in the form of a six-feet-five inches broad-shouldered young man, neutralized the would-be adversary with a tight grip of the neck and a demand for an apology.

The next day, Lampis found a four-room apartment with bedroom, living room, dining room, and kitchen, at 835 Cornelia Avenue. It was convenient for their transportation. They signed a lease for one year, at eighty-five dollars a month. Not bad! Privacy, security, and only one block from the bus stop for Nick and two blocks from the elevated train station for Lampis.

Aunt Artemis gave them an old couch that opened into a bed, and the rest of the furniture came from the Salvation Army – a single bed without boards, a dining room table with four chairs, and a couch for the living room. He slept in the dining room, on the single bed. Nick took the bedroom. The dining room served, in addition, as a study. Nick went along with whatever he suggested.

They quit their jobs one week before school started. Nick just shrugged his shoulders when asked about the reaction of his boss when he announced that he was quitting. The Western Electric Assembly-Line boss and especially the man that hired him acted betrayed.

"You told us you were not going back to school!"

No sympathy or remorse came from him. "If you were offered a scholarship (a conscionable distortion of the truth) by the University of Chicago, would you not go back to school?" He also said, "I didn't know when I applied for the job that I would go back, but I was hoping."

The personnel director walked the other way without a goodbye or even an angry "good luck."

The Assembly-Line boss shook his hand with unquestionable sincerity. "I wish you all the luck in the world."

Lampis helped Nick with registration, under Dr. Argoe's guidance and in spite of the forceful interference by Mr. Slotky, who had blatantly cheated him from an A in his chemistry class three years ago and apparently still held a grudge, told him in a condescending, if not scornful, tone: "You have to come back tomorrow and then we'll see, maybe I'll just throw you out."

He remonstrated to Dr. Argoe who, without a word, marched in rightful indignation to the registration line.

"Are you ignoring the rules?" Slotky asked Dr. Argoe.

"Your rules? Every time!" Dr. Argoe replied.

His own registration was simple and efficient. Microbiology 201, Biochemistry 201, Zoology 204, and Histology 301. A heavy schedule, to be sure, but necessary for a B.S. in Microbiology in June. His commitment was unwavering, and he never stopped for an inventory of his reserves. The reverses of last year and particularly of the summer were nearly forgotten. In contrast, his winning experience with the encounters in Pittsburgh and with the "hillbillies" enhanced his self-confidence. He had been accepted by the University of Illinois Medical School and there'd be no reason he would not be accepted again next year; his grades had come up after a dismal beginning. He had found a job – two jobs! – in the midst of a recession even if he had to lie; he had won a fist-fight by a knockout, and he had heard from Dr. Majarakis, a surgeon at Henrotin Hospital with his MD and a PhD from the University of Chicago, "I will be delighted and proud to write a letter of recommendation for you; I am proud to know you."

Hesitating, when initially approached with the explanation, "I hardly know you," Dr. Majarakis offered to take him out to Sunday brunch and "spend a couple of hours with you to learn more about you."

Dr. Majarakis' remarks more than neutralized the pain from an encounter with a Greek "old-timer" at Uncle Nick's store.

Uncle Nick had told the old-timer with undisguised pride, that "This young man is studying under scholarship at the University of Chicago."

"Why don't you go to work and send some money to your father who's croaking from starvation? You're going to school as if there aren't enough American young people to fill the American schools. You insolent, lazy, new-comer bums are all alike!" This uncouth man had shouted at Lampis.

Lampis checked his impulses to deck this insolent man and replied calmly, "I am working hard not to fail my parents but to meet their expectations of me."

"Please leave and never come back," Uncle Nick told the man firmly, taking the nearly-full plate from him.

Uncle Nick's boundless goodness, jovial disposition, and invariably encouraging attitude provided a valuable moral support. Lampis counted his blessings: his health, his youth, Dr. Argoe, Mr. Savoy, Nick Demos, his other true friends, Uncle Nick – enough to overcome any obstacles.

He plunged back in his studies with renewed confidence. But for good measure, and in spite of the enormous, for him, expenses, he applied to twelve Medical Schools (Harvard, Columbia, Rochester, Johns Hopkins, Cincinnati, Tulane, Duke, Washington at St. Louis, Northwestern, Illinois, Chicago Medical School, and the University of Chicago).

Uncle Jim called from Galesburg. "Tony is homesick and would like to come live with his cousins."

Lampis received this news with jubilation. Of course, he would find a job for Tony, but the three of them together – it would be wonderful! They had been inseparable when little, Tony always with the two younger cousins, George and Nick, and the older brother Nick with the two older; his sister and him.

It did not take long to find a job for Tony, at the Florsheim shoe factory, after visiting several places, in answer to Newspaper ads, and a skirmish with a Personnel Director at Hotpoint, who, after looking at the name and place of origin, on the application form, advised him, "We have no openings."

Lampis had taken time from his studies and was angry. "This is today's paper," he said, pointing to the ad. "Your sign up front reads Help Wanted."

The response was curt: "We're not hiring Greeks!"

"What kind of discrimination is this? Why don't you state that in your ad, huh?"

The answer, offered apologetically in the privacy of a small office, diffused his anger.

"We're hiring people who are likely to stay with us for a long time. Greeks don't; by the time they're trained, they've saved enough money to start some kind of business and they leave. I hope you understand."

Nick was a lot happier with Tony around. They established some routines, dividing labor and expenses fairly. Saturdays were "cleaning days." One had the kitchen and the bathroom, another the floors and dusting the furniture, and the third had the windows and the laundry. They rotated and inspected each other's work – just like in the Army. They probably had the cleanest apartment in the complex. They played pranks on each other and did practically everything together. Their poverty and deprivation didn't bother them much.

Tony had brought him some good luck. He was doing well and had fun in school. Northwestern, Washington, and Duke sent him the "second part" of their two-part application system, which meant he had a fifty percent chance of being selected. The University of Illinois requested an interview. His confidence soared again, and the "what ifs" vanished. The individual attention from all his professors, without exception, and the noble competition, with a comfortable comradery, cultivated a sense of belonging. A devastating blow from an "F" in the Biochemistry test was averted after Dr. Evans, the Professor and Chairman of the Department called him to his office for an explanation of his failure. He pointed out to Dr. Evans that he had given the correct answer to a question worth forty points, but he was given a zero.

"But you don't tell us how you arrived at your answer. Do you know how?"

"Of course, I do," Lampis replied confidently.

"All right, show me on the blackboard," Dr. Evans requested.

Lampis went to the board, traced all the reactions and equations out in detail, and turned to look at Dr. Evans, who simply put a 4 in front of the 0 on the paper and in his book and announced, "It's an A-minus. I'll see you in class."

He left wondering whether any other school supported students as much in realizing their potential. His prayers that he remained here for Medical School became almost obsessive.

The interview at the University of Illinois almost assured him of his acceptance. He made certain that they had his new address by requesting and tearing up the old cards. His optimism from his interview at the University of Chicago was more cautious.

The quarter was over before he knew it and just in time for work at the post-office. He was discouraged when told that he had to report every morning, that they were not hiring for the entire holiday season. He found work every day, even on the day he was to leave by train, for an interview at Tulane University. He was there at 5:00 A.M., shivering in the cold with a couple of dozen other men, when the foreman came to announce, "I need three men to load trucks."

He did not hesitate a moment, not taking a chance for the relative comfort of mail-sorting. He loaded trucks for eight hours, without a break and rushed home to take a bath and change before rushing to board the train at 4:00 P.M. He had a tough time mustering enough strength to get out of the bathtub, and he left in a hurry, without a bite, for the train. He would travel all night. The interviews were scheduled for 8:00 A.M. the next day.

He made it to the train, just in time, running at full speed from the ticket counter. His only luggage was his shaving kit. He walked the aisle panting and looking for an empty seat so he could stretch and relax, but not finding one, he finally sat next to an old man, across from a very pretty young woman. He hoped that this old man would fall asleep and let him sleep also. It wasn't to be. No sooner than the train pulled out of the station, his seatmate retrieved a half-pint of whiskey out of his breast-pocket, took a prolonged slug and offered the bottle to him. His polite refusal with a "thank you" and the confession that he had not eaten or drank anything in twenty-four hours (repeated two to three times) offended the seatmate gravely, provoking a demand for an explanation as to why he thought he was better and attracting the attention of all the passengers within earshot. The smile from the pretty young woman infuriated the drunk who concluded that they "are making fun of him."

Lampis avoided further confrontations by leaving with the pretty young girl for the lounge. She was a Sophomore at Northwestern, returning home to New Orleans for the holidays.

When his hunger overcame the pleasure of the young lady's company, he took her back to her seat to make sure he did not miss the call to dinner. The drunk was standing in the aisle, exchanging obscene insults with a counterpart in a woman about sixty years old – she had provided the excuse for him to leave earlier, when she walked in the aisle with a profuse greeting for everybody, eliciting an equally profuse response from the drunk. The conductor took the woman away and goaded the still cursing and threatening drunk to his seat. The young man from Notre Dame, sitting directly in front, finally stood up and smashed his fist in the drunk's face. The conductor returned, apologizing to everybody, and took the drunk away.

Lampis had missed the call to dinner, but there was a snack car about six cars to the front, he was advised. He left the girl to go to the snack bark to get something to eat. First things first? Hardly. He was famished.

He found the car and sat at the counter, only to be told "Sorry, mister, can't serve you."

"But I thought you served until eleven," he protested.

"We are, but not you, mister," he was told again, firmly.

"Why not? I am hungrier than any of these people here. I am starved," he remonstrated with a smile, adding, "I'll pay!"

"Do these people look like you, Mister? Look around."

Only then did he realize that they were all black. Quickly he replied, "Yes, they're all human beings, like me. The only difference is that they're eating and I am not."

The man looked at him intently for about a minute and finally announced slowly," All right, Mister, I'll serve you, but you pay now, and if a conductor comes through the doors, you just leave; we're in Tennessee, Mister, and this car is for Negroes only."

A young man was posted at one door and charged with the responsibility to "watch both doors and give the signal, if a conductor was coming." His hunger was suppressed – the best tasting ham sandwich he ever had! – but his indignation was irrepressible. He walked back to his seat slowly. He was tired, too. Everybody was sleeping. He had the seat all to himself, with the drunk gone, and the clanking of the wheels soon lulled him to sleep – a deep, dreamless sleep.

Stiff and sore at about 4:00 P.M., he bid goodbye to the pretty girl, after he helped carry her luggage to her waiting parents and headed for the YMCA not far from the train station.

He walked the deserted streets, mustering all his strength for a brisk military pace. His tiredness, anxiety for the interviews, and flashes of all his momentous experiences in the last twenty-four hours left no room for reflections from the encounters with a man sleeping on the sidewalk, his back against the wall, or with the two young women giggling and supporting each other in their unsteady steps with high heels (these images came back vividly, later, when Nick and Tony asked him about his impressions from New Orleans). He paid four dollars for the upper bunk in a four-bunk room, at the YMCA, but the groans and moans of the man below kept him awake.

The sights of New Orleans in daylight with the street-car and bus rides to the campus of Tulane University stimulated him to full alertness and self-assurance. Each of the three interviewers seemed reassuring, particularly the last, who wanted to know what he thought of the causes of the great schism between the Catholic and the Eastern Orthodox churches and emphasized, at the end, that a "B average at the University of Chicago is equivalent to an A+++ at any other school." The two other candidates, from Texas, that he met between interviews, seemed subdued. They gave him a ride to the city and parted company.

His desire to see more of the city, before leaving in the afternoon was curbed by tiredness. He went to a movie instead, but all he saw was the part of the newsreel in which the Chicago Bears were humiliated by the New York Giants in the Championship game. He slept for two-and-one-half hours at the movie and all the way back to Chicago on the train.

CHAPTER 24
New Horizons

TONY AND NICK WERE ASLEEP when he returned from New Orleans. He was asleep when they left for work. He was awakened at eight o'clock by a telephone call from the House Mother of the B-J Dormitories at the University of Chicago.

"You have a letter here, from the University of Illinois Medical School."

"I'll come get it," he replied, aroused to full alertness. He checked his excitement at the thought that "it must be a letter of acceptance," and rushed out for an encounter with the "big moment."

"Congratulations," the letter started. The rest was read at a glance.

"I made it," he declared uninhibitedly to the House Mother, pointing to the letter.

"Congratulations," she said.

He raced across the Midway and down 59th Street to Cottage Grove for the bus. The wait for the bus was too long, the bus ride too slow, and the train was too slow. He read "Congratulations" on every page of the *Sun-Times*. He raced to the empty apartment, dropped on his knees as soon as he entered and stretched his arms heavenward to cry, "Thank you God, thank you!"

He couldn't wait for Nick and Tony to come home to share his joy with them. He called Uncle Nick whose voice crackled with his congratulations. He wrote his parents, full of excitement, a brief letter. He could not concentrate. He went for a walk to the Lake and barely managed to keep from shouting, "I made it. I made it!" The drab apartment building looked elegant. The bundled-up old ladies, pushing their carts, looked beautiful.

Nick and Tony hugged him, kissed him and cried. They shared his joy fully that day, and the next day, when a telegram came from Tulane, and the following day when yet another acceptance came from the University of Cincinnati. And just to think that he was afraid that he may not make it. Had he ever had, or will he ever have, a happier Christmas Holiday? He had two weeks to answer. He decided to wait until he could talk to Dr. Dorothea Miller before sending a fifty-dollar money order to hold his place.

Dr. Miller congratulated him warmly and requested that he allow her to "Think about it until tomorrow."

His telephone rang at 1:00 A.M. some ten hours after he talked to Dr. Miller.

"Congratulations," Dr. Miller announced, "You've been accepted at our Medical School. We want you to stay here. Dean Ceithaml wants to see you at eight o'clock this morning."

"Thank you, thank you," he kept repeating even after he hung up and rushed to wake Nick and Tony. They stayed up for two hours, too excited to go back to sleep, sometimes talking, sometimes just smiling at each other, and all together asking, "Why did Dean Ceithaml want to see him first thing in the morning?"

Dean Ceithaml's fatherly smile, warm handshake, and laconic expressions inspired unconditional trust and a vow to never disappoint this man. "Congratulations on your acceptance by our Medical School. You are one of five students who have been selected for the Basking Scholarship; that includes full tuition plus one hundred dollars," Dean Ceithaml announced. He paused, "If you need any assistance, financial or otherwise, you just let me know."

The handshake conveyed heart-felt congratulations, re-assurance and confidence. "I want to see you again, in about a month. Goodbye!"

Lampis struggled to put together a few words to express his gratitude, appropriate for Dean Ceithaml, and managed to say, "Thank you, sir. I will strive to prove that I deserve this honor and faith in me."

He floated down the stairs, glided across the street, heading east on Ellis Avenue to his Microbiology class and burst into the classroom. "I am in, I'm in Medical School here, with a scholarship, too!" He wanted to share his joy with everybody, he could not contain it. Everybody looked beautiful, even the girl that Richard was "going to marry to ensure making it to school and to work on time, every morning."

He made no attempt at moderating his excitement or at controlling his impatience to go home for a celebration with Nick and Tony and for his sacred obligation to write to his parents.

Uncle Nick, Dr. Argoe, Mr. Savoy and all his friends, whom he called after the initial jubilation with Nick and Tony, were "very proud" of him. After the letter to his parents, he wrote to all the other schools, with the proper expression of gratitude, to withdraw his application. The suspense had ended. He had scaled new heights and looking back, appreciated the steepness of the climb more than at any other time. A few months less than six years ago, he had been dashing to the American Consulate, the Police Department, the Exit Department and finally to the Sea-port in a frantic effort to escape from despair and to keep a distant dream in sight. He had succeeded in escaping then, and in pursuing his dream. He had drawn strength from his parents' sacrifices and faith in him, and he had been sustained by the resolve to ignore the obstacles of discrimination and deprivations. He had found inspiration in Nick Demos's, Dr. Argoe's, Mr. Savoy's, Mr. Anderson's, and Mrs. Karanikas's support, and he had looked for sustenance in the encouragement from his friends during the most difficult years. They all shared his joy. His gratitude was extended to all of them, individually, and collectively. His dream of gliding over the apple orchard, in full blossom, returned, and his daydreams occupied a great deal of the time in his breaks from studying. Four years from now...

The response from Washington University and Duke University was warm and congratulatory, about his acceptance by, and his choice, to stay at the University of Chicago, "a great school," as well as complimentary with the assurance that "we would have enjoyed having you in our school!"

The letters from Tulane, Cincinnati, and Illinois also expressed congratulations and wishes for success or greater achievements. Those from Columbia, Rochester, and Johns Hopkins expressed appreciation for the prompt notification of his withdrawal, as well as congratulations for his acceptance by the University of Chicago. Harvard replied with just a card, "your request is acknowledged." – nothing more. He read indifference or resentment in Northwestern's reply. Had Chicago Medical School received his request for withdrawal before mailing its rejection? "We regret to advise you that the Admissions Committee decided not to consider your application." No dent to his pride from this rejection. He actually enjoyed it! After being accepted or considered by the top Medical Schools in the Country, he's rejected by Chicago Medical School

His euphoria raised his level of concentration and efficiency to higher levels with seemingly less effort. He was enjoying his assignments or projects in the Biochemistry and Microbiology Laboratories, found time to help some of his classmates with their problems, and challenged the assistants to find anything wrong in his work when showing surprise that he had finished already. Concepts were easier to grasp, principles clearer in their analyses, extrapolations not difficult to follow, and reviews shrugged off as superfluous or unnecessary. Doubts about good grades, if ever raised, were dismissed. And the excursions along the shore of Lake Michigan became a ritual in rewarding meditation.

He laughed easier. The days were brighter; and he walked with a resolute pace. The candle that his parents lit at the Monastery while giving thanks to St. Nicholas, after receiving his glad tidings, illuminated his memories of love and toil as much as it brightened his way to his cherished, lofty goals. This euphoria was not lessened by the resentful, if not cynical and hostile, remarks by his uncles, such as "that Masonic, Communist School where they use people for guineas pigs," or "big deal," and by Aunt Helen's all-too-obvious frustration in her repeating "Northwestern, a much better school, wouldn't even look at him;" but a mixture of emotions, ranging from simple disappointment to outright contempt, with a good measure of pity and bitterness, was inevitable. The word "congratulations" never reached their lips, if ever conceived in their hearts.

The winter quarter ended in the way it began, with the rewards of a solid performance and a consequent re-invigoration for new challenges. In the weeklong interval between Winter and Spring quarters, he reflected on events and emotional reactions, ventured into fantasizing about the rewards from the achievements in Medical School, and retraced the courses of evolution of encounters into friendships. He spent more time with Tony, talking in the living room, going for walks or grocery-shopping and visiting friends. Nick was busy with his studies, well into the second semester of his first year at Wright Junior College, joining only during his brief breaks and meal-time. Their conversations ranged from reminiscing to politics to plans for the future. Sports and girls were not included for lack of interest and of means for pursuits, respectively.

The final quarter of his undergraduate studies, with its heavy schedule of four courses – Bacteriology, Parasitology, Histology, and Virology – and new acquaintances among his classmates fortified his self-esteem and confidence. Having developed better study habits, he had become more efficient in the use of his time and he felt tireless. And luck was still on his side. A mere acquaintance in Organic Chemistry last year worked next to him in Histology. Sharing information, exchanging ideas, walking out of the Laboratory together, and eventually finding out that they would be classmates in Medical School forged a strong friendship. He was quite convinced that he performed better because of his friendship with Ivan – he was tireless; his grades "stayed up there;" and he felt more comfortable among his classmates.

The disappointment in Dr. Friedman, his Bacteriology Professor, who refused to change his grade after adding fifteen points from a page he had completely missed, was particularly painful since (a) that addition made his grade the highest in the class, (b) he considered that a gross injustice, and (c) he had liked Dr. Friedman.

"If I were to grade your paper all over again, I may knock some points off," Dr. Friedman argued.

Lampis challenged him with his own logic: "You have already graded my paper, along with the rest, and admitted to having missed a whole page, found no mistakes in that page, and added fifteen points to the original seventy-nine; you have also announced that the highest grade was ninety-nine; I deserve an A."

"You deserve what I give you," Dr. Friedman replied curtly.

Dr. Friedman's response was reminiscent of Dr. Slotky's and Dr. Weingarten's verdicts. On his way to Dean Ceithaml's office for remonstration, he could not help but contrast Dr. Friedman's unfairness with Dr. Evan's understanding.

Dean Ceithaml's initial response "What do you care what grade you get from Dr. Friedman? You're in our Medical School with a Scholarship, aren't you?"

"It's a matter of principle, Dean Ceithaml. It's the injustice."

"The matter will be looked into."

Lampis was sent on his way with a pat on the shoulder.

He found out later that his grade had been changed to an A.

In just a few days, he would receive his first degree, a Bachelor of Science in Microbiology, and gain new momentum for the giant leap into the Medical School Curriculum in the fall.

Dean Ccithaml called him to his office, after his remonstration against Dr. Friedman. "I wanted to say that I'm pleased with your work, that's all," he said, and added, as an afterthought, "only one job for this summer, not two!"

The Carillon bells of Mitchell Tower, of the Lutheran Seminary, and of the Rockefeller Chapel set his soul resonating and carried his spirits to heights beyond the reach of mundane experiences. The cap and gown, put on in the basement of the Rockefeller Chapel, conferred the serenity and solemnity of the event and the exhilaration of victory in a noble cause, and carried him to the gilded clouds.

Lampis marched with the rest of the graduates slowly, silently, reverently, in a column of twos, looking straight ahead, from the basement, outside and inside the Chapel. The sound of the Carillon bells was replaced with organ music. He reflected as he took his seat, that this was the largest organ in the world – equaled only by that of the Riverside Church in New York – and here he was receiving a degree from one of the greatest universities in the world.

He wished that his parents were here to reap the fruit of their labors and sacrifices, and he concentrated in transferring his parents' images and expressions in the countenance of Dr. Argoe, who had gracefully accepted his invitation to represent them. Nick and Tony watched from the side.

The Chancellor's speech, starting with congratulations for a just reward in a strong challenge and a difficult task, continuing with reminders of their commitment and of their legacy, and emphasizing their sacred obligation to persevere in the pursuit of Truth and Excellence, summarized his preoccupations with his obsessions in the last several years. He appreciated that this achievement was just one more rung up the ladder of his climb – high enough for a broader view and for a deep sigh of satisfaction and of humility.

He walked up the aisle and up the steps to the podium to receive his diploma.

"Congratulations," the Chancellor said, smiling at him, giving him the diploma and shaking his other hand. The handshake conveyed a torrent of messages, a torrent that should carry him over boulders and dams, precipitous falls, and torturous routes to tranquil coasts and beyond stormy oceans, in search of the Truth, of the ultimate in human dignity, and of the fulfillment of his destiny.

He could not see the moisture in the gleam of nick's and Tony's eyes, glancing at them as he came down the steps. Nor could he juxtapose Dr. Argoe's memories of his own graduation, so many years ago, to the pride in his protégé. Clutching his diploma with reverence and affection, he took his seat and waited solemnly for the end of the ceremony. He identified with everyone who received his or her diploma and felt the exhortations with each "congratulations" swell to the point of floating his very essence to the ceiling of the Rockefeller Chapel.

The melodies of the organ saturated the chapel and the souls in it with its celestial messages. One row followed the other solemnly, serenely, into the aisle and out to the lawn were embraces, jubilation, and tears of joy overwhelmed inhibitions of propriety. Then hands extended in every direction, with friends introducing friends to their families, graduates congratulating graduates, and the returned smiles made the day even brighter.

Nick and Tony cried. Dr. Argoe exhorted him to "bigger and better achievements," glowing with pride. After a few pictures to commemorate the big event, Dr. Argoe left. His ecstasy would have been incomplete if he did not take Nick and Tony on a tour of the campus to show them where he belonged. They seemed impressed, but his heart sank when he realized that he had left his diploma in the basement of Reynold's Club. The last few hours, with all the enormity of the emotions and the momentous resurgence of dedications, had distracted him from even his most tangible and precious possession.

He appreciated the attendant's good humor as he handed him his diploma, saying, "I'd have a tough time convincing people that this is my name, if I couldn't pronounce it."

His relief was expressed with a deep sigh, his gratitude with a repetitious, "Thank you."

The chatting while walking to the Elevated Train Station and on the train, was sporadic and punctuated by irregular intervals. His thoughts, in these intervals, leaped from childhood memories to more recent encounters, back and forth, from the seeds of his intellectual awareness to the sprout, the growth and the blossoms – the fruits were still to come.

The ride home brought back memories of Marie Wendt, the girl that he met on this train a few months earlier, who had charmed him with her dancing eyes, and who had recently sent him a clipping of "Freddy," after she moved back to Minneapolis. In the cartoon, Freddy was asking his mother to remind him when it's time to marry – Marie writing underneath, "Your mother forgot, didn't she?" And that brought back his parent's image, with tears of joy and pride. He imagined them embracing him, wiping each other's tears, and walking to the Monastery, a half-hour's brisk walk, to light a candle of thanks to St. Nicholas, the patron of their cluster of villages. He tried to swallow the lump, raised to his throat, at the thought that he was not failing them.

Lampis followed Dean Ceithaml's advice and did not look for a second job, after he had secured one in the Microbiology Laboratory – eight hours a day, five days a week, Monday through Friday, and every fourth Saturday. He planned his schedule, for evenings and weekends according to his priorities, and for the first time since his separation from the Army – he would not be discharged until a total of six years from the time of his separation had been completed – he was able to relax.

He enjoyed his job among dedicated, considerate, and gentle people. His eagerness to learn and to please was rewarded by their eagerness to teach him and to share his excitement. He came home to his humble apartment for a Spartan meal, to relate stories from work and to share a laugh with Nick and Tony, or even play a prank on one or both of them.

He went for walks alone or with one or both of them; visited Uncle Nick at least every other weekend, strengthened his bond with the family of his father's grandson, who had just moved from Athens to Chicago and chatted with a friend, Nick Katris, at a produce store. They reminisced about their experiences in the army and mostly shared their excitement about starting Dental School and Medical School, respectively. They had lost contact with each other, after his withdrawal from his uncle's environment, met accidentally again, and now were re-acquainted. Nick had seen combat in Korea but had not lost the purity or sincerity of his personality. He would be starting Dental School at Northwestern.

There was no air-conditioner or TV in his apartment and as a consequence, he saw a lot of movie in the cheap neighborhood air-conditioned theaters, to find some relief from his hay-fever in late August and early September. He enjoyed the respite, but was also impatient for the next, long hard battle. He was still obsessed with the laurels of his final victory. Lying down at night, he would lock his hands behind his head, - an old habit – recalling the procession to Rockefeller Chapel, with all the Carillon bells ringing, and dream of another such day, only more glorious, in four years, when his most cherished dream would come true; he would try to anticipate the new challenges and think of alternatives in overcoming or circumventing new difficulties; and he would prepare for new acquaintances and friendships. Not infrequently, these thoughts continued into dreams after he fell asleep.

He could not avoid comparing this summer's pleasures with last summer's tribulations. Sometimes, last summer seemed to have receded into the remote past or to be fading slowly like a bad dream. The agony of finding a job, the disappointment and sometimes humiliation in being turned away, the exhaustion from going to school and working two full-time jobs – one at the assembly line – and the uncertainty about his future had fostered discouragement and had driven him closer to despair. The encounter with Dr. Majarakis, who treated him to a Sunday brunch for an intimate exposure before writing a letter of recommendation in his behalf, and the highest grade in the Physics course at the Navy Pier (University of Illinois) had been his rescuing experiences. He had stamina to spare, but he had to plan carefully to keep some reserves in store. He avoided expenses beyond the absolutely essential, fulfilling his needs for diversion by a simple walk along the Lakefront or a visit with some of his friends. His shyness with girls served him well in conforming with his frugal plans and austerity. The relative monotony of this summer was a most welcome relief and never reached the borders of boredom.

His brother Nick registered for the second year at Wright Junior College, without his help this time, and plunged into his studies in earnest. Within a week, Lampis attended a wine-and-cheese reception for his School of Medicine entering class at the University of Chicago. He listened to the orientation descriptions of the campus and of the curriculum, and prepared or braced for the new challenges.

He met some of his classmates and was impressed by their maturity, intelligence, and self-confidence as much as by the absence of any signs of arrogance or pretense. The faculty members, without exception, made them feel welcome and at home. He had heard names like Dragsted, Palmer, Jacobson, Lindsay, Evans, and Wissler pronounced with reverence or awe; shaking their hands and anticipating listening to or following their exhortations evoked a feeling of pride and humility, at the same time – pride in the special privilege to be in this place and humility in assessing the expectations of him. He greeted those who came from the University of Chicago – fourteen of the seventy-two – shared his joy with them and mingled with those who came from other schools across the Nation. He felt an instant bond with all of them but made no hasty decisions as to who was likely to be his close friend. He already had one in Ivan. He simply enjoyed the gathering and prepared for the plunge in his studies with a new vigor.

CHAPTER 25
The Initiation

REGISTRATION WAS SIMPLE. The courses were the same for everybody in the class, but he was exempt from Biochemistry and Histology – he had taken these courses for the B.S. in Microbiology last year – and he had to find two other courses. A course in Genetics appeared interesting. He searched for another acceptable course, found one in Anthropology, but a week later, the assignments seemed so heavy or overwhelming that he panicked, thinking he'd have a hard time catching up, and he dropped it. In its place, he chose to work in the Bacteriology Research laboratory of Dr. C. P. Miller.

He had a full schedule and appreciated Dean Ceithaml's admonition to not seek employment. "We want you to concentrate on your studies. If you need help, you come to us. We'll find the money that you need."

Once classes started, with a brief introduction for each, there was no time for reflection, contemplation, or socializing. The assignments came heavy, and the expectations were clear and uncompromising. "You're here because you're exceptional; we seldom make a mistake in choosing our students; we expect that you do your best to make sure you're not one of our rare mistakes." That was the message repeated and reverberated in classrooms, laboratories, and hallways. The initiation was harsh and the challenge called for intense concentration and for all reserves in readiness. His classmates, like him, all retreated to the security of concentrating in the pursuit of their predestined goal, allotting some mostly unplanned breaks for forming and strengthening new connections/friendships – some of which were sealed with the first handshake. Sharing some of their diverse background experiences, mostly at lunch in the cafeteria, or waiting in the hallway before a lecture, broadened the horizons of dreams and fortified their determination to reach the summit in their climb for their destiny. Respect and trust for each other were expressed with eye contact and hand waves.

The relatively small size of the class – seventy-two in all, with seven respectable and inspiring young women – helped in the budding and promising of new friendships and partnerships. The class in Anatomy, with the alphabetical assignment of four in each group, was the most demanding in fortifying individual and "team" perseverance, with frequent summoning of reserves, for the first and the next incision on the body of the cadaver. Exchanges of thoughts and conclusions were limited to the observations with each incision and identification of muscles or organs. Emotional reactions were suppressed – except for one nightmare that was shared with his old friend Nick Demos, who related, in response, a similar nightmare from his Anatomy experience six years ago. The support from and for each other in the team (David, Robert, and Charles) proved sustaining and fortifying.

The lectures and discussions in the Genetics, ranging from DNA to chromosomes, were intellectually stimulating and challenging, with questions and discussions of theories or evidence about the consequences of "mutations," "survival of the fittest," and "evolution" repeated in the classroom and in the hallways. Curiosity and satiety seemed indeterminable in that course; but the anticipated better understanding of "Heredity" was even more rewarding.

Working in Dr. Miller's laboratory had its own special rewards. Dr. Miller had impressed him at the first interview with his knowledge of Greek History and Geography, as much as with his dignity. Margo, Dr. Miller's assistant, was serious, helpful, dedicated to Science, and aloof. Leslie, the PhD candidate cried uncontrollably at the extent of Dr. Miller's corrections and recommendations after a review of her thesis.

Lampis inoculated, sacrificed, and eviscerated hundreds of white mice; smeared and incubated hundreds of Petri dishes; and spent interminable hours looking through the microscope. The most demanding task proved to be the collection, classification, and tabulation of data. "Facts, Organization, and finally Conclusions – no extrapolation," Dr. Miller had emphasized. No room for cursory perusals or hasty conclusions "in this Laboratory or in Science," Margo echoed.

He hardly saw his brother or cousin Tony. He still commuted by the Elevated Train and Bus to the North Side, spent every weekend studying and limited his social contacts to telephone calls.

His first test in Anatomy, coming after a nightmare, was a near-disaster with a grade of C and prompted a stern note from Dean Ceithaml: "It behooves you to do better. You're expected at my office at 10:30 A.M., Tuesday."

He could not decide whether he was more disappointed in himself or in that he had failed Dean Ceithaml. He had no trouble deciding that Dean Ceithaml would not accept the nightmare as a legitimate excuse. (He had dreamed that he had gone back to the Anatomy Laboratory to catch up on his dissection late in the evening. He was alone in a quiet room, with a mellow light from a dangling light bulb. He looked around, shivers traveling up his spine and raising his hair on end. He found enough courage to proceed, after half convincing himself that he had just imagined the movement and the sigh. After the first cut, his cadaver protested, "You're hurting me," and after an interminable moment, sat up, swung his legs on the opposite side of the table, stepped down, and began to walk toward the door, with dissected flaps dangling and with the head still wrapped completely in formaldehyde-soaked bandages. "What am I going to do?" he thought, "without a cadaver? I'll throw him over my shoulders and bring him back; he'd be too weak to resist; maybe I'll have to kill him again, will I be prosecuted? After all, he was dead!" His predicament was resolved by the cadaver who, before reaching the door, turned around, walked unfailingly to his table, climbed on it, lay on it, face up and sighed: "I am so tired!" Lampis woke up in a drenching sweat. He could not go back to sleep. He took a bath, dressed and went for a walk to the Lake at 2:30 A.M.).

Dean Ceithaml's countenance was far less stern than his note. His advice was fatherly and almost apologetic. "I know you can and will do better," he emphasized and added, "Maybe you're working too hard; when was the last time you went out? Go out. Take a break!"

Lampis had braced himself for a stern lecture and firm recrimination. He was relieved and almost elated after this meeting.

He followed Dean Ceithaml's advice and worked up enough courage to ask Elsa to dinner. He had met her stepping out of the bus, after helping her pull her dress down, blown up over her head by a gust of wind. They had talked, as they walked together and for a while before parting – they had parted with the hesitant and non-committal, "I'll see you again."

His prayers for another meeting on the bus had been answered repeatedly, and she had expressed fascination at his work when she visited him in Dr. Miller's Laboratory. She was beautiful, intelligent and charming. She accepted his invitation for dinner readily and with an expression of trust. He took her to a Greek nightclub, after dinner at a restaurant next door, and apologized for both. The next and final date was to a movie where she squeezed his hand and clung to him during a suspenseful scene. After he found out in their conversation and from his classmate and new friend David Anderson, that her father, a Lutheran Minister, had violently objected to her liaison with the son of a Greek priest while she was a student at Augustana College, he felt quite uncomfortable as a surrogate and at the thought of causing more hurt. David Anderson, who had expressed disbelief that she had gone out with him – she had "turned down everybody that asked her," David assured him – encouraged him, to "stay with her. You'll never, ever find a girl like Elsa." (She was David's Housemaster's Secretary, and he knew her quite well).

He did not follow David's advice. Instead, he concentrated in trying to persuade David to stay in Medical School rather than leave for the Lutheran School of Theology on campus.

He "got back in the groove," and before long, Dean Ceithaml told him he was "pleased" and to "keep up the good work." David Anderson and Ken Walgren, David's roommate, became his close new friends. Ivan Diamond, his classmate and friend for the last two years, invited him to his humble apartment for dinner a couple of times. But he still had no confidant. In spite of his classmates' sincerity and the support from Dean Ceithaml, he had not managed to overcome the recurring feeling of loneliness.

He longed for the comfort of a close relationship but was afraid of rejection and kept his contacts at the polite, discreet level of propriety. Nick was too preoccupied with his own problems, kept to himself, and showed little emotion to even milestone events, probably still homesick. Tony was more responsive, but of questionable understanding, and consequently spared of his emotional turmoil. Cousin John, his roommate for the first two years of Gymnasium, had moved to Chicago and lent an understanding ear, usually with the telephone receiver on it, but even then he was hesitant to burden John with his emotional strains, and he let the conversations revolve around memories or problems with John's brother Nick (John, cousin Takis, and he had made a precipitous visit last summer to Flint, Michigan, to extricate Nick from the nets of a conniving divorcee, the mother of two children and the subject of an extensive gossip.) His old, faithful friend Nick Demos, now a resident at Passavant Hospital, was there with the right advice every time, but discretion, with a good dose of pride, dictated that he must rely on his own strength and judgment.

The first quarter came to an end with the holidays. He had fared quite well, with A's in Genetics and in Research Microbiology, and a B in Gross Anatomy. He continued to work in Dr. Miller's Laboratory – research was going on during the holidays, too – and secured a job in the Microbiology Laboratory. He worked at least ten hours every day on weekdays and a few hours on Saturdays and Sundays, but he managed to relax in the evenings. His brother Nick was doing quite well, too, better after the dramatic confrontation, in which Nick's swing of a fist was neutralized with an arm lock when Lampis had torn up the "borrowed" copy of the coming-up Math Test. Nick had secured a job, too, but would not divulge what type of a job until he was forced, with the threat of another wrestling match, to show his hands (he had been hiding his hands behind his back for days); with tears in his eyes, Nick showed the blisters and the bleeding on his palms, from shoveling screws and nuts for hours without a break.

They did not exchange Christmas presents – just wishes, handshakes and embraces. Their entertainment was limited to visiting Chris Sakellaropoulos on Christmas and Uncle Nick Apostal on New Years' Day, to observe the tradition of wishing "Chronia Polla" (Many years, or Many happy returns) for Chris's and Uncle Nick's son, Bill's Name Day, respectively. They celebrated New Year's Eve by going downtown to observe the crowds, returning home after the revelries at midnight, by paying only one fare. (Nick went to the Elevated Train Station, bought one ticket, waited until the next train came, and moved out with the crowd, taking three transfer tickets). His guilt was counterbalanced by Nick's cleverness.

They reminisced again, a lot about Christmas in the past: the tolls of the Church bells in the middle of the night; yiayia's (grandmother's) version of the birth of Jesus; the hiding in dirt huts in the forest during the occupation; the starvation in Athens; the fear of going home during the civil war. They were destitute now, but they had a warm apartment, a bed (they had bought a set of twin beds), their health, the will and capacity to work hard, and a future. They looked back only to see how far they had come and to sap new vigor from their roots. They did not put up a Christmas tree – they could not afford one – but felt no less Christian, with no bitterness or guile in their hearts.

He was back in school on January 2, with a schedule similar to that of the first quarter: Gross Anatomy, Physiology, and Microbiology Research. Waiting on the platform of the Elevated Train Station, in subzero temperatures, on a windy day in the Windy City, stimulated his ingenuity. He had timed his arrival at the Station, to avoid a lengthy wait and to estimate the distance from his position to the door of the train when it came to a stop, to minimize his exposure to the cold. His worst frustration came when two bulky ladies walked, side by side at a snail's pace, blocking his way up the stairs and making him miss his train. On the way to school, he reviewed his notes, planned his experiments, or even daydreamed. He frequently slept on his way home, missing his stop on two or three occasions and paying the price of another ticket to get to the South-bound tracks. On one occasion, a young woman had fallen asleep, and probably in a dream, had cuddled up to him; he woke her up, feeling embarrassed. Blushing, she rushed to the other side of the tracks at the end of the line. He never saw her again. He'd see the same faces frequently, and after a few encounters, exchanged greetings or smiles with them.

He had the same partners in Anatomy; one of them, Bob Anderson, was married and somewhat enviable for that. Another, Charles Attig, was serious and of the same age as he, making the two of them among the oldest in the class. The fourth, David Anderson, who had given up the idea of going to the Lutheran School of Theology, remained one of his closest friends. The two Andersons had an appreciable sense of humor and enjoyed a laugh with him. Dissecting their human cadaver had become routine, not evoking shivers or fright when touching or moving a hand.

In Physiology, he had two partners, one of whom, John Hotchkiss, was so compulsive that they were never able to finish until three, four, or even five hours after everybody else had finished and the room had emptied out. They worked mostly on dogs and rabbits, sacrificing most of them at the end of the experiment. His main regret from sacrificing these animals was that he could not take the rabbits home to cook. He was among those – more than a few – who had some trouble in the first few weeks, with Respiratory Physiology, requiring special tutoring, in small groups of threes or fours, by the assistants and by Dr. Perkins, the Professor. Losing his notes, on one occasion, on the train, caused embarrassment, frustration, and a lot of extra work. Dr. Perkins was wonderful with small groups, much more effective than as a lecturer, and emphasized that it was he that was failing as a teacher, not they as students. Once the basic principles and concepts were made clearer and understood, in those special tutoring sessions, he found the rest of the material and subjects easy to follow. He was relieved and reassured when advised that he did not have to come back for the special tutoring sessions.

Dean Ceithaml called him to his office – he called everybody – just to see how he was doing, whether he had established any close friendships, and whether he needed any help. He was again encouraged to take a break from time to time, meet with friends, attend a lecture in Literature, History, or any field not related to Medicine – "there is so much going on, on campus, take advantage of it!"

He did not hesitate, in response to Dean Ceithaml's question what he thought of his classmates, to state that he was skeptical about the motives of three of them, that he had detected some mercenary attitudes. Dean Ceithaml did not inquire further – he just commented, "We cannot claim infallibility in our selections. We have made mistakes in the past, but we try hard to not repeat them. We'll talk about those three again in your last year."

Once again, he left Dean Ceithaml's office with a buoyant step and a light heart, and he walked out into a brighter-lit path to the future, a secure world, and a welcoming society.

The weekly group discussions in Psychiatry, based on the student's observations and conclusions from their contact with their assigned pregnant women in the Obstetrics Clinics, were intellectually stimulating and fascinating. He began to wonder whether he should become a Psychiatrist. His "patient," a young, moderately overweight black woman with a B.S. degree in Biochemistry, who acted superior to her "uneducated" but pleasant and hard-working husband, was entirely unemotional about her pregnancy, quite blasé, and accommodating. Her husband, in contrast, was personable, excited, and communicative. Lampis was to follow her through her pregnancy, be present at delivery, and visit her at home two or three times afterwards to observe the transition and adjustment. The Psychiatrist, Dr. Aldrich, listened attentively, guided the discussion, and made his own brief comments at the end of the hour-long but seemingly short seminars.

Another attempt at a relationship with a member of the opposite sex ended in a disappointment. He had met Natalie in the Anthropology class and was attracted to her as much by her physical beauty – rather rare on the University of Chicago campus – as by her self-confidence and assertiveness. After two relatively brief meetings, he concluded that she preferred more expensive, if not fancy, places for an evening out, and he did not call her again (He found out, many years later, that he was wrong, and had inadvertently offended her); nor would he try anybody else. Priorities, reality and necessity dictated that he confined all his energy and efforts to studying, with diversion limited to walks, an occasional visit to Uncle Nick, and a movie in a local theater with brother Nick and/or cousin Tony. He still wore the pants with the half-dollar size hole, from sitting two years ago on the bench where the sulfuric acid had been spilled, grateful for the long jacket fashion and cautious to not bend over. His Army overcoat, dyed dark blue last year, continued to serve him well, especially in his walks to the Lakeshore.

The end of the second quarter, with a solid performance after a shabby start in Physiology, was followed by a week's welcome rest. He did nothing more than write his parents and his Uncle Vasiles, take inventory of what he had accomplished, and gather momentum for the third and final quarter of the first year. He had to improve his performance to secure the renewal of his scholarship. He had concluded, from casual conversations, that all the other four "Baskind Scholars," had done better than he had, and that he must prove at least their equal.

He had the opportunity to meet all twenty "Baskind Scholars," five from each class, at a reception by Dean Ceithaml, with Dr. Baskind present. He was impressed with all of the scholars and felt a special bond with all of them, reverence and gratitude for Dr. Baskind, and a growing admiration for Dean Ceithaml. He weighed his expectations of himself against those of him by all who had invested in him.

His new partners in Physiology, one of whom, Owen Rennert, was also a "Basking Scholar," were efficient, methodical, and confident. He enjoyed working with them, exchanging notes, dividing the work, meeting to discuss their findings and even playing jokes on each other. They let Martha try to prove that she was "a better man" in handling alcohol, when studying diuresis, but desisted from reminding her of the consequences. He had to guide her to her Dormitory and practically carry her to her room, with the Housemother on his heels, to ensure that proprieties were not transgressed.

He found Neuro-Anatomy more interesting or fascinating than Gross Anatomy, working alone and next to his old and trusted friend Ivan Diamond! He had no doubt that he would pull an "A" or that he would retain everything he was learning. Professor Gersh, always present, walked from desk to desk, inviting questions. He was an imposing and, at the same time, inspiring figure. The urge or obsession to establish a personal contact or achieve recognition from this man kept him quite busy. In Professor Gersh's benevolent, perennial smile, he read the realization of a dream and the fulfillment of a mission to disseminate knowledge and to cultivate young scientific minds. One more example to follow; another man he must not fail.

He reflected often, on his good fortune at being at this great University, listening to and guided by so many outstanding teachers, and preparing for the total dedication to the noblest profession. Unfailingly, he thought of his parents' dreams and sacrifices, of his conviction that his dreams coincided with theirs, and of a day that he'll walk with them in and around campus to show them "his school." Whenever he had a chance, he walked in the quadrangle just to see groups of students with or without their instructor; sitting on the ground, in the sun or in the shade of a tree, continuing with their "round table" discussions and oblivious to their surroundings; or he'd stroll along the midway, from the Classics building to the International House, punctuating his thinking or day-dreaming with the collection of images of couples with locked arms or hands, of a girl pushing strands of her hair behind her ear, of the grace of Ida Noyes Hall, or of a lone student totally lost in his thoughts. At least once-a-week he met for lunch and a chat at the C-shop with Peter Karavites, "an old friend" from Wright Junior College, now a graduate student in History, to exchange their respective experiences from their studies, to discuss politics and to turn their backs to the entrance to avoid recognition and, consequently, invasion, by "Parlapippas." These meetings with Peter were followed, invariably, by a feeling of re-identification, catharsis, and re-invigoration. They occasionally wondered what "mysteries or secrets were harbored in the mind or kept in the briefcase of the Parlapippas," (blabbering pipe) Adamantios Androutsopoulos, who walked on the campus, from time to time, now approaching, now avoiding students of Greek origin or descent. They were amused by his superciliousness, annoyed by his approaches, and ambivalent about future encounters with this unfathomable character.

The casual encounters with other students of Greek descent, in the classroom, the quadrangles, the C-shop, and the Library, led to the consensus for establishing a Greek Club. The need for sponsorship by two members of the faculty was easily met in the enthusiastic support of Dr. Metropolis of the Fermi Institute and of Dr. Catravas, from the Department of Biochemistry. Before the end of the Spring quarter, they had organized their Club, elected their officers, and planned their activities, starting with a wonderful "get-acquainted gathering," at Ida Noyes Hall. He was impressed with practically every one of the students and proud to be one of the founders. The presence of their sponsors added as much seriousness as ambition to make their Club rewarding and exemplary. He had not participated in group activities since the Army and now enjoyed the exhilaration from camaraderie with intellectual stimulation. He faced the final examinations not only with confidence, but also with a light heart and he was not disappointed in his performance.

One year down, three to go. Most of his classmates scattered across the country, returning to their homes. Some, with jobs on campus, stayed. He returned to the Microbiology Laboratory and continued his research assignments with Dr. Miller. His name appeared in the abstracts, prepared mainly by Margo, for presentation at the meeting of the Federated Societies for Biological Sciences at Atlantic City. He was excited and grateful but also somewhat embarrassed in the belief that he did not deserve it. He still had difficulties in distinguishing rewards from favors. He had worked, but he did not contribute much in ideas or designs in the experiments. Margo assured him that she and Dr. Miller knew he observed it.

He felt at home in the Microbiology Laboratory, learning a great deal about Clinical Microbiology, becoming an expert at killing guinea pigs humanely, with one stroke, and refusing to accept that Ed, his coworker and a Veterinarian from

Estonia, had a drinking problem. He was entertained with stories of Mrs. Kleiber's incredible accident-proneness and couldn't control his laughter when recalling a stack of cultured petri dishes, carried in her left hand with the arm nearly fully extended and the right hand on top of the stack under her chin, scattered in the hallway; when remembering her standing on the windowsill trying to open the window by pulling the lower half up and hitting her chin with it; or when told of her falling among garbage cans on a cart rounding a corner in the hallway. He tried to remember these incidents and other stories Ed had related whenever he was overcome with sadness at the thought of never seeing Ed again, after Ed was fired.

He had a good relationship with all his coworkers, and he always looked forward to a long evening walk with his brother and cousin.

The old lady living directly above them seemed to be getting her exercises by moving her furniture around; who knows, she may have also been studying the vibrations of her windows – or even theirs – by turning her radio or TV on full blast. She hardly ever smiled when they carried her groceries upstairs or her garbage downstairs. They had accepted her idiosyncrasies, but when advised that their rent would be raised, they decided to move to a third-floor apartment, with no one above them, one block away.

They carried their meager furniture up the street and up the stairs, sighing with relief and convinced that the noise from the elevated train, about fifty yards away, would be much more tolerable, even with open windows, than the ruckus by the old lady. He invited Helene to visit him in his new apartment – they had reestablished contact after a year's total silence – and was as frustrated as he had been at their previous meeting.

Incredibly, the old lady directly below them, knocked on the doors of all the other tenants to advise them that "these young men on the third floor are too noisy, bringing women all the time and partying all night," – the same old lady above them in the old apartment had moved in the apartment below them.

Always obsessed with being fair to others, he requested of his brother and cousin to take their shoes off upon entering their apartment and to walk lightly. His old theory that "maybe the old lady is deaf, that's why she turns her TV on full blast," was shattered when she banged against her ceiling, presumably with a broomstick, at practically every movement, however light, they made. After a while of this tip-toeing, Nick and Tony had had enough and decided on revenge – with entertainment. Not only would they move freely and frequently from the east end of the living room to the west end of the continuous dining room, with the old lady's banging under them as they moved, they would also stand at diagonally opposite ends, tapping, alternately, with their feet, and exhausting the old lady with running back and forth, banging at the site of the tapping. Whether she tired or admitted defeat after her unsuccessful attempt to have them evicted by circulating a petition among the other tenants – no one signed it! - she acquiesced.

The lady in the next apartment, whose husband traveled a great deal and who felt safe with three young men living next door to her, frequently left her ten-year-old daughter with them, when she went on errands, and had a lot to do in foiling the old lady's efforts. She assured the tenants that "You'll never find more decent, considerate, or kind young men," and that the old lady's allegations "had not a grain of truth in them."

They returned to their usual quiet ways and were intrigued by the fact that they never heard the old lady's TV or radio at any time after she moved to the apartment below them.

Summer was coming to an end and his eagerness to return to school increased to the level of impatience. He had missed his friends, also, perhaps the more when walking around campus after work. The prospect of Nick's moving to Urbana, to attend the University of Illinois, and of the increased expenses in maintaining the apartment with Tony aroused some concern and apprehension.

How would Nick manage alone? He had mentioned something about sharing an apartment with another student from Wright but had not elaborated. He'd miss him, but he had to brace himself. The problem of maintaining the apartment was solved by cousin John's decision to join them, first at the apartment, and shortly thereafter, at a small house in Near-North Chicago, on Sedgewick Street, with a relative of the owner, Mr. Danigelis – the house in which beautiful Diane Danigelis, the Miss Illinois of two years ago, had grown up.

The heavy schedule with Pathology, Neurophysiology, and a graduate course in Endocrine Physiology – he was exempt from Bacteriology – all with demanding laboratory assignments, proved more demanding than he had anticipated; the additional load of the required Psychiatry course and the elective sessions in Religion in Medicine, the last usually held late in the evening, led him to the conclusion that moving on campus would make it easier for him.

He rented an attic room with kitchen privileges, in a small house on Ellis Avenue, near 55th Street. The landlady was discreet, quite hospitable, and respectful of his privacy; her husband, usually there in the morning, was of few words, civil, and attentive to his attractive, seventeen-year-old daughter. Lampis felt alone, isolated. He avoided taking breaks from studying to prevent the feeling of loneliness from overwhelming him. He distanced himself from his friends, stopped visiting Uncle Nick, made his visits with Tony and John brief, and began to have difficulty in concentrating.

The contact with his brother Nick was maintained with regular, once-a-week scheduled and brief telephone calls. They inquired about each other's health and performance or difficulties with their studies, about their correspondence with their parents, and about any new plans or leads for work during the Holiday break. They could not afford lengthy conversations. He did not voice his apprehensions about Nick's adjustment to his new environment, nor did Nick's usual laconic and mystical answers dispel them.

He was surprised and worried when his landlady left a note under his door: "Nick called and wants you to call him back. It's important!"

Nick did not apologize. "I am worried about Tony who has quit his job, was not looking for work, started to smoke, and just planned to register for Unemployment Compensation. I don't like the company he keeps. You must talk to him in person, as soon as possible. Don't put it off. Call him tonight and plan to meet him tomorrow. Good night and good luck."

Tony agreed to meet him at a restaurant at State Street and Chicago Avenue, the Northwest corner, and was waiting for him, cigarette in hand and uneasy. "What's happening? Why did you want to see me?"

"I missed you, Tony. I long to be with you again. Tell me, how are you?"

"I am tired. I didn't like my job. I'll take it easy for a while."

"When are you going to start looking for another job?"

"I don't know. I'll register for Unemployment Compensation and wait for a while."

Lampis's patience was thinning out. "Don't light another cigarette, Tony! Not now, not ever! Why did you come to this country, Tony? My understanding was that you came to work, not to be a parasite. Look into my eyes, Tony! We share the same family name that's known for hard work, honesty and decency; you cannot dishonor it, Tony! If you don't want to work, I'll find money to pay for your ticket to go back to Greece. You cannot shame the name."

He was stern and did not keep his voice low. Tony's eyes filled with tears, his hands trembling, and his Adam's apple rising to the chin.

The silence that followed was interrupted by the waitress. "Would there be anything else?" She may have paraphrased: "Is there anything I can do?"

"No thank you! There'll be nothing else."

They parted with a handshake and no words. He had no regrets – only apprehensions about Tony's innocence and vulnerability. He must maintain a closer contact and ask for John's help. His words kept reverberating. Tony's tearful eyes and expression of guilt followed him on the subway-train ride, the bus ride, and along his walk to his room. He stood in front of the house, in the quiet of the night, reflected on this last nightmare, and heaved a deep sigh before entering.

Convinced that his feeling of not belonging in this house with this family, was shared, he gathered enough courage to tell his landlady. She graciously agreed that "You'll probably be more comfortable in the Dormitories."

He procrastinated, reasoning that it would be better to wait until the end of the Quarter. Their relationship remained discreet, polite and quite formal. He was embarrassed when the young girl walked out of his bathroom naked, and he wondered why she did not seem embarrassed, a half-hour later, at breakfast. She knew he had seen her! He resolved to be more careful, listening for footsteps before coming out of his room.

He gradually re-adjusted to his new environment, was able to concentrate without effort and for longer periods of time and began enjoying studying once again. He worked furiously at his final paper in Endocrine Physiology and could not contain his conviction that he will get an "A." His landlady was also sure he'll get an A. "You'll get straight A's the way you study – a typical University of Chicago student – did I tell you I graduated from the University of Chicago? So did my husband – maybe we'll never leave this campus."

The appreciation that all of his friends and classmates seemed to have become more serious and withdrawn, also made him wonder whether this was a phase that everybody goes through in the second year, or whether this marked the beginning of a new direction in their lives. They all looked obsessed with their studies, as if this was their last chance, minimized their social contacts, and shared less and less of their individual experiences or pursuits. Still, they managed, without obvious effort, to stay above petty competitiveness, to challenge each other only at the intellectual level and to maintain a relationship of trust and respect. His own comfort with his classmates increased to the level of security. All his sentiments remained confined in thought and deliberation – expression would take more of an effort than his reserves would allow at this time. The indirect invitation from his landlady for a closer relationship, in her statement "I have trouble divining your thoughts," passed unanswered, though deeply appreciated. Perhaps when these sentiments became a burden, he'd look to this serene and perceptive lady for relief.

The quarter was coming to a furious close. Reviewing for finals, writing papers, anticipating performance and comments placed heavy demands on his reserves. The information about the need for "a couple of volunteers" to take part in an experiment with "Room and Board, plus a small stipend," as a reward, distracted him briefly – long enough to make specific inquiries and sign up – from his frenetic schedule. The relief from the financial worries helped in summoning and maintaining his powers of concentration. He'd make the move after the final examinations. His landlady was gracious and understanding, as expected. He was almost euphoric with another quarter behind, the anticipation of spending the holidays with his brother and cousin, and the new impetus from "his experiments."

The disappointment from the "B" in Endocrine Physiology was not soothed by his Professor's explanation that "this would be an A paper for an undergraduate student, but not at the graduate level." He still thought he deserved an A. (Years later, after reviewing his paper, having accidentally come across it in a drawer, he would agree with his Professor!) Overall, he was quite pleased. He was not worried about the renewal of his Scholarship, and he decided not to return to the Post-Office for work.

He was "welcome to come back and work as many hours as you wish," in the Microbiology Laboratory of the Hospitals, with Sundays, Christmas, and New Year's Day off all day, and Christmas Eve and New Year's Eve, half the day off.

He'd have plenty of time to rest. The exchange of minor or inexpensive gifts with his brother and cousin would satisfy the need to observe tradition. Again, a Christmas tree would be an expense they could hardly afford or even think of.

The eighth Christmas away from home was much better than the first seven. He was closer to his goal; he had been able to erase or suppress some of the early negative impressions; he had formed new strong bonds; and more importantly, he felt that he had found a new home. Inescapably, or deliberately, he recounted the milestones in the last seven years and concluded firmly that his good Fates had definitely been at his side and kept the bad Fates at bay. His determination and sacrifices were bearing fruit. He found sustenance in the fruit of his labors, in the faith in him among old and new friends, and in the prayers of his family. This was a truly joyous Christmas Season. He did not have to overcome last year's insecurity or the previous year's suspense. He shared only joy and happy memories with his brother and cousin. He was more concerned about Nick's new challenges than his own. The only shadow was from Nick's uncertainty whether he would "make it" at the University of Illinois. Nick still guarded the privacy of his thoughts, choosing to overcome his difficulties without assistance.

He enjoyed his work and his encounters. He visited Dr. Miller's Laboratory, and he anticipated the beginning of the new quarter with the new excursions in Pathology, his assisting in Microbiology, teaching his own classmates, and the moving to a Hospital room with a sense of impatience.

His visits to Uncle Nick and the parents of his father's godson made the Holiday Season more complete than he had expected. Having not seen Uncle Gus had left a void even after his appreciation that a likely encounter with Aunt Helen may be upsetting or that a simple or goodwill visit may be misconstrued as begging for a Christmas gift. Uncle Gus had paid him a couple of visits last year, suggesting during one of these visits, that he should start thinking about marriage and adding, "A few families, with marriageable age daughters, had expressed a genuine interest in you." Uncle Gus had apparently had second thoughts – or even regrets – about his past behavior towards him and wished to make amends. He had thanked Uncle Gus, asked him to convey his appreciation to "these families, whoever they were," and advised him, with finality, that he was not considering marriage – not yet, anyhow! Uncle Gus had pleaded that he keep an open mind and he "not end up like me!" He had felt closer to Uncle Gus now than ever before, but he could not overcome his hesitations to visit him.

The walks to the frozen shores of Lake Michigan answered his needs to scatter and recall his thoughts, to be totally alone, to re-assert his separate existence, to even be carried away with his train of memories and aspirations, to a far-away promised land. The calls came with the whistle of the wind through the naked branches, the dreams and memories from the mist of the Lake, the light to his path from the reflection of the moon in the water, or the far away city lights. He reached in for strength, stretched out to embrace his escaping self, and stepped from star to star for a wider view.

"Were you at the Lake again?" Nick or Tony would ask.

He would nod "yes" and wait for the next question.

"How far did you go?"

How would he know? How could he measure the distance from star to star?

"You were gone a long time again."

He would wait until most of his thoughts caught up with him – some of them invariably left behind in the mist of the Lake and among the starts, to be retrieved the following night – before being able to answer concretely or connect the question to the questioner.

They, Tony and Nick, indicated they understood him, and he was content.

He moved to a Hospital Room, I-423, sharing it with a patient. Most of the patients in I-4 had hematologic malignancies – Leukemia, Lymphoma, Multiple Myeloma, etc. – and were quite ill. He had known that in advance and had braced himself.

He was instructed carefully, on the scope and goals of the experiment, in the routine that he must unfailingly follow, and in the expectations from him. He studied his diet alternatives, all salt-free, before making his commitment for the same breakfast, lunch, and dinner for the duration of the experiment. He would have no difficulty, he assured the dietitian and the Resident in charge, in complying with the dietary restrictions and in collecting every drop of his urine. (He would conceal his bottle in a shopping bag whenever venturing away). He planned to be away all day, going back only for his meals and to stay at the Library until it closed; the patients, his roommate included, should be asleep by then; he would draw the partition to not disturb his roommate, and he could stay up as late as he wanted; or if the patients were restless, he would go to the cafeteria, in the farthest corner, to study. He had it all figured out and felt quite comfortable.

The assignments were heavy from the first day. No need for lengthy introductions and orientation. Dr. Wissler, Dr. Fitch, and Dr. Spargo, in Pathology, inspired respect and high expectations. Pharmacology added a new dimension to Physiology and Biochemistry, stimulated a new fascination, and scattered the fear of mysticism about drugs and medications.

He did not experience any discomfort when introduced to his classmates as the Assistant in Parasitology, and he looked forward to helping them in the laboratory. Treated with the proper respect and deference by his classmates, fostered a new relationship with clearly drawn lines and defined comfort. He moved from desk to desk, answering or asking questions, explaining observations, or amplifying on some conclusions. He never sensed any hints for favoritism or leniency.

The new course in Psychiatry included the assignment of evaluation and follow-up of a patient in the "Home for the Incurables" with the reports and discussions in the weekly sessions (six or seven students per session). His patient in the "Home for the Incurables" repeated a few times that he had missed him during the holidays and anticipated his return with some impatience, evoking a heavy feeling of guilt from the realization that he had not thought of this unfortunate, half-forgotten, man for more than two weeks. He resumed his studies with enthusiasm and a new vigor, meeting each challenge and rising to every occasion. He enjoyed Pathology the most and began to entertain the thought of becoming a pathologist. Psychiatry still fascinated him, but he questioned whether he may not be happier studying people's tissues rather than psyches. His Professor's obvious satisfaction with his performance made the choice more difficult. The escape from these conflicts was relatively easy with the reasonable argument, "I must wait; no need to rush to make a commitment."

He spent more time in his room after his roommate was discharged and the bed remained empty. He felt far more comfortable in having the room to himself. He could concentrate more in privacy, and the breaks with Naomi's visits were more enjoyable – and longer – than walking out in the hallways. Naomi's purity, sweet soft singing, openness and genuine interest in everything she did set her apart and high above everybody else on the floor – or everywhere! She checked his blood pressure, pulse, and temperature, just like every other patient's (was he a patient?), left the room lit up with her smile, and stopped by, "Oh, just for a short visit," before going home. She always declined his offer to walk her home, after the 3:00P.M. – 11:00P.M. shift, and he always thought, "What a wonderful girl!" They became well-acquainted, still discreet with each other, and he missed her on her days off.

Saturdays were spent mostly in a different room, where he'd drink four or five liters of water within fifteen minutes and have intravenous fluids run at a rapid rate in both arms, for five hours. He was allowed to deviate from his diet from Saturday evening through Sunday evening, and he invariably regained the five pounds he had lost during the week. It wasn't exactly fun, but thanks to his friends who'd come to stay with him, it wasn't that bad, either. They would talk about their studies, their plans, and occasionally about girls. One of his friends, Paul, who was a year ahead in Medical School, confided that he had met a "wonderful, wonderful girl!" who had displaced every other girl that he had ever met from his thoughts. He was happy for Paul – and curious! Paul could not conceal her identity: "She works on your floor," he said, expecting him to guess.

"Is it Naomi?" Lampis asked without hesitation.

"Yes!" Paul replied, his eyes sparkling and his face beaming. "Isn't she marvelous?"

He reached for Paul's hand and entreated: "Don't ever let her go, Paul!"

They didn't say much after that – just smiled in utter happiness. Paul was as pure as she was. How wonderful that their benevolent Fates drew them together.

Naomi looked even more angelic on Monday when she walked in his room and declared, "I am so happy that you and Paul are good friends!"

He took her in his arms and told her that he was even happier that her and Paul's path had come together. From then on, Paul would frequently come with her for a visit, but she still refused to be walked home. ("The Nurses' Home" was four blocks east of the hospital and one block south across the Midway). She had "never hurt anybody and God would not let anybody hurt" her. She was a Lutheran minister's daughter, like Elsa! He and Paul, both of little faith, worried to despair and would follow some thirty feet behind without her knowing, of course, just in case God was "preoccupied" with somebody or something else. When and if she found out, they would assure her that "God had made us do it."

The excitement in the Pathology Course was difficult to contain or express. While peering through the microscope, the mysteries of the diseases were dispelled. The voice of Dr. Wissler, of Dr. Fitch, or of Dr. Spargo, dispelled the lingering, even at this stage, fears of impotence before nature's omnipotence or deities' depths of omniscience and stimulated scientific understanding starting with tangible fundamentals. He refrained his fascination with discipline and restraint, lest he be led far afield by a stampede of his curiosities. Sharing his excitement with some of his classmates increased his insatiability and strengthened his argument that sleep was a waste of time. His excursions from his books or from discussions with teachers and classmates became less frequent, and when pursued more often, were directed to answering questions plaguing him in his childhood and early teenage years; why did bodies become emaciated with starvation and swollen after death? Why did he go out in the hot sun and shake with chills before burning with fever when suffering from Malaria? Why did the scavengers not die from feeding on infected and decomposing carcasses? The inevitable connections of the memories with the scenes of their creation were severed for now, but the links were kept in reserve for a possible future retrieval for some other, useful, purpose.

The understanding of the disease processes, through the microscope, peering at slides of tissue specimens, fascinated and stimulated him; it also transported him to the bedside of the afflicted person to witness the suffering and the fading hope for recovery, to feel the pain of the loved and loving ones, and to buckle under the weight of helplessness. Burdened with these recurring excursions beyond the microscope and wishing to reconnect the tissue with the organ and the organ with the body, he requested that he be allowed to spend some extra time in the morgue, attending and helping with autopsies.

Dissecting his cadaver one and one-half years ago, had prepared him only partly to the process of cutting and removing the organs from a naked body on a table, that had moved or stirred limbs and emotions only a few hours earlier, and placing them in jars. He looked for fortifications in methodical and deliberate actions of his mentors, for support in reasoning, and for fulfillment in the anticipation of correlating his gross anatomic observation with the histological finding and further, gathering knowledge for conquering disease in the future. He kept repeating, "This is a dead body, not a dead person; the person was carried in the memories of his or her loved ones, wholesome and intact; the person could not be cut or dissected," but he still felt a chill up his spine and a light cold perspiration on his forehead. Discussing his experiences and reactions with his closest friends offered a partial catharsis; succumbing to his roommate's curiosity – he had a roommate now – would be sinful or sacrilegious. He did not keep count of the number nor did he retain the names of the autopsies he attended or assisted in; the former might have been disrespectful to the memories of the individuality among family and friends; the latter would have been sacrilege, the name belonging to the person, not the body. But he knew that he "had enough of this" when the quarter was over. Was he fulfilled or relieved? He could not honestly decide. In contrast, he was insatiable in peering at slides under the microscope, and he registered for an additional elective course in Pathology.

The appeal of Psychiatry had not diminished, but the lures of Pathology were more and more difficult to resist. A few "spectacular," according to some of his classmates, diagnoses, from a series of slides only, raised him in the eyes of his impressionable classmates and were rewarded by an offer from the Distinguished Professor and Chairman, Dr. Wissler, for a two-year diversion toward a Ph.D. in Pathology, before completing the Curriculum for the M.D.

Honored and grateful, Lampis requested, "a little time to think about it."

He deliberated carefully and intently but did not solicit advice. Dean Ceithaml emphasized that the decision was his alone. His love for Pathology did not exclude potential rivals in clinical medicine or other fields of research, and the loss of five years (two years during the war, one year between graduating Gymnasium and immigrating to the United States, and two years in the Army) coupled with his fixed sights on the M.D. finally swayed him toward staying on course and fortified him to decline Dr. Wissler's offer. Should his love for Pathology prevail over the temptations from the other fields of Medicine, he could pursue a PhD in Pathology after acquiring his M.D. His gratitude and admiration for Dr. Wissler were raised to even higher levels after his expression of trust and respect for his decision along with an invitation to work on some "exciting Research projects," in the Department.

All this, plus the renewal of his Baskind Scholarship, swelled his gratitude for the benevolent Fates that guided him to this great university, from his obscure, tucked away little village in Southern Greece, beyond his imaginable horizons and unfettered dreams. His father wrote that he made the customary pilgrimage to the Monastery of St. Nicholas to offer his thanks by lighting a candle.

He continued to imagine his parents embracing and looking into each other's tearful eyes with expressions such as "our boy is following in God's paths, in answer to our prayers; may the Lord sustain him"

CHAPTER 26

THE G.I. BILL WAS COMING TO AN END, with the end of this academic year. His savings from the G.I. Bill during the "Guinea Pig" tenure and last summer's work did not amount to much and would soon be exhausted. His Scholarship covered tuition only (tuition had gone up!) and the taxing demands of the clinical years would not leave time for a job. Whom could he turn to?

Dean Ceithaml did not change his tune. "You just concentrate on your studies."

He would continue his course, to the exclusion of practically all social contacts and outside activities, to raising frugality to new levels, to redefining the "absolute essentials." Having survived the long war years, having grown up with rationing of the essentials, he should have no great difficulty. One day-at-a-time, with the blinders well secured against peripheral vision distractions, with steps on firm ground and sturdy rungs, and with the goading of his obsession, he would stretch for the reach and reap of the fruit of his dreams and of his labors. He guarded against distractions and warded off temptations, recalling his appreciated vulnerabilities and not forgetting to redraw the line between skepticism and cynicism.

The frequent visits of Peter, a new friend, to his laboratory desk, though sometimes distracting, provided another outlet for expressing his fascination and enthusiasm with the observations through the microscope and his extrapolation to the disease processes. Trusting that this erudite and articulate new friend, an intern in Oral surgery, would not misunderstand enthusiasm in his explanation for showing-off, he would describe and elaborate on what he discovered in his slides during these brief encounters in the laboratory and later at lunch. Peter appeared well versed in literature and the Arts, with a sizeable dose of conceit, making their conversations stimulating and challenging. The prospect of sharing a room, a condition that Peter had requested for his participating as a subject in the same experiment, aroused some ambivalence and led to his emphasizing that he would not have much time for socializing.

The encounter with Carol, an old acquaintance from Wright Junior College stirred another, unanticipated as well as fulfilling, array of emotions. A timid wave from behind the desk in the Medical Alumni Office as he passed by it on his way to the Student's Lounge, and the look from the deep blue, big, almond eyes, brought back the memory of their first encounter with a Déjà vu impact.

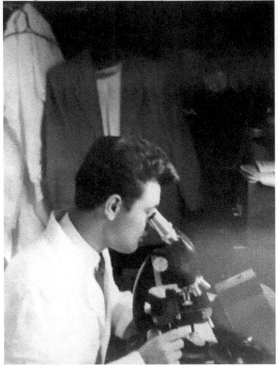

"Congratulations, I heard about your perfect paper in Chemistry," she had called out to him, sitting on a stairway at Wright Junior College, four-and-one-half years ago. He sat next to her, at her invitation, to hear how happy she was, being in love with "a wonderful Greek boy" and that she knew about his scholarship from the University of Chicago. He had been flattered, then.

He was happy to see her again, but he noticed a change in her eyes. Still beautiful, they conveyed a lingering pain and a plea for a friendship. She was a graduate student, living off campus with two other students.

The friendship blossomed routed in unconditional trust and respect. He could read Carol's thoughts and divine what was to follow simply by looking into her eyes. He prayed that sharing her torment with him would help the healing of the wounds that she had suffered in trying to hurt her parents, after their uncompromising objections to her love for a Greek boy. ("His parents also," she emphasized, as if in a desperate effort to shift some of the anger away from her parents, "had objected to his attachment to a Jewish girl"). She was regaining her self-esteem from her academic achievements and from the respect of her teachers and fellow students.

She would look up, from behind her desk, as he approached her office, recognizing his steps in the hallway. He would stop at the door to her office or step inside for a few minutes, exchange smiles, convey his sentiments with words and gestures and turn around to wave once again as he left for the classroom or the Laboratory. He knew that each encounter for a few minutes revealed more of him to her – and vice versa – than others may waste a life-time trying to accomplish. The two Saturday evenings in her apartment, with dinner and conversation, transferred them across the barriers of fear for misunderstanding to a sunlit field of trust. She knew his schedule and his resolve to walk to her office during his breaks, and she waited for him. He had not appreciated that he was whistling the tune of 'La Mobile' every time he saw her until Ivan squeezed his shoulder one day and told him, smiling, "You just saw Carol."

The preparation for the clinical years, starting with the art and science of History-taking and the methodical approach to Physical Examination, carried him to within sight of the gilded cloud at the summit. The white coat with his name tag on the left breast, the reflex hammer and the tuning fork in one side pocket, the ophthalmoscope in the other, the flash light and the tongue blades in the breast pocket, and most importantly, the stethoscope around the neck – everybody must have taken notice – heralded the transition from the books and the laboratories to the intimate or sacred contact and trust of the welfare and life of another, any other, human being and of society. He and his classmates practiced on one another, under the close supervision of their instructors, before their introduction to patients, with the repeated emphasis on gentleness, thoroughness, respect for the dignity of the examined and importance of organization of the gathered information. His blushing and disarticulation after examining an attractive and teasing young woman amused his classmates, but his instructor appeared "very understanding." She had some…murmurs!

His roommate was preparing for his return to Greece. He understood the excitement and anticipation but felt no envy – not even jealousy. The distance between them had increased to unbridgeable and even immeasurable, by any standards, lengths, after the Carol incident. The conflict between his early promise to buy "this guy's" Hi-Fi – he would not think of him with a name – and his desire to erase every memory of him was difficult to solve. Breaking a promise, even to a scoundrel, may lower him to eye-level to someone he preferred looking down from a rooftop. Touching a contaminated object may bring back memories of painful emotions. The decision that he could disassociate this lifeless object from unpleasant memories, or that he could turn these memories to fortifications for future encounters with evil, finally swayed him toward keeping his promise.

He had introduced his roommate to Carol and had harbored the delusions that he would experience a vicarious pleasure, similar to his own real pleasure, in hearing about their evening together. Instead, he had locked himself in the bathroom to relieve - or magnify? – his anguish in sobbing, after witnessing the display of primitive and sadistic gratification at the neutralization or consumption of the prey. His impulse to pounce on this animal was thwarted by the risk of his expulsion from Medical School. He walked out of the room and wandered around the quiet campus. He returned around 2:30 A.M. and found his roommate sleeping. His torments kept him awake most of the night and drove him to another long walk, returning after his roommate had left.

Lampis stayed away from his room as much as possible, leaving as soon as the roommate walked in, with hardly any exchanges or acknowledgements. He could not confide in any of his friends, mainly for lack of strength, and tried to find an escape in studying harder in the library.

He did not know how he'd react to Carol at their next encounter, whether to see her as soon as possible or wait until he mustered enough strength and compassion to comfort her. He became aware of his decision to go to her only when he stopped at the door of her office. She raised her eyes, flooded with tears, to look at him from behind the desk. He walked to her, their eyes locked. He spread his arms and she stood up. He took her in his arms. She threw her arms around his neck. They squeezed tightly and cried together. He wiped her eyes and kissed her hand without exchanging a word. He did not whistle 'La Mobile' walking down the hallway, even after his conclusion that he loved and respected her more than ever. He continued his routine, needed, visits to her, and it was not long before he started whistling his favorite tune again. The roommate's presence faded but was not extinguished.

He could not overlook the similarities between his roommate and himself. He, like his roommate, had come to this country in the pursuit of a dream. He was alone, like his roommate was. He had vowed to go back to the same country when his studies were completed, as his roommate had allegedly vowed. They liked the same music – classical – and they were of the same gender. The similarities ended there. Feeling uncomfortable even with these few similarities, he looked for disparities and kept repeating them. The roommate had been supported throughout his years of study by his family and had spent the summers on breaks, resting and recuperating, while he had been supporting his family and had no chance of contemplating recuperation. The roommate had inherited a Home and was returning to it. He had found a new Home. The roommate was contrasting and separating the past with the present, longed to return, and looked back for security and comfort. While he tapped the past to feed the springs for watering new fields, he gathered momentum for a next leap across new boundaries, and he strained to tie his earliest memories in a well-defined small world with the subsequent whirling and dismembering experiences of his late childhood and teenage years, to the chariot of his visions. Had the roommate had any positive influences? Or had the negative confrontations strengthened his convictions? He was praying for the latter and that their paths would not cross again.

Lampis continued meeting with his friend Pete occasionally at the C-shop, for a cup of coffee and a stroll in the Quadrangles, or along the Midway. Pete, almost an antithesis of the roommate – who, incidentally, had come from the same city in Greece – had never been tainted by selfishness, had an aversion to hypocrisy, and achieved intellectual maturity well ahead of his chronological age. Their discussions ranged from philosophy to girls, with a pursuit of the former and a respectful distance from the latter.

Attending the gatherings of the "Greek Students' Club," with all these frightfully bright and idealistic students, discussing ideas and concepts or plans for a future without end, was re-invigorating and relaxing at the same time. The parting handshakes transmitted strength in both direction, trust in the attainments of their respective goals, and a commitment to stay on course and together beyond the "until we meet again."

"This is my home," Lampis repeated, as he strolled among the arches, gazed at the gargoyles, and raised his eyes to the towers of the Gothic buildings. He was secure within the massive walls, among the stately elms in the Quadrangles, along the Midway from Lying-In Hospital to the International House. A group of students sitting in a circle on the ground with the Professor directing or encouraging a discussion, a few individual students deeply absorbed in thought or in the books on their laps; a fleeting interlude of a smile or a wave with a greeting and the chimes of the Mitchell Tower bells all reinforced his feelings that he belonged here.

The memory of his promises to return to Greece when his studies were ended did not evoke self-recrimination or a sense of betrayal. His studies would never be completed, and he must find the best possible places or environment for these studies. He had no doubt that his parents and family would understand or approve with pride. These thoughts checked his impatience and fortified his endurance.

⁓⁓ ⁓⁓ ⁓⁓

A brief encounter with the family of a young woman, who had stirred, transiently and irrationally, "inappropriate" desires, made him aware of changes in his evaluations of her that he had not appreciated. He inquired about her politely, expressed polite satisfaction that she was in college in Alabama, promised that he would set up an appointment with Dr. Frank Newell for her father who was losing his vision in the "good eye," and wondered about his reaction if he saw her again. He felt in control and was in a position to help. Her parents were composed in their distress, and Dr. Newell was magnificent in his delivering the dreadful, irrevocable message.

"Unfortunately, the destructive process cannot be reversed or checked and total loss of vision will follow soon," Dr. Newell said. "I am very sorry." He conveyed the message with an admirable mixture of sincerity, compassion, and finality.

The parting handshake and mutual respect, expressed in their eyes, made the pronouncement of "Thank you," somewhat anticlimactic.

Lampis had witnessed dignity in helplessness and compassion in a harsh sentence. He reflected on Mr. Chaculas' clinging to a last ray of hope and his strength in accepting the ultimate pronouncement that he must live in absolute darkness for the rest of his life. He marveled at Dr. Newell's gift in blotting out that last ray of hope and fending off despair with one stroke. The interview, examination, and delivery of the ultimate conclusion seemed methodical, precise, deliberate, definitive, relatively brief and yet totally complete. Had it been longer, had the explanations been embellished, had the conclusions been presented not directly, Mr. Chaculas would have been denied the opportunity to assess and understand his own strength – he may have suffered an insult to his self-esteem and dignity.

Dr. Newell became one of Lampis's idols. The list was lengthening.

Lampis talked about his experience with his best friends among his classmates and with Pete. He appreciated the inevitability of his facing dilemmas similar to that of Dr. Newell's and prayed for the acquisition and fortitude to emulate Dr. Newell. Fleetingly, more than once, he also wondered whether his old friend in Alabama appreciated her father's strength and dignity. *She'll probably call me to thank me, and I'll probably see her again* – was this logic or hope?

Whether this logic was correct or his hope was realized, she did call. The conversation was brief, formal, and confined to her father's misfortune; the etiquette of inquiring about each other's studies was not forgotten, and the "maybe we'll see each other in the summer" non-committal. Had Naomi's presence during the conversation – he had taken the call at the Nurse's Station – influenced the tone and the length of this conversation? Naomi's comment "Maybe I can meet her, too," expressed her curiosity and questions: "Who is she?"; "What does she mean to you?"; "Is she pretty?"; "Is she nice?" Her comment – and implied questions – remained unanswered. The comparison was inevitable. Paul was so lucky – deservedly, of course!

The final quarter of the Second year was coming to an end. The approach of the final examinations was anticipated with eagerness, not apprehension, for the final leap from Basic Sciences to Clinical Medicine. He could not share his excitement with his classmates; they may be struggling with the harnessing of their own excitement. He talked to Dr. Peroutsea, who could relate to it, to his cousins Tony and John, who could share it, and to Naomi who could understand and appreciate it. His concentration and assimilation had been so unhampered and distilled that a cursory review of the notes and textbooks was all he needed for the final examinations. He felt light-hearted. His circle of good friends had widened. His scholarship had been renewed. Additional financial assistance, if needed, was promised by Dean Ceithaml – Dean Ceithaml made no empty promises, nor empty warnings, nor empty praises, nor empty anything! He was secure and securely on his way. His goal was in clear sight.

Dr. Peroutsea had been a comforting and inspiring friend. Having just completed her residence in Plastic Surgery at the University of Wisconsin, she took a part-time job as Director of the Employee Health Service at the University of Chicago. He had met her when she examined him for his "pre-employment physical" for his job in the Microbiology Laboratories. She, also, became a trusted friend. Young, attractive, personable, and open-minded, she offered her time and advice without "strings attached." Her laughter always lifted his spirits. Her calling him "Lambrako," an affectionate name only his father had used for him (he had never told her that!), served as a reminder to visit her at work, more frequently than discretion perhaps allowed. Her stories about her youth and student days in Athens, having been spent only a few blocks from his Uncle Vasiles' home, fascinated and entertained him. Her faith and trust in him enhanced his confidence and self-esteem even though he felt she was exaggerating in repeating: "Look, you've got everything, looks, youth, intelligence, personality, the support and springboard of a great University, everything; your future is secure and glorious."

If commitments or hesitation delayed a visit, she'd reprimand him always with a smile.

"I hope it was your studies that kept you away from me. I missed you, Lambrako."

He would respond to her inquiries openly and without reservations. She was probably able to divine his secrets, anyhow. When Tony was sick, she came to see him and was offended when offered payment. He wanted to share her with his Greek friends, some of whom he took to her office to meet, and he shared with them the wish that she and Dr. Catravas, also single, could meet. But he had never engaged in match-making before and felt embarrassed at the thought.

His contact with his brother Nick was limited, at regular intervals, and brief. They could not afford the price of lengthy telephone conversations. He trusted in Nick's demonstrated sense of responsibility but could not totally dispense his concerns about his vulnerability to manipulation by glib tongues or possible surrender to disguised unscrupulousness. Their conversations were limited to exchanges of inquiries about their studies and news from home. Home, in one sense at least, would always be where the parents are. They talked more when they met for Easter, and each felt re-assured about the other. Tony was an integral part of the "Trinity," the separation by distance and pursuits notwithstanding. They understood each other with a brief eye contact, with a shrug of the shoulders, with a hand gesture, or with a smile or a frown. They never argued or even raised their voices. Reminiscing was their most cherished – and cheapest – entertainment. Never mentioning money or wealth in their dreams of the future, never aware of envy for those who lived in luxury, and never thirsting for power may have reflected their naivety or deprivations during their childhood and adolescence but was also salutary in confronting reality. He dismissed comments about biases against foreigners in general and Greeks in particular as remnants of ignorance among the uninformed; he neutralized arguments like "Northwestern University has a quota of five students of Greek descent, even if it happened that the top five hundred candidates were of Greek descent, for the entering class of 128 in Medical school," with the argument "That may be an isolated example." He also dismissed thoughts and arguments that he was oblivious to facts or denying reality. Nick may have not shared his views but seemed determined to ignore, or, if confronted, overcome these or any biases, however prevalent. Tony was comforted in the knowledge of his cousins' courage and reciprocated with the strength of his innocence and faith in the goodness of all people.

The distance from his uncles was lengthening, but his resentment, never allowed to grow out of control, had withered and faded. He had neither the time nor the inclination to dwell in negative appraisals. He was riding high on the tide, with his gaze fixed on sandy shores and sun-lit ridges beyond. If he looked back, his vision would penetrate through the temporary dark shades to focus on the illuminating images from his parents' strength, from the rewards in honesty, and from the lightheartedness after tasting the fruits of his labor.

He had cultivated rationalization only to the point of usefulness, when confronted with difficult or impossible choices. He could do as well in the Basic Sciences part of the National Boards two years from now. He could not afford the one-hundred-dollar fee for the Boards at this stage. Plus, he could use a little rest.

In a genuine effort at reconciliation, he visited Uncle Bill and offered to help out at the store in the three-week interval between the end of the Academic year and the beginning of his Clinical year in the Summer. His sense of accomplishment seemed to gain a special significance from the simple word "clinical," His old friend, John, the drunk, who happened to be there, and was still sober, with his usual perceptiveness appreciated the importance of this milestone and raised his glass: "Clinical! I'll drink to that and your continued success." Lampis thanked him and shook hands with some of the other old acquaintances who offered their hands, smiles, and good wishes. Two older ladies joined in, adding, "How lucky we are, coming here on a day you're visiting."

Uncle Bill went about his business, staying out of it all, and when Lampis asked him again, replied curtly, "We don't need your help here."

Lampis was not hurt or insulted. He understood. Uncle Bill had never learned manners, did not have the strength or the desire to rise above grudges, and probably resented the goodwill he had just witnessed. He truly felt sorry for Uncle Bill and accepted his hopelessness, contrary to his nature. He made no resolutions about when or whether he'll ever be back.

Nick, the realist, who would have probably advised against the visit and the offer, if consulted, shrugged his shoulders. "What did you expect? Maybe you learned your lesson now."

There was no hint of malice or resentment in Nick's response, but the uneasiness about his older brother's naivety was quite evident.

The break between quarters was brief. His confidence after the final examinations was unshakable and especially fortified with the renewal of his scholarship. He chose to continue in the next three quarters and have the final, Spring quarter off. He worked in the Microbiology Laboratory during the day and returned to his habitual long walks along the Shores of Lake Michigan, with Tony and Nick, or alone, to gather new strength for the demands of the next nine months. His preoccupation with the excitement of the adventure into Clinical Medicine, with the thoughts of tomorrow, and with the effort to imagine these shores before the arrival of the White Man, allowed little time for conversation. If he ventured to express his thoughts, he did as if talking to himself, discouraging a response. He frequently forgot to turn back; when finally reminded, he would plead for just a little further. The return seemed to take much longer, in contrast to the trips to his maternal grandmother's, when he was a little boy, and he would, as if in compensation, become more talkative. His sleep would be more restful, and the recurring dreams of his childhood and adolescence, standing on a sunlit ridge without a shadow and gliding over the treetops of an apple-tree grove in blossom, returned. The drabness and monotony of the brick apartment buildings contrasted with his dreams but did not sadden him. Instead, they created the illusion of their being the foundations of a bridge, on their rooftops, to the fields of his dreams.

The visits to Uncle Nick opened the windows for a look at his father in his childhood and youth, raised him to levity and laughter, and unfettered him from the weights of the "what ifs."

No one could tell or invent a joke, dispel sadness, or disseminate laughter like Uncle Nick could. Cousin John would double over, holding his belly and walk away with his laugh turning his face to a red-beet color and finally exploding through his eyes in tears. They'd stay late, and they, his brother and cousin Tony, would sometime be the only ones on the elevated train and the bus – first the train, then the bus – on the way home, repeating Uncle Nick's stories or quips and laughing all the way. Some of the bus drivers seemed envious, some indifferent, and some annoyed.

The interlude came to an end, full of memories, with the apprehensions and anticipations hardly abated – only pushed aside temporarily. Starting with Psychiatry and Pediatrics may make the transition somewhat easier, he reasoned again, grateful that the Dean had approved of his choice of sequence: Psychiatry, Pediatrics, Surgery, Medicine, than an off-quarter, leaving OB-GYN for the first quarter of the final or four-quarter full year. He wondered whether his dream-love with Pediatrics or his love affair with Psychiatry would be rekindled and flare up again to burn his bridges for a return to Pathology, or consume him with desires for adventures into new, unexplored fields. His passion for Pathology was not diminishing, and his return to the Laboratory for research was anticipated with impatience.

Living with his brother and cousin would necessitate wasting two to three hours on the elevated train and buses. He had to use every minute of his time to the maximum benefit. He had assumed that he'd have no trouble finding a room in a dormitory. When told that all the dormitories open for the summer were filled, and expressing his anxiety to one of his classmates, he was informed that this classmate and his two roommates would be glad to have him in their apartment until the fall Quarter, when the fourth roommate would return. Just a few blocks from campus, on 53rd and Dorchester, with his own room, among trusted and respected friends, four more friends in the next apartment, this arrangement seemed, even if temporary, as perfect as he could expect. And just as he expected, his roommates respected each other's privacy and needs, carried out their assignments in keeping the apartment clean and neat, showed the proper deference and respect for each other's friends, male or female, and studied quietly late into the night. The walk to campus, in the morning, was refreshing and stimulating. The walk back, late at night, not devoid of apprehension, with the senses of hearing and vision at full alert, not dissimilar to his experience in his flight from his village, eleven years ago to escape capture by the communist guerrillas.

He had trouble maintaining his early fascination with Psychiatry or recapturing his even earlier fantasizing about being a Pediatrician. The absence of inspirational guidance in the contact with or evaluation of patients and the distance of the Psychiatry Faculty contrasted strikingly with the first two years. The conceived relegation of the relationship between students and patients to the authoritative and condescending, or even hostile, Nursing Staff aroused resentment and created alienation with the consequent total disenchantment. The impatience for "this to be over," was magnified by his friends sharing his disenchantment.

The repeated ventures to divine what was going on in the minds of non-communicative patients and cryptic Psychiatrists added to the frustration and lengthened the chain of "What-do-I-do-now's." He attended the lectures, reviewed the charts, interviewed the patients, and played solitaire along-side his classmates.

The stimulation and whatever excitement was generated came from his discussions with his friends rather than from the attending Psychiatrists – with the exception of Dr. Woodward's discussions that were stimulating, well attended, and – everybody agreed – "made a lot of sense."

Some of the discussions by the other Psychiatrists – Dr. Aldrich had receded out of sight – reminded him of his training in interrogating prisoners of war with the frequent "What-do-you-think of this?" and "What-do-you-make of that?" The growing resentment for the Nursing Staff's assumed authority over the students finally pushed Ivan to remind the Head Nurse that her position did not entitle her to "bossing Medical Students around."

The undeserved, stern, reprimand, individually, from the Dean's office, after a two-day deeply disturbing and depressing exposure with an overnight stay at the Manteno State Psychiatric Institute, added insult to injury and raised a collective indignation and righteous protest.

The dismal and dehumanizing, for patients and attendants, conditions at "Manteno State" left Lampis and his classmates in a shock of disbelief. Here, in the latter half of the 20th Century, he saw hundreds of patients herded from place to place and corralled in narrow spaces; they were locked in large spaces devoid of anything even remotely resembling a human habitat and forgotten by society, family and assigned attendants. The crop of heads, through holes in boards covering bathtubs, with the rest of the bodies immersed in ice, of those condemned to cryotherapy; the fright and screams of those strapped to their beds – and anticipating their turn – in two rows along the length of the room, witnessing the convulsions of their fellow-unfortunates; the images of the torturer Psychiatrist in the form of a plump, middle-aged woman with a heavy accent and a heavier hand in pushing the buttons of her torture toy, after her sadistic assistant stuck her electrodes in the scalps of those whose lot fell for this type of punishment; the expressions of helplessness and resignation of those staring at the high ceiling of another chamber before falling into coma after the second robot delivered the insulin injection offered by the first robot in a syringe – why were they discarded to this pit of oblivion? - ; the encounters with so many who had lost their identity and seemed unaware of their existence; the dismissal of those picked for an interview or demonstration, with a wave of the hand and the suspected restraint for a swift kick; and the tirade, bordering on belligerence and poorly concealed vengeance, of the "famous" Psychoanalyst about the students' offensive and deplorable behavior the previous evening (he and his classmates had played three innings of softball, sang softly to the tunes of Tony's guitar for about one hour, and kept their conversation low to ensure that the other occupants of the building were not disturbed) – all combined to plunge their spirits and hearts down to depths from where even their bellows of despair would not be heard. And they remained silent. The "goodbye" and "I'll see you tomorrow" ended the nightmare for now. He, and he was sure his friends, would not be able to keep this nightmare from returning.

The vindication from the Dean's response, after an objective assessment of the events, did not soothe the feelings for the Department of Psychiatry – nor did the Faculty alter its initial stand. He and his classmates were convinced that the false accusation of being rowdy and disruptive during their night stay at Manteno State influenced, or even determined, their final grade. He did not inquire of his classmates to compare their indignation with his, but his became widely known after his loud protest to Dr. Daniels, an Associate Professor, in the gift shop: "I am not a C student, I do not accept a C, and I am totally disenchanted with Psychiatry."

A few days later, Dean Ceithaml assured him: "We know you're not a C student – and you'll prove it again."

Unfortunately, he did not prove it with Pediatrics, and his conviction that a personality conflict with one of the Attending Physicians, from their first encounter, influenced his performance for the rest of the quarter, was not enough to raise him from the depths of a new depression. He had become defensive, compulsive, and withdrawn. The thought that he may not be suited for Medicine was not in accord with his concepts of a physician, and his conclusion that "maybe I should stay with Pathology" did not provide much comfort. He wanted the conflict to be stronger, the choice much more difficult, and the final decision not at all easy.

He had repeated to his family and to himself, through the years, his dream and resolve to become a Pediatrician before starting Medical School. His fascination with and enthusiasm for the basic sciences distracted him –

temporarily, he reasoned – from his ultimate goal; but the infatuation, perceived as "head over heels" love for Pathology, coming from the temptation from Psychiatry, raised some questions about his old commitment to Pediatrics. He soothed his conscience pangs by repeating that he had not made an irrevocable commitment, that a nurtured dream may also fade when awakening to the challenges of a new love, that he had not betrayed a principle or violated a sacred oath. He will compare the gratification from overcoming the frustrations in fighting disease and curing children with his experiences from the efforts in assimilating the principles of the basic sciences and with his exhilaration in drawing the correct conclusion in applying these principles. He would also look to his instructors and professors for these gratifications and enrich his experience with vicariousness. He would identify with the suffering and resigned child, as well as with the agonizing parents. And if the rewards from meeting these challenges raise him to a level higher than he had risen before, he'll embrace Pediatrics.

He studied "Nelson's Textbook" of Pediatrics; he listened attentively and took lengthy notes at the lectures; he tried to question the mothers with objectivity and compassion; and he looked to the Attending Physicians for inspirations, as well as for traits to emulate. He felt uncomfortable with his conclusion that Dr. Grosman was "detached;" helpless in not being able to relieve or share Dr. Mila Pierce's pain in treated children with leukemia and awestruck before Dr. Dorfman's depth of knowledge and explanations of the most complex pathological processes in simple understandable analyses. His admiration to Dr. Buchanan grew with each encounter. His visits to La Rabida Hospital transferred him from the bedside of the bedridden child to a future with constant reminders of physical limitations, special care, and precautions, protectiveness, and a telescoped lifespan. He understood the disease processes, and he ached when observing them in a child. To soothe his aching, he frequently disassociated the disease from the child, to the disappointment of his instructors and to his own embarrassment. His appreciation of the growth of conflicts, from within and with the inevitable personality clashes, began to interfere with his concentration and, consequently, his performance. The gratification from the "lab-work (Urinalysis, blood counts, stool examinations) fortified his conclusion that Pediatrics had lost out to Pathology. He felt more comfortable in the laboratory than at the bedside, and he longed to go back to the Petri dish and the microscope.

His job as a phlebotomist (blood-drawer) from 6:00 A.M. to 7:30 A.M. in spite of its routine, served as a catalyst for his frustrations, as much as it did in providing a little extra money.

Lampis was disappointed in himself that he was angry at the Psychiatrist's or resentful of a Pediatrician's apparent hostility – disappointed most of all, in that he was unable to suppress the suspicion that his foreign origin was the cause of the Pediatrician's hostility. He appreciated, in a self-evaluation, that he showed more empathy or compassion than objective evaluation in his contact with the

Psychiatric patients, that he may have extrapolated from his own conflicts or solutions, that he should have not allowed the blatantly seductive manipulation of one of the Psychologists – made worse by her being the wife of a senior student he had known for the last five years! – to upset him during one of the last one-on-one evaluations, and that he should have given answers from his own conclusions and not tried to guess what answers his examiners would have liked better.

He was fully aware that he did not make young mothers comfortable, that he tried to emulate the Interns and Residents in their approach to children rather than follow his own inclinations, and that his reticence, out of deference, in questioning the diagnostic or therapeutic process may have been misinterpreted as ignorance or lack of interest. Still, he felt he was wronged, if not deliberately, at least nonchalantly.

The repeated admonitions from the Faculty and Staff in the Department of Pathology, from Chairman down to technicians, and from Dr. C. P. Miler's Laboratory, "Don't be discouraged, this is your first exposure to Clinical Medicine," helped to guide him from self-recrimination and resentment to re-assertion and new resolutions. He reflected repeatedly on what he did or what went wrong to avoid making the same mistakes again, and once again, he folded his wings and sought shelter in solitude in the crevices of memories from past hard blows. He recounted the ways he was able to rise again and to find strength for a new and higher climb. One way was to remind himself that he can do it – after all, it wasn't just good luck that brought him this far; another, that he had to "get angry;" another, to learn from and capitalize on past experiences; and yet another, to discern distractions and to avoid excuses and rationalizations.

He appreciated his brother's and cousin's concern, and he felt remorse that he let them down. Nick had had his own problems at the University of Illinois, mainly strong personality conflicts, and a shaken self-confidence. Tony appeared hurt for both of them and equally frustrated in not knowing how to help.

Lampis was grateful for Naomi's confidence – "I am not in the least worried about you," she had announced without the faintest hint of doubt.

Paul seconded Naomi's note of confidence, and the lift from Ivan's belief in him finally began to tear the curtains of self-doubt and self-recriminations.

He looked for stepping stones in amusing experiences or re-assuring encounters but found them weak for the length of the needed leaps and too far apart – like the baby with the anal artresia, the exhilarated and bewildered mother, the almost comico-tragic sequence of the fecal spray, and the embarrassed gratitude of the sprayed, pretty young resident for covering her with his coat and walking her home; the bet of his friend that he would take the prettiest Resident, Dr. Capour, out to dinner; or his walking past the panic-stricken and pleading Head-Nurse, to take the hand of the belligerent and furniture-smashing Mrs. Storey, to sit next to her and let her cry on his shoulder, and to desperately try to regain her trust by risking the returning Head-Nurse's wrath in resolutely blocking her approach, with a large syringe, to his patient. (Mrs. Storey had become his instant patient, and he found out later that the Head-Nurse's concepts of "inappropriate and obstructive behavior," coupled with the seductive Psychologist's report, had played a major role in the determination of his final grade.)

The solace, coming from his remonstrations, and the corroboration from his classmates that there will be a drastic change in the structure of teaching and guiding of students in Psychiatry, was a major contributor to his recovery from the right-left blows to the chin. He was staggered but was not knocked out. Slowly, he emerged from the shadows of self-deprecation onto his pre-defined path, gathered strength during the break of one week between quarters, and returned into the green fields of his dreams full of restored confidence.

He moved to the Dormitories, Hutchinson Commons, before the start of the Surgery quarter, but his first negative reactions to his graduate-student roommate, who seemed aloof and hardly polite, became stronger than the odor from a stack of pipes in a room with permanently shut windows. His conclusion that his roommate had an aversion to or phobia of fresh air, closing and latching the windows as soon as he found them open, was followed by his early decision within one week, to request a transfer to another room. His heavy and demanding schedule dictated that there must be no distraction.

Luckily, there was an empty room for two, with him the only occupant for the present, and the additional benefit of kitchen privileges, in Foster Hall. He was content and re-invigorated once again, his confidence buttressed by his ability to store and recount accurately the information (History and Physical Examination) from four consecutive patients at the end of the day.

In all of his twenty-nine years, Lampis reflected, he had never had the total privacy he enjoyed now. Of course, he did have some privacy in his first year at the University with his separate room, except for the same entrance through John Schoenberger's room, and he was grateful for John's friendship and discretion, but he still had to be on his guard not to disturb or distract John in any way.

Now he had this large room to himself. He could turn his music on louder when taking a break. He could have all the lights on late into the night, and he did not have to tip-toe when moving around. He did his kitchen-cleaning duty, at his turn, late at night, always after midnight to avoid distraction and interference. He quickly regimented his activities and was pleased with his efficiency. His schedule – and his strained finances – did not allow for much diversion, and the occasional or rare excursions beyond his confines potentiated his recoil into his shell.

Barbara's pure Iowa charm and challenge, after a late dinner in her apartment – he had to call her three times to apologize for being late and appreciated her understanding – and another brief encounter, reminded him of his vulnerability and fortified his defenses. He would simply avoid her. He enjoyed the brief coffee breaks with Edie in open and non-presumptuous exchanges – Edie was engaged, appeared happy, and provided a sharp contrast to Barbara. He found some vicarious pleasure in John's excitement about Connie, and he reminded himself that he must be content with vicarious pleasures for now.

His routine, starting at 6:00 A.M., stretching into the early hours of the next morning, and cramped with unanticipated surprises, kept him "in high gear" and steady on course. His temporary self-doubts had vanished and his self-confidence had been completely restored. His admiration for the miracle-performing, perfectly composed Attending Surgeons, was curtailed only by his determination to compare this admiration with his assessment of the virtues of other disciplines. He idolized Dr. William Adams in Thoracic Surgery, stood in awe before Dr. Vermullen's encyclopedic knowledge, found Dr. Newell's depth of discourse in any field of Medicine scholarly, was impressed with the Senior Resident's composure and the Junior Resident's ambitions, and was reminded of the assumed high expectations with respect and encouragement. Efficiency, competence, compassion, intellectual honesty, dignity, ambition – displayed in the classroom, the operating room, and the patient's room without effort – left plenty of room for discussion and no room for idleness. If this was not having a good time, then what was?

Dr. Adam's invitation, "Come closer, hold this, now look at this," or "What do you think of that?" not only presented a unique opportunity to learn and extrapolate, but also conveyed a wish to share in the excitement. Everything was exciting! There was no such thing as a "routine case!" or "not exciting case." In fact, they were reminded that the terms "patient" or "case" should be used only when deliberately concealing the individual's identity or disassociating the individual from his or her problems. Otherwise, it must always be "Mr. Smith with such and such a problem," or "Mrs. Jones with this or that complaint," – just as they were admonished to be specific, precise, and deferential. The bonds, formed from sharing stimulation or excitement, from example and advice, from guidance and challenge, seemed strong as well as encompassing, secure as well as promising. The illustrious names, engraved under portraits or on plaques, were pronounced with reverence or were used as examples for the rewards in the pursuit of scientific truth and excellence.

Holding the retractors or handing instruments would have been boring, had his curiosity not been continuously maintained and the explanations or questioning of the Attending Surgeon kept his mind racing. During the irregular and unanticipated interludes, he tried to correlate what he was witnessing now with what he had learned from dissecting his cadaver two years earlier or helping with the autopsies six months ago. The bodies he dissected or cut up then were dead and would never hurt again; but these bodies were living and would hurt from his cutting and from what they had endured. He shuddered every time, and wondered sometimes, whether his attempts to convince himself that repeating, "This cutting and the pain that goes with it is helping them," had been expressed aloud. He was reassured when he appreciated that nobody was looking at him.

Lampis had heard "We're treating human beings, not diseases," practically every day for the last six months, and he had seen it in practice continuously. He was beginning to feel as a part of the team, sharing in the efforts, the suspense for the final outcome, and the joy of success. Shaking the hand of the patient and the family, when sending her or him home, erased all the pain and the agony from the fight with the disease. Waving the last goodbye fanned and re-invigorated the strength to "carry on." No wonder he felt tireless. Accepting defeat and surrendering to helplessness was humbling and painful. Repeating, "We did everything possible," was neither soothing nor relieving – and was invariably followed by, "We must keep working harder and harder to reduce these experiences to a minimum."

Hearing this again, after a visit to Bessie Savoy, the wife of his revered Chemistry Professor at Wright Junior College, fastened the blinders against distractions even more firmly (She had pleaded with him to "come back tomorrow," unable to suppress or conceal the pain from her widespread and consuming cancer of the breast). The next time he saw her was on the autopsy table – and a few times in his nightmares.

His desire to gain more knowledge and strength – and to test his reserves – for future encounters with this dreadful disease neutralized Mr. Savoy's suggestion that he not attend the autopsy. He confessed to Mr. Savoy, much later, that he had not followed his suggestion and that he walked out after one quick look, omitting the description of the shivers at the sight of yesterday's expressive and today's lifeless face. Can anyone, he wondered, fortify or buttress himself enough for this kind of encounter? Or would he ever challenge himself in this way again?

His acceptance of an invitation for a cup of coffee, during a brief break, after an exhilarating experience in Dr. William Adam's operating room, by a simple, pleasant and fatherly, inquiring man, was rewarded by an undreamed-of-encounter. Answering this gentle man's inquiries while walking with him in the hallways, he had been unable to check his wish to catch a glimpse of the famous man after hearing the greeting "Good morning, Dr. Huggins," and was content with the knowledge where Dr. Huggins worked.

He continued to wonder "What Dr. Huggins looked like," riding the elevator down. He had graciously accepted the offer of his companion to "Just have a seat, I'll treat today," and answered more questions about his origin, his past, and his plans, while sipping coffee. When a distinguished, gray-aired professor walked to their table and addressed his companion as "Dr. Huggins," he instinctively stood up and felt awestricken that his companion was none other than Dr. Huggins.

Dr. Huggins stood up also, not instinctively, but comfortingly, and offered his hand: "Yes, Dr. Anagnostopoulos, I am Dr. Huggins; let's sit down and enjoy our coffee and each other's company for the remaining few minutes."

Lampis managed, in those few minutes, to tell the attentive Dr. Huggins that he had come from Greece alone in the pursuit of a dream; that his dream had never included a treat from Dr. Huggins, and that he was thrilled from his exposure to Surgery, and that he prayed he would never fail his patrons and his mentors.

He took his leave, along with the advice of Dr. Huggins, "Keep a reign on your dreams and look for the greatest thrills in scientific discovery." He carried the emanation of warmth and trust in the clasp of his hand by both Dr. Huggins' hands, and floated out of the cafeteria, through the hallway and up to the classroom for the lecture.

"Who was the distinguished gentleman you were sitting with in the cafeteria?" asked Ivan when he sat next to him.

"Oh, that was Dr. Charley Huggins," he answered nonchalantly as he could manage.

"Do you know Dr. Huggins?" Ivan could not contain his excitement. "He was a Nobel Prize winner."

"Now I do! He bought me coffee."

"You have to tell me all about it after the lecture."

Neither one could wait. After Ivan, he enjoyed immensely repeating his story to some other friends.

The weeks rolled by, one after another, and his knowledge, excitement and confidence snow-balled. He anticipated the oral examinations, at the end of the quarter, with less apprehension than some of his classmates. And he felt a big boost when one of the better and hardest working students confided in him that his answers to a "hypothetical case" were not correct or even close.

"Can you, are you at liberty to tell me about the hypothetical case?" After he was told the case, he asked his friend "Was one of your answers 'spontaneous pneumothorax?' That's the only correct answer."

His friend was devastated. "How did you know?"

"Just think: 22 years old, healthy male student…"

His friend left and came back inconsolable. "You were right. Why didn't I think of it?"

"Maybe because you were too tired and uptight; did you sleep at all last night?" (He remembered that this friend had slept for twenty-three hours and, waking up Sunday morning, missed the final exam in Pharmacology, having not slept, rumor had it, all week preparing for the finals).

His own oral exams the following day were "a breeze" and brought smiles from his examiners.

"You weren't worried, were you?" asked Dr. Rigler and added, without wating for an answer: "If you were, I'd be disappointed."

He had two full weeks to rest between the fall and the winter quarter, during the Holidays. He would work in the Microbiology Laboratory, every single day, but knowing his work and being in a comfortable environment would contribute to relaxation and recuperation. He would register for the next quarter on Friday afternoon, after the final oral examinations. He did not anticipate a fateful encounter.

CHAPTER 27

LAMPIS RAISED HIS EYES, after filling the registration forms, and met the eyes of the young woman sitting across the desk. They exchanged smiles, introductions and handshakes, looking into each other's eyes while he was trying to divine whether she was "for real" and what she was thinking.

"I'm free for a piece of pie and a cup of coffee. Are you?" he asked her.

She was.

Their hands locked. They walked across the Quadrangles, talking, stopping to look at each other, smiling, stretching their joined hands to avoid stepping in a puddle, and heading for the C-shop. Had the manager not reminded them that "the C-shop closes at 9:00 P.M.," they may have spent the entire night talking. A small piece of pie and their conversation suppressed the pangs of hunger and all other thoughts, except those for each other.

She remembered that she was leaving for home, Philadelphia, early in the morning. He walked her to the Dormitory, across the street from his own. They parted with a gentle, fleeting, timid kiss on the lips, with her promise that she would call him on January 2, the day of her return, and with his swirling emotions. Had he ever experience this all-consuming emotion before? He was sure he hadn't. Would he be able to sleep tonight? To his surprise the next morning, he had slept soundly. Not to his surprise, she kept displacing all other thoughts the next day and every day. He could not wait for January 2. He could not stop talking about her, repeating the same expressions to whomever was listening and entertaining Nick and Tony, who began to tease him: "Tell us about Judy; how many days? We lost count."

He was not surprised when he returned to the Dormitories, after the orientation and assignments to the various services of Internal Medicine, to find a new roommate. Robert, a graduate student in Economics, having just come from the University of Minnesota, seemed reserved, polite, private, and apprehensive. They exchanged formalities, each re-assuring the other "You'll do well. Don't worry. You're here, aren't you?" and went their separate and not-so parallel ways.

The impatiently awaited telephone call did not come. The phone at the end of the hallway rang a few times, but each time it was for someone else. Maybe tomorrow night. He knew that he would not return to his room until late in the evening, and he hoped that she remembered to page him at the Hospital if she could not find him in his room.

His schedule was quite heavy; Lecture at 7:00 A.M., every weekday; teaching rounds from 8:00 A.M. to noon; the "noon Lecture" from 12:00 to 1:00; and finally, the work-up of the assigned patients with complete History and Physical examination, blood counts, urinalysis, review of all other Laboratory studies, the write-up with the long Differential Diagnosis, and the recommended additional studies to establish the Final Diagnosis and to rule out all other possibilities. The mid-afternoon Lectures were optional but few dared not to attend.

The average number of new patients they would have to work-up, they were told, would be forty-five, or about four per week, in the twelve-week quarter. The preparation to organize the acquired information, to list the Differential Diagnoses in their order of likelihood, from the most to the least, and to prepare the arguments in defense of their conclusion would require concentration, thinking, and extensive reading.

He was assigned his first patient next day, and he had to hold his ground in the salvos of cross-fire from the Intern, the Resident, and the Attending Physician the following day. He sought shelter in the Library to lick his wounds, to soothe his bruises, and to forget his stings by reviewing and expanding on what he had learned.

His old, reliable friend, Ivan, tried to assure him, "You did OK, better than OK," but he was staggered.

If only Judy would call. She still had not called. He ran to the nearest phone in the Hospital when paged and to the Dormitory phone when it rang, only to hang up or turn it over to another student, heavy hearted, every time. He did not have her number; she was going to move to an apartment and he did not have the new number. What happened? Had she not come back? Was she ill? Did she simply forget about him? Or worse yet, could she be amusing herself wondering how he'd be running to the phone?

Again, Ivan asked him to be patient, "She'll call. Just wait."

Lampis was in the Student Lounge for a brief respite of classical music and relaxation when he heard his page. It was not she.

"You have a new patient," the lady in charge of assigning patients to students said. "Her name is Judy Harness. She's in room I-324."

"Her name is what?" he asked, feeling stunned.

She repeated it slowly.

"Coincidence," he said, trying to reassure himself. "How old is Judy Harness?" He tried to fortify himself by repeating the name.

"She's 24," the lady replied, accommodatingly. "Still a coincidence?"

His heart began to throb. "What does Judy do?" he managed to ask again, after a pause for composure.

The lady had not hung up. "Doctor," she replied, "you can ask all of your questions to Judy."

"Please," he intoned, "I may know her."

"She's a student, a graduate student."

He felt a light, cold perspiration and his strength draining. "Where?" he asked, praying she was from Northwestern, or Loyola, or the University of Illinois, or even farther.

"At this University," she said, and added compassionately, "Do you know Judy?"

"I think I do, thank you." He hung up. He sat on the closest chair, recapturing flashes of their conversation, her smile, her green eyes, the touch of her hand. "That's why she did not call. She is in I-324. Maybe it's something minor and they did not have any other room for her. Or maybe there is another twenty-four-year-old graduate student at this University named Judy Harkness. Oh, my God." He was beginning to face the pain after feeling stunned. He walked to the student directory and looked at it. "H comes before G, and before I; I-324; and before J, oh yes, Judy, no-, no-, no-, back to H; only one Harness, Judy." He looked again. Just one.

He called Ivan. "Could you come to the Student Lounge?"

Lampis did not wait long.

"What's up?" Ivan's concern was apparent.

"Remember Judy, the girl I was talking to you about?" He was inarticulate. "She's a patient in I-324, and she was assigned to me. I was assigned to her. I can't take her!"

"I'll take her; maybe they put her there because there was no other room in the Hospital." Ivan was reading his thoughts. "I'll go see her now. I'll call you when I'm finished."

"OK, thanks, Ivan. It couldn't be!"

What could he do in the next hour or so? He went for coffee. It tasted terrible, and everybody was so unfriendly. He went to the Library but could not concentrate. What could he talk about if he went to the Microbiology Laboratory? He went to the Bookstore, the Humanities section; "Oh yes, *Vanity Fair*. What was it about? The Greek Tragedies. I am Greek. Is this not a tragedy? Aristophanes – how insensitive!"

Lampis returned to the Student Lounge, sank in an easy chair and waited for Ivan's call.

"This is WFMT, 98.7 on the FM dial. We have just heard Beethoven's 6th, the Pastoral. Eugene Ormandy conducting, and the Philadelphia Orchestra."

Did he hear it? That was the first record he ever bought!

"Hi Pete. I'm OK."

Pete had not responded to his greeting, then asked: "Are you OK?"

"Yeah, I'm OK. How are you? I'm waiting for Ivan to call me."

Pete seemed unsure that he was "OK" but chose to leave him in his deliberations whether or not he was "OK."

He picked up the phone before the second ring: "Ivan? I'll wait for you here in the Student Lounge." He walked to his chair, then turned around and walked to the hallway, facing the East end from where Ivan would be coming.

"What's taking him so long?" He chased all thoughts away, blank, void, abysmal. Weightlessness but nailed to a dead tree-trunk, swaying with the gusts of the memories and dreams of two weeks ago.

Ivan walked toward him, with a sterile stare just in front of his feet. After feeling the bond of friendship and the empathy from Ivan's hand on his shoulder, unable to wait longer, he asked, "Did you see her?"

"Does Judy mean much to you?"

"I haven't thought of anything else since I met her. She's the one, Ivan!"

Ivan squeezed his shoulder. "Brace yourself. She's a very sick young woman," he articulated slowly, and stopped.

"Is it leukemia? Acute? Myelogenous? What's her hemoglobin?" He chased after his questions, not waiting for Ivan's reply. He stopped, held his breath and faced Ivan. "Is it?" he implored and waited this time.

Ivan took his time. "It is! Acute Myeloblastic leukemia, with extensive infiltration of her breasts. The diagnosis was established from a breast biopsy." Ivan stopped and seemed to be struggling to find something more to say.

The admonition, "brace yourself," kept reverberating, now faint, now forceful, until interrupted by an echo from far away.

"She asked me whether I knew you. I told her we're close friends."

The echo stopped somewhere in the immense void between the two friends.

"What?" he asked. "Of course, we're close friends."

"She wants you to wait a couple of days before you go to see her. She needs a little time. You come to dinner with us tonight. I'll call my wife. In the meantime, get busy, find something to do."

"She's going to die, Ivan!" The answer came with a firm squeeze on the shoulder and it meant, "brace yourself."

Lampis declined the offer for dinner. Instead, he went to the Library and stayed until ushered out at 11:00 P.M., when the Library closed, reading everything he could find on Acute Myeloblastic Leukemia. Back in his room, he reviewed the chapter in his textbook and decided it was…a good summary. He did not wish to burden his roommate who appeared worried.

The four hours of sleep, from 2:00 A.M. to 6:00 A.M. seemed to have not interrupted his thinking, having been restless, dreamless and merciless. He did not recall how he arrived at the classroom, nor anything after going to bed last night. He sat next to Ivan, as usual.

Instead of saying "Good morning," he sputtered, "It's so terrible, are her parents here?"

Ivan nodded. "Yes, her parents flew in from Philadelphia last night."

Somehow, he had no difficulty concentrating during the lecture or later during the discussion with rounds. Ivan thought he was exceptionally sharp and on his toes. But he seemed to have run out of reserves halfway through the noon lecture. He was distracted by the slightest noise and annoyed by the snoring or the sight of the diversity in slumping of those who had fallen asleep. He even felt self-contempt for having found amusing, in the past, this sonorous somnolence, and the undecipherable notes taken during those noon lectures. The biting into the apples and crunching of the lunch bags were particularly offensive and sacrilegious. He didn't get much out of this lecture.

The new patient, assigned to him in the afternoon, taxed his patience with his long stories in answer to the simplest questions, but the time spent in taking a complete history and, later, in selecting the pertinent information for his write-up, kept his mind from focusing on Judy. He stayed up late again, concentrating or organizing his thoughts for the arguments in support of his final Diagnosis, against all other differential Diagnoses, and for the quiz to follow.

When finished, yesterday's events crashed on him with a full force. "It cannot be true! It was just a dreadful dream!"

Denial didn't help. If he could just cry.

The repeated gusts of wind, the occasional noise of a passing car, the tick-tack of his alarm clock would not let him go to sleep. When awakened by his alarm clock, he decided he had just fallen asleep. He lay in bed, with his hands locked behind his head, eyes closed, and mind blank for another half-hour.

Lampis rushed off, remembering that he had not had his cereal after he arrived at the Hospital. During the lecture, he rehearsed his presentation and responses to anticipated questions. Still, he managed to take a few notes and exchange a few whispers with Ivan. He did not join in the laughter after a witty remark by the lecturer. He looked at Ivan with gratitude for understanding. They walked the hallways to meet with their "attending," talking abstractedly about the lecture. Not a word about Judy. Thinking about her was painful enough – and both knew that the other was thinking about her.

He presented his patient, careful to emphasize the pertinent information, to avoid wordiness or repetition, and to establish the premises for his conclusions. He was interrupted quite frequently and politely for clarification of a statement, but his train of thought was not derailed. In the quiz that followed, for a good half hour, he held his ground. The Attending Physician, the venerable and benevolent Dr. Wright Adams, seemed pleased with his organization, presentation, and answers. Ivan was proud, and Ellen, the third member of the "three-student group" told him that she'd be glad if she performed half as well the next day. The Resident and Intern nodded approvingly. Fleetingly, he thought, "Judy will be proud of me, when Ivan tells her," and he choked.

During the noon lecture, he was so absorbed and took notes furiously, that he was surprised when he heard the customary "Any questions?" signaling the end of the lecture.

After a brief respite and a hot dog, with Ivan at the Gift shop, he started for the Library when he heard his page. He picked up the phone.

"This is Dr. Herbelscheimer, how are you?"

"Fine, thanks." He wondered what she wanted.

"You've been on campus for a long time, and I understand that you have a lot of friends. Round up your friends. We need a lot of blood for Judy. She may start bleeding any moment."

"I'll get busy," he answered. "Thank you." He headed for the Blood Bank.

A pint of blood lighter, but with a heavier heart, he started making telephone calls, starting Alphabetically from the Student Directory. The wound deepened every call. Only the few sick expressed their regrets. All the rest headed directly for the Blood Bank. He asked them all to pass the word, and he checked the names of those he had reached. Later, he would try to call those he had failed to reach.

Lampis stopped to see Dr. Herbelscheimer to advise her of the response to his calls, but mainly to ask her why she had called him.

"Judy told me about you when she came to the Student Health Service, the first day." Dr. Herbelscheimer was the Director of the Student Health Service. "She was so excited about her encounter with you!"

He listened.

"Such a wonderful young lady; one could read so much in her eyes: purity, gentleness, generosity, sweetness, love and more. I could add dreams of happiness in a happy world. I didn't, because it wasn't there the second time I saw her, after the Diagnosis was related to her. We're going to lose her, soon, very soon, I am afraid." She spoke slowly, haltingly, looking away from him to the left upper corner of the room. Then she stood up and offered him her hand. "You've done just as I expected of you. The Blood Bank called me to tell me there is a steady stream of students, starting with you, to donate their blood. Don't go see her yet. You look pretty bad. Wait until tomorrow."

He promised he'd wait until tomorrow, repeating the inadequate expression "It's so terrible," firs aloud, and then multiple times in his thoughts.

He went to the Microbiology Laboratory to plead with his friends there to "Donate a unit of blood for Judy," and then to the Library to repeat his plea to everybody there. Everybody left his or her books open, on the table, and headed for the Blood Bank. He fought the tears back and managed to swallow the choking knot in his throat with the memory of the ancient Greek proverb, "Ouden kakon amighes kalou ("Not one evil is separated from good"). He remembered one of his sadistic teachers in the Gymnasium uttering this proverb at an encounter in a bookstore where he and the other two members of the "first triumvirate," as they were known throughout the Gymnasium, asked to "borrow" some books. They had been suspended, along with the entire class, for three days for conspiring to boycott classes on the first day after the final examination, on Sunday of the first semester, and they had decided to write and plan to stage two new plays for Independence Day to raise money for their school. "Ouden Kakon Amighes Kalou," (Not one good is separated from evil), he had replied, indignantly, - "insolently," his teacher later remarked.

He wondered what this man's reaction would be in witnessing this supreme, spontaneous display of nobility among his friends and classmates. Pride in and gratitude for his friends transferred him across the bridge from grief to hope – grief from Judy's imminent death, hope for the future of humanity with his friends lighting the ascending path.

All these thoughts and events of the day, returning, in no orderly sequence and frequently simultaneously, lulled him to a deep, badly needed sleep.

He managed to have breakfast the following morning. He had forgotten to have dinner the previous night, and he was famished. He had remembered to drink plenty of liquids after donating his pint of blood. On the way to class, he thought: "Judy is not to walk these paths again, won't gaze at these magnificent awe-inspiring gothic buildings; won't sit at the C-bench on a sunny spring day, or under an elm tree with her books in front of her; won't sit across the table in the C-shop so he can absorb her thoughts by looking into her eyes."

He'll never see her pushing aside a wisp of her hair, teasing the playful breeze.

After he sat down in the classroom, he tried to remember whom he had passed and greeted or did not greet on his way. "Are you going to see Judy today?" Ivan asked, and added, "She's ready, she said, if you are!"

Lampis had to brace himself during class, during teaching rounds, and with every stir of self-awareness.

Ellen wanted to know "What's happening to him?"

"I'll tell you later," Ivan replied.

Lampis walked halfway to I-324 on the I corridor in mid-afternoon but turned around and sought refuge in a Men's washroom. He waited. He did not cry; he just groaned. He stiffened-up and walked back. He knocked on her door gently.

"Come in," she answered.

He opened the door, took four steps and stopped. She stood at the foot of the bed, in a full-length robe. They looked at each other for a whole interminable moment.

She smiled and spoke first. "I had dreamed of you when I was fourteen, and I kept waiting for you, and now that I met you, I am going to die. At least my dream came true."

She spread her arms, halfway out, halfway up. The next move was his. He walked up to her, took her hands, looking into her eyes.

She smiled.

He took her in his arms. They embraced tightly, her heaving chest pressing against his heaving chest. She cried softly, resting her head on his shoulder. He kept chewing his lower lip to transfer the pain to a more tolerable level. He wanted to spare her from his agonizing emotions.

They sat on her bed, next to and facing each other, holding both hands.

"Ivan told me you were terrific, day before yesterday; I was so happy and proud; just as I expected from my dream and from our real-life encounter. He tells me you've been friends for many years. I hope you'll be friends forever."

He kept looking into her eyes, squeezing her hands and listening. He wanted to store her voice and every word she uttered, clearly and permanently. He wanted to illuminate his existence and aspirations with the moist gleam of her eyes. He finally managed to say that he wished to meet her parents.

She was elated. "They're eager to meet you also," she answered. "Can you be here tomorrow, at the same time?"

They embraced tightly. He kissed her on the cheek, gently, and they parted.

He would never see her again. The next morning, she lapsed into a coma, having bled in her brain, and she died about twelve hours later. He never met her parents.

Ivan told him, "All the nurses were crying. Everybody was crying."

Lampis still could not cry. If only he could transport himself to the summit of the ruins of the Castle, about five kilometers southwest of his village, and groan from the depths of his soul, to hear his groans echo in the ravines and gorges, to scare the crows and the evil spirits, to make the reptiles crawl in deep crevices, to challenge Zeus to a duel!

He plunged into his studies with a determination that he had never been aware of before. He was also unaware that he was trying to recover from the knee-buckling blow of some avenging Fate. Not infrequently, he would look up from his books or away from his mentors to see her smiling and comforting eyes – across the table at the C-shop or sitting on her bed. And he would compare every girl he ever knew or met with Judy. She always won, sometimes leaving him with a sense of guilty for a blasphemous comparison.

His friends, Ivan, Phil, Charley, and David, may never know, and never be able to estimate the support their friendship gave him. Their availability, their understanding, and their discretion were always unfailingly, timely and correct.

Ivan, his "partner," self-confident and mature, kept assuring and re-assuring him about his performance. David, with his conflict between the love for his fiancée and the affection for his narrow-minded father offered a distraction with vicarious pleasures and suffering. Phil infected him with enthusiasm and excitement about each day's new discoveries in books and in discussions about patients. Charley's confession of an adventure, starting with an incidental meeting in the cafeteria, followed by an excursion to "The Gate of Horn," and ending with an impasse, placed him in the position of the confidante and big brother. (He hoped he relieved Charley of his guilt but failed to give or evoke enough strength for a way out of his impasse).

His roommate became more and more preoccupied and even withdrawn but remained discreet and considerate. They seemed never to have time to share their concerns or thoughts, and consequently, develop a close relationship, or any relationship. The mutual respect, developing with the first encounter, never changed, and when, late one night, Robert advised him that he had requested a private room, that he needed to be alone, he was neither surprised nor offended. He assured Robert that he understood, wished him well, and expressed his confidence in his overcoming his difficulties after re-adjusting to the new environment and "the spirit of the University." In spite of their "good-night" exchanges, neither had a good night. Robert's sighs and turns reminded Lampis every time to suppress his own, but he was unable to recall in the morning whether he finally went to sleep before or after Robert stopped sighing and turning.

He had the room to himself again, but only for a few days. He was advised that he had to move to another, single room that "two other students will move to his room."

The new room was much smaller, facing East to the street instead of West to the Quadrangles, on the second floor. But it didn't really matter, since he spent little time, other than a few hours of sleep, in it. He would leave at 6:45 A.M. and not return until 11:15 P.M., after the Library closed. Most of the time he'd leave without breakfast. The "five more minutes," after turning the alarm clock off, stretched into a half hour. (He reasoned that if he moved the alarm clock to the corner by the door, he would stay up after walking across the room to turn it off. This proved wrong. He still went back to bed for "five more minutes.") Leaving the window open in the morning for fresh air and lightening the weight of fatigue with the help of a cold room, when he returned at night, worked for a while – until a snow storm, coming from the East, filled his room with snow, sparing his bed, because of its position in the corner against the wall on the same side but away from the window.

After that incident, he would open the window for about one hour after he returned. The heat was turned off at midnight and on again, with the inevitable banging of the pipes, at 6:00 A.M. He had become accustomed to the banging and his sleep was hardly disturbed. Occasionally, his concentration and intensity, or even the lecturer's charisma, were not enough to stem the tide of sleep during the lecture. He'd be embarrassed and grateful for Ivan's nudge, and he'd look around to see whether anyone else had noticed.

Ivan never gave him a chance to reciprocate, and on one occasion, he slipped.

Dr. Louis Cohen's lecture on Hypertension had been introduced with the presentation of a young woman of twenty-eight years, whose uncontrollable high blood pressure had frustrated her physicians before she came to the University, and the students appreciated that her femoral pulses were weak.

He was awakened by a loud snap of the pointer on the podium followed by a stern command: "Wake him up, Diamond!"

Shaking his head after Ivan's elbow thrust – not a nudge this time – Lampis heard the question, "What's your diagnosis?"

Ivan's whisper, "I think it's coarctation of the Aorta," filling the void between the utterance and the snap of the pointer with diminishing reverberations, was retrieved before it faded.

"Coarctation of the Aorta," Lampis replied.

Dr. Cohen, appearing dumbfounded, dropped his pointer and looked at his audience and declared, "I'll be damned! I swear to you, he was sound asleep, and he still comes up with the correct diagnosis!"

Ivan, proud of Lampis, and not appreciating the saving impact of his whisper, reached to his left to shake hands.

The Quadrangles were deserted, except by the familiar shadows of the trees, swaying with the blowing wind, when returning to his room. Whether there was anyone else crossing the sidewalks or under the arches, in the early morning, he was hardly aware. He was always rushing, except on Sundays. The alarm clock went off at 6:00 A.M., on Saturdays and Sundays, also. But then, he always had breakfast on the weekend, and he would never miss Dr. Buchanan's Pediatric Neurology Lecture at 7:30 A.M. every Saturday. He had to arrive early, or he would not find a seat. If inadvertently delayed, he had to sit in the aisle or stand in the back of the room. Dr. Buchanan's entrance would signal the beginning of an absolute silence for the duration of the lecture. Everyone sat at the edge of his or her seat, spellbound. The child, frequently brought in for the demonstration of the neurological disorder to be discussed, would raise its eyes, after a gentle caress and a smile from Dr. Buchanan, with the countenance of looking at God. The end of the lecture was followed by a confusion of sighs of fulfillment, surprise after a look at the clock, and craving for more. No one stirred until the sound of Dr. Buchanan's footsteps faded in the hallway and no words were uttered until the room emptied and the milling in the hallway began to disperse with exclamations such as "Unbelievable," "Unfathomable," "Beyond perfection," etc.

Sundays were relatively more leisurely, with more of a chance to "catch-up" with reading and discussions with classmates, a call to a friend, or a stroll in the Quadrangles for a revival from the cold breeze or a spiritual transcendence from the chimes of Carillon bells of Mitchell Towers, the Lutheran Seminary or the Rockefeller Chapel.

The weeks followed each other so quickly that he was almost startled. He had to plan for his "off-quarter." The obvious option was to return to the Microbiology Laboratory for full-time work with the rest of the time spent on some Research Projects in Dr. Wissler's or Dr. Fitch's Laboratories. The temptation for an "Externship," at a Community Hospital, such as St. George's, with a relatively good salary and the opportunity to test his acquired clinical skills made his decision quite difficult – that's what he told Dr. Herbelscheimer in an encounter during his break for the main staple of a hot dog lunch at the Gift Shop. The third choice suggested by Dr. Herbelscheimer, he had never dreamed of.

"Why don't you go to Greece to see your parents?" she asked. "If you're just like the rest of our students, you won't have another chance for five to seven years, with one more year of school, then a year of Internship, then three or more years of Residency, then maybe a Fellowship! This is a splendid opportunity."

"But I don't have a penny to my name. I am poorer than a church-mouse," he replied, laughing at the cliché.

Dr. Herbelscheimer was resourceful and must have known about Dean Ceithaml's sensitive chords. "Go see Dean Ceithaml," she advised with a persuasive expression.

He related this conversation to an old friend, Electra, at a brief meeting for coffee, at the end of the day, asking indirectly for advice.

"Go," Electra said emphatically, and without waiting for a response, she added, "I'll give you some money."

Lampis choked, not only at the generosity and sincerity of her offer – he had decided, at their first meeting nearly six years ago, when she was only nineteen, that she was all-pure, all-honest, and most sensitive to other people's needs – but also at the realization that she wanted to help him enjoy what she never had a chance to (her parents had died when she was ten years old, leaving her to the care of a fourteen-year-old brother and to the Providence of God, through the kindness of neighbors and friends; there were no relatives!). Her offer was so spontaneous and sincere that he was afraid that she may be offended if he did not accept it.

After swallowing the oversize lump in his throat, he managed to utter: "I'll accept it as a loan, with the understanding that I cannot pay it back for about two years."

"OK," she agreed. "Whenever you can."

He kissed her on the cheek and walked out of the cafeteria. She refused his offer to walk her to the Bus-Stop on Cottage Grove and 59th.

"You have work to do," she said. "Go to the Library or to your patients. I'll see you when you have a few minutes. You call me."

He felt a sense of guilt for allowing the not-unexpected question, "Is she for real?" to surface, and then concluded, "I'll proclaim to the four winds that there are angels." What else could she be? Orphaned at the age of ten and raised by her brother George, who was just a few years older, helping others – she still worked at the Immigrant's Protective League, where he had met her for the first time – and working on her Master's in Social Work. His self-assessment and self-esteem must, from now on, be measured by Electra's standards.

Following Dr. Herbelscheimer's advice, or directive, he went to see Dean Ceithaml the next day and related the conversation with her.

"Good idea," Dean Ceithaml answered. "What's the fare for the ship?"

"About two hundred and ninety dollars."

"Be here at 8:00 A.M. tomorrow." Dean Ceithaml looked at his appointment book, stood up, and extended his hand for a shake. "Goodbye."

Lampis thanked the man he revered from the first countenance on the day he had walked in this office a little over three years earlier and walked out with the anticipation that the next morning would be momentous. He had no trouble concentrating during the lectures, the teaching rounds, and his studying. He would do whatever Dean Ceithaml advised him.

"I am here to see the Dean," he reported to the secretary.

"Oh yes," she answered. "He left this for you. He's at a meeting now." She gave him a sealed envelope.

He opened it. She was looking away. Inside was a check for $1,000 and a note: "Have an enjoyable visit with your parents. We'll see you when you come back. P.S. This is a loan. You have ten years after internship, to pay it, no interest."

The secretary looked up, probably wondering why he was still there, and smiled.

"Thank you," he said, not necessarily to her. She smiled again and turned her attention to her work. He was ecstatic, grateful, overwhelmed, but kept it all to himself – until evening, when he shared it with his brother Nick and cousin Tony in a brief telephone conversation with each – though some of his ecstasy must have overflowed in his call to a Travel Agency to make his reservations on the *Olympia* or the *Queen Frederika*, whichever sailed first after the end of the quarter. His excitement reached its Zenith when he was advised that the *Olympia* would sail on March 25, Greek Independence Day, exactly one week after the end of the Quarter.

His euphoria in the next few weeks was apparent to all his friends, some of whom wanted to know who the girl was that he was in love with, and his stamina or endurance seemed to have passed beyond all physical and physiological boundaries. His self-confidence surged to a new height. The bonds with his classmates and friends grew even stronger. His respect and reverence for his teachers rose above veneration – and it was in this state of mind that the quarter and the academic year came to an end.

He moved out of the Dormitories – all his possessions amounting to his books, a few records, and his Hi-Fi, aside from the clothes on his back – to cousin John's apartment. John and another cousin, Symeon, had bought an apartment building with a Bar-Lounge and a small Restaurant on the ground floor, across the street from Wrigley Field. John was almost as excited as he about his trip to Greece. They stayed up late into the night, reminiscing, reassessing their strengths and weaknesses, bringing their respective goals into a clear focus, and exhorting each other to stay on course. Watching one afternoon a drunk staggering, falling, picking himself up off the sidewalk three or four times before finally giving up trying to walk and sitting with his back against a door, evoked a spontaneous laugh at first. After a moment's reflection, a heap of self-deprecation arose in him for being amused by human decadence.

His brother Nick came up from Urbana, the University of Illinois campus, for the weekend, to say goodbye. They spent the next two days going for long walks and visiting friends and relatives. Sometimes, they talked a great deal, recounting their experiences together, bringing each other up to date with their respective accomplishments and mishaps, and daring to look into the future beyond, "What comes next." Sometimes, they walked or rode the Bus or the Elevated Train in silence. He could not decide whether Nick's tears at the time of their parting, at 4:30 A.M., Monday morning – Nick had to be back for classes – were stirred by envy or the loss of his companionship for the next three months.

He had not had any contact with his uncles for well over a year. Anticipating a great deal of discomfort in answering his mother's inquiries about her brothers with, "I don't know. I have not seen them for over a year," he repeated to himself, "I have to rise above pettiness," or "Maybe they've had a change of heart."

Having mustered enough courage, Lampis ventured a visit.

Uncle Gus nodded. "Have a good trip." He walked away and down to the basement.

Uncle Bill refused to acknowledge Lampis' presence and when pressed, refused to shake his hand. "My hand is clean and pure," he protested.

No response. No greeting for his sister.

Asking for more punishment, Lampis decided to walk to Uncle Bill's house to see Aunt Helen and the children. The doorbell was not answered. That was the last straw.

Packing did not present much of a problem – just one small suitcase, the same that he brought from Greece, with hardly more in it than nine years ago. He had no doubt about his parents and relatives not expecting any gifts, about the total identification of their priorities with his. Had they not given their blessings when he announced his decision to emigrate to America for the sole purpose of pursuing a higher education, of becoming a Physician? Had they not encouraged him and prayed for him through all his years of toil? Had they not, unfailingly, expressed delight and happiness at his reports of progress, asking for more of the same and nothing else from him?

CHAPTER 28
The Pilgrimage

THE TRAIN RIDE TO NEW YORK reawakened memories of the ride, in the opposite direction, nine years ago. The contrast, especially in anticipations, was unavoidable. He was now foreseeing the smiles, embraces, and tears of joy, instead of fortifying himself, then, for all possible reactions. This was a round trip; that was a one-way trip, with dreams and no promises. The landscape was cheerful, inviting, even possessive. Nine years ago, it was distant, detached, and benevolently accommodating. He was sure he was smiling in his sleep – his sleep overtook his thoughts and flooded his mind with dreams of sunlit ridges, lightly misted valleys, and clouds pierced by snow-covered mountain-peaks.

Lampis had left for New York two days before sailing day, so he could spend some time with his friend Takis, now a graduate student at New York University, and meeting with Gerry and Edie, Gerry had taken Edie to New York to meet his mother. He had not seen Takis for almost two years, after Takis' graduation from the University of Illinois. Only now he realized how much he had missed him – his innocence, his sincerity, his trust. They had shared their joys and disappointments, their dreams, their stale loaf of bread, but they had never commiserated. He had forged a strong friendship with Edie and Gerry before they met each other and fell in love at first sight.

Finding Takis' one-bedroom apartment did not present a problem. Takis had been working late as a waiter and could not meet him at the Train Station. He was also busy with classes and did not have much time. They had to "make the most of it" in the time in between.

They talked, bringing each other up to date and projecting on their respective future challenges, venturing out only to Macy's to buy a shot-gun for his father. One hundred and twenty-five dollars was a small fortune but knowing how much his father wanted it and remembering that almost everyone else in the village had a better gun than his father, he would make this ultimate sacrifice.

Meeting with Gerry and Edie was a fulfilling, exhilarating and moving experience. The warmth, purity, and pervasiveness of love spread in all directions and erased formalities or hesitations. Gerry's mother and sister exemplified the

297

virtues of nobility in spirit and hospitality at their best. Their love for and pride in Gerry was obviously further enriched by his bringing Edie into the bosom of their family. Gerry seemed ecstatically happy. Edie looked as if she had reached the threshold of her destiny. And he felt uniquely privileged to be among them.

The spectacular whirlwind tour in New York City, including the view from atop the Empire State Building, with Gerry's methodical and impeccable guidance, left Lampis with crowded and jammed impressions. He tried to take everything in, and left the assessment or grading of his impressions, even the "wows," for later. Later, he would separate, before grading, human ingenuity and ambition from elements of human reactions, monuments to human potentials or vanity from elements of human dignity, the conquest of nature from the ennoblement of character. And after all the categorization and grading, he would conclude that the encounter in Gerry's mother's apartment was the highlight of the day or, more accurately, one of the highlights of his life.

Takis went with him to the port, right up to the ship, where they parted. They kissed each other on both cheeks, fully aware, and in defiance of drawing stares from the dock workers and the port authorities. Takis did not conceal his envy, nor was he able to suppress his vicarious joy.

Lampis climbed aboard, feeling lighthearted and buoyant.

The *Olympia* appeared more majestic, in comparison to the *Nea Hellas* – young, confident, defiant, and adventurous. He remembered the *Nea Hellas* as sturdy, determined, undaunted, and seasoned. The faces of the crew looked familiar; the commitment to sea and the unknown, the security in having made the right choice, the combination of cheerfulness and dedication to a purpose were the same he had seen nine years ago, even if the features were different. His cabin was roomier than it had been on the *Nea Hellas*. He chose the top bunk again. He liked climbing it.

This is an auspicious day, March 25th, Greek Independence Day, he thought, and most fitting for a salute to the Statue of Liberty. He will not miss it this time. He paced the deck, facing the Statue and recited silently the Hymn to Liberty, the Greek National Anthem, until it came into full view. He screened his arms and cried aloud in Greek: "Haere, oh, haere, Lefteria" ("Hail, oh, hail Liberty"). He turned around to face them and recited from the same Hymn to Liberty "From the heart, Washington's land rejoiced, remembering the iron fetters binding it, also." The Greeks among the crowd applauded.

Lampis stared at the Statue in awe, before its majesty and message, shivering at the memory that twenty years ago, Liberty and Human dignity were threatened with extinction, and he sighed with gratitude and relief at the thought that those dedicated to the service and preservation of Liberty and of Human Dignity had prevailed. His pride swelled with the tributes paid to the country of his birth when it raised the standards of the Heritage and defied Mussolini and Hitler, when only England had remained, alone, in the way of totalitarianism. He remained on deck, facing the Statue, long after distance and mist had shrouded it from his view, repeating the verses of the Hymn of Liberty and reflecting that his Ancestors had challenged not only the might of the invincible Ottoman Empire (the "sick man of Europe" was just some wishful thinking) but also the doctrines of Metternich and the Holy Alliance.

Two young women stopped to greet him as he strolled on deck, succumbing to their curiosity, they confessed, to know what his salute was and what it meant. Mary's smile was an invitation to "go on." Dorothy's blushing betrayed shyness. He remembered to introduce himself, and after a proper handshake, he decided he'd spend as much time as they would allow with them. They were close friends, had just graduated from the University of Oregon, and were fulfilling a dream to travel to Greece and Italy.

"What did your salute to the Statue of Liberty mean?" Mary repeated.

Translating the words was easy, explaining his sentiments were more taxing; and understanding his overcoming inhibitions was difficult, even for him.

Mary, the more forward of the two, suggested, "People deprived of Liberty may appreciate it more!"

Had he been among those people?

"Your slight accent," she suggested again, "tells us that you may have been." And she followed, before he could answer, with "Had you ever despaired?" Did the Statue of Liberty revive memories of hopes?"

He may have kept her in suspense while he was re-arranging the surging and overlapping memories to relate them in some sequence. And he had to rein his emotions. Following the swells and retreating to the ripples on their sides, he summoned and recited his experiences of a single day: the bullhorn declaration, "The immortal city of Athens is free! Zeto e Eleftheria, Zeto e Ellas!" ("Long live Liberty, long live Hellas); the teacher raising his clenched fists over his head and shouting in response, "Zeto!"; the students rushing through the door and echoing their "Zeto!"; his outdistancing his classmates in running and in shouting "Lefteria, Lefteria!" ("Freedom, freedom!"); his Aunt Violeta at the door, cuddling the blue and white Greek flag, and after a shower of kisses, handing him the flag and pleading, "Climb on the roof and hoist it as high as you can;" the church-bell tolls answering church-bell tolls; the hugging of friends and strangers; the crowds with banners in orderly procession singing songs of freedom and of defiance to oppressors and conquerors; the blue-and-white flags on roof-tops or on balconies; the rush for a view of and the sobbing from the sight of the Greek flag, instead of the hubristic and desecrating Swastika; the submergence of the pain and agony from watching children die of starvation, burning of villages, and mass executions; the confusion of dreams and unrestrainable plans for the future.

Mary and Dorothy listened. Mary looked at him intently, and Dorothy started at her hands on the rail. He stopped and looked into Mary's flooded blue eyes.

Dorothy glanced at him and fixed her gaze straight ahead at the horizon, "You witnessed and experienced all that? How old were you?"

"I was fourteen years old, chronologically," he emphasized. "Emotionally, I was five, uninhibited; having survived through deprivations, starvation, illnesses, and cross-firing bullets, I felt old."

"We'd like to hear more about your experiences and your life," Mary ventured to say, after a nod from Dorothy, touching his hand. "We'll see you later. Hope we're sitting at the same table. Goodbye."

He was flattered by their attentiveness, appreciative of their openness, and somewhat perplexed by their "surprise" in his insisting that he was a Medical Student and not a History or Literature Student. A forgotten accidental encounter with one of his professors of Literature in Gymnasium, in Athens, re-emerged vividly.

"You are going to study Literature, are you not?" his professor asked rather imploringly.

"No, my mission is to study Medicine."

"Think it over. Don't make any hasty or impulsive decisions."

⁓ ⁓ ⁓

Walking alone with the gentle, cool, breeze on his face or a stronger wind pushing his shoulders from behind, he let his thoughts scatter unstrung and disconnected. The gales during the voyage in the opposite direction, nine years ago; Kalliope's hair flowing in the wind; the bleating of the ewe on the slope across the ravine; the resolution of "the first triumvirate" to become physicians; Aunt Christitsa's sparkling blue eyes; Dr. Dorothea Miller's call at 1:00 A.M.; Dean Ceithaml's admonition "It behooves you to do better;" Gerry and Edie holding hands; his jumping from stone to stone across the creek; the lonely walks along the shores of Lake Michigan. He made no effort to connect or organize these thoughts, and he was surprised how long he had walked when a sudden void made him aware of the present.

The void and the sudden awareness of how long he had walked revived his bordering-on-fright discomfort after an experience initiated by an intense memory from the sight of a bush or from hearing a movement in a symphony, followed by a strange taste and salivation, with his desperate effort to suppress the memory and the taste, and culminating in total lack of awareness while continuing to walk or carrying on with whatever task at hand.

The hope that this experience would not return and an unexplained fear in confiding this most private mystical transcendence had buried it deep in his subconscious until he witnessed his symptoms in one of his patients. He had not had one of these seizures, classifying them now as Psychomotor Epilepsy, for seven and one-half years, but he was frightened again.

He had related his symptoms to Dr. Schulman, a Professor of Neurology. Dr. Schulman agreed with his self-diagnosis, suggested that there was a good chance they would not return, after such a long interval, but that he must not consider a career in Surgery. Was he cured? How? What was the cause? Was it Malaria? Was it the fall from the porch after the German soldier's punch? – he remembered the big lump on the back of his head after regaining consciousness – or was it hereditary? (both grandfathers had suffered from seizures, the paternal in youth, the maternal in old age, and cousin Eleni was having them now – he was bringing some Dilantin to Eleni). He hoped that it was due to Malaria, and that he was cured.

Nine years ago, he was reaching into the stores of his memories, in a deliberate or subconscious effort, to secure a continuity with his past. The abrupt end to his fragmented childhood and adolescence, the frantic rush to gather all the documents and to procure the Police affidavits, the exasperating encounters with resentful or blatantly hostile petty officials contrasted with the polite, encouraging and promising encounters with the personnel at the American Consulate. The suspense of whether he was going to be ready before the sailing of the *Nea Hellas* had not left any room for re-adjustment or mental preparation. He had faced a "fait accompli," of his own making, of course, to which he had to adjust. And for that, he needed strength from within. There was no other source, except in the memories of his fragmented and tumultuous childhood and adolescence. He had to anchor his existence to its beginnings to avoid going adrift. He mustered strength from the memories of events that had molded his individuality and guided him in his struggle for survival and to keep in reserve for the struggles that lay ahead.

He was now going back to revisit the family and places of his inspirations and springboards, to give an account of himself, and to renew his vows to his commitment. He had not quite reached his destiny, but he was in clear sight of the summit in his ascent. He was comfortable in his beliefs that he had not compromised his principles and that he had not betrayed the trust of those who inspired him. He would welcome and enjoy retrieving some of these memories again, now and in the future, for nourishment or refreshment, to sustain him through struggle and to shield him from contentment. He was humbly pleased in the inventory of his accomplishments and fully aware of what remained unaccomplished.

He would not count the lifeboats and the portholes while walking the decks, on this voyage, hear ominous messages from the clanking of the steel-ropes on the mast, see the menace in the surge of the mountainous waves. He would not have to defy, with an unbuttoned halfway down shirt, the sprays of the hissing gales. He had not conquered all his fears, but he had overcome many adversities, relying on his determination and perseverance. The motto of the "Companies of Mountain Raids," the equivalent of the British Commandos in the Greek Army, "He who dares wins," had become his silent battle cry. His vanquished adversaries had retreated behind the memories of his advances. His horizons were illuminated by images of Dr. Argoe, Mr. Savoy, Dr. Dorothea Miller, Dean Ceithaml, Dr. Herbelsheimer, and so many others. He started counting these images, instead of the portholes, some flashing from a faraway distance – all smiling, all inspiring, all holding the banner of his ancestors, "Aeim Aristevein: ("Strive for Excellence"). The clanking of the steel-rope against the mast would now echo with the sounds of strings of joy in renouncing the remnants of superstition. The swelling of the waves would arise from the bouncing of the sea nymphs and of the mermaids' dancing to the tunes of benevolent Tritons. He would spread his arms to embrace the gales, to assimilate their forces; and he would transform the spray into a mist for a rainbow from one outstretched hand to the other. He would stand at the bow of the ship, longing to hear the song of the Sirens.

Odysseus had longed for twenty years to see the smoke rising from the hearth of his home. He had flushed-out Achilles, enticed Philoctetes, conquered Troy, tricked Aias (Ajax), challenged Poseidon, turned down immortality, but never gave up his vision of "the rising smoke."

Lampis was not Odysseus, but he, too, had not given up his vision, and he was close to his "rising smoke," with his blinders securely on against distractions, and with his armor locked to ward off the arrows and spears penetrating or sideswiping his shield. Defiance had served him, also, well. He must remember that. He was not offered immortality in exchange of anything but had been tempted by promises of wealth and security, and by the lures of vanity and lust.

The Bell to dinner interrupted his thoughts. Mary suggested that he must be hungry. He had forgotten, and now that she reminded him, he was famished. She appeared curious about his thinking or day-dreaming but was also discreet to not inquire. He was not ready to share his thoughts. Would he ever be?

The smooth waves followed each other from the sides of the ship to the horizon, lowering their crests, transforming into ripples further away and reflecting the sunset at the edge of the horizon. The reflection of the clouds, densely compressed against the surface of the ocean at the limits of his vision, with the purple gradually fading to gray, lay still and glistening in the distance, quivered with the ripples, and finally bounced as it approached the side of the ship. Mary and Dorothy would wait for him in silence. The gap between the last memory of a bright sunset behind the peaks of Tsemberou (the kerchiefed mountain) and this display of unfathomable beauty (for his benefit?) was spanned, without shades or shadows of any other events. He was carried from one end of the ship to the other, and back, by efforts he did not recognize, hypnotized by the perpetual undulation of the waves, the dancing lights, and the call to penetrate beyond his awareness. He managed, with the summons of all his reserves of strength, to pull his existence back to one speaking entity between Mary and Dorothy and to beg their forgiveness for his distractedness. Dorothy's prolonged look into his eyes pleaded for explanations or confessions. Mary's smile was followed by, "I am afraid and regret that you see more than I can; can you tell one what you see? I'll try to follow you."

He raised his right hand and pointed to a dim star. "Look," he said, and lowered his hand slowly, pointing to the layered clouds, to the apex of the triangle of rosy light and more slowly, to the water directly below them. Then he spread his arms out to claim all that expanded before him.

"I see," Mary answered, "but I still wish I could see as much as you do."

The first day concluded with a walk to gaze at the stars. Mary and Dorothy were tired after the concert, following "the incredible dinner," and retired early. The soft, cool breeze, the splashes of the torn or parting waves, the brightness of the stars transferred him back to childhood memories when he would lie on the ground after the harvest, trying to capture God among or beyond the stars, or explaining divinations of astrologers and poets. The attempt to

retrieve images from the travel in opposite direction, nine years ago, could not be sustained, fading after a furtive glimpse. He was not disturbed at the realization that he could not maintain continuity of thought, beyond a few links, to forge a chain to or from his soul. The dominance of a star, a change in the force of the breeze, the flutter of the flag, the unexpected rise and collapse of a wave, the trail of a falling star, one after another, cleaved his thoughts and redirected his drifting attention.

"Do you know what time it is?" a member of the crew asked, emerging from the door to the lounge.

Before answering, Lampis wondered aloud: "The bright star there," he pointed, "is it still there?"

"I can still see it," the man answered, looking perplexed.

"I can see it, too. I can see the light that was generated maybe eons ago, and by the time the light reached us, the star may have exploded or froze into a rock."

The man repeated his original question: "Do you know what time it is? It's two-thirty. Good night."

The hallways, like the decks, were deserted. Instead of the gentle splashing of the waves, he heard a muffled, unanticipated, creaking, as if the ship swayed slightly; instead of stars he saw dim lights. His eyelids were heavier. His thoughts were submerged. He enjoyed the gentle rocking of the ship, lying in his bed, and was lulled by retrieving the sounds of the waves, the fluttering flag, the whispers of the breeze.

When he looked out his porthole, the waves appeared tame, sparkling in the sun and following each other to eternity. He could follow them only so far; he could not stretch to eternity. Besides, he rationalized, he was not reaching out, he was going back to his roots, to restore his inner strength, to draw from the deep wells of his lost childhood and adolescence. Then, on his way back, he'll ride the waves to where the clouds rested, folded, on the ocean's surface, to cover the sun as it blushed red behind them. He'll race ahead of the breeze and he'll call the Fates to join him.

Had he ever felt this free before? How was it that he had shed all burden, that he started whistling, that he condensed time and all of his existence into this moment? How did he find security in stepping from hardship to hardship, in grasping promises rooted only in dreams, in chasing after a prayer to his own soul – that's transgression of logic, isn't it?

Lampis was almost surprised in his realization that he was dressed and ready for breakfast. He hardly remembered having shaved, showered and dressed, but before he could explain or understand his surprise, he was carried away by the dancing nymphs born of the unction of sunlight and smooth waves, to the shores of the land of his birth. He was deposited in a cove where no one had set foot before, with clear sparkling water at his feet, ageless protective cliffs to his right and left, and a winding path in front of him leading straight up to the clear blue sky. He witnessed the birth of the nymphs, he was transfigured with the touch of their hands to his outstretched fingers, he glided among and with them, listening to their humming songs, and was content in imagining their beauty behind the veils of mist and sunlight. He read "Welcome" in the swaying of the wild flowers growing in the crags of the cliffs; he was purified by the waters at his bare fee; he drew strength from sapping the roots of the pine trees; and he anticipated intoxication from the fragrance of the Thyme along the path rising to the peak of the mountain piercing the sky.

"Daydreaming again?" Mary asked, who with Dorothy, waited for him at the entrance to the dining room.

"Is that what it's called?" he asked himself before replying. "I get carried away, almost physically."

The small talk was brief. Mary and Dorothy looked rested, and excited.

"We've never been on a ship before, and this is magnificent," Mary said.

Breakfast was "perfect," in variety, taste, and nutrition; he was "beginning to think like a doctor," Mary observed. The stewards, according to Mary, were "perfectly civilized."

The conversation ranged from exchanging information, including past experiences and plans, for the sake of better acquaintance, to world politics and philosophy. Dorothy talked the least, he the most. Mary raised the questions.

"We could continue strolling on the deck, it's such a beautiful day," he suggested.

He could not resist relating the memories of his voyage in the opposite direction, nine years ago. They seemed envious, or at least enjoying a vicarious experience. He wondered whether their often-repeated expression "unbelievable" stemmed from admiration or skepticism. The contrasts of his emotions then and now, starting with the apprehension of venturing into the unknown then, and returning to the security of Love now, separated by events in a continuous struggle to stave off despair and to keep exhilaration within the bounds of decency, and heightened by the absence of distractions, served to unite two aspects of his personality that he had not appreciated before this time. The contrast in the weather, stormy and menacing then, but calm and pleasant now, seemed appropriate or fitting for the respective emotions.

He was not sure how many of his thoughts he expressed to Mary and Dorothy. Mary's comment at one point, "You're not talking," suggested that he had been consumed in his thoughts and that he may have been rude. His apologies evoked smiles and a light giggle. How precious these timeless moments are, strolling along the decks of a ship, in the middle of a calm ocean; caressed by a gentle cool breeze in the center of a wide horizon; detached from cares and beyond pursuits; choosing or discarding memories with no regrets; equating time with the ripples and the waves of the ocean; understanding life in the reflection of light from the waves or the eternal message of the wind from the ocean to the shores; and conquering or ignoring Time with reflections, assimilations, and abandon.

Absorbed in his thoughts, he was, most of the time, oblivious to the other passengers walking the decks, mostly in pairs, and enjoying the sunshine, the cool breeze and their conversation. He was often embarrassed in returning their greetings after they had already passed several paces behind him. They all seemed lighthearted, happy, and friendly – all except the pretty blond girl who seemed preoccupied, distant, and as if struggling to keep from crying. The resemblance, in looks and sorrow, with the blond girl with the thick curls seeking solace in loneliness or prayer on the deck of the *Nea Hellas*, revived empathy and helplessness. He had never learned the name of the first girl or what caused her pain.

Would he ever know the reason for this girl's torments?

Her parents seemed quiet, also in pain, and withdrawn – hardly even talking to each other. They did not attend the dances, sitting apart and quietly in the lounge, and only nodded in response to greetings. They strolled on the decks, in silence, usually next to each other, but not touching, or they stood leaning against the rails at the stern, occasionally touching each other or squeezing each other's hand, without talking, as if to transfer reassurance about sharing in the torment.

The young man from North Caroling, going to Greece to bring a bride back, charmed everyone as much with his radiant personality as with his strong Southern accent. He made acquaintances at the first encounter, groups formed spontaneously and laughter was heard from all directions, subdued or restrained within sight or hearing of the couple and their pretty blond daughter. Their apparent sadness or grief dampened merriment and evoked respect and deference for their privacy.

"Why don't you approach and invite the girl to join us?" Mary asked Lampis.

The deliberation about the advisability to respect their choice to remain apart or to make an attempt to draw them into the group was concluded with Mary's recommendation

Lampis approached the parents and introduced himself. He learned the name of the daughter, Bobbie.

"We would like to invite Bobbie to join us," he said.

The parents looked at each other in appreciation and with a timid sign of gratitude. Bobbie looked at them with a hesitant plea to accept the invitation.

They nodded in consent and half-pleaded, half-commanded "Go ahead, we'll join you later."

Lampis had hardly finished introducing her to the rest of the group when the parents joined and introduced themselves. After a few minutes, the parents excused themselves, asking their daughter to stay, and walked away holding hands.

Bobbie followed them with her eyes until they turned to wave and smile at her.

The conversation was light, getting-acquainted type, polite and deferential. When she left about one half-hour later, to find her parents with the promise to return, everybody agreed "she's a nice girl."

Their circle widened, with diverse personalities blending in merriment while observing propriety. Bobbie began to smile and soon infected her parents with "socializing."

Two girls from Gary, Indiana, with their Greek-American accent and idioms, overcame their initial reticence and giggled without blushing. Another girl from Pennsylvania could not keep her eyes off a handsome young musician. Expressions such as "We'll never forget this trip," or "Isn't this like a dream?" were repeated with every encounter.

He divided his time between socializing, solitude, and reading in the Library. He sought his solitude at the stern of the bow of the ship, to retrieve memories or to chase after his dreams. He looked for company to share a laugh or to "get to know them." His approach to Bobbie was more deliberate and in readiness for a halt or a retreat. Her revelation, with tears and pauses, that her only sister had just died explained the pain in her and her parents – they had decided on this trip to Italy to be together, away from everything and everybody. Will he ever learn how to comfort people in pain? To find the right words? To redirect their thoughts? He had known pain and suffering from early childhood; he remembered how his pain was soothed by love and kindness; he had admired those who had the gift of soothing grief with hope or reason; and he had chosen Medicine to ease pain and suffering. But how can he lighten Bobbie's and her parents' grief? Would praying help?

Each day, from the last view of the Statue of Liberty, seemed a repeat: bright sunrise, echoing God's command, "Let there be light;" a calm and smooth ocean, in deference to Poseidon's caresses of a Nereid' gentle breezes to show Aeolus' benevolence; glorious sunsets, Apollo's crown of victory; a canopy of stars, blinking and winking as if sending messages to each other. An occasional white cloud, rising above the horizon, conveyed its "bon voyage," wishes by spreading out, thinning, and vanishing in perpetuity. The soft splashing of the waves against the sides of the ship, more like affectionate touching in the night, whispered tales of encounters with gods and men. The long, narrow and gradually fanning out white band from the stern faded in gray and in dreams of old Nereus. And he prayed for more of the same, hoping to capture displays of omnipotence and frivolities in the contests between Divinities and Nature. His unbridled thoughts, spreading from his earliest to the most recent memories, distracted him, frequently and without warning, from the calls in the arches of droplets, from the mist where ocean and sky came together, from the sway of the mast.

His new friends seemed to know when to join him and when to leave him in his solitude. He did not share the thoughts of his solitude, storing them for appropriate rearrangement and interconnection at "some other time." He had been labeled a "loner" before, but he did not feel uncomfortable with that label, bound by his father's admonitions, "better alone than in bad company." There was nothing bad in this company. He was just hoping that his new acquaintances did not misinterpret his need to be alone as snobbishness.

Mary's curiosity about his missing, or longing for, the girl he left behind was apparently satisfied with his answer, "There is no girl in my life," but she was still puzzled about his desire to be alone. The girls from Gary were less discreet, but he hoped that he had managed to refuse their invitations without offending them.

He did not refuse Bobbie's timid request that she join him in his walk around the deck, on two occasions, but they hardly talked. Once, they stopped at the stern, leaned with their backs against the rails, about two feet from each other and gazed across the ocean, without a word for a long time, before she finally asked – was she mustering courage all this time? – "Will you give me your address? I'd like to write to you; to stay in contact."

"I am flattered," he told her, "and hope to prove worthy of your trust." His confidence in relating to someone in grief was quite shaky. He began to feel uncomfortable, but there was no way out, except in the hope that Bobbie would start the conversation.

After another long pause, she timidly asked: "What made you choose the University of Chicago?" and without waiting for his answer, she added: "I hear it's the hardest school – and no football."

"It's very hard, and I found out the hard way," he replied. He talked and she listened, asking more questions and eventually showing signs of distance from the recent overwhelming grief.

Her parents, holding hands, smiled as they met them walking in the opposite direction, reminding him, at the third encounter, to listen for the bell-call for dinner. She hadn't registered for this semester, because of her sister's terminal illness – here she stopped talking for half the length of the ship, reached for his hand, and he offered her his handkerchief – but she was going back in the Fall to continue with her third-year of college, a small Liberal Arts College in Missouri. She withdrew her hand, crossed her arms across her chest and begged him to continue with the recounting of his experience. "Was the Army a good or positive experience for you?"

"I made the best of it," he replied, and related some frivolities, such as bumping the Commanding General's car while looking at the legs of a WAC, making a date with a six-feet tall girl, or antagonizing and outwitting Captain

Kloeper. Before long, she was laughing, all the way to the Dining Room. Her parents fixed their gaze on her, smiled, and raised their glasses. He pulled and pushed her chair under her, wished them "Bon Apetit" and walked to his table. He knew they were following him with their eyes. He hoped they trusted him.

Mary was curious, again. "Who molded you this way, your parents, your teachers, or was it God's hand?"

Lampis had never learned how to handle compliments without blushing or interpreting them as teasing. Dorothy's timid looks apologized for her friend's forwardness. Mary seemed totally comfortable and as if never in need to apologize or in fear of being misunderstood, challenging her companions to follow her example. The comparison and contact with the girls he had met at the University of Chicago Campus was unavoidable. Where they were driven, assertive, or forceful, challenging, and unsettling, she was unpretentious, inviting, charming and comforting. Where they were trying to divine their future seemed to span a wide horizon, her course followed a straight path to contentment, a fixed goal, and security. If he had a choice, what would it be? Luckily that choice could wait. For now, he would learn from Mary and Dorothy, from Bobbie and her parents, from the Gary Indiana girls, from the omnipotence of the ocean, from the mysteries of the falling stars. He would gather and store all he saw and heard, walking the decks or sharing a moment, reflecting and expanding while lying in his bunk at night and letting dreams transport him to the gates of fulfillment.

Who molded him this way? Who put the final touches? His father's strength? His mother's sacrifices? His grandfather's benevolence? His grandmother's fairy tales? The echoes of the goat-herder's whistle? The morning mist in the ravines? The ascension of the tree-line to the snow-covered slopes of Taygetus? The awe from the stories of the heroes who defied the Turks? The echoes of the church bells from hill-top to hill-top? When did the molding begin? When did the final touches starts? And is this his final form? If it was, would he be content with it? Was the question "Who molded you this way?" loaded with approval or suggestive of the need for improvement? If Mary did approve of this molding, he'd be quite comfortable – for now.

He lost contact with and interest in time again. He looked at his watch only when somebody asked, "What time is it?" He traveled back to different stages of his childhood and adolescence, retrieved the memories of some fateful events or decisions, recaptured the bright images of idols and mentors, and even wondered whether he confused experiences with fantasies. In these moments of uncertainty, he would concentrate more intently on the sequence of events, and, inescapably, relive the experience with all its agony or reward. He did not think of writing, and if anyone asked him what he was thinking about, he would answer vaguely with the intent of discouraging further inquiries. He spent more time alone, frequently declining invitations to join a group or have a drink at the bar. He had to be frugal, with his limited cash. Bobbie was mixing quite freely with the young crowd now, and Mary had taken to writing in her diary, letters to her fiancé, or articles for a local paper to submit when she returned. The ocean remained calm and benevolent, the clouds condensed against the edge of the horizon, and the breezes caressed affectionately – all conducive to reflection, abandon, and introspection. The anticipated encounters in Greece, the plans or dreams for the near and the distant future, and the inventory of his strengths and weaknesses returned with the monotony of the wave-splashing and gentle rocking of the ship while lying in his bed at night.

The passage through the Straits of Gibraltar, The Pillars of Heracles – profaned to Hercules by the irreverent Latins and their successors – was closer to the reposing African coast. The defiant cliffs, or "pillars" on the European side rose perpendicularly from the surface of the sea to support a few scrawny trees in a landward stretching ridge. Heracles had gone beyond this coast to bring back the bulls of Geriones, he told Mary and Bobbie.

"And you went beyond these coasts in search of a new life, not bulls, and you'll bring joy to your mother and father," Mary replied. Bobbie and her parents wanted to hear more about Heracles, taking turns looking at the cliffs through binoculars. He obliged, starting with the encounter, sitting on a rock at its crossroads, with the beautiful, bejeweled young woman promising power, wealthy, and glory; the next encounter, still sitting on the same rock, with the simply dressed, humble, young woman warning of toil, obstacles, pain, derisions, and anguish – all that and more in the pursuit of what was right and a clear conscience. "Follow me," the first young woman implored. "You should follow me," the second young woman suggested. Heracles had made his decision but wished to know their names. "They call me Vice," the first woman declared defiantly. "I am Virtue," the second announced. Heracles stepped down from the rock, took the hand of the second girl and pleaded, "Guide me, don't let me lose sight of you; I'll follow you."

Lampis had an audience now. Some people asked for an "encore," when he finished.

Bobbie decided she was going to take a course in Greek Mythology and wondered whether Heracles may have really lived. He wondered, too, but concluded that there must have been a good man with that name, growing in statue from inspirations and retold stories, to a demigod. He also wondered, not aloud, why the two Greek-American girls from Gary, Indiana walked away to stand apart, facing the coast of Africa.

He related a few more stories of Heracles' tasks, then switched to his memories of these coasts, gathered nine years ago traveling westward. The memories of Kalliope came back most vividly. "Look at me, look into my eyes," she had implored. "What do you see?" she had begged, and then walked away with the verdict, "you're helpless," after his stumbling, "I see…"

He strained to see the chapel at the base of the cliff in the cove, the fisherman rowing toward the shore, the flock of doves circling over a cluster of tiny white buildings. The chapel was still there, further away this time, as if in proportion to the time of the first memory, but all the other memories had to remain unreinforced. A majestic Liner, sailing west, sounded its horn, as it approached, was greeted in return, with the reply of a horn and waving of handkerchiefs, and left a white trail fanning out and fading toward them. Was there someone just like him on that ship, with all the difficulties of harnessing and explaining or rationalizing all his emotions? If there was, he hoped this other person would have more strength and more experience than he had – or still has.

The anticipation of approaching and disembarking in Naples stirred excitement and brought some sadness. He had missed his chance to visit Pompeii nine years ago – he had not money for the bus fare – but the Fates had had a change of Heart in the interval. He infected everyone with his excitement. Everyone but Bobbie and her parents whose sadness about "parting from all these wonderful, wonderful people," in turn, infected everyone else. Had they only known, they repeated frequently, they would have planned to go to Greece to be with the rest for two more days.

He danced with Bobbie more than with the rest of his new friends put together. Her shyness, deference, and sadness combined to suppress even the trite exchanges, to taint the smile with sorrow, and to translate the rhythm of her steps to "Farewell, Farewell, Farewell." Her parents danced for the first time, holding each other tightly and conveying a deep trust in each other, with their frequent glances. He danced a slow tango with the mother and was grateful to hear her say, "I wish I could meet your mother." Hugs and kisses and "Thank you's" at the end of the night forged stronger bonds and strengthened the promises, "We'll never forget you!"

Lying on his back, with his habit of hands locked behind his head – somehow this position seemed to help his concentration – he recalled the sequence of the day's events, to its final stage. The inevitable question, "Will I ever see Bobbie again?" remained unanswered. The timid question, "Could I fall in love with her?" was answered without hesitation: "Of course I could, easily, with all her pure and good qualities, but I am not ready yet. I must keep my emotions in harness, including regrets."

They'll be parting tomorrow, most likely forever. He envisioned embraces, tears, promises, and "thank you's"; then a final turn for a final wave.

The excitement about the visit to Pompeii, kept in check by the events of the day, displaced all other emotions and thoughts. He could hardly wait. The pictures that he had studied in his books, with fascination, transported him easily to the empty streets, among the ghost building, and to the napping theater at the edge of the city. He was alone. No sounds other than those of his footsteps, the breeze through the gaping windows, and the chirping of sparrows. The mellow light, the fleeting, faint, messages from the distant past, and the receding awareness of his own minute significance carried him, imperceptibly, across the boundaries of awareness to the oblivion of sleep.

His awareness was abruptly restored by the bright sunshine, silent seagulls that ignored each other, and an indistinct shore-line through the mist in the distance.

The decks were crowded. The excitement was infectious.

Mary's eyes sparkled, and her smile reflected a surge of sentiments.

Dorothy blushed with her appreciation of the inadequacy of her expression "It's like a dream."

Bobbie's eyes were moist and the grip of her father's hand firm.

Lampis had no chance, nor did he try, to be alone to recall or relate that Naples was a Greek City, Neapolis, that Pompeii was a Greek City before the Romans decided to honor the great man after they had destroyed him, by renaming a beautiful city after him. The thoughts did surface, but disconnectedly. The shores became gradually more distinct, with blurred objects taking the shapes of trees, buildings, and mountains in the background. The ship slowed for a gentle encounter; the crescendo of the horns of the tugboats conveyed their welcome greetings in their marine language.

The Italian flag was raised alongside the Greek flag and the passengers began to wave at the land. The few people at the pier, walking or standing, seemed to be repeating what they did from time immemorial, as if knowing what to expect and what to accept as pre-ordained. The monotonous hub of the city gradually began to undulate and eventually to be punctuated by horns, whistles, and finally voices. The tranquility of the voyage across the ocean and into the bosom of the Mediterranean retreated in bewilderment. The search for the horizon was arrested by mountain ridges in a haze.

The ship glided, sideways, with the pull of tugboats toward the Pier. The lines were skillfully and effortlessly thrown from the ship to the Pier and looped around the moorings, then secured as the side of the ship pressed the tires against the Pier, gently, as if in an embrace of reunion. Gates opened on both sides, and the tide of emotions flowed across the bridges. The anticipated embraces, tears, and promises were profuse and uninhibited. Bobbie and her parents hugged and thanked everyone, in turn, going to Greece, and expressed their "eternal gratitude."

The last farewell, conveyed with a wave of a hand, a smile of fulfillment, and eyes glistening with tears, was a repeat of last night's sentiments. The three of them, the two parents and their daughter, turned around and kept waving, walking backwards for a few steps, before following the customs official to the opposite end of the building.

He turned to Mary and Dorothy: "You are going to Pompeii, aren't you?" he asked, knowing the answer and hoping for distraction.

"What a silly question, yes, we are," Mary answered.

They strolled on the decks for a while, on the side of the land, talking little and capturing, for keeps, as much as they could within sight or hearing. Perhaps, he thought, Mary and Dorothy captured more, not distracted by memories and the inevitable contrasts between then and now. The sky was gray and low then, bright and clear now. The Vesuvius was hiding, perhaps in remorse, then, showing a sleeping or remorseful benevolence now. No urchins on the pier begging for cigarettes now, and no Costas to be entertained by the degradation of humanity scrambling for a cigarette or even a butt. Orderliness and purpose now, instead of confusion and abandon then; restoration of the faith in the goodness of the human race and pride now, instead of the struggle to contain despair and indignation then. He kept these thoughts to himself, not wishing to tarnish the images Mary and Dorothy were storing.

Deeply preoccupied with the anticipation of the pilgrimage in Pompeii, he retained only sparse and loosely contained images of the Journey from Naples. The guide, with his heavy Italian musical accent, but fluent scholarly English, carried him from age to age, back and forth, using the ruins of antiquity and of the medieval times as stepping stones or catapults. He was close enough to the guide to read total commitment to, and full enjoyment of, his work, between sentences and in the deliberate pauses, in the expressions of sparkling eyes and of changing smiles. He excused the giggles in the back of the bus with the conclusion that they could not hear or see what he could from his position – and he could hear and see all that the guide related; and more: the marching armies; the chariots; the neighing horses; the hoarse commands; the clouds of dust; the peddlers; the slaves in the fields; the crosses on the Armour of gathering crusaders; the exaltations of the victors; the chains of the captives; the blasphemies against the Pantheon, and the trampling underfoot of the fundamental teachings of Christianity.

The dark-gray barren slopes of Vesuvius rose before them like the walls and boundaries of hell or of Death's kingdom. Venturing beyond or behind these boundaries raised fears of witnessing the torment of sinful souls, of memories for the rest of one's life, or even of no return. The bus came to a stop, after a few hairpin turns up the slope, at a fairly spacious square lined by souvenir shops, close to each other, and a broad entrance to the Museum in the South-west corner. The clusters of tourists moved silently, following the guides, rarely exchanging glances, and deliberating about the advisability of bringing home a souvenir from Death's domain. The shopkeepers seemed subdued, merely showing their offerings and shying from bargaining, as if in fear of offending a watchful spirit.

The guide led the way, talking animatedly and with deep reverence. His group followed, stepping on ground and stones polished or pulverized by countless feet of visitors through the ages. The sight of the majestic ruins of the buried and unearthed city halted movement, arrested all thought, and demanded total surrender to the echoes of the past with its glories and its despair. He recognized some of the buildings and landscapes from pictures and reality. Pictures satisfied curiosity or even aroused admiration. Reality, stark and disciplined, displayed and unfolded the remnants of human thought and ambition during stages of unsuppressed or insuppressible instinctive adventures.

Last night's anticipated images were magnified in the three dimensions of visual assimilation and storage, of restoration of what had been with the cooperation of knowledge and imagination, and of bridging the last days of hope and despair with today's reflections. The guide's narratives and demonstrations made it all much easier.

He walked along the avenue were the Greeks and Romans strolled or paraded, pressed his hand where they had leaned, to refresh with running water; looked through the gaping windows or doors inside and beyond their dwellings; and admired their expressions of beauty and behavior in their paintings. He had managed to suppress his disappointment in the behavior of some members of his group by concentrating harder on the guide's discourses, but their progressively louder and coarser demonstrations or ignorance and uncouthness, in imitating the guide's accent to entertain each other, drove him to go off by himself. His indignation interfered with his ability to concentrate, and his fear of being identified with the uncouth and irreverent led to the conclusion that he would gain more by reflecting alone and away from everyone.

He roamed the avenues and side streets until he came to the theater at the edge of the city. He sat at the furthest marble seat and let his imagination transfer him to witnessing tragedies or comedies but stirred it away from the duels of gladiators or roars of starved beasts at the sight of their trembling and helpless prey. He looked at his watch occasionally, mustering the strength to return to the present, to time his return to the bus. He would apologize to and thank the guide in private – he'd be the last one off the bus. He stood up for a last view and a grateful farewell before strolling slowly and deliberately alone, back to the bus.

The guide continued, in his determination to enlighten his audience, in the remaining time, with his scholarly recounting of events and changes through the centuries while the rudeness in the rear of the bus was still mounting and difficult to ignore.

Lampis listened, reflected, and asked a few questions. He was flattered with the guide's frequent addresses to him and interpreted these addresses as signs of appreciation for his attentiveness and understanding. He filled-in much of what was left blank on the way to Pompeii, but he still felt cheated. He would have to come back, he declared to the guide, after thanking him for his guidance and inspiration and after apologizing for having strayed during the tour of the city. The handshake was warm, with a firm grip of both hands and the promise to never forget.

There was no time for a stroll through the city of Naples. The ship would sail in about one hour. He walked the decks alone, retrieving and reliving the memories of nine years ago. He thought of the barefoot, blond, blue-eyed young woman with the baby in her arms, of the frustrated policeman trying to direct the chaotic traffic, of his posing for a picture in front of the castle to send to his parents, of his unsatisfied curiosity about a Greek at the post office having decided to settle in Naples. He gazed at the sun, losing its brightness and turning from orange-red to purple in the fiery haze before submerging in the Mediterranean. He imagined the thick gray-yellow clouds of ash and vapors, from the explosions of Vesuvius that buried Pompeii. He could see the boiling shores form the flow of lava into the sea and the total darkness away from the yellowish, hellish glow at the summit and the slopes of Vesuvius.

The ship pulled away from the shore, slowly, gently, and smoothly. It sent its farewells, the sound of its horn, across the waves, riding the gentle breezes. The lights of the city receded toward the horizon. The bell-call to dinner, more welcome than at any time since New York, changed his thoughts from the past to the present, two more dinners, eight meals in all, after tonight, before disembarking in Piraeus.

The excitement at the Dining Room, fanned by the impressions from Pompeii or Naples, and by the anticipation of reaching their destination, was pervasive. Only one unhappy memory: the parting with Bobbie, so long ago, early in the morning. Mary's and Dorothy's excitement conveyed the joy of the realization of a dream; that of the Gary, Indiana girls some apprehension or insecurity; the acceptance by the young man from North Carolina, of the pre-ordained course. Conversation ranged from subject to subject, with frequent returns and continued from the Dining Room to the Decks and to the Lounge. No attempt at dominance or impressiveness – just sharing thoughts, dreams, and ideas. The music was nostalgic, romantic, and inviting to dance with abandon. The escapes to the past were obscured; the lights to the future appeared dim. 'Now' was reigning unchallenged.

The "short walk" with Dorothy and Mary on deck turned quite long, and much longer before they finally surrendered to tiredness. A side-ways half-moon rose steadily from the East. The stars appeared denser and brighter on the West. Lights flickered in clusters on the left along the shores; a soft gray darkness thickened gradually on the right. No repetition, even on the right the lights from the coast appeared at irregular intervals and spreads, and the darkness on the right approached and receded with the rising and dipping crest of the waves. Morpheus must have accepted defeat and retreated to revise his strategy for the next encounter. The return of memories, from his early childhood to the excursion in Pompeii, displacing each other and vying for dominance, erased time from his awareness. The same, vivid, memories surfaced and resurfaced again, as if goaded by a single-minded divinity to remind him who he was and that he must remain humble. Somehow, logic wedged between these memories and prevailed with the argument that he must go to bed to enjoy what tomorrow may have in store. He gathered and condensed the memories of the last day before surrendering to Morpheus, the God of sleep.

The next day was long, longer with the frequent consultation of the watch. No land in sight; some ships in the distance, appearing adrift; the sun followed its familiar path, ever so slowly; no seagulls; the waves and the spray from them indifferent; the exchanges at the brief encounters restrained. What happened to last night's excitement? He could not explain even his own inertia. He tried the Library, his walks, the recollection of fateful life events. No change. Why couldn't today be tomorrow? He hoped that tomorrow was a better day. The inventory at the end, in his bunk, showed emptiness, or worse yet, waste. The last return of the thought "One more night," took so long to complete, that sleep overtook it before it was completed.

The next thought, six hours later, was "one more morning." He was surprised to see the decks rather crowded. Everybody seemed cheerful, and yet restrained by inner, private thoughts. He paced the length of the upper and second decks, with unplanned, spontaneous stops of at least several minutes, his mind wandering from memories to explanations, to vague plans, before he became aware of a mass movement to the doors for the descent to the Dining Room for breakfast.

Lampis waited for one last stroll in total solitude. The need to re-assert his individual, separate existence had never changed, and the dubious reference to him as "a loner" never disturbed him. He was neither the captive nor the master of this ship riding the waves. He was just a distinct individual, a thinking entity. He did not bother to characterize his thoughts as serious or light to measure his journey through life in length or in terms of events.

He almost missed breakfast.

"How do you contain your excitement?" Mary asked, and continued: "To see your mother and father again, after six-and-one-half years, to stand in the places that inspired you, to hear the sounds and voices of your childhood. You must be near bursting with excitement!"

"I am," he replied, "but I had to bottle it up for the last moment. I did not wish the last moment to be an anticlimax."

"It's our last day together. Chances are we'll never see each other again," Mary emphasized. "I'd like to know more about you, so I'll be asking you a lot of questions; if I seem indiscreet, please stop me."

They talked all day, Dorothy being the continuous listener, and Mary and he taking turns in asking and answering questions.

Dorothy talked about her forthcoming wedding in the fall, her fiancé's leather business, her column in a local paper, her plans for the future, and cursorily, very cursorily, about her past.

Lampis talked mostly about his past, matter-of-factly about his struggles and difficulties, hesitantly about his successes or accomplishments, and tactfully about his adversaries. When pressed, he explained why there was no romance in his life.

"No relationship lasted long enough to evolve into a romantic one, since I had little, if anything, to offer," he replied. "I had never had the background or preparation, being obsessed with my academic pursuits, nor the time and means to engage in the natural desires. Besides, I am quite convinced that I am not romantically or physically attractive to women, and if some of the women found me interesting, it was because they felt safe in my intellectual presence or in their decision that my acquaintance would be short-lived. Whenever I forgot all that and ventured out, naively misinterpreting some girl's attentions, I was hurt, and recoiled in the protective shell of my studies."

"All the girls are charmed with you," Mary countered.

He repeated that it was because they felt safe and that he should be grateful he had other interests. Dorothy never commented, probably agreeing with him, but not wishing to lower his self-esteem, in this particular part of his personality, even more.

He had never been in the company of young women for so long, so many hours, so many days, and he felt quite comfortable. He reflected again; is it because he'd never see them again? Would he feel and behave differently if he were to see them again? He had answered all of Mary's questions, directly elaborating only at her prodding and trying to avoid repetition and embellishment. In the late evening, they walked in silence, most of the time, or exchanged brief comments about their joint experiences and repeating "What a wonderful experience this has been!"

No one was in the mood for dancing. The musicians appeared distracted, looking straight ahead and as if straight through the walls to the stern of the ship and beyond. Conversation was sparse and slightly above whispers.

He started counting the hours. The hands of the watch seemed to move slowly. Would he be able to sleep tonight? Would he know, without any announcement, that they had entered the Greek waters? Would it be rude to excuse himself and walk the decks alone?

Dorothy looked at her watch.

"What time is it?" Mary asked.

Lampis decided that they were ready to be excused. After the proper hesitation, he offered to walk them to their cabin. They accepted, graciously, and they strolled slowly and silently.

"Our last evening together!" Mary intoned, and after a moment, with a pleading smile, added, "I hear the University of Oregon Medical Center has a good reputation. Would you consider coming to Portland for your Internship and Residency?"

"I would consider it," he promised, and bid them goodnight.

The breeze was a bit more than gentle and invigorating. The sky was crowded with stars in a profusion of messages to each other with their blinking. The Mediterranean Sea heaved rhythmically, with frequent unexpected punctuations and sighs. The pale reflection of the lights on deck and through the portholes, uneven in intervals and in brightness, circled the ship in a mellow halo. The seductiveness of the songs of the Sirens changed from subtle to overpowering and from bow to stern. His efforts to reclaim control of his thoughts were neutralized by a sudden change in the force of the breeze, a fine spray from a playful sea nymph, a sense of insignificance at the center of the dark horizon outlined by extinguished and relit stars. He surrendered to memories of lying on his back in a freshly harvested field, with the smell of the wheat shafts, marveling at the stars;

to dreams of building a house on a hilltop surrounded by apple and pear trees in perpetual blossom; to the lyrics of Lord Byron's poems. He fought the temptation to envision his family's tears and embraces in welcoming him "home." He stood at the bow, gripping the rail, not to transfer the squeeze to his tear ducts, as he had done nine years ago, but to draw strength from the omnipotence and the legends of the Mediterranean. He stretched the moment to the ends of his comprehension of time, and he traveled ahead, far beyond the reaches of the ship, to the lair of his still untamed – if tamable – dreams. He faced in the opposite direction at the stern, feet apart and arms stretched out, to embrace all of his past, to summon his encounters for inspirational guidance, and to offer thanks to the Benevolent spirits for their protection. His thoughts traveled far and wide, mostly unbridled, colliding and condensing haphazardly to return home with an awakening impact before scattering with the breeze beyond the limits of the horizon. Orderliness in his thoughts, at this time, was unattainable, even if desirable – it would draw limits to his concept of life, separating memories from dreams and creating a space difficult to bridge with logic.

He strained for the flashes from a Light-house, after the rocking of the ship made his walk along the decks resemble the walk of the Paratroopers in Fayetteville, North Carolina, on the first weekend after pay-day. He reasoned that the ship may be approaching the dreaded Cape Maleas. After the flashes to the left, became regular and predictable, he retrieved his logic to guide him to his cabin for a few hours of sleep. He was in Greek waters now. He struggled to contain his excitement, trying, in a last resort, to imagine how his little nieces would react to him. He knew, from their pictures, that they were pretty. He fell asleep with their bright images before him, after a deep, knotted sigh.

CHAPTER 29

THE SIGHT, THROUGH THE PORTHOLE, of jagged coastlines, with overlapping asymmetric ridges rising behind them, of tufts of white lazily drifting clouds in a bright blue sky, of deep-blue waters with snow-white caps like a vast, torn Greek flag, and of effortlessly gliding seagulls stirred emotions and sentiments to lift him, with the lump in his throat, to heights of inexpressible happiness.

Lampis repacked his suitcase swiftly. His ascent to the deck for a wider view was slower than he would like, with the narrow hallways rather crowded by a mass exodus for breakfast – the last meal on the ship. The view was much wider and clearer. Isolated white buildings, homes on the slopes near the shores or chapels on hilltops, the identification proofs of the soul of Greece, sent out the message of "Welcome back, son!" The message echoed in a continuum, from slope to slope and spread inland through the ravines and the gorges. He waved at the land of his birth, with a plea for recognition as a worthy son. Smiles and 'wows' spread from bow to stern and from deck to deck, uninterrupted or even intensified by the announcement, over the loudspeakers, of the need to fill-out the Customs Declaration before disembarking.

Breakfast was hurried and quiet. Mary and Dorothy had not done their packing, and he wanted to hear more of the welcome signs. He thanked and shook hands with the stewards, apologizing with embarrassment for the meagerness of his tip, rushed to his cabin to pick-up his suitcase and returned to the deck for more handshakes and hugs – there would be no time for farewells in the Custom House. He promised Mary and Dorothy that he would spend an evening with them in Athens.

The *Olympia* slowed to a drifting pace. The tug-boats surrounded it and began to pull it, reminding him of his fascination as a child, of a tiny ant pulling a beetle. His eyes combed the Pier, before he could see faces clearly, looking for a couple with two small children and a crowd around and behind them.

His heart throbbed up to his throat when he saw a little girl in a red coat with a bouquet of flowers in one hand and the other hand held by a man's hand, a baby with her arms around a mother's neck standing next to the little girl with the red coat, and a small crowd surrounding them. He pointed them to Mary and Dorothy: "That's my family; the little girls are my sister's children!" Then he pointed to the spot where, nine years ago, his sister had shaken with uncontrollable sobs, afraid she'd never see her older brother again.

Mary and Dorothy were moved to tears.

After one more long, last look, Lampis swiftly disembarked, unable to restrain his desire to rush to his family, to take them and hold them in his arms. He could not see them from that side of the ship, but their image stayed with him, blurring everything else out – until he caught a glimpse of his Kalos K'agathos (Good and Benevolent) Uncle George, the husband of his father's sister, on the pier; he had always been deeply appreciative of and grateful for his genuine love.

Uncle George began to wave wildly and cry uninhibitedly: "My boy, my boy, welcome, my boy."

Lampis hastened to him, swinging his suitcase, for a prolonged, tight embrace, mixing tears with kisses on the cheeks and declarations of eternal love.

"Let's go through customs quickly," Uncle George said, when he was able to, "and not keep the others waiting." He picked up the suitcase and hurried to a well-acquainted official for a speedy, cursory inspection (Uncle George had worked at the Customs House as a porter for many years).

The official complied, looking inside the suitcase. "This is a used shotgun," he said.

"No, it's a new gun," Lampis replied. (Would he ever bring his father a used shotgun?) Then he realized that the official wanted to minimize the duty.

"This is a *used* shotgun," the official repeated, stamping the "Declaration" with the 'all-clear' stamp and wishing them warmly and genuinely, "A joyful reunion and stay."

Mary and Dorothy, right behind him, were waved on with a "Kalos elthate" (Welcome) and "Kale diamone" (A joyful stay).

Lampis ran ahead of Uncle George to the open arms of his family, embracing first his mother, then his father, and in rapid successions, his sister, brother, brother-in-law, nieces and the rest of the relatives and friends. The older of his little nieces, not quite five years old, offered him her bouquet of flowers and a gentle, timid kiss, followed with the question, "How is Eisenhower?" (After all, he was coming from America and must have daily contact with Eisenhower). The younger one, one-and-one-half years old, clung to her mother's neck and ordered him "Get away from here!"

After this unceremonious rejection, he had another round of hugs, kisses, and declarations of love and devotion from the other members of the family and friends. The tears of joy flowed copiously, and the sighs attracted the attention of the milling crowd on the Pier. He was fully aware of the conflict, among the members of his family, between the desire to hold on to him and the fear of offending another possessed by the same desire. He touched one, looked at another, smiling uninterruptedly, and tried to leave no one out.

His brother George took charge. "We must go now," soothing those who would return to their home with "we'll all get together again soon." Uncle George would have to stay at work. Aunt Nikki, with her little daughter, would take the bus to her home. Uncle Vasiles and his family, along with Takis, his boyhood friend, would take the subway. The immediate family would take two taxis. More embraces, tears, and profuse affections before parting. The question, in his mind, "Have I ever known happiness greater than this?" remained unanswered or lost in the answers to their questions, from all directions: "How was your voyage?"; Did you encounter any storms?"; "How did *Olympia* compare with *Nea Hellas*?"; "Did you find some good company among the passengers?"

He assured them repeatedly that he had a wonderful time on the ship; that the weather had been perfect, and that he had met some truly decent and friendly people.

In the excitement of the reunion, both questions and answers seemed forgotten and repeated in the taxi on the way to his sister's home. He tried to listen, to respond, and to look out the window for familiar landmarks. If this were a dream, he wished it to be as vivid as possible. His mother on his left and his father on his right, squeezed his hand in turn or together. His brother, sitting next to the driver, after giving his instructions, turned around and beamed continuously. The inquiries about Nick, the third son, held back up to now, followed in rapid succession. The reassurance that he was well and doing well in school turned the tear faucets on once again – if there was another outlet for the emotions, aroused by separation from and pride in someone so dear, he could not think of it. He concluded that some of the hugs and hand-squeezing were meant for Nick, but he reveled in them just the same. The absence of their youngest child may be more painful now with the other three near them. He blocked the thoughts of their pain at the inevitable separation again, in about two months, from the two sons now with them.

He sensed a vicarious excitement in the Taxi driver's discreet questions, "How long have you been away from home? Where do you live in America? How does it feel to be back again, in the bosom of your family?" The last question did not need an answer. It was obviously asked to show that he, the taxi driver, knew, and to suggest, "think of nothing else at this time."

The handshake and the brightness in the Taxi driver's eyes conveyed the message, "Thank you for the privilege of witnessing the joy of your reunion." The wave of the hand while driving away slowly was a touching encore. Lampis knew that the Taxi driver couldn't wait to return home to tell his family about what he had witnessed and experienced.

They climbed the spotless, white-marbled, spiral stairway to his sister's tiny, cozy rooftop apartment, exchanging phrases and sentences with meanings for broader or deeper than the words in them, smiling all the while. They walked out on the spacious open patio to let their happiness spread across the brightly sunlit city to the mountain ridges, to translate the humming of the city-traffic as the echo to the resonance of their ecstasy, and to raise their eyes to heaven for a soul lifting, "Thank you."

His sister's disciplined and directed bursts of energy in preparing for the expected visitors, in treating everyone with the perfect beverages or gestures, and in caring for her little children spread an infectious merriment with spontaneous laughter and exclamations. Katerina's, the older of the two nieces, intrusions for attention with her cute uninhibited questions or announcements, added a new dimension to the all-consuming happiness. Demetra's, the little one, commands, "Get away from here," were rendered weak and unobeyable by her own sweet smile. The brother-in-law scurried about, laughing and gesticulating, trying to help and sometimes, inadvertently, getting in the way.

Hugs and kisses from the parents were offered to whomever was near at the moment of the recurring urge. The void of nine years was quickly filled. He was fully awake in a dream of ecstasy and fulfillment. He did not think of the beginning of this happiness, nor did he foresee an end. He was too engrossed in the moment.

The stream of visitors started within a half-hour after his arrival, the most impatient unable to stem their eagerness and the most restrained hoping to have a better chance for intimacy with fewer people around at the end of the day. The purity and spontaneity of their demonstration of love saturated his soul to sustain him forever. He was insatiable in absorbing the attention and affection displayed for him, and he never wondered whether he deserved it all, taking it, as it were, for granted. He would not deny them their prerogative to give it – or himself – the right to take it all.

The next few days were spent in bliss, bringing his family up to date, elaborating on his positive memories and skipping over the painful recollections. He was particularly careful to spare his mother from any negative references to her brothers. He visited with close friends and relatives in his sister's or their own homes. He made his pilgrimage to the Acropolis and the Agora; he walked the streets where death and terror roamed in 1944, and he measured his stature against his image of his deprived childhood or turbulent adolescence.

A walk through the National Gardens with his father brought him closer to expectations from him, beyond the Academic or Professional goals, such as sharing his life with the right woman and perpetuating his essence through children. Facing stark reality, he told his father that he had relegated this phase of his life to a lower priority, until his studies were completed. "I had no time for socializing and acquaintances with eligible girls, especially Greek girls. Would you and Mother be disappointed if I married a non-Greek girl?"

His father stopped, placed his hands on his son's shoulders and delivered his pure and sincere sentiments: "So long as she reciprocates to your pure and unselfish devotion, so long as she can share in your trials and triumphs, so long as she can inspire trust and respect, she can be Greek, Turkish, white, black, or yellow; we'll lavish our blessings and share your happiness."

The reflection from his father's eyes reignited an old, cherished thought: "How fortunate I am to have this man for my father."

321

His brother George was working and could not, regretfully, he said, go to the village with him. He would join them for Easter, along with their sister's and Uncle Vasiles' families. He would be alone, of the four children, with his parents, to listen to every word from their lips, to follow them in their excursions to the past, to divine their hopes and dreams, and to confide in or confess to – within the boundaries of discretion and decency – his experiences and aspirations. He would be lulled to sleep with their whispers from the adjoining room; he would be awakened by his mother's caresses, and he would fill his day with the sound of their voices.

The country-side, on the way to the village, strewn with a profusion of colors from the flowers, and fragrant from the blossoms, spread the glory of the Spring. The cloudless clear sky mirrored its blueness in the sea, and the sea, as if in gratitude, took the blueness to its depths to intensify it. The pine trees swayed in the light breeze to send a greeting across the slope. The Cypress trees tipped their topmost branches to acknowledge the rapture of beauty in the fields carpeted with poppies. The lemon and orange trees, in full blossom, dominated the plains with their fragrance. The ruins of the castles reposed in sunlight and in their glories of the past. The younger passengers in the bus began to sing, initially softly and then freely, enticing the older ones to join them. And he was carried ahead of the bus, with the wings of his youthful imagination and nostalgia to his beginnings.

The bus was immediately surrounded when coming to a stop at the village square. He swirled from one embrace to another, was moved to tears by tears, and drew a deep breath to revitalize his existence and his dreams. He was carried to the steps of his home, the place of his birth and for so long the center of his world, with the lift from the "Welcome Home" echoes. On the solid stone-slab across the top of the door he read his grandfather's name, identical to his own, and the year the house was built – 1900. He knew that his grandfather's ever-present spirit was welcoming him, also, and that his grandmother was sprinkling him with her blessings, just the way she did a few minutes before she passed away.

He climbed the steps reverently, as if approaching for the sacrament of the Holy Communion, and heard his mother's sigh: "Our home, your home." He entered the Inner Sanctum, the sanctuary of his childhood, studied the changes since his last visit, and embraced his parents again for a deeper or more permanent engraving of their love from this reunion. The closest relatives and friends poured in, all beaming and ebullient, filling the house and his heart with boundless joy. His mother scurried to offer them drinks and sweets. They responded with their heartfelt "Kalos ton dechthekate" (an idiomatic Greek expression meaning, roughly, "May your receiving him fill you with joy.") He answered the question, "How long are you going to stay with us?" often twice to the same person, acknowledged their "Kalos elthes" ("Welcome") and their "Es ygeian" (to health), and read pure joy in their faces and gestures.

Their stay was inversely proportional to their closeness to the family – the closer the ties the longer the stay. Some, at the end, were asked to stay for dinner.

Most declined politely. Uncle George and his family decided to stay, only to keep them company while Kostas and Demetroula promised to return. Uncle George and Aunt Antonia asked about Tony, their son, and wiped their tears with relief and assurance, after listening to his stories about the fun and absolute trust he and his brother Nick shared with Tony, when living together.

Mother seemed super-efficient, entertaining her guests and preparing for dinner, without effort. Father just beamed with pride and joy. Cousin Nick, private and self-effacing as usual, sat apart, taking everything in, deferring with respect and glowing with inner joy. Having had experienced and anticipated this kind of love and attention, he was not overwhelmed. He just enjoyed it to the fullest. And he knew there would be more of the same.

Each day, after the first exhilarating experience, brought more happiness, with the inevitable rekindling of memories from encounters and excursions to his childhood's playgrounds, to the fields where he worked, to the hilltops from which he strained to expand his horizons, to the ravines whose mist shrouded his secret thoughts, to the vineyards, where the nymphs danced at high noon, and to the fountains frequented by benevolent spirits. He divined only the extent of his good fortune from the flight of the birds; he resisted hypnotism from the distant cry of the owl in the moonlit night; he stirred his greed for more of the nightingale's song; and he sighed at his limitations in smelling every flower individually. He shared some of his thoughts in some of his long walks, with his father, and he reminisced with cousin Nick. He listened to their stories, their recounts of their daily cares, their plans for tomorrow and next month, their prayers for the preservation of good health.

He was invited into every house, as he strolled through the village, the doors always open and the genuine smiles enticing. The repeated references to his being "always a good boy" made him blush, feeling grateful for their good memories of him. He felt that they all claimed him as their own son and that he belonged to all of them. The years that had separated him from them had erased all petty confrontations and strengthened, or even magnified, the memories of shared joys. Their example even when not neighborly, had helped to mold his character and keep him on his path. This humble village was not just his cradle; it was also – and still is - his springboard or launching pad.

The resurfacing of the attempts at humiliation and breaking his spirit ("putting him in his place," as his Aunt Helen would insist) by his uncles in Chicago, from his mother's inquiries and Uncle Nicholas's curiosity, reopened his wounds, but briefly. The love and trust he was enjoying now was the perfect, ultimate cure.

Uncle Nicholas vented his anger by blaming it all on the "evil Helen," but this anger was not enough to stem a flood of tears.

His mother shook her head and hugged him lovingly. "St. Nicholas's protection will defeat all of your adversaries."

Lampis did not think of the struggles for survival or in overcoming setbacks, of the all-consuming concentration in his studies, or of the apprehensions about living-up to his expectations. But he was impatient for questions about his friends and mentors at school. He wanted his family to know about the great men and women who inspired him, guided him, and buttressed his self-esteem; about the purity and selfishness of his friends among his classmates; about his great fortune in studying at one of the world's best Universities; and even about his successive loves for the different fields of medicine: Pediatrics, Psychiatry, Pathology, Surgery, Internal Medicine, and Radiology. All these questions were asked; and all his answers were rewarded by the all-telling response: "Glory be to God."

The sun was as bright as Nostalgia had illuminated it. The breezes whispered, from branch to branch and from tree to tree, the eternal mysteries he had tried to divine in his childish imagination. The white clouds drifted across the blue skies carrying his early curiosity about what lay beyond the mountains. And the incessant revelry of the brooks, in their flowing over rocks or changing directions when encountering the roots of the Plane tree, repeated the messages gathered along their course from the blossom-studded slopes to entrust to the sea that carried him to his dreams.

The Vespers, during Holy week, transferred him back to the transcendental elations of his early childhood, to the hopes for deliverance from the inferno of the war, and to the escapes from sentimentalism, deprivation or despair. In the solemnity of the supplications, in the reverence of the congregation, in the flickering light of the candles, his soul rose high above substance to seek the link between existence and eternity. The priest of his childhood seemed to have never lost his direct connection with God – if God was listening to all the other supplications. He must be especially pleased hearing from Father Elias. For just one brief moment he wondered whether his father thought of anything else while chanting. The piety of the women, lifting their little children to light the candle and kiss the icon of Jesus with the crown of thorns, spread a message of grief, humility, and dim hope for deliverance. The right hand of the old men, along the single row of pews against the walls, seemed to be making the sign of the cross automatically and independently of the suspended thoughts in their minds.

The momentary distractions of his wandering spirit did not lessen the intensity of his concentration – they provided the connections between body and soul. His own crossing himself, along and concurrently with the rest of the congregation, tied him to the purest and most benevolent of their wishes. The end of the Service filled the church with whispers, probably of greetings or plans to talk outside. The sexton moved silently and reverently, extinguishing the candles. The Priest tidied his inner sanctum, with an occasional glance to the altar boys to show his appreciation and to remind them to stay quiet. Most of the congregation milled outside for a few minutes, until the priest came out. The parting wishes, "Kale anastase," ("May Resurrection day be a happy day") in the star-lit square in front of the church, did not distract from the song of the nightingales rising up from the ravines and from the rustling of leaves descending from the Plane tree; they just swelled the anticipation for Resurrection Day. The walk home, slow and deliberate in the starlight, sanctified all he had witnessed and carried him close to transfiguration to a spirit springing from hilltop to hilltop, gliding over the gorges and leaping along the Milky-way.

He returned to the balcony to marvel at the stars, to listen to the nightingales, to retrieve memories, to dispense with the boundaries of time. The soft footsteps of his mother, hesitating at the door, came back from distant memories and ended at his side. The gentle touch on his hand was followed by a deep, fragmented crescendo sigh and after pausing to gather strength, her reverent question, "Remember?"

Sensing that she remembered his standing at this same spot the night before his leaving, maybe for the last time, nine years ago, he turned and took her in his arms, kissing her on the forehead. "I remember."

"Glory to Thee, Oh Lord," she sighed again, warming his chest with her breath. No more words, for an eternity of bliss; just sustenance from each other's heartbeat and squeeze.

"One day closer to Resurrection," she said, with a celestial kiss to his cheek. She left him, as if in full respect for his quest of solitude.

The anticipation of Uncle Vasiles' arrival lengthened the days and brightened the memories of the joy from special love that united them. The anticipation of Resurrection encompassed the merriment in celebrating among loved ones, the cracking of the red-dyed eggs, the clinking glasses of wine with the toast of "Christos Aneste" ("Christ has risen"), the dancing at the village square, the house vibrating with song and laughter. The memories of deeply-rooted and ever-flowing Love were segregated in the inner-sanctum of his existence; they'd never be in need of resurrection; they'd never die!

This same eagerness of Uncle Vasiles' arrival interrupted his trance during the Holy Friday services with: "Where is he? What tranquility and inspiration would his indelible smile transmit?"

The intonations of "Kyrie Eleisons" outside the church when starting out to carry the flower-decorated and candle-lit symbol of Christ's burial, the epitaphios, along the main street of the village, will not reach heaven without the lift from Uncle Vasiles's voice. Still, the delivered from all unholy and even mundane thoughts – and unified in goodness and reverence – congregation revived, with its chanting, in rotation, the sorrow of Mary and of the Disciples, and the innocent, childhood fantasies of witnessing the taking down from the cross and of carrying the limp body, with arms dangling, to the tomb.

Uncle Vasiles' arrival, a few minutes before the procession was to start, transported his soul to a new summit, closer to the stars, where the chants suspended and undulated in a canopy over the flickering candle-flames.

Lampis followed the procession, next to his uncle and in the midst of his family, carried in mid-air in solemnity and reverence. The stars trembled lightly, as if with the breeze, the fragrance of wildflowers and burning beeswax diffused in the darkness; and the priest's intonations, followed by the congregation's "Kyrie Eleisons," saturated the homes along the route of the procession. The lit lanterns in front of the houses cast shredded, faded, shadows of posts and flower-pots; the dogs must have curled-up somewhere out of sigh; and the bulks of the mountains, from all sides, appeared to have drawn-in, to be part of this solemn commemoration. The boys in front, carrying the 'Hexapteryga,' knew when to stop for the next prayer or intonation. The silent crowd clustered around the 'epitaphios,' and the 'Kyria Eleisons' resonated, without echoes, once again. The final stop, under a pear-tree in full-blossom, blended the spirit of lamenting humanity with the spring resurgence of nature's beauty.

The return to church seemed, comparatively, hurried; the whispers less restrained' the intonations more ritualistic; and the footsteps heavier with a vague sense of sacrilege. The entry into the church, under the hoisted 'epitaphios' was preceded and followed by total silence. All the candles were extinguished. The congregation waited, as it did every year, in suspense. The priest emerged from the inner sanctum, crossed his arms over his chest, bowed humbly, delivered his last prayers, without raising his eyes, and finally reminded his flock – as if it needed reminding – of the Resurrection services.

The filing out of the church was quiet, reverently subdued. Greetings were exchanged, and acknowledged with nods and half-smiles, after the awe-laden kiss on the canvas commemorating the burial of Christ and picking off a flower from the 'epitaphios.' Even outside the church, conversation was carried out in whispers, and the excitement from the arrival of relatives and friends from far-away places was restrained or stored for resurrection on Resurrection day. Aunt Violetta seemed unable to control the resurgence of her emotions, beaming, hugging, and smiling – in spite of the lateness of the hour and the long, adventurous travel from Athens.

The family cluster grew and moved slowly from the church yard, stopping for a few minutes in front of the house for a rehash of the arrangements for the celebration of Resurrection Day. Another round of hugs and kisses followed, along with the wishes for 'Kale Anastase,' and the cluster dispersed.

The call to the balcony from the outline of the mountain peaks and the songs of the nightingales, overwhelmed the urge to follow the example of the rest of the family and to retire for the night. The spread of the moment carried him, along with the song of the nightingales and the whispers from the mulberry tree, above and beyond the mountain ridges, away from self-awareness, across a gentle transition from star-lit nights to the mellow-mist light of dawn, to the other side of the long shadow of the lone evergreen on a hilltop. No thought of the past, only a receding image and hum of the crowd chanting 'Kyrie Eleison.' No venture into tomorrow, the magnitude of the moment all-consuming. No surrender to tiredness, only an end to the moment with the mother's plea echoing from the remote past: "Don't stay up too late."

The day after the entombment of Christ – or was it the day before Resurrection? – seemed suspended and was supposed to be uneventful, between reflection and anticipation. Reflection unveiled sadness and self-recrimination. Anticipation stimulated preparations and restrained impatience. The long walks with Uncle Vasiles and brother George to the old vineyards and to the river-valley to reminisce, the shorter walks to the cemetery with Aunt Violetta to pay the due respects to Papou (grandfather) and Yiayia (grandmother), and the encounters along the way stirred old emotions and engraved new memories. Walking and exchanging thoughts along the sun-lit ridges, or slopes, reinforced the conviction that Uncle Vasiles cast a long shadow, that "wherever Vasiles walked, even the thorns blossomed," – how perceptive and appreciative these villagers are, he thought. Brother George walked straight, shoulders back and chin high, talking matter-of-factly about his resolution to travel to the United States for advanced studies. They walked among the grapevines and imagined Papou bent over, planting and nourishing them or building the stone-fence all around the vineyard; they knelt to drink from the water flowing into the hollowed stone; they were revived in their covenant to carry and pass on the legacy of the Family; and they stood at the hilltop to gaze at whole tufts of clouds crowning the peaks of the mountains or to gather sights, fragrance, and sounds for storage and wealth. The bleating of the mother-ewes and the mother-goats for their lambs or kids silenced the song of the birds and stilled the breeze, the deep sigh from venturing to understand and from guilt brought no relief; the hope that the lamb or kid was frolicking at the edge of a terrace, temporarily out of sight, and not hanging lifeless and skinned to be roasted tomorrow, could not tear the veil of dark remorse. The anticipation of the festivities was displaced by thoughts such as "What if I were that mother?"

The gathering at the dinner table was subdued. Conversation seemed inappropriate, if not sacrilegious. The events of the day were related, in response, laconically (this part of the country was used to be part of Laconia, the Spartan domain, known as Skyritis) and deferentially. Mother's and Aunt Violeta's footsteps, to and from the kitchen, were counted with respect and affection. The silverware's encounter with the plate was noiseless. The toast to "Kale Anastase" ("Happy Resurrection Day") was restrained – cheerfulness was held in store. But the memories could not be suppressed.

Lampis had only a few memories of joyful or comfortable gathering on this day. After the innocent first ten years of his life, came the fears and deprivations of the war, the occupation, the civil war, his escape to the new World, and his grappling with open or undercover foes. His father seemed to be reading him, with moist eyes. His uncle's smile brightened his early memories. Aunt Violetta, always practical, suggested they rest their "eyes and mind" before the bell's toll.

The fields bathed in a mellow, misty light. He lay, weightless, swaying with the whispers among the pines and the rustling from oak to poplar, lifted with the pull of the stars, transported in infinity, unaware of his dimensions. The bell tolls carried him over ravines and ridges to the bliss of timelessness, delivering him to vying forces of consciousness and oblivion. His mother's voice echoed from the Galaxy and spread across the limits of his visions, then returned to resonate from the chord of his existence in a clear, sweet motherly sound: "The bell is tolling!"

He reached for her hand to sap sustenance and bliss. Her kiss, deposited with the second tolling of the bell, swirled him wider and wider, then closer and closer to her bosom.

"Yes, Mother. I'll be ready in a minute." He had no concept of the length of the minute, having just returned from eternity, but her smile left no space for contemplation.

Lampis washed and dressed mechanically, and then realized that everyone else was ready, candle in hand for church. Didn't they go to bed? He had just lay down, he'd hardly closed his eyes before the bell tolled.

Everyone repeated, "Are you ready? Let's go!"

Everyone touched everyone else, with a hand on a shoulder, a pat on the back of the hand, a gentle squeeze of the arm, a smile. They descended the stairs and walked to church in silence, in a cluster shrouded in affection and bonded in trust.

They lit their candles, made the sign of the cross, kissed the icon and took their place in silence, nodded to the people next to them, and waited to be transported. The priest's silhouette moved noiselessly in the inner sanctum. A muffled cough restored, temporarily, the element of corporeal existence. The cantor's recounting of the three women's ascent to Calvary Hill and worrying about their weakness in removing the tombstone seemed to carry the whole congregation behind the three women in silent, transcendental litany.

The sexton shuffled quietly from one site to another, straightening candles, motioning to the curious boys to step back, and glancing at the priest to anticipate his next move.

The candles and lamps, one by one, were extinguished by the sexton and the faithful, after a nod from the priest. Total darkness, except for a faint light flickering in the inner sanctum, as if from the moon behind a tattered cloud, far in the East.

The priest emerged with his lit candle, his face illuminated by the halo of the candlelight, stopped at the "beautiful gate" and chanted: "Behold, darkness and dawn," stretched out his hand with the candle in front and intoned: "Come ye, receive the light, from the inextinguishable light…"

Those closest to him stepped forward and lit their candles, then turned around to pass the light among all the faithful. Silence, again, amid the flickering lights; anticipation.

The priest raised his hand heavenward and, in a voice that may have not been his own, chanted: "Christ has risen from the dead…" The congregation repeatedly chanted this hymn, rising to carry their candlelight to the stars and to join with the multitudes throughout the land in spreading the message to the Universe.

Lampis joined his voice with the rest, his existence retrieved, expressed in this chant, and confined within the walls of the church. Here, he had received his forty-day blessing, baptism, and his first communion. He lifted his eyes from his candle to look at his family, to store the glow from their faces, to stretch his elbow out to touch the one next to him for a corporeal contact with bliss.

The hymns and intoning followed from one constellation to another, the reading of the Gospel was heard from an opening in the gates of heaven, and the finale "Christ has risen," with the response, "Truly He has," stirred the congregation to exchange smiles before filing to receive the small piece of bread, the antidoron (instead of gift), and to hear a personal "Christ has risen."

More glances, more smiles, more handshakes, and "Christ has risen," on the way out, the hugs and kisses reserved for the encounters in the church yard, first with the immediate family members, and then with whoever happened to be the closest.

The milling around in the church yard, with hugs and good wishes all around, continued for about fifteen minutes. The stars in the east began to fade. Only the brighter ones refused to surrender to the ascending yellow-purple light from behind the dark gray outline of the stretched-out ridges. The women – and some men – cupped their hands over their lit candles to protect them from the light breeze, to keep them burning, and bring the holy light to their homes. The chatter, full of merriment, was not interrupted by laughter or buoyance; it resulted from the overflow of joy and deliverance from the daily cares. The bursts of fire-crackers and boys' bragging left no echoes and hardly any memories – except, perhaps among them. The dim light from the windows of the church conveyed a message of tranquility and spiritual peace.

Mother reached the house first. She stood at the open door and spread her arms to embrace each and all with smiles and loves. Her example was followed quickly and the house reverberated with repeated vocalizations of "Christ has risen" and "Truly He has." They gathered around the table, mother, sister, and Aunt Violetta bringing the red eggs and the rest vying to guess and pick the egg with the hardest shell. Several times they chanted, "Christ has risen," before cracking egg against egg and laughter from winners and losers.

The special soup, prepared only on Easter Sunday, and the yogurt that followed, were tastier following the fasting during Holy week. The antics of the little nieces, looking angelic in their Easter dresses and courting attention, accentuated the pervasive happiness.

Father raised his glass to the pictures of Grandfather and Grandmother and toasted: "To you, blessed be your memory, we are indebted for all this happiness!"

The "Amens" were followed with the clinking of the glasses and the finale of a chorus of "Christ has risen."

They all helped clear the table – all except Father, who had never practiced it. They made their make-shift beds again and retired "for an hour or two" before resuming their festivities at sunrise.

Uncle Vasiles and brother-in-law George were up and ready for a walk in the country. The sun had just emerged from behind the peak of St. Christopher. The dome of the blue sky rested on the mountain ridges. The fields displayed their finest and brightest spreads of flower beds. The slopes ascended to their crowns of scattered majestic oaks. The valleys and ravines receded in the mist but spread heavenward the song of the nightingales and blackbirds. The noisy sparrows darted from trees to roofs, carrying in their beaks straw or stick for their nests. The dew on the grass blades sparkled from the sunray. The exhilarated redstart, perched in full view – at the top of the lone oak in an open field and defying the hawk – repeated "Christ has risen" in its own language. The fragrance of the wild flowers and blossomed trees came in waves with the light breeze and overlapped at the turns along the path on the slope. Brother-in-law George's weakness in suppressing the urge to express his inspirations or sentiments disrupted the others' concentration in assimilating all that surrounded them. Uncle Vasiles lagged behind, marveling, reminiscing, and comparing the present with the past images. Brother George walked ahead, hands clasped behind his back, lost in thought, or surrendered to the omnipotence of Nature in the Spring and barely aware of the others' presence.

He flitted from one thought to another, from awe to marvel, from a sigh to a cry of infinite joy, from the swaying branch before him to the mystery in the ruins of the distant castle. No effort in, no tiredness from the walk. Their appetite for more grew insatiable, turning into greed. They absorbed so much and missed much more. But the others must be waiting.

Father stood at the balcony, scanning slopes and ridges, spanning his assertiveness from early memories to reaping the rewards of his labors and dreams and in total awareness of the magnitude or importance of the moment.

"Did you enjoy your walk?" Mother asked, smiling and displaying her vicarious pleasure, before their response.

Expressions of joy, with gestures, words, and smiles filled the house and their hearts. No one could sit still. Touching, teasing, joining in merriment circled around the table, and around the room with every encounter. The exchange of stories and the sharing of memories followed one another in a sequence seemingly unconnected and ending with "How did we get to this subject?"

Happiness was experienced or expressed in so many ways. What else can one name all this?

The table was set again. More red eggs, salad, cheese, fresh-baked Easter bread, roasted spring lamb, wine from Grandfather's vineyard. Kings couldn't possibly have enjoyed a better feast or known more bliss. Luckily, no one asked who was the happiest; there'd be quite an unsettled contest, from four-year old Katerina to the Patriarch.

The afternoon services of Love, with the aura of summation or crowning of the glorious events of the day, had no hints of anticlimax. The air seemed more festive and less solemn. The priest appeared in a light of celestial exhilaration.

The congregation lifted above all earthly cares. The candle-lights illuminated the very essence of human existence. The last "Christ has risen" rose to the ceiling and spread out through the open doors, to mix with the triumphant bell-tolls.

More handshakes, more kisses on both cheeks, and more exclamations for "this beautiful, wonderful day."

The musicians tuned their instruments, sitting on the stone fence around the old Plane tree, oblivious to the milling and merriment around them. They waited patiently, in observance of the old tradition, for the priest to emerge from the church and lead the first dance.

The priest shook hands, right and left, placed himself at the lead of the quickly-formed circle of dancers and led the dance, gracefully and in dignity, for one full turn, then sat at the terrace against the church to enjoy the dance of his "flock."

The traditional three circles were formed in an orderly way, as if rehearsed, and the dance started in its full vigor. The young displayed their vitality and grace, the mature their strength and discipline, and the old their dignity and pride.

Lampis joined hands with his family and held the handkerchief for his father's favorite song, the 'Karangouna.' No one could dance it like his father could.

Lampis did not compete with his father when his turn came, dancing to the Tsamiko, 'The Willow Tree.' Whether happiness or abandon overcame his inherent shyness or the inspiration of Spring and his youth dispersed his inhibitions, he danced as if among nymphs and satyrs.

His Aunt Violetta wanted him to go "on and on."

"I did not remember you ever dancing this beautifully," his father told him.

His pleasure in giving his family a new dimension of pride in him lifted him above the higher branches of the Plane tree. Lampis moved to the end of the semicircle, and watched his sister, brother-in-law, brother, uncle, aunt and cousins taking the lead in a succession with his father guiding them. It seemed that all spectator eyes focused on his family.

The bills, from ten to one-hundred drachmas, kept filling the musicians' basket.

Young women turned and twisted gracefully, and the older women and men reminisced about their feats without envy. On and on they danced until dusk.

When the music stopped, smiles, good wishes, and handshakes were exchanged with sincerity and goodwill, once again. The musicians packed their instruments neatly, waved happily and gratefully, and mingled among the joyous crowd.

His father's erect posture and square shoulders; his mother's smiles and sparkling eyes; his uncle's reflection of all the day's fulfillments; his aunt's exuberance expressed in hugs and tearful eyes; his sister's girlish giggles; his niece's dashing from one to another…all and more, displaced all memories of hardship or sorrow of the past.

They walked to their home, arm-in-arm, turning around to transmit their individual bliss to each other, or to absorb more happiness, before crossing the doorway to the confines of intimacy, trust, and sharing. The small talk, the reminiscing, the invitation for a repetition of a well-known story served no purpose other than to strengthen their bonds beyond vulnerability.

Sleep came easily and carried him back to his familiar sunlit, flower-strewn, stretching to infinity, ridge, where he cast no shadow, heard no sound, and felt weightless.

The festive mood continued the next day, with church services at St. George's church in the adjoining village and a visit to Aunt Christitsa's home. He remembered that this tradition was very old and must be observed. The walk down to the creek, across the bridge, and up along the slope was anticipated with strained patience and eagerness for Aunt Christitsa's glowing smile and sparkling blue eyes. She'd meet them at the steps to the patio, with spread arms, beaming. Looking into her eyes – she always looked into your eyes – led to a revelation of boundless love, to unconditional surrender. Her assertiveness, always challenging to the strong and intimidating to the weak, added a new dimension to the joy from their being together and justified, fully, her nickname of 'The Captain.' Her happiness appeared unmatchable. The exchanges of trivial amenities conveyed deep commitments to each other and an open view of each individual's path. He cherished this encounter, as he had so many times in his childhood and adolescence and prayed for more of the same. The parting, as in the past, made his steps lighter and the day brighter.

The pilgrimage to the Monastery and to the ruins of the castle was planned carefully and anticipated eagerly. The memories of his past excursions and explorations carried him ahead of the start of the next day, as he lay with his hands clasped behind his head. He longed to climb the steep steps to the top of the ruins to follow the gorges and the succession of the cliffs to their twisting out of sight, to listen to the bells of a flock of goats or the chirping of the partridges, to descend to the cisterns of the middle ages, to carry a branch of bay, to be anointed with the dew on the blossomed clover. The vivid memories gave way to imaginations of new discoveries, and the fascination from these discoveries blended with the dreams in a restful sleep.

The walk along the winding road; the leaps from stone to stone across the sparkling waters of the broad creek; the stops to listen to the song of the nightingales and of the blackbirds; the sharing of fascination with the fragrance of the wild flowers or with the strength and endurance of the scattered Oak trees; and finally, the view of the Monastery with the white-washed fortress-walls flanked by tall, dark, cypress trees, the cupola and the belfry, each with a cross as its crown, reflecting glory in the morning sun; all in an overlapping sequence delivered him from the confines of his comprehensions to the door-steps of transcendence. All he could say to the others was "Stop. Look. Reflect."

Aunt Violetta squeezed his arm. "You must be seeing a lot more than I can; more than my brother Metsos who is a poet; tell me."

He couldn't. He could only feel it.

The rest of the walk was in total silence; even whispers would be sacrilegious. The light breeze bent the wheat in successive gentle waves and spread the mixed fragrance of chamomile with the aroma of the blossomed apple and scrub pear-trees; the swallows darted low barely above the flower beds or shut up against the blue sky to flutter their wings in tribute to Spring; the rocky slopes to the West, straight across, rose unevenly to a stretched-out proud ridge. The lizard, with a cricket in its jaws, hid under a rock; the vineyard to the left promised a good harvest in a few months. The fortress walls began to tell stories from their gun-holes and from the rampart at the top.

The gate, flung wide open to welcome pilgrims or suppliants, revealed a courtyard in a profusion of roses, potted flowers, and Jasmine vines winding along the rails of the stairways and patios. The dark-robed, radiant nuns with the Mother Superior at the front, welcomed them, guided them up the stairs to the inside of the church to light their candles and kiss the Holy Icons, and after a brief ritual, offered their traditional hospitality; red-dyed eggs, Easter-bread, and liquor, along the simple benches against the walls under the patio. The Mother Superior, sitting next to him wanted to know all about her godson, his brother Nick while maintaining everybody's attention, giving instructions to the nuns and not neglecting the children.

The tour of the Chapel where the members of the "Peloponnesian Elders" took the oath to gain freedom or die, of the room where their Declaration and their appeal to the "Christian Powers of Europe" was signed, and of the tunnel leading from the fortress to the forest, either to escape or to secure provisions during a siege, brought back what he felt, every time, as a child: the towering superhuman figures of the fighters in the revolution of 1821. He shared what he could express with his uncle and brother, storing the rest for standards and measures against achievements of other men of different ages and places. He saw, from the Balcony, the Byzantines and the Franks in their armor, on horseback, the Turkish ranks in their ferocity following a Dervish with a swirling sword, and the freedom-fighters dancing defiantly on the hilltops. He heard the hoarse commands, the neighing of the horses, the war cries, the spirit-lifting songs – all in a few minutes when alone, before he heard "Are you going to the castle?"

The paths they followed, after the pleas to be careful and the blessing from the Nuns, had been trotted for centuries by travelers, marauders, pilgrims, laborers, and warriors. If he could only divine what the oak-trees and the rocks had witnessed. His little cousins, with their boy-scout experiences, showed off at every chance. His Uncle reminisced aloud, entertaining everybody, himself probably the most. His brother leaped from rock to rock or across water-ruts and waited for the rest to catch-up. He followed the butterfly's abandon, the bee's deliberate visits from flower to flower, the direction of the breeze from the waves of the curtsying flowered branches. He was carried by the anticipation of the succession of Nature's revelation at the next turn. And he tried to retrieve his soul from its wanderings in the deep gorges and along the limits of his perception.

The confines of the narrow path, with thick brush on both sides, helped his concentration when needed or desired. The openness of the field, with the rows of stone fences and the luxuriant clover and wild flowers, lured thought and soul away to spread high and low among the souls and spirits of those who named this place "The Upper City," centuries ago. The 'City' was restored only in his imagination – no trace of it, anywhere! The dwellers of this "upper city" had vanished into oblivions, from massacres or displacement, long before the Monastery, an arm-stretch away from where he stood, rose to dominate with its beauty all that human senses can encompass. The camera focused on it, even before the thought "We have to remember it this way" was formed.

He tried to jump from rock to rock and to step only on naked ground, revering the clover the wild flowers. He resisted the temptation to pick the red poppies; and he swallowed hard remembering Marigoula, carried away with reveling, on a spring day eighteen years ago, standing on a big rock and calling aloud with all her strength, "Mama," then shaking with sobs. Her mother had died a month earlier. He did not relate this memory to Euripides, Marigoula's older half-brother, same mother, different fathers. Euripides had come along with his wife. Lampis prayed for one of Euripides' inimitable witty one-liners to bring him back from eighteen years ago.

The ruins of the tiny Chapel along the slope on the way to the castle provided shelter to lizards and challenges to the snails; the fragrance of the flowers, sprouting out from the spaces between the wall-stones and where the roof once rested, replaced the aroma of the incense. He remembered some of the names of the Saints from his grandfather's stories, impressing his uncle and Euripides.

The conquest of the summit of the castle was rewarded by the coolness of the breeze on his face, the rise of the song of the birds from the Plane trees lining the meandering creek below the precipice, the display of nature's immortality on the defiant cliffs and the repetition of his echo "long live." He assured his stunned younger cousins there was more to come. He would not tell them, not yet, about the time he was tempted when sixteen years old to cast himself off the cliff to find out how much of his past he could recapture before hitting the steeply sloping shining rock just above the creek. He only told them about throwing large rocks or pushing boulders to hear the hiss in the fall and to see them explode with the impact.

The descent to the cistern, the "discoveries" of the remnants of frescoes, the walk along and on top of the walls of the fortress invigorated body and imagination, unleashed exclamations, and evoked regrets for the lack of written records. His young cousins resented their father's frequent admonitions to be careful – they seemed insatiable. He told them all he knew and about some of his encounters in his excursions or escapes, estimating the height of the cliffs, carrying them along the winding trails and fascinating them with the repetitiousness of the echoes of his whistles or calls. He walked along the top of the inner and taller of the three concentric walls to the corner to conquer all before him and to rise above humble or petty encounters. He stood at the edge, spread his arms to embrace the breeze, looked down to the top of the trees retreating on the steep slopes to the merging of the two deep ravines, and strained to fathom time and space from creation to dissolution. His uncle's pleas to come down, lest his cousins would follow him, retrieved him from his wanderings.

Following a different path, on the way back, he looked for the little cave where he retreated, in a rainy afternoon, ten years ago. When he found it, he saw himself standing at the entrance, with raindrops on his hair and face, absorbing and blending his existence with the softness of the rain, the song of the birds, the whistles of the goat-heard, the fragrance of the wildflower, the shroud of the mist over the Plane trees in the ravine, and the gilded clouds drifting to cover a patch of blue sky. He listened to his uncle's story of his grandmother striking the dirge and crying when Grandfather's plow lifted a flat stone covering a full skeleton.

"God only knows whether this human being had anybody cry for him or her," she answered to Grandfather when asked why she was crying.

"It seems that he or she was properly buried," Grandfather had reasoned, and replaced the stone over the skeleton, taking his hat off to show respect and beg forgiveness. "This skeleton," Uncle Vasiles concluded, "Must have been centuries old and maybe of an enemy, since he was buried in a place all by himself."

The pre-occupation with not missing anything, sharing impressions and memories, and engraving the profusion of surging sentiments made their walk back effortless and short. The brief rest at the hill of and next to the ruins of St. George's Chapel stimulated repetitions of stories about the ringing of the bell, suspended deep in a covered and forgotten well, on St. George's day, about grandfather's perseverance, in his childhood, in locating the well by the resonance of the hollow ground from his stumping and jumping, and about the ringing of the bell at sunset to remind those in the fields to return to safety in their fortressed towns.

Their already stimulated appetite was satisfied with their provisions, from the hospitable nuns, of bread, cheese, roasted lamb, red-dyed boiled eggs, and wine. Taking turns in kneeling to drink from the spring fountain at the root of the Plane tree strengthened their bonds with new sentiments for posterity. The spread of glances and smiles from each other and across all their vision could encompass, the stir from the exclamations of ultimate pure pleasure, and the inevitable transfer of wish to passion for a repeat tethered them to this place and time permanently – only the appreciation of the time shown on their watches and promises to be back at the Monastery, where the others were waiting, gave them strength to strain for a release.

At the Monastery, they found everyone overwhelmed again with the beauty of this sacred and historical place. The excitement of the young cousins was impossible to contain, as they interrupted conversation and contemplation. His dilemma in participating or drifting aside to reflect on his individual harvests of memories and inspirations did not grow into a conflict. He participated with relish and reflected insatiably – all the way back to the village.

The mellowing sunset light and the gilded clouds resting on Tsemberou, the eternal mountain of his childhood's west horizon, spread a weightless mantle over the day's – and his life's – memorable and already nostalgic events. Relating these events to each other would be anticlimactic, if not violating their sanctity. Consequently, the evening was rather quiet, individual recollections and reflections punctuated by simple questions and answers and not interrupted by conversations. Their tiredness seemed blissful and quite apparent.

The visitors did not stay long, as if out of deference. The exchange of "good nights" with tight hugs and gentle kisses, all around, ended the day of a journey in the Elysian fields. The epilogue was engraved from his gazing at the stars, from his deciphering the whispers of the breeze in the mulberry tree, and from his rising heavenward to the song of the nightingales. He tip-toed to his bed, listened for more messages from the gently-rustling vine-leaves across the base of his window and was lulled to surrender, unconditionally, to Morpheus.

CHAPTER 30

AUNT GIANNOULA'S SCOLDING OF THE CHICKENS and reprimands to her goats, with the clanking of her pans to re-assert her authority, every morning after dawn, served as the alarm-clock and the first stimulus to conversation. She was not going to change her routine for "those lazy Athenians who sleep until noon!" And they, he among "those Athenians," weren't going to allow this minor nuisance to spoil their day.

The sun lit the cloudless blue skies from mountain-top to mountain-top, shrouded the ridges with a thin haze, studded the slopes with the glimmering shadows of the trees, whitened the mist in the ravines, and reflected in the dew-drops on flowers and leaves. The breeze reveled in tipping the tops of the cypress trees, in swaying the blossomed branches of the crab-apple trees, in spreading waves across the wheat fields, and in carrying the song of the birds or the bleating of the ewes. The flow of the water in the winding creek carried its hum over the smooth pebbles and rocks in its bed, greeted the cyclamens at every turn, and sparkled in its encounters with the sun rays penetrating through the branches of the Plane trees. The fragrance of the wild rose dominated in the shadowy steep banks; the defiant thorns challenged the bees and the butterflies across the barren fields; and the pear trees displayed their glory, in full blossom, to all who could see.

Each day revealed new worlds of beauty, sprouted new joys, and added to the happiness of the day before. The steady approach of the day of separation and of commitment of all the collection of joy and happiness to memories cast a light shadow of sadness, but fleetingly. The repetition of the promise to return, whether to himself or to the others, prompted by the encounters of moist eyes or the flight of the swallow, was followed by vows to never sever his roots. The toast with the clinking of the wine-glasses at dinner, changed from "Christos Aneste" ("Christ is risen") to "Kale antamose" (Happy reunion), from celebration to bracing for the goody-byes – a natural sequence in a family with a full past of separations and reunions.

The departure of Uncle Vasiles' family and of the two Georges – brother and brother-in-law – unfolded a rich array of memories with each hug and each reassertion of "We had a wonderful time." He could not recall, nor could he imagine, a happier Easter Holiday. His sister, with the two little daughters would stay a little longer. The emptiness, if it ever developed, would be filled with the chatter and antics of the little girls. He'd visit some of the relatives to listen to familiar stories and find security in the old bonds. He'd revisit the fields, the vineyards, and the hide-outs. He'd sort out his memories to draw strength from the good and lessons from the bad. He'd whistle old tunes when alone and bring fresh wild flowers to his mother.

The extra week with his two little nieces was filled with games, giggles, and joy. He chased them, threw them high in the air, tickled them and repeated fairy tales he had heard from his grandmother. Their little arms around his neck and their cheek pressed against his cheek spiraled him heavenward. Watching them bounce on the bed or chase after the chickens condensed the whole world to a few meters' diameter. He shared his joy in them with the visiting and visited relatives. He started and ended each day with a gentle kiss on their heads as they lay asleep next to each other. And he was sad to see them climb into the taxi for the return to Athens.

The trip around Peloponnesus had not been planned until after his sister and her two little daughters left to return to Athens. The view of the snowy slopes and ragged peaks of Taygetus, stretching across and raising the boundaries of the horizon in the south, beckoned with a lure for a pilgrimage to the glory of Sparta and the mourning of Mystras. His childhood curiosity - whether the people in the villages of Taygetus were aware of his trying to see or imagine them climbing the stairs in their homes or dancing in their village square – returned and changed into the desire to see his village from their villages. The southwest barriers to the rim of the sky dome revived the memories of the swarms of German bombers flying to bomb the port city of Kalamata nineteen years ago and aroused the curiosity to see how that city looked, having risen from its ashes.

The taxi fare, being very cheap, did not challenge his frugality. The summoned taxi driver, Spyros, from the near village of Kollinae, an old acquaintance from his first two years at the Gymnasium, was affordable in price and tolerable in his poor-taste wise-cracks. During the breaks in Spyros' monologue, he could anticipate the new revelations of the glory of Spring, at the next turn of the winding road up the slope or along the hill-ridges, with more excitement. Monotony was a remote, vague concept. No order in the pine forest, the swaying heather in blossom, the fields of poppies, the swooping of the swallows, the slivers of white clouds, the succession of mountain peaks or the direction of the gorges.

Cousin Nikos responded occasionally and laconically, not in deference to their visit to Laconia, but conforming to his character – probably a vestige of his ancient Laconic heritage.

Some memories, long suppressed, but awakened by certain landmarks, rose above his rapture with nature's beauty and Spyros' poorly connected stories; the white-washed house with the blue window shutters on the sloped, where his mother was born and where he had spent summer days; the house of the feared thief Balaskas, executed by the EAM resistance fighters; the cross-roads where the German conqueror, expressionless and stern, drove by without a glance at him and his mother; and finally, Monodendri – the lone tree – where the German forces executed one hundred and eighteen hostages – among them Dr. Karvounis, who rejected the offer to be spared and chose to die with the rest.

Lampis asked Spyros to stop, so he could pay his respects at the single cross marking the site of the execution. They stood in silence, staring at the low dense bushes and at the rocks, some polished by rain and age, and some lichen-patched, jutting among them.

Trying to swallow the hard lump in his throat pumped the tears down his cheeks. Returning to the taxi and back from that accursed black day of sixteen years ago, still in silence, he noticed other people, some with handkerchiefs to their eyes, revering the memory of the sacrifice. He had heard the rattle of the machine guns; he'd witnessed the fall of the bodies, brother next to brother; he'd seen the blood trickling and squirting; he'd convulsed with the agonal kicks and spasms of limbs and of arching backs; and he'd segregated the murderous robot soldiers, turning their backs to walk away and mount their trucks, from the human race. He had ached for the grieving mothers and fathers, and he shuddered at the thought of measuring their grief – whether for one son or for four sons (one mother had lost four sons, two others lost three each, and two more, lost two each!). He had wondered whether the survivors in these families were sustained by faith, by hatred, or by resignation. But he did not relate any of his torments to the others.

The slow climb along the winding road to the ridge of the mountain revealed nothing. The vast space to the end of his vision was devoid of life, of movement, of substance – just emptiness. If Nikos or Spyros talked, he did not hear them. He was aware of his own existence only because he was aching.

The view from the summit, facing south and all one could encompass with only a slight turn of the head, spread an array of slopes, valleys, and mist in the distance, with the brightness of the sunlight bridging the gorges, dancing in waves across the terraced wheat fields or sparkling exclamations among the quivering leaves of the poplar and olive trees. The fragrance of the orange and lemon blossoms rose up the side of the mountain on the wings of the playful breeze. The meandering of Eurotas River among orange groves, with its ripples reflecting old glories and tranquility, receded in the south.

The groans of the taxi engines in the ascent changed to a soft hissing going down-hill. He needed all of that and more of a sustained effort to relieve the pain from the wounds of Monodendri.

The succession of images of groves of orange and lemon trees in blossom, of flower and vegetable gardens, of white-washed houses with patios and window-sills lined with flower pots, and of people engaged in grave conversations or laughing eventually pushed the past, agonizing or glorious, out of cognizance. Almost suddenly, there was no time for memories or contemplations; no space for other events or places for comparison or contrast. Had he not been in the confines of the taxi-cab, he might have become diluted – or oversaturated to a burst – by the succession and intensity of the overlapping displays of beauty. Cousin Nikos remained, expectantly, quiet. Spyros kept discreetly silent. He knew he missed a great deal – he would just have to come back some day. The waving of the people along the road conveyed a combination of greetings and an invitation to return. He must come back.

The city of Sparta opened its wide boulevards before them – tranquil, clean, fragrant, welcoming. The reception of the hotel extended hospitality, warmth and unreserved trust. The encounters with the Spartans, on the streets or in stores, confirmed the oft-repeated observation that "The people of Sparta are polite and civilized." Roaming the streets, lined with trees and spotless, in late afternoon and evening, allowed fleetingly, for the wandering of the imagination to the time when Leonidas marched out for the ultimate sacrifice in the altar of Freedom; when their shapely and proud young maidens – the phaenomerides or thigh revealers, as the rest of the Greeks enviously, rather than condescendingly, called them – held off and beat the furious attacks of Kind Pyrros of Epiros; or when the two benevolent brothers Agis and Kleomenes persuaded the people to recognize the rights of the Perioekioe and the Helots. The visit to the site of the excavations a walking distance from the modern city, aroused, again, sentiments of reverence for his heritage. Remnants of the Hellenistic and Roman eras, they served more as reminders of decline, of the faults rather than the virtues of tradition, of resignation or even of decadence.

The profusion of fragrance, enjoyed in the outdoor restaurant at dinner and through the open window at the Hotel, competed with the dense stars across the dome of the sky and with the serenading band of young men. Surrendering to sleep came only after having exhausted all his reserves in fighting it.

He had anticipated a new surge of pride from the reflections of strength and endurance in the monuments of Byzantine culture in a Christian world, whipped into submission to mysticism and superstition. Instead, the ruins of the palace with the gaping roof and windows, the spiritual vibrations from the carvings and mosaics of St. Demetrios' church at its feet, and the treasure-chest of relics from a defiant faith in the church of Pantanasa, tucked permanently away on the steep slope, - transferred him to fields strewn with reminders of decline, despair, and pleadings to divinity for deliverance. The stretch of ramparts across the ridge and summit symbolized a retreat from fertile grounds, not a citadel of freedom – a place where men trusted the natural barriers and the goodwill of Christ, not in the strength and dignity of free men. The deference and hospitality of the nuns of the Pantanassa echoed a mixture of submission and compliance from the dark past. The throne at St. Demetrios where the last emperor of the Byzantine Empire – or what was left of it – was crowned, seemed suspended in emptiness and a symbol of the Fates' mockery. This notable Emperor would die fighting as a simple soldier on the ramparts of Constantinople. Climbing and descending on stone-paved streets, where infantry and cavalry of the crusaders crowded with heavy loads of loot, taken in the name of Christ, from the schismatics or heretics, he heard the clamor and revelry mixed with pleading and bewailing. The lizard flitted at the sight of the cat. Resting on a flower, the butterfly fanned its wings slowly and rhythmically. The souls and spirits of the past, unseen, fled before him through the ruins.

He could not decide whether he wished to come back.

Reaching the summit and walking on top of the massive fortification walls to the very edge over a sheer cliff, about a mile above the now-foaming, now sparkling waters of a rushing stream, failed to change his reflections. Had he been able to push the thoughts of human suffering, of surrender to the impostors of God's anointed, and of the despair at the sight of dying Hopes, he may have overcome his timidity or inhibition to assert his existence by calling, with all his strength, the nymph Taygete from among the evergreens on the steep slopes of the mountain, rising to the West and named after Her; he may have cheered the Byzantines for having remembered their heritage and summoned their valor to route the Franks in the valley to the south-west; he may have strained to hear the triumphant cries of the legendary Freedom fighter Zaharias in chasing the panic-stricken Turks. He did gather, summoning some reserves, from his scanning in all directions, images of nature's glorious displays, of echoes from a proud past, of laments for submitting to ephemeral gratification, and of re-awakening of the consciousness of Freedom's rewards.

The descent to vine-shaded Restaurant porches, from the peak of the day's journey, added links to some disconnected impressions: Here an old woman harvesting wild oats with her sickle; there a donkey grazing at the end of its stretched tether; further down a tourist or scholar reflecting and contemplating across the plain the gently rising slopes of Mount Parnon; and below in the shades of the olive and pine trees, monuments of greatness and decay.

The worked-up appetite suddenly took command, was appeased by an appropriately Spartan snack, and acquiesced; the appetite for the venture over the Mount Taygetus mounted.

The return to Sparta, along a gently winding road through olive groves, orange gardens, and flower-carpeted fields, contrasted with the climb over ancient paved paths and with the anticipated ascent through the evergreen-flanked or wonder-unfolding road over Taygetus. They did not waste time. They, Lampis and Nikos, had to be in Kalamata before sun-down.

As they drove out of the city headed west, the urge to wave goodbye to the people of Sparta was insuppressible. The response, with a smile, conveyed a clear message: "It was nice to have you with us, have a safe trip, and come back." He wished he could have stayed longer and vowed to return. In two days, he'd stored enough memories to anchor him in this now tranquil harbor of glory and noble spirit forever. He recognized, among those waving back, Lycourgos, Leonidas, Agis, and Kleomenes, again and again. The perioekioe stopped and stretched to their full height to re-assert their command of existence and future. A flock of doves circled to the far right and perched on a lone oak tree.

This was peace.

The ascent to Mount Taygetus was gradual; the view to the right wider and expansive; the anticipation of reaching the clouds, unfolding down from the summit, growing; the desire for one last revelation from Trype, where the ancient Spartans cast the deformed or handicapped infants off into the gorge below, following the commands of Lykourgos, according to some sources (How was Agisilaos, lame from birth, spared, he questioned?) consuming; the need for a deep breath of lemon-blossom fragrance, mixed with the scent of pine, overpowering. They stopped; he walked to the edge of the road and traveled across space and time, without fear of severance from his own existence.

The winding road split massive rock formation, edged along steep slopes, crossed over sparkling books, skirted open fields strewn with bright swaying wildflower, and turned away from precipices. A beautiful view was succeeded by a breathtaking sight, and the overlapping of wonders left no room or time for comparisons. The purity of the thin mountain-air carried the fragrance of the pine and of the 'mountain-tea' to beyond the recognized senses. The groans of the taxi were muffled by the concentration in capturing the whispers from pine to pine and the messages from the past.

The scattered clusters of houses on steep slopes or near the edge of a precipice, the narrow and lost behind ridges dirt-roads, the lone chapels on widely separated cliffs, and the terraced fields, framed by eternal evergreens, repeated and echoed tales of escapes from the invaders, of sacrifices to the altars of Freedom, and of resurgence of strength to overcome submission to Fate and to rise to a pre-ordained destiny of noble ends. The Franks, the Venetians, the Turks, and more recently, the German conquerors had repeated, among their ranks, that they disdained subjugating these villagers, camouflaging their cowardice with bravado; when challenged to the point of derision, they ventured out in large hordes to pillage and burn, to defile sacred grounds, and to hurry back in their fortresses boasting of their triumphs and staining history. He captured the ascent of small crowds from the valleys to defensible ridges; he witnessed the frenzied building of houses around a church; he followed the sentinel to a point of a clear view; he heard the goading of the plowman and reached out to help the old woman carry her sack of grain; he spanned the width of the slopes; he measured the depth of each gorge; and he felt anchored to a past of struggle and of oblivion to mortal confines.

He returned to his own personal confines, pitting, temporarily, his insignificance against the ages of human challenges to gods and nature when cousin Nikos finally asked, "Are we approaching Kalamata?"

He reasoned that since the olive trees stretched to greet the pine trees, they must have descended low enough to approach Kalamata. The curves of the road were wider, with longer and longer straight stretches to allow the taxi-driver to speed up. The encounters with shepherds and farmers became more frequent, and the villages seemed to be drawing closer to each other. Cousin Nikos was impatient to get out of the taxi, not feeling well.

"We're almost there," the driver assured them.

The city of Kalamata was still numbed and stunned from the blows of the war. The reminders of the tilted and rusting hulks of ships in its harbors and of roofless buildings with gaping windows from the bombings of the Luftwaffe nineteen years ago, of gutted roads by the traffic of tanks and heavy artillery for eight years, until nine years ago, and of black-clad old women in mourning for lost sons cast an oppressive shadow of defeat. There were no signs of gathering strength for a revival, of stretching for a full awakening. The return to his greetings conveyed envy, but not resentment, with a message, "You're lucky, you're not from here."

The smiles were restrained, the gestures measured, the responses to inquiries brief and discouraging for conversation.

Lampis walked along the shore, watching the seagulls gliding or perching on the masts of the sunken ships, estimating the intervals between the splashes of the waves, looking for rainbows, and recoiling from excursions to memories and dreams.

Cousin Nikos felt better, his headache relieved. A simple meal on a broad sidewalk in front of the restaurant, reminiscing about their childhood in a different era, and anticipating their travel to Pylos and Olympia did not dim the near-ecstasy images gathered in crossing over Mount Taygetus. The promenade along the shore, in the late evening, unveiled more of a surrender to dull deities. Older couples, with clutched arms, walked in silence, looking straight ahead. Children dashed across the street and into the crowds, as if being chased by prankster-demons. Young girls frowned at some imaginary temptation. No music to be heard. No laughter to echo.

A small boat bobbed as if on an uneven teeter-totter. The play of the light and the gentle ripples in the sea seemed tame and timid. The surf crept-up on the beach and retreated apologetically. The thick gray across the bay shielded the lures for travel and muffled the song of the sirens. He, too, retreated before some of his own desires and fantasies, lest he commit sacrilege. Yet, his strolls seemed to carry him to more temptations.

A brief visit to Aunt Vasilo's, his mother's sister's house and the encounter with cousins he had never met before, marred his wishes for more pleasant memories with some remorse for failing to arouse any new sentiments. He censured his judgmental conclusions but failed to neutralize them. He confessed to Nikos, and Nikos absolved him.

Pylos reposed on the tranquil shore, its bay facing the long island of Sphacteria, and was lost in the memories of Nestor's feasts and boastings. The grandeur of its palaces was left to the imagination. The bare skeletons of its circling walls and the worn floors of the palaces or dwellings invited for a journey with Nestor to far-away Troy for adventure and for a glimpse of glory; to sail beyond Sphacteria and out of sight of land; to marvel at the strength and beauty of Achilles and Aias; to turn away from the arrogance of Agamemnon; to try to unravel Odysseus' plans; to listen to Nestor's endless stories about "When men were men," stealing the cattle of the Elians or dispatching an adversary. The bright and cloudless blue sky, the deep-blue waters lifting Sphacteria above their gentle waves, and the caressing breeze revealed and reflected the glories and the sacrileges of the past in Calypso's legacy.

Sphacteria beckoned with the sun-bathed cliffs and the secrets of her shores. The small boat, puffing its shoulder up to the rocky wall, promised lasting memories. The boatman's smile and handshake initiated the desired memories. They glided over the joyous waves, with no white-caps, and tried to penetrate the depths of Navarino's bay waters in search of the remains of the Turko-Egyptian fleet and of the Ottoman empire.

The boatman assured them that some of the sunken ships were still intact, for one hundred and fifteen years, until the German bombardments in 1941; he pointed to a few planks near the shores of Sphacteria and displayed a feeling of horror in relating the origin of the name of the island. "Three thousand men were put to the sword on this island! ("sphazein" meant the dispatching with the sword or knife).

The cries of the seagulls may still be echoing the distant groans of the dying on this tranquil, uninhabited island.

Two sheer white cliffs, rising perpendicularly out of the deep blue waters, each with a white wreath of spray encircling its base, stood apart, joined by the ends of a rainbow, to the south of Sphacteria, and unstained by the horrors of the war and the carnage that soaked its soil. Gentle splashes soothed the southern tip of the island. The eastern shore stretched to their left, as they rowed parallel to it, beckoning for a human footprint. The sparkling of the morning-sun with the ripples of the tame waves, veiled the face of the past below the brows of the shrub and rusty rocks. The remains of the Turko-Egyptian fleet revealed their secrets only to those who reveled in History.

They entered into the bosom of the enclave, leaped onto the rocky shore, watched the crabs scurrying into crevices, shaded their eyes against the sun when facing East, and walked toward the summit. They jumped from stone-to-stone, exchanging laconic phrases like, "be careful" or "imagine one hundred or three thousand years ago."

They stood at the summit, bathed in sunlight and caressed by the breeze, to gaze at the shores of the mainland, saturated with mist and memories, and to stretch for a grasp of what lay beyond the haze to the West.

The boatman waved, with his hands crossing above his head. Was he sharing, vicariously, in their ecstasy, or was he reminding them that it was time to go? They were carried, weightless, along the narrow paths, gutted by the rain-waters, and from stone to stone, by the pull of the anticipated new discoveries. The answer "indescribable" to the boatman's inquiry, "How was it?" left no reserves or excuses for conversation. Rowing back across the straits, with his thoughts anchored to the rocks of Sphacteria, brought Pylos closer from Nestor's age to now and to tomorrow.

Lampis leaped off the boat onto the Pier, shook the hand of the boatman and read in his eyes "You made my day!" he stored one last wide-angle picture of this story-packed ground and agreed with Nikos that it was time to go.

The overlapping revelations of olive-groves, white-washed villages, ruins of castles, crowning peaks, flocks of sheep on slopes, winding brooks, and thickets of shrub left no room for reflection or anticipation and made the trip seem longer than expected. He had not talked to any of the other passengers on the bus, and wondered, at the end, why no one sang.

The landscapes, in the bus-ride from Pyrgos to Olympia, receded behind without an imprint. The anticipation of the pilgrimage to the temple of Zeus and the stadium of the Olympic games, of marveling at the sight of Hermes of Praxiteles, and of roaming among the ruins and the spirits of the glorious past seemed to erase images and sounds along the way, as soon as they were formed. His heart-beat pumped a lump to his throat. He watched the chariots in convoys with young men standing and gazing silently in the distance; he shared the pride of the fathers of the young men; and he sensed the honor, along with the reins, in the grip of the charioteer. A new procession came into view with each turn of the road. And finally, the modern little town of Olympia spread the pride and the splendor of its heritage before visitors and pilgrims.

They found a room on the first floor, with a window opening to a garden of blossoming lemon and orange trees. The first, few deep-breaths were intoxicating; the next few transported him to the Elysian fields. He could not wait. The Alsos, with its majestic pines, to the South-East was calling; the Alpheus to the South-Southwest was luring; the poplars were nodding and whispering, "Come to us."

They walked in silence and reverence to the sacred grounds, and they wandered among the columns of the temple of Zeus and of the palaistra (wresting or training grounds), in awe and in a trance. Phideias' statue of Zeus, sitting on his throne, appeared before him, just as Pausanias described it: "Either Zeus came down and showed himself to Phideias, or Phideias ascended to the summit of Olympia to see Zeus in all his glory."

They crossed the gate that carried the athletes to the stadium and stood before the stand where the Ellanodikae (Greek judges) crowned the victors with the wreath of olive branches. He turned to see Diagoras carried on the shoulders of his three victorious sons, and he heard the roaring and the chanting of the crowd, "Die now Diagoras, what other glory or happiness could you possibly wish for?" He felt the throb of his heart expanding his chest at the sight of Diagoras slumped dead on his son's shoulders.

The fragments of the columns and statues in the walls of the ruins of a Byzantine church raised a sigh of sadness and shame at the realization that the destruction and desecration of noble human aims and achievements was carried out, in the name of Christianity, by the Byzantine emperors Theodosius the Great, and Theodosius the Small – long after the Celts and Allarich and before the pagan Slavs made their inroads.

He walked and turned to look again. He stopped and listened to the messages in the eternal whispers among the pine-trees and the laurels; and he followed the course of the Alpheus to the end of his horizon. The museum, at the top of the hill, inhaled and exhaled silent visitors. They walked slowly, he to fortify his soul for the ultimate gratification and Nikos lost in silence. He had always, from his early awareness, left the best for last. He borrowed Nike's wings, at the entrance, to fly for one more look, over the ruins of the temples and the gymnasia, spread out from the foot of the hill, before entering the museum. He strolled and stopped, smiled and stopped, along the displays of the statues and friezes, still leaving the best for last. He finally stood before Hermes. Hermes looked straight ahead. His gaze fixed at infinity, with a mission; His perfect body relaxed after the journey, leaning on a tree stump, with every part reflecting, in addition to perfection, human dignity and divine purpose; the left side made one smile back, the right side announced, "It's time to rest;" the front transfixed one's admiration to inexpressible emotions.

He circled around it, again and again, and once more, as if tethered.

An attractive young woman sat on a bench about twenty feet in front of the statue. "I had the same dilemma," she said in English, smiling. "Sit here for a while. Maybe, eventually, we can, together, find the strength to move, before they usher us out."

He smiled back and sat next to her in silence. He studied and marveled at the contours of the statue's flexed muscles of the left half of the body, limbs, and torso; he followed the relaxed outlines of muscles and joints of the right half to the conclusion of perfection; he lost his breath in gazing at the power of beauty; he returned to every part for an insatiable 'encore;' and, unable to gather enough words to express his admiration, he turned to the young woman to ask for help from a smile.

Responding or sharing her sentiments, Karen obliged with the hoped-for smile. All they could say when they finally gathered enough strength to move, was "Can you ever imagine anything as beautiful?"

They walked alongside each other outside of the Museum, before she asked, "How was it saved from the Germans?"

"They buried it," he told her, "and defied the German's threat to execute ten men if the statue was not produced. The Germans finally gave up after executing fifty people."

She could not believe it. They asked the first souvenir shop owner; he confirmed it.

"Some of these men were my relatives," a salesman at a small clothing store half-bragged, half-demurred.

When the waiter at the coffee-shop emphasized, "That's what happened," Karen wept. They hardly talked about anything else; just Hermes and his survival through fanaticism, barbarism, and the ages. They parted with the memories of their encounter and without the exchange of personal pursuits or addresses.

He felt guilty leaving Nikos out, even though he related to him some of his exchanges with Karen. Nikos, as expected, was understanding: "You could go with her and show her around for a while. She's pretty," he said, blushing. She had wandered off to rejoin some friends.

Lampis and Nikos strolled along, visiting some souvenir shops. They bought some small, inexpensive replicas for their parents before stopping at a restaurant for another 'Spartan meal.' He could not stop talking, and Nikos hung on every word, about the day's experiences and rewards.

The experience of their return to their room could have not possibly been anticipated. They had left their window open. Through it spilled the mellow light of a full moon, the fragrance of the lemon and orange blossoms, and the song of a chorus of nightingales vying with each other in serenading their mates. They did not desecrate the night by turning the light on. They absorbed all they could, sitting by the open window and returning to their beds to lie awake through the night for more and more. Morpheus, undoubtedly distracted by the very same enchantments, took his time before rising from the gentle currents of the Alpheos, carrying breezes, whispers, and rustlings to lure them to His domain of oblivion and of unexpected gratifications or disturbing encounters.

When awakened, they wondered whether they both had the same dream. They vowed to remember this dream. Whatever followed would be anticlimactic.

———

The trip to Patras certainly was anticlimactic in spite of the exuberance of Spring; of expansive carpets of deep red dense poppies, spread over fields of rolling hills with olive branches tipping like dominoes; of rising above tree-tops, belfries and of mountain-tops poking the edges of blue sky at each turn of the road.

The city of Patras lay on its side along the shore, its right shoulder supporting the Acropolis. A Hotel on the harbor promised easy access to the strolling grounds in the evening, a quiet night, and a pleasant view of the sunlit slopes in the morning. He deferred the resolution of his conflict about visiting Petros, his ex-roommate and Carol's defiler, until the next day. Carol's moist blue eyes sparked in his memory, igniting pain, longing, and indignation, all at the same time. The long walk along the shore, past warehouses and gardens, soothed the pain and displaced, on the return, all images or perceptions with the concentration in fathoming and storing all the beauty of the sunset.

There were no ghosts like those in Kalamata. This city seemed, somehow, severed from the past and flirting with the future. Its harbor was cluttered with ships of the American 6th Fleet; the streets, surrounding and stretching out of the harbor, soon became crowded with groups or clusters of sailors – some polite, some boisterous, some in search of entertainment, some looking for gifts for their dear ones back home.

Nostalgia, of a different kind, dominated his thoughts for 'back-home' for a brief while. The escapes from regimentation when in the Army brought back smiles and the urge to tell Nikos all about them. He was interrupted by an argument between an unscrupulous store-keeper and a polite, confused sailor. The sailor questioned why he was charged three times the amount of the price-tag. He and Nikos stepped in, on the side of the sailor. Nikos barely contained his rage; and after the purchase of the item at a discount, they headed for the Tourist Police. They returned to find the shop locked up and the shop-keeper arrested. There!

A new destination the next day: a pilgrimage to Mega Spylaion (Great Cavern) and Aghia Lavra (Santa Laura). The train ride along the shore on the left, through olive groves and orange gardens, with the green mountain slopes rising nearly straight up on the right, added memories and inspirations vying for first place with those from the slopes of Mount Taygetus. Could this be surpassed? It was, by the ride on the "toothed railway" train from Diakofto to Kalavyrta, climbing in the narrow, deep gorges with the sheer cliffs, allowing the view of only a narrow strip of blue sky; by the crawling along the side of a cliff, with the opposite cliff as close as the stretch of the arm from the window; by the stopping in the shade of thick, ageless plane trees; and by the drawing out a triumphant whistle at the end of the line.

He ignored the occasional chills and the lingering aches, in his determination to miss nothing. The three-kilometer hike up the very steep slopes to Mega Spylaion suppressed all the aches. The mild perspiration and warmth were attributed to the efforts of the climb; the soreness of the throat to panting. With his gaze fixed at the towering belfry, with a simple cross as its crown, he was carried aloft, transported and deposited at the gates of the sacred, and sanctified in faith and mission grounds of the Monastery.

A narrow, stone-paved yard hung over a cliff, with its foundation resting on a few strips of terraced gardens. The windows seemed to be carved out of the cliff hanging above, in five tiers. Directly in front, perched on top of a jutting out second cliff, was a square building with a cross on its roof, a sentinel and guardian for the parent cloister.

The visit to the church, deep in the cavern, overwhelmed him with a sacramental reverence for the power of God in the eyes of the believers and with the sympathy for the frustration of the skeptics. He and Nikos lit their candles; followed the shadow of the monk crossing himself and bowing before the austere wide-eyes Byzantine icons; were penetrated by the now benevolent, now punishing stare from these same icons; marveled at the art of the chandeliers and of the carvings of the icon stand; and retreated slowly and in awe, to the daylight.

The monk who served them coffee and toast obliged in relating the history of this Monastery, from its establishment in the 7th century A.D. to its contributions in the wars against the conquerors. The remotest the related events, the more profuse the apologies for missing details. The eye-witness of the hanging and of the lowering from the ropes of eighteen monks, from the windows and balconies of the sentinel building on the next cliff, was described matter-of-factly, all bitterness or hatred against the Germans erased by time or rationalized away with religious convictions. The sin of pride was concealed below the black robes and the furrowed forehead, in relating these stories and in showing them the largest oak wine barrel in Greece.

The next pilgrimage to Aghia Lavra, the site of the official Declaration of the Revolution against the Ottoman Empire, by the Bishop of Patras, in the midst of the Liturgy celebrating the Annunciation of Virgin Mary, required extra-strong fortification against the tide of the surge of emotions. He did not talk and did not listen to the eager-to-please taxi-driver. The sacred and sanctified interior appeared majestic, yet humble, before its accomplished titanic mission. He was carried aloft by his own sentiments, and stood before the Beautiful Gate, the entrance to the Inner Sanctum, and he tried to capture, with his imagination, the moment Bishop Germanos stepped out of the Inner Sanctum holding the banner 'Liberty or Death,' and challenging "Who wants my flag, what hand deserves it?" Lampis felt pushed forward by the surge of a crowd with outstretched hands to take the flag. He owed them, the carriers of the banner, so much, and he reflected: forty-five years earlier the cry "Give me Liberty or give me Death!" that reverberated across his adopted country.

When they returned to Kalavrita – they had just passed through on their way from Mega Spylaion to Aghia Lavra – the aches became more intense, the soreness of the throat intensified, and swallowing required effort. The rest in the shadow of the giant plane tree and the cool lemonade did not help much; nor did the long shadow of the lone, huge, cross at the site where all of the captured male inhabitants, above the age of twelve, to the number 1238, were executed in retaliation for a German defeat on the battlefield. The reminders of this terrible event – the cross, the women in black, the absence of smiles – intensified his apprehension of imminent illness and made him decide to change his plans of making the round of Peloponnesus and return home. The first taxi driver asked for an exorbitant fee, far beyond their means' and when they heard him telling the other taxi-drivers about, "these two young men who seem desperate to get home," they decided that waiting until morning was the better choice and to tell the taxi-drivers that their greed did not serve them very well. They retired to a boarding room in a widow's house.

The night was terrible for him with chills and a high fever and for Nikos with keeping a vigil, helpless. The train ride to Diacofto and on to Corinth and Tripolis the next morning, left only memories of chills, shivers, a burning fever and a painful throat. He made his own diagnosis of acute streptococcal tonsillitis, took some penicillin in Tripolis, and returned home to his worried parents. A violent cough, with some blood, caused some panic in his parents that he could hardly alleviate. His rapid recovery, after the coughing up of blood, brought relief to all, especially his parents.

His brother George returned from Athens, having resigned from his employment, to spend some time with the parents before leaving for America. Mother's light steps turned into shuffling; her shoulders drooped, her smile could not veil her sadness, and her eyes remained moist. Now all three of her sons will be far away in America. She hugged them at every encounter, and looked into their eyes to drive her love for and faith in them deeper into their hearts. They did not read any pleading in her moist eyes. There was no remorse in her sighs; bitterness against the Fates was unthinkable.

Father's strength was unwavering, buttressed by his 'philosophizing' and his belief in that 'the pre-ordained is impossible to circumvent,' his chin was up and his shoulders still seemed to support the firmament without tilting, but supporting Mother required more strength.

Father pointed to the fledgling swallows, perched close to each other on the clothes-line, with his right arm tenderly around Mother's shoulders. "Look, Mother. Learn a lesson from them. They left the nest; they'll come back tonight and tomorrow night; they'll fly to the telephone-wires, across the street, they'll come back again; they'll fly farther and farther, and finally, they won't come back; the nest will remain empty."

That did not help much. It just furrowed her forehead and heaved her chest.

They all had to find ways to keep busy. Lampis and his brother George built new flower troughs at the edge of the patio and made the rounds of places to harvest childhood memories and repeat the vows to return.

Father rode-off on Kitsos in quest of an oracle for the answer to, "When will we see our sons again?"

Mother lit the candle and crossed herself before the Holy Icons.

Cousin Nikos stood at the top of the stairway, lost somewhere across the space before him and the past behind him. They returned greetings and were reminded of the remaining days. They read in each other's eyes, "We'll be back."

Aunt Maritsa, who was traveling with them to join her sons in Chicago, counted the days, swinging from the joy in anticipating embracing her sons again to the grief in uprooting "A life of sixty years," and in the foreboding thought that she may never come back.

Friends and relatives "Couldn't resist the impulse," – that's what they said – for yet another "brief visit." These visits were, for the most part, brief and sometimes quiet, but the messages were clear and profound – all compressed in one sentence: "We won't forget you."

After the visitors left, he'd walk to the balcony.

He inhaled deeply to absorb the fragrance of the spring-flowers. He listened intently for the calls from the owls and the rustling in the mulberry trees. He tried to divine the celestial messages and his destiny from the stars and from the outlines of the hill-ridges at night or from the flight of the swallows in the morning. He caressed the railing of the balcony and the twisted trunk of the vine. His imagination carried him where his steps could not. He knelt on the rocks at the edge of the creek and bent down to drink from the fountain of youth. He followed his nostalgic drives to make new imprints along the paths of his boyhood and of juvenile escapades and escapes. And he bargained with his Fates to strengthen his bonds with the past and to pave his future paths with full awareness of all encounters.

He kept reminding his mother that he had kept his promise and had been back twice since making the fateful decision to go to America, hoping that his new promise to return would lighten her sadness with hope.

The farewells to him nine and six-and-one-half years ago and sending off their youngest across the seas four years ago must have been heart-rending to his parents. Parting with two sons now and not knowing when they're going to see them again must have drained them, their deep faith in God and in them not-withstanding.

Mother's tears could not be stemmed.

Father's discreet sighs resonated beyond the confines of their home.

Sister wept quietly in the kitchen and scolded her little girls for no reason.

Brother-in-law George paced back and forth on the Veranda or kept watering his flower-pots to near-drowning. The little girls seemed subdued and cried, not knowing why.

Trying to cheer each other with recalling some of the happiest experiences or funniest mishaps provided only a temporary reprieve. The plea "Write often, your letters will be our sustenance," was repeated endlessly.

The big party, the evening before sailing, with his sister's unmatchable delicacies and with the buoyancy of unrestrained display of affection, lifted everyone's spirits to optimism. They laughed, teased, sang and danced. Even Mother enjoyed it. No tears or remorse when saying good-night; no goodbyes; only promises to "See you at the port tomorrow."

He was quite certain they all slept well.

The Ocean Liner, the *Olympia*, beckoned with a display of its white majesty and exhaling a thin white-gray smoke from its chimneys. The flag fluttered and flapped in the direction of the drifting light smoke. The crew worked deliberately, on board or at the pier, oblivious to those behind the gates waiting to be carried away to a new life of promises. Separate clusters of people, with those departing in the center, touched and hugged, and wiped tears.

When the gates opened, those departing started to move resolutely, slowly and orderly. Most turned around for one more wave and a blow of a kiss; some just stared at the *Olympia*. The crew reacted politely, deferentially and, when needed, compassionately.

Lampis was an old hand at this; he wondered how George felt, or how much effort he exerted to maintain his proverbial control; but he was more pre-occupied with Aunt Maritsa's sentiments or turmoil.

She had ventured away from the village only to other villages nearby to visit friends or relatives, to Tripolis occasionally, and to Athens once in her lifetime. She had never seen a ship. And here she was boarding one to carry her to a new world across the vast seas and oceans. She talked little, wiped her eyes frequently, clung now to him, now to George, or to both at the same time, and crossed herself as she climbed on board. He resisted the temptation to tell her about the wonders of the New World or the joy of her reunion with her sons, concentrating instead in reassuring her about the comforts and the safety of the ship. Her blue eyes sparkled with anticipated joy and with a flood of tears.

After being shown to their cabin, they returned on deck – he did not climb the mast this time – and waved at their family, as well as at the crowd along the pier and the shore, and at the firmament of Greece. The waving became more furious as the horns bellowed their goodbyes and the *Olympia*, the Giant, was pulled away by the midget tugboats. The crowd on the piers remained transfixed, probably until the masts of the *Olympia* were lost beyond the horizon and in the mist of the sea.

They paced the decks slowly, with Aunt Maritsa between them, greeting and introducing themselves to other passengers, straining for a closer contact with the receding shores, and scanning the waves for escorting dolphins. The returning memories were pushed back to make room for the storage of new ones, but he could not resist looking for Kalliope's smile or wonder, "What is she doing now?" Fortunately, sailing was smooth and Aunt Maritsa seemed transported with this undreamed-of experience. Her occasionalquestions were either amusing or stimulating. Her trust had no boundaries.

The sun was descending behind the mountains and the sea turning dark near the shores when the chimes called for dinner. Aunt Maritsa stood, for a moment, in awe, as they entered the expansive dining room. She "had never seen anything like it," she exclaimed. At the table, she was overwhelmed with the succession of the courses, trying to share what was placed before her with them – an old maternal instinct reinforced with a habit from the lengthy deprivation during the war (she did not break this habit through their voyage).

The two young women across the hall from their cabin seemed shy and reserved, lowering their eyes after a polite greeting and stepping aside to let him and George pass. Most of the passengers were returning to America after a visit to Greece and segregated from the "New Emigrants," as if they belonged to a separate caste. He and George were also shunned but were rather grateful for the opportunity to get re-acquainted. George, a mere boy of sixteen when they parted, was now a man who had served in the Army and had earned a University degree, through his determination while working full-time.

Still exploring each other and reserved, they shied from relating intimate relationships or experiences other than those they shared and found safety in discussing plans for the future or, less often, in reminiscing about past struggles, setbacks and overcoming adversity. He hoped that in the next ten days of close contact, they would develop a new understanding and a stronger trust based on respect. 'Formality' and 'etiquette,' dictated by prudence in appreciation of nine years of separation and of evolution from adolescence to adulthood, guided their exchanges of thoughts or sentiments. Their brief breaks from each other were to reflect on their individual emotions and, often, to judge each other's evolution of character. They did not neglect Aunt Maritsa, returning to her frequently and guarding against misusing her discretion.

The weather was most cooperative and benevolent, with hardly any rocking or swaying of the ship. They spent most of the day walking the decks; the evenings would be divided between attending concerts or dances and marveling at the stars. He found reminiscing about his first voyage more and more difficult to resist, but he frequently succumbed – rationalizing that he must – for the comparison.

The stay in the port of Naples was brief, and leaving Aunt Maritsa alone for a tour of the city would be improper. They observed from the deck and listened to the muffled humming of the traffic in the city spreading out before them. Vesuvius covered the shame and guilt of its infernal crimes in a thick tuft of gray clouds. The medieval palace to the left contained and guarded the mysticism and superstitions of the past. Had the impressions of his first visit been so deeply engraved to keep returning with the intensity of leaving no space for new revelations? The memories of his first visit succeeded one another without a pause for reflection, as he scanned the streets receding from the port, but the image of the barefoot blue-eyes blonde young woman with the baby in her arms kept returning; her hair flowing back in the breeze; her smile' her melodic sweet voice; the touch of her hand; the parting of their fingers; the last wave of goodbye or 'arrivederci' from across the street. Could George comprehend the impact of this encounter or understand the force of his impulse and the drain in his reserves to stem this impulse – to go out, back to that intersection to see her again?

They walked to the side, facing the pier. The Italian passengers began boarding the ship; some were wiping their eyes with handkerchiefs or tight fists; some had bent shoulders under the weight of grief; some were walking to surrender' and some, very few, were defiant. The waves from the crowd on the pier stirred the wails and fanned the prayers.

Aunt Maritsa took her handkerchief to wipe her tears and muffle her sobs. Divining his and George's curiosity, she answered, "All those mothers, and fathers, and sisters…" and she just cried some more.

The repeated sequence of fetching Aunt Maritsa before going to breakfast, of the strolls on the decks, of the visits to the lounge or the Library, of the now familiar faces of fellow-passengers and crew, and of the response to the chimes calling for dinner or supper established a routine but did not promote boredom. Distractions with conversation, hypnotism from following the rise and dipping of the waves or drift of the smoke from the chimney, retrieving memories and planning for the future or even fantasizing carried them far beyond the ship and crowded the days. Aunt Maritsa waited patiently for them, wherever they left her, afraid she may get lost if she ventured away by herself. She counted the days, asking every day for confirmation, and seemed in full control of her emotions. The transfer of some of their sentiments from Mother to Aunt Maritsa, made easy because of her closeness since their early memories, was soothing the pain of separation. His faith in George's strength and resolution, firm from the very beginning, was fortified steadily with their close contact and became unshakable. George was a realist and did not harbor any delusions, revealing no vulnerability – or hiding it well! – to sentimentalism and, in that respect at least, appearing stronger than his older brother. Their observations or inspirations from watching the waves or the stars converged only after listening to each other. Filial affection expanded in a new dimension with the mushrooming of mutual respect. And he hoped that George's prayers for the perpetuation of this relationship were as fervent as his own.

The Atlantic Ocean, still benevolent and tranquil since the crossing in the opposite direction, heaved gentle waves and capped them with white sprays in disharmony, to the end of the horizon, to show its goodwill and to remind them of its omnipotence. He did not have to defy the gale with an open shirt at the bow or to brave the tilting and tossing like he did nine years ago. Perhaps Athena appealed to Zeus, and Poseidon was intimidated by his more powerful brother.

The days succeeded one another with more sunshine, more of the same haze in the horizon, and more gratitude for Aeolos' slumber. The walks along the decks, leisurely and effortlessly, carried him to the remote past and the distant future, to encounters with menacing demons and with luring sirens, and to passions for the nymphs and for the muses of grace and of inspiration. Sharing his transports with George proved challenging, with new thoughts or fantasies displacing those he struggled to express. He ventured occasionally to inquire about George's thoughts or excursions and wondered whether he heard recounting of old plans or rehearsals of prospective endeavors rather than inexpressible sentiments.

The depressing memories of oppression, hopelessness and surrender from the visit to Lisbon would raise a sigh of relief or gratitude, every time they resurfaced, in that the *Olympia* had not followed the exact course of *Nea Hellas*. He prayed that these memories will be compressed in a dark corner by bright images of banners of liberty and by the strength of resurrected human dignity if he ever visited that City again.

In contrast, he was disappointed in that he did not have a chance to relive the inspirational messages from the welcoming coast and inviting slopes of Nova

Scotia, to be re-anointed by the mist form the union of a gentle breeze with the crest of a benevolent waves, and to be reborn from the soil and the foundations of Halifax. He hoped that when he returned – and he must – nothing will have changed so that he may reflect on the immortality of nobility in the human spirit and on the calls of destiny.

The approach to New York resurfaced his sentiments of nine years ago. He expressed some to George, but in deference to George's individuality, retreated to allow George to dwell on his own. The tranquility of this voyage contrasted strongly with the storms of his emotions and of the ocean nine years ago. The shores of the land of his birth and of his adopted home were much closer this time.

He left home and he was coming home.

George would have to decide alone where home was.

They admired the Statue of Liberty together and when satiated, shifted their gaze to the shoreline and skyline of New York City, from inspiration and promise to challenge and reward. The bright day and the tame waters lured them slowly to the welcoming gates of the New World. Perhaps, George had seen it all in the movies, perhaps that made the transfer from spectator to the personal, close encounter smoother, but the leap from one life to another may tax his reserves of strength and push the limits of his resolve.

The process through the Custom's House was orderly, uneventful. He was in control. Aunt Maritsa was numbed from all that unfolded before her and clung to him trustingly, frequently asking, "What did he say?" even though the "he" was talking to someone else. George saved his questions for later; for the present, it seemed he was intent on gathering it all in.

The two taxi-rides, from the Custom's House to a restaurant and from the restaurant to the train station left them only partly educated, in spite of the taxi-drivers' determination or commitment to their mission to educated all the "out-of-towners." And the cashier's uncouthness, refusing to accept the American Express check and threatening to call the police, left both Aunt Maritsa and George wondering whether this may be "typical American."

Lampis pushed Aunt Maritsa's seat back, after settling down in the train and before long, she was blissfully sound asleep. George lasted a little longer.

Lampis leaned back, closed his eyes and spanned all that transpired between boarding the ship in New York and this moment. He dwelled on his gratitude to Dr. Herbelsheimer, for her idea and urging him to visit his parents, to Dean Ceithaml for the generous moral and financial support, and to Electra for her sacrifice to help in his time of need. From all that, he concluded that he had enough reserves for "the last stretch." Just a few days to readjust and classes would start again. He anticipated meeting his friends and sharing each other's experiences in this ten-week interval. He prayed that their experiences were rich, also. After images began to overlap, displace each other in disarray, recede and blur, he woke up in Indiana, near Illinois – that's what the conductor said. The landscape did not look familiar, yet he felt the buoyancy of "returning" where he belonged. An impetuous surge of a feeling of guilt was suppressed with the force of "I have not deserted the ranks of my heroes. I have not betrayed the trust in me. I am following my destiny!"

Aunt Maritsa was overwhelmed with the approach to the realization of her dreams to be with her sons. She kept wiping her eyes and repeating, "Are we almost there? How long yet?"

The train slowed down. The passengers began to stir. He squeezed Aunt Maritsa's hand to reassure her and to feel her heart-throb. She kissed him and turned to George to hug him, also. He pulled their luggage down and anticipated the encounter of mother and sons. The inevitable contrast of this reunion with his mother's parting with her sons hardened the lump in his throat. He prayed that his mother also will reunite with her three sons in some not-too-distant day, just like Aunt Maritsa did.

Lampis walked to the exit, passing three decades of visions, revitalizations, and renewals of vows while refocusing on his goals. His confidence in reaching these goals was expressed in the simple sentence "We're here!" He delivered Aunt Maritsa to her sons; he presented George to the youngest brother, Nick, and to all the cousins, and he stepped on a new milestone in his life. He heard all the questions from all directions and repeated his answers: "The voyage was marvelous; we all enjoyed it; everybody's well and you have greetings from everybody." The details were left for later. George strolled with confidence, neither awed nor overwhelmed.

The memories of nine years ago returned in detail, with a vivid impact, half-frightening him with the thought of the return of his psychomotor seizures. Lampis pushed the images of his uncles into oblivion with a nudge at Tony's ribs and leaped across the span between the 'then and now' with just one step away to the side.

Dearborn Street, stretching straight to the North and lined with imposing strong buildings, would now take him to a destination, not the unknown.

Lampis stood erect to be recognized and to accept the "welcomes" and the challenges. He turned to repeat, "We'll see you again," and entered one of his cousins' car.

CHAPTER 31
At the Foregates

LAMPIS SETTLED IN A NEW APARTMENT in their old neighborhood, with his brothers and cousin Tony. Accustomed to frugality, by necessity, they did not venture beyond the bare essentials in furnishing or personal articles. They agreed on a schedule and rotation of "duties" to maintain cleanliness and neatness, amused themselves with jokes and pranks, and eventually succumbed to the pressure of "modern civilization" to buy a second-hand black-and-white TV.

Nick, back from the University of Illinois at Urbana, for the summer, had already found a job and helped George find one, too. Their entertainment revolved around exchanging stories about their day's experiences, walking to the Lake-shore, and visiting with cousins John and Symeon just three blocks away. Now-and-then, on weekends, they'd take public transportation to Uncle Nick's home. George adjusted very quickly, undeterred in his determination by the monotonous assembly-line work at a bakery or by being robbed at the subway station just a few days after starting to work, responded to his new names, "the mustached-one" and "the other one," coined, derogatorily, by their dear uncles, and concentrated on mastering the English language.

Whether relaxed and reinvigorated after his experiences in Greece, or inspired with the anticipation of the crowning of his efforts, Lampis was more relaxed and more efficient with his studies and with his research. He shared with his classmates his excitement from his "discoveries" of fluorescent labeling of antibodies to "Erlich's Ascites" tumor cells and of chromosome aberration in these same cells; listened to their "discoveries" and plans; and exchanged information about hospitals for internships.

He worked in the Clinical Microbiology Laboratory on weekends and in the Employee Health Service three afternoons per week, and he still had time and energy for establishing and exploring new friendships – within the boundaries and constraints of his severely limited financial means. The new level of his self-confidence, he reminded himself, must rest on the frequent reassessment of reality.

Obstetrics and Gynecology had not aroused much enthusiasm, but he tried to keep an "open mind." His reverence for human life, strengthened from his observations of and contact with the perils of disease during his exposure to the other disciplines of Medicine and from the deep hurt in crossing Judy's path, gained yet another dimension from the first cry of the baby and from the expression of ultimate happiness on the mother's face at the sight of her baby. The irrepressible exchanges of ecstasy, in the mother's smiles and sparkling eyes of the doctor and his assistant – their smiles not apparent under their masks, but reflected in their eyes – conveyed, back and forth, the exuberance of emotions at witnessing a 'miracle;' the "congratulations" and "Thank you's" echoed "let there be light."

Lampis envied the doctor's moment of depositing the baby on the mother's bosom with the charge, "It's yours to love, to nourish, to protect."

Would he wish to be in this doctor's place? he thought. Would looking forward to witnessing or even participating in another 'miracle' be fulfilling for him? Or would the challenge of confronting and conquering disease provide a greater satisfaction?

The anticipation of excitement from the first cry, growing with each centimeter of cervical dilation, was uncontrollable. Practicing tying surgical knots on the back of a chair or the leg of a table, reading Novac's textbook, or listening to the Residents' stories and witty remarks did not make the cervix dilate any faster. But when the anticipated cry was heard, when the glow from the mother's face illuminated the room, the moment expanded to occupy all of his awareness and to displace memories, thoughts and dreams. The comparatively anti-climactic ritual of cleaning the baby and handing it to the gleaming, beautiful mother – every new mother looked most beautiful – stirred the desire for more of the same experience to insatiable dimensions.

The obvious fulfillment and deep satisfaction displayed in a Senior Resident's description of experiences, show of gentleness with a touch and reassurance to a woman in labor, and rewards of respect from the nurses at every encounter was discussed among the students, more than once, with the conclusion, "That's how I'd like to be" – until, one dreadful day, a rung to the ladder to exhilarating heights snapped, and the plunge to the depths of despair and helplessness was followed by a recurring nightmare.

"Everything is going very well," the mother-to-be was reassured. She smiled in gratitude and waited for the next contraction. He sat with the admired Resident, asking questions, listening to answers, and anticipating the next round of happiness.

"Something is wrong. I can't hear the fetal heart-tones," the frightened panting nurse sputtered.

They rushed out, transferred the young woman in labor to the delivery room, and worked furiously. He responded to requests to "hold this;" "move that," and "hand me that," without thinking and without remembering, in a painful interminable suspense. Finally, the baby was delivered. No cry this time – not after the removal of the meconium from the mouth, the gentle slap on the buttocks, the mouth-to-mouth respiration, the rhythmic compressions to the chest on-and-on. The agonizing moments stretched out. The silence pushed the walls from the sides, the floor from below, the ceiling from above to compress all that mattered to the hope for a spontaneous heave of the baby's chest.

The Resident summoned all his strength and reserves to pronounce "We lost the baby."

The mother managed to ask for her baby, clutched it and burst out in sobs. The nurse squeezed the mother's hand and let her own tears flow.

Lampis just stood there, crushed and devastated, hearing "We lost the baby. We lost the baby." He watched the Resident suturing the episiotomy and repeated, after the Resident and the Nurse, "I am sorry. I am sorry."

He walked out of the delivery room without another word. The hallway was empty, lifeless. The door to the dressing room creaked, as if to cry also. He slammed his locker door, after dressing mechanically, and decided to take the stairway; he was afraid that he may start sobbing in the elevator with all the people around. He'd walk down the stairs slowly, out of sight, and out to the Midway.

After closing the door behind him and a few steps down, he stopped. In front of him sat someone with a white coat and hunched shoulders, clutching his head in his hands. Should he turn around and walk away silently? Should he pass by discreetly? He could not move. Hearing the sighs and sobs from the heap in front of him, he felt the lump in his throat swelling and choking; his chest began to heave. He carried his crushing burden and deposited it next to the Resident, who turned for a quick glance with dulled-from-pain and flooded-with-tears blue eyes. He also clutched his face with both hands, surrendering to the surging sobs and tasting the saltiness of his tears in the corner of his mouth. His right shoulder and thigh touched the Resident's left shoulder and thigh to share and transfer, back-and-forth, each other's anguish and grief.

The janitor, coming up the stairs with a bucket and a mop, stopped for a moment, then turned around and walked down again. The sound of the closing door jarred them to stand up, clasp each other's hands, nod without a word, and walk in opposite directions.

Lampis headed for the Gift Shop but ended up in the bookstore. He decided to go to the Library but found himself in the dark, fluorescent Microbiology room, staring at and beyond the slides of fluorescent tumor cells. He walked out to look for Ivan, but he turned around and walked away, after just waving at him. The attempts to escape with retrieving memories of his journey to and encounters in Greece were aborted or failed. A long walk along the Midway or along the arches in the Quadrangle may help.

The lure of Internal Medicine remained the strongest. But his enjoyment of and performance in an elective Radiology course suggested that, perhaps performing well, without the burdens of a direct, emotional stress may be more gratifying. The applause by his fellow-students and Radiology Residents for his correct diagnosis in difficult cases, at the Wednesday evening Radiology Conference, frequently tipped the balance toward Radiology. And what about the excitement of scientific discovery and fulfillment, promised by Pathology and Research? Fortunately, time was not running out. He still had at least one year before making the final decision.

The Wednesday evening Conferences, 7:00P.M. to 8:30P.M. for third and fourth year Medical Students, were as stimulating as they were rewarding. The students who volunteered to participate would write their names on slips of paper; the third-year students wrote on yellow, and the fourth-year students wrote on white. The Chief Radiology Resident, who had chosen x-rays with pathologically established diagnoses, would pull a yellow and a white slip and call the names. The third-year student sat at the Chairman's left and the fourth-year student at his right.

After the x-rays were put on the viewer, the third-year student was handed the pointer and expected to identify and describe the lesion or abnormality, list his deferential diagnoses and arrive at his conclusions. The fourth-year student would take over to agree, present his arguments and conclusions, and extrapolate about prognosis. The Chairman would add his comments and correlate roentgenologic with clinical findings. A correct diagnosis was followed by the traditional applause of snapping fingers in both hands; a missed diagnosis by a student who was expected to do better and who 'could take it' was followed by hissing – both in direct proportion to the challenge and the remoteness of the correct diagnosis, respectively. The third-year and the more sensitive fourth year students were only applauded. A rare miss by the Chairman raised the roof with the hissing. Lampis' luck was holding up. His name was called every Wednesday, and he had more finger-snapping than hissing, enjoying it all. And the Chairman did not deliberate long, before agreeing to the Students' request for the continuation of the conference during the breaks between academic quarters, including the Holidays.

Distraction from his studies and his plans came from many directions and unexpectedly, spanned a wide spectrum from exhilaration to self-deprecation, and stirred hopes for success or raised fears of rejection. He shared all his experiences and emotions with his brothers and Cousin Tony, keeping hardly any secrets. Nick, the youngest brother, frequently reprimanded him for his vulnerability and naivety. George displayed, not so subtly, some reserve. They all seemed to understand, but not espouse or even approve, of his sentimentalism, to set limits on vicarious pleasures or burdens, to use logic to the detriment of emotion.

The old question of whether he was blessed or cursed to love without restraint resurfaced and kept him awake at night. It was a blessing when transported at Gerry's and Edith's wedding; maybe a curse when not answering the door and watching Uncle Gus walk away in rejection (he had a lot of work to do, and Uncle Gus would continue with his pontificating monologue on his favorite Theologian's doctrine for hours!); definitely a blessing in the anticipation of watching David walking with Karen, holding hands; probably a curse in listening to Charley's dilemma.

In spite of all these strong distractions, he stayed on course. He returned to his studies, his research, his work. He sat at the furthest corner in the cafeteria, concentrating on his assignments and the findings of his experiments. He declined invitations to parties, partly to avoid the embarrassment of being offered a ride. And he had no difficulty in mustering the strength to ignore Barbara's leaning on his shoulder and breathing in his ear, in the dark room while he was unleashing his excitement about the fluorescence on the tumor cells' surface. He risked, or admitted to, being labelled weak or timid in his social contacts, to camouflage his Achilles' heels with flimsy excuses and clumsy escapes or by venturing only in what appeared to be safe territory. And he promised to show his brother Nick and his ally, Uncle Gus, who were convinced that the territory he considered safe may be "full of traps," how they had underestimated his strengths.

After all his retrenchments, Lampis felt secure and content. He knew he was performing well in his studies. His sponsor, Dr. Fitch, shared his enthusiasm about his research, tugging at the reins of scientific accuracy by reminding him of the need for repetition and quantification to keep from drawing premature conclusions. He was assured by his boss's, at the Employee Health Service, confidence and affection for him, by her husband, Dr. Gotsis. His friendship with Betsy, the daughter of one of his idols among his professors, was blossoming into a cherished platonic relationship. The responses to his requests for letters of recommendation I his application for his Internship were invariably enthusiastic. He felt closer to his friends in his class and made new friends. They were all more relaxed and enjoying each other's company. All was going well, until one Thursday morning, just before the 8:00 A.M. lecture when suddenly all seemed on the brink of collapse.

Dr. Robert Page, the Associate Dean, took him aside in the hallway to remind him, in a fatherly, caring tone. "I know how much you have invested and sacrificed to reach this stage. Be very careful with the female patients. An incident in the Employee Health Service has come to my attention."

"I have always been very careful, and never transgressed from propriety," Lampis protested.

"I assure you that you are not being reprimanded, that the complaint or report will not be related to anyone, and that I mean to protect you by reminding you to be very, very careful."

Lampis could not concentrate, talk, eat, or drink for the rest of the day. He was frightened, in spite of Dr. Page's assurances, that this vicious slander would go on his record. He felt his paranoia growing to encompass every young woman, including Betsy, whom he had examined in the Employee Health Service. Who could be so vicious to invent such a lie or so deranged to distort a proper examination to a perverted approach? He was crushed and devastated.

He tossed and turned in bed and then paced the floor all night. He must find out from Dr. Page, who she was – first thing in the morning.

Dr. Page did not appear surprised to find him waiting at his office. "I have not slept all night, either," he admitted, but he was bound to not reveal the name, just as he was bound to not relate this incident to anyone else.

The hopes of detecting a change in Dr. Page's expression were not realized when allowed to relate the incident of the black girl walking stark-naked from behind the curtain to ask him a question (he had sent her back to put a gown on when lifting his eyes from filling out the form to realize she was naked) or the ex-model who insisted that he write down that her breasts were normal after refusing to allow him to examine her breasts (his suggestion, in the presence of a nurse, that she be examined by Dr. Perutsea, the lady Physician in charge, evoked a response, shocking the nurse with throwing off her gown and sneering: "Here, you're dying to fondle my breasts, have your fun!" He was surprised that she was hired, even after her profuse apologies, and that she had the audacity to sit at his table, in the corner of the cafeteria when there were plenty of unoccupied tables).

Dr. Page's final words were, "Go back to your work and be very careful and let me know of this girl's next move."

Lampis remembered her "next move" only a few minutes later in the hallway

Bob walked toward him but didn't see him in the hallway. He shook his head and repeated, "I just can't believe it!'

"Are you talking to yourself, Bob?" Lampis asked him.

Bob stopped and looked at him intently. "She was talking about you! She threatened to take care of me just like she did of the guy with the long name; it must be you she was talking about!"

Lampis grabbed and squeezed Bob's arm. "Who is she, Bob?"

"That, that audiologist; she threw her arms around me when the nurse walked out of the room, after the examination, and I pulled back and walked out; that's when she threatened me."

"Threw her arms around me" …That's it! The flash! Last Friday, Lampis had been concentrating on the design of his next encounter walking down the hallway when rounding the corner, she bumped into him accidentally, he thought, and threw her arms around him. He had apologized for not looking where he was going and pushed her gently aside; she was holding on to him, chuckling and looking at him. Although he did not turn around after walking away, he knew she was standing there.

"Would you please," he implored, pulling Bob's arm, "repeat what you told me to Dr. Page?"

"I should, before Dr. Page hears a different story," Bob replied.

They walked to the elevator, rode up from the second to the fifth floor, and knocked on Dr. Page's door, not exchanging another word. They were invited in and asked to sit down.

"Would you please tell Dr. Page what you told me?" Lampis asked Bob.

"Before you start, what did he tell you?" Dr. Page asked, pointing to Lampis.

"Nothing! He just suggested or pleaded that I repeat to you what I told him. Not another word," Bob replied.

"Go ahead, please," Dr. Page said.

Bob repeated the story, emphasizing, "I just walked out; I didn't know what she was up to. I didn't want to offend her. I just walked out and she threatened me!" He was white.

Dr. Page tapped the back of his pencil on his desk slowly. He just sat there, waiting. "Thanks for coming to me," he said, after an interminable minute or so.

He stood up and extended his hand first to Bob, then to Lampis. "Thanks again," Dr. Page repeated with a half-bitter, full of conflicting emotions – that's what Lampis read – smile. "Now let's all go to work. We've all learned a good lesson."

When they walked out, Bob asked: "What did she do to you? How did she take care of you?"

"It's a long story! Let's go for a cup of coffee. I'll tell you."

They had about twenty minutes before starting at their respective clinics. He related his story. Bob filled the pauses with repetitions of, "I can't believe it!" "Can you believe it?", "It's incredible." "Our Guardian Angels must be watching over us."

"We must be good guys," Lampis concluded and Bob concurred.

They stood up and embraced, right there in the middle of the cafeteria.

Now he was euphoric. He had been exonerated. He wanted to call his brothers, but they were at work. Whom could he call? Nobody! It was time to go to work. He will tell his brothers and Tony all about it in the evening. His emotions ranged from disbelief, to indignation, to rage, to gratitude – the last for Bob and Dr. Page.

Ivan, sitting next to him in the classroom, noticed the frowns and the stares in space and expressed his concern. And he dwelt at length in his deep appreciations for Ivan's friendship.

Lampis was starting at the Ear, Nose, and Throat Clinic, where she worked, the following Monday. He resolved to act as if nothing had ever happened when he met her to see what her next move would be. He could not control his patience when his first patient needed an audiogram. Good chance he'll see her now. He took his request to the Clinic Coordinator.

"Sorry, this will have to wait about one week," she advised him, and added, "we are short of help. We have only one audiologist."

"Why?" he inquired.

"The other one was fired by Dr. Page on Friday. He just walked down here and fired her; on the spot. Nobody knows why," she answered, shrugging her shoulders.

Lampis suppressed his impulse to declare, "I know why." Instead, he said, "Thank you," and walked back to his patient. Was he thanking her, Bob Caplan, Dr. Page, or God?

He did not take long to recover, erasing his indignation, banishing this woman from the ranks of the decent women that he knew and was meeting or greeting, and giving himself some credit for acting the way he did. He was light-hearted again, but the advice, "be very, very careful," struck a chord with every new encounter, and he kept repeating, "I will. I must."

The new girl he'd met at the far corner of the cafeteria, seemed pure and innocent – that's what he saw in those moist, beautiful eyes looking at him. Will he see her again? Or was she visiting someone in the hospital? When he found out where she worked, after he saw her again in the hallway, he asked one of the girls that he knew in the Medical Records department to introduce him to her.

"Sure, I'll be glad to. Just come to my party Friday evening. She'll be there," she said, a little too eagerly.

He went to the party. "Where is she?" he asked the hostess.

"She's not here. I didn't invite her. Do I look that dumb? Have a drink. I'll introduce you to my friends." She followed through with a mischievous coquettish smile.

How successful he was in pretending that he had a good time, he did not know. The ride on the bus and then the elevated train was long. He had wasted all this time, but he was not angry. He was flattered.

Rotating through the outpatient Clinical Services – Medicine, Surgery, Pediatrics, Obstetrics, Gynecology, including their respective sub-specialties – was stimulating, challenging, and rewarding. The one-on-one contact with Residents and members of the senior Faculty purified humility and raised self-esteem and ambitions. The Socratic dialogue tapped unrecognized or underestimated strengths, aroused latent thinking powers, and guided to new sources of knowledge and gratification. The enrichment from the ending rotation was stored, and the venture to the next was anticipated with greed for more.

The schedule and pace were regular and predictable, in comparison to last year's. Consequently, he could plan for the hours at the Library, the time in the Laboratory, and the meetings or excursions with his friends. His discipline did not lax; nor did his enthusiasm for his studies, and his excitement from his observations and 'discoveries' in his 'research.' His main interlude remained in the realm of walking in the Quadrangles or to the C-Shop, attending lectures in Sociology or Archeology, or drifting aimlessly with memories and dreams.

The challenge from 'the x-ray of the week' for students, House staff and Faculty, excepting Radiology, was anticipated and brief, but the reward from a correct diagnosis, lasting. Ten out of twelve in the Summer quarter, tying him for first place with one of his Professors may have been just good luck, but a repeat in the Fall quarter, tying him for first place again, with one of the Senior Residents, half-convinced him that maybe he was better than he thought. If that holds up, then Radiology may win.

Somehow, he had become superefficient in his studies and work. He'd finish all his assignments and still have time to spend a few hours with Marian on Friday evening, Barbara – not the one that was breathing in his ear in the darkroom! – Saturday evening, and Helene, Sunday afternoon. They all knew about each other; he had not made any commitments; he was not 'cheating.' He procrastinated in making a choice.

Marian was too young; Barbara was too Catholic, and Helene was too temperamental. Maybe they would go their separate ways when convinced that he was non-committal and too poor. Then nobody would get hurt. That's how he rationalized his lack of courage or know-how to sever the ties. He finally thought he'd gather the strength to tell Marian after the AKK Fraternity party before Christmas; and Barbara after the play on New Year's Eve; and Helene sometime before "buckling-down" to study for his Comprehensive Exams at the end of May.

The meetings of the Greek-Students Club, with members ranging from the first year of Undergraduate School to PhD candidates, in all fields and Professional Schools (School of Medicine and School of Law) were as stimulating and entertaining as they were rewarding. He accepted the nomination for President and took his position very seriously, in planning lectures, inviting members of the faculty, and soliciting everybody's help. The occasional intruders – one of them was quite regular – from the outside, were invited to return and offer suggestions. The full schedule, planned with the help of his 'officers,' was accepted with enthusiasm.

The holiday season came and went. He buckled down as he had planned, and started reviewing all the material and subjects covered in the four years of Medical School. He did not follow through with his plans to loosen his ties with Marian, Barbara, and Helene. He hoped that meeting them less frequently, every second or third week-end, would make them conclude that he was losing interest. But they were "so understanding" that he fell back to his convenient procrastination.

The suspense in waiting for the announcement of the Matching-Program results for the Internship began to build up. He was perplexed about the lack of invitations for personal interviews at the University of Chicago, his first choice, or the effect of his decline to go to Philadelphia General Hospital, his second choice, for the interviews (he could not afford the fare, he had advised them) with the selection committee.

He reasoned that they knew him well enough at the University of Chicago, and they had letters of recommendation at Philadelphia General. He was confident about the University of Illinois, his third choice. "We'd love to have you with us," all three of his interviewers told him (he had enjoyed that interview and his meeting with Bea, who sang so sweetly about a deep love and cried while driving him home. She was "very special" he had told her, about two years ago, but their paths had crossed a little too early.)

He felt equally confident about Duke University, his fourth and last choice, judging from the tone of the letter advising him of the receipt of his application and of the letters of recommendation (was Agape still single? Was she still in Durham?)

Vacillating between Internal Medicine, Pathology, and Radiology, he had applied for the Rotating Internship. Dean Ceithaml advised him, "Go away to see how they do things in other places and stay away from places where supervision was inadequate or could not offer ways and means for reflection. You've been on the campus long enough, maybe too long. Get a taste of and tap some other good place. You can always come back."

Still, Lampis would rather stay. This was home.

Marian was drawn closer to him, working in the Hospital and seeing him every day - she brought lunch for him, or gave him her own, too – clutching his arm at each encounter. Barbara prayed fervently for what was best as well as for the salvation of his soul. Helen's response was "You'll stay here, but whatever happens, happens." And he resolved that whatever happens, he'll make the best of it.

In the meantime, he adhered to his 'regimentation' of preparing for the "Clinics,' attending the lectures and conferences, reviewing for the 'comprehensive exams,' working on his research projects, and meeting with friends, most often with Pete or Takis and quite frequently with Athan and Electra, for excursions into History, Political Sciences or Social Sciences (their respective fields).

The unexpected and unanticipated interlude with the visit of Queen Frederica of Greece to the campus proved very exciting and memorable. He and the officers of the Greek Students' Club were invited to a reception in her honor. They lined-up in one of the rooms at Ida Noyes Hall. He had never met Royalty before – he had written her once, to appeal to her for intervention in fairness in the evaluation of the Candidates to the Greek Military Medical Academy – but he was not uneasy. When she extended her hand, after he was introduced by the escorting Chancellor Lawrence Kimpton, he took it and bowed respectfully. She held his hand and talked to him in fluent and articulate Greek – her enemies had been arguing that "she doesn't even speak Greek" – inquiring about his background and his plans for the future and urging him to cherish his Heritage and to not forget his duties.

The thrust of a hand between him and his Vice President standing next to him and the repetitious, "Megaliotate," ("Your Majesty") distracted him long enough to reason "The Queen is holding my hand, Athan's hand should be facing the other way."

Chancellor Kimpton whispered, "Who is he?"

After a quick glance, Lampis answered, "I don't know." This ended the distraction but not the conversation with the Queen. (This frequent intruder, known in their close circle as Parlapipas (the blabbering wind-pipe) protested vehemently, in a subsequent encounter: "You told the Chancellor you did not know who I was."

Undaunted, Lampis answered, "You expected me to turn my back to the Queen to recognize you, who was not even invited and did not belong there?" (Even if he could imagine that this "parlapipas," Adamantios Androutsopoulos, would one day become a Prime-Minister during the dictatorship in Greece, he would have answered the same way).

A most memorable interlude, he concluded.

The day of the announcement of the 'Internship Matching' came, after a sleepless night.

"This is it, good luck," he repeated and heard echoing as he followed the tense crowd into P-117, past hardly composed wives, fiancées, and girlfriends, at about ten-to-seven in the morning. He saw between Ivan and Phil. The silence was oppressive. His thoughts were disconnected, irretrievable.

Dr. Page came in from the back door and walked to the podium. He stood there for the longest minute, opened his folder, wished them "good morning," and declared, "Most of you did well – first or second choice," then started to read the names and the institutions that matched.

"He's reading alphabetically; I am next," he thought quickly after the first name was called. His heart sank a little deeper when he heard his name followed by "Philadelphia General" – that was his second choice. Why? What happened? Was it that ex-model woman? Was he wrong about his conclusions of being well-liked here? Well, it's final, and it's not the end of the world. (He found the answer on the day after his graduation when emptying his locker. The application for the Internship had never been submitted. It was there, in his locker. He could not blame anyone but himself).

Ivan's and Phil's congratulations and assurances that "Philadelphia General is a great place," were pushed back by his thoughts and questions. He recognized them, after missing the next four names in the A's and a couple of B's, and thanked them, adding, "I hope you're right."

They all listened again. Some of his close friends' names he registered in his mind; some of the others he was not sure that he had heard.

"Ivan Diamond, New England Medical Center; Phil Eaton, Barnes Hospital."

He must concentrate harder to find out who else was going to Philadelphia General Hospital. He had counted three, by the end: Donald Goldstone, David Gormley, and Lauren Pachman. Had he missed any? Lauren was a good friend; he'd spent long hours with her learning and experimenting with fluorescent microscopy in the dark room; he had had dinner with her and her roommate, Holly Moore, at their apartment. He hoped to get to know David and Don better at PGH.

Dr. Page ended with "Those of you who did not hear your name or did not match, please come see me in my office," and walked out. Silence again, for about a minute; then all stood up and rushed out, to those waiting in the hallway.

Lampis heard, "Tell me. Tell me. Where? Where?"

He saw hugging, wiping of tears, milling around, clusters.

Marian was waiting, eyes moist, right hand clenched to her stomach. He walked to her, unclenched her right hand, looked into her moist eyes and delivered: "It's Philadelphia General!"

Her hand limp in his gentle grip, eyes dulled by the flooding of tears and lips tight at the corners, she stared at and beyond him for a long-long moment, before resting her chin on his right shoulder, raising her arms slowly to embrace him, and relieving her conflicting emotions in soft, restrained sobs. He reciprocated with a tight squeeze in the hope of expressing his appreciation for her feelings and his acceptance of the decrees of his Fates. But this Acceptance was not transferred to her.

She rested her chin on his right shoulder and cried. "This is the end! It's goodbye; at least I got to know you."

A few minutes later, after regaining her composure, she confessed, "Maybe it's better this way."

Acceptance was not made much easier with the repetitions of, "It's a great Hospital. Lauren is going there. Dean Ceithaml recommended that I go away. It's a great opportunity to be exposed to a different environment."

The question, "Why not the University of Chicago?" – his first choice – plagued him and puzzled some of his teachers. And he could not overcome his hesitation to ask Dr. Page. He was not faced with decision-making difficulties. Resolved: will share a room with David Gormley in the Doctor's Home; will eat whatever was served in the Cafeteria; will work hard and enjoy it; must go to the Philadelphia Orchestra to watch Eugene Ormandy conduct; brace for new challenges or even the possibility of not returning to Chicago.

Lampis escaped from these thoughts by plunging into his studies with a two-fold purpose; prepare for the final comprehensive exams, still or only four months away, and avoid hearing "We'll miss you," in social encounters. He fortified for the separation from his close friends, among his classmates. He'd been through enough separations to know that some may be final and painful, that he must brace for the summons to his reserves to sustain him or to re-enforce his determination, and that he must start now to explore ways and means to make the new transition not just smooth and tolerable but momentous for new ventures.

The distractions and vicarious excitement in listening to the wedding plans among some of his close friends; the excursions to an aimless ride around or out of the city with Marian on Friday evenings (she "commandeered" her father's car); the solitary long walks either along the Midway, past the Museum of Science and Industry to the "Point" to scatter and retrieve thoughts and dreams across the Lake; and the returning calls to reach for the North Star and for tranquility along the North Shore; all of these and some from unexpected encounters were interrupted or followed by the resurging questions: "Where will I be next year and the next year? Will I ever come back to all this that's part of me?"

The escapes to the Laboratory, to his mice and to the dark room with the Fluorescent Microscopy, carried him to detachment from past and future, transferred him to fields of consuming questions from his observations and left him stranded in search of answers. Barbara's warm breath in his left ear, her leaning on his shoulder and her pleas, "Show me," were stored for interludes in times of merriment or distress in the future. Counting of the chromosomes and correlating with the size of the tumor cell or contrasting the fluorescence of the smaller and larger cells was the top priority for now.

But the prospect of leaving all this behind, or storing it to feed and make his nostalgia grow, returned every night, before Morpheus came to his rescue, until the end of the Winter Quarter.

CHAPTER 32

THE WEEK BETWEEN QUARTERS, his final "break" as a student on this campus, was crammed with visits to friends and relatives, with a concentrated, frenzied effort to gather and classify more information from his experiments, and with his gathering strength for the separation and for the next climb in three months.

When alone, he reflected on the memories from last year, reassessed his strengths and weaknesses, made new resolutions, and drifted with fantasies and hopes to sunny fields crisscrossed with gentle brooks and stretching to a circle of white clouds. Recoiling to the present, his apprehensions, stemming from and revolving around the questions, "How ready, how prepared am I to treat people with complex and life-threatening diseases, to reassure or comfort their families, withstand the pain of losing the battle, losing a life?" nearly overwhelmed him.

Sharing his apprehensions and identifying them with those of his classmates in the cafeteria or in the Student-Lounge offered some but not enough comfort; expressing them to his brothers and cousin was a plea for their prayers; and taking refuge in the company of Marian, or more reluctantly, of Barbara or Helene shielded him, however transiently, from the darts of his self-doubts.

The inventory at the end of the week left him staring at a lot of blanks, looking for support from his mentors, and praying for strength. The remorse from and self-incrimination for having not used his time more efficiently was inevitable and difficult to soothe with rationalizations. His only, partial comfort was found in repeating "I hope I have learned a lesson."

The final Quarter, with assignments to Outpatient Clinics and with regularly scheduled morning and noon lectures, differed from the last two Quarters in that camaraderie expanded and bonds strengthened, with more frequent meetings to exchange ideas about the preparation for the Comprehensive Examinations, to share excitement from their research projects, and to support each other when needed. These meetings and the daily one-to-one encounters with the Attending Physicians fortified his resolve to meet the challenges of Internship, and beyond that, of Residency. He was puzzled and flattered in concluding that his teachers and friends had more confidence in him than he in himself.

The Emergency Room assignments provided an opportunity to test his knowledge and skills on the 'firing line.' It also provided a new field to cultivate and harvest experience for sustenance during the skirmishes or battles with the unforeseen or unexplained illnesses and complications. He chose Saturday night for two reasons: (1) he could sleep on Sunday and be ready for Monday, and (2) he had heard that Saturday nights were the busiest. In his eagerness to get the most out of it, he showed up early, stayed close to the Residents, volunteered to do all the 'scut-work,' and did not leave until he was practically chased out.

The inevitable heartbreaks, after frenzied efforts to save a life, took a heavy toll, driving him to wander aimlessly around campus, to withdrawal, and to the Laboratory for a reprieve with his mice and slides. The frequent 'triumphs' changed him with a lasting and contagious euphoria for the rest of the week. And the 'routine' cases made him wonder about the definition and perception of 'routine.'

He shared his experience with his friends and inquired about theirs for a more complete fulfillment. And he reasoned that going without sleep from early Saturday morning until late Sunday night should prepare him for the demands and strains of Internship. He was never bored, looking for ways to help or asking the Residents to explain their conclusions and recommended treatment or to elaborate on the precautions to prevent complications. He moved from room to room, to the Nursing Station, to the X-ray Viewing Box, and he sat down only to write his notes. The discussions with the Residents were carried on standing in the hallway or at the Nursing Station. And the repeated admonitions to treat the individual patient as an individual, with full respect and dignity, to never allow objectivity replace or displace compassion, and to integrate the clinical with the laboratory findings were echoing 'loud and clear' in the evaluation of every new patient. He came 'closer and closer' to feeling like a doctor with each successive night in the Emergency Room, the intellectually challenging and the physically taxing tasks taking a tool that others appreciated more than he did.

"You look tired," Sheila commented on late Sunday morning when he met her for brunch. (He had met Sheila a few weeks earlier when he drew her blood for a test in a research project – she was a volunteer – and he was fascinated by her intelligence, self-confidence, and beauty).

"I had a rough night," he admitted, "pulling pellets out of a man's rear-end with forceps, something like tweezers. I lost count. He was full of them!"

Sheila started to laugh and kept on laughing, almost hysterically.

He was tired and became annoyed. "It's not funny, Sheila; not for the man that was shot, not for me who had to spend the whole night pulling the pellets."

"I am laughing," Sheila replied, pushing with both hands on her stomach to prevent cramping, "because I did it; one of my friends and I did it; we took a good aim."

"You did that?" he almost shouted, jumping off his seat and staring down on her in disbelief and contempt, "and here I am having brunch with someone that shoots people full of pellets just for fun, for a good laugh."

He was ready to walk away without a goodbye when she reached out and grabbed his right wrist.

"Sit down and give me a chance to explain, please," she pleaded. "It was not for fun, it was in desperation." Her voice undulated with the apparent profusion of emotions, from frustration to anger, to satisfaction, to remorse, to guilt, and to a plea for understanding. "This man started coming across the street from our building, at dusk, about two weeks ago, standing there and dropping his pants."

He knew that she lived in a building with efficiency apartments on the second floor rented to girls only, with business stores on the first floor.

"We called the Campus Police, but we were told, 'It's off campus, out of our jurisdiction, call the City Police.' We did, but nothing was done; we called again and again, still nothing. We had had it and decided to take matters into our own hands. My friend and I borrowed two shotguns, hid about fifty yards away behind some bushes, and when he dropped his pants, we fired away, four barrels."

She stopped, squeezed his hand across the table, looked into his eyes, as if begging for trust and understanding and started to cry.

Not knowing how to respond, he returned the squeeze of the hand and started to laugh, uncontrollably. She was laughing again.

The waitress came to their booth, stood perplexed for a moment, shrugged her shoulders and walked away. She'd come back later for their order. He asked for a repeat of Sheila's story, repeated and embellished his story of pellet-pulling, and they laughed some more.

Two Saturday nights later, he treated another 'Sheila victim,' for leg and hip fractures. This time the act was not 'premeditated.' The 'victim,' a peeping Tom or potentially worse, had climbed onto the overhang and parted the curtains of the open window, at about one o'clock in the morning as Sheila was getting ready for bed. She screamed in fright; he turned to run and fell on the sidewalk, breaking both legs and the right hip.

"Enough of your adventures, Sheila," he remonstrated the next day. "Move back to the dormitory or keep your windows shut and nailed, or better yet, let's publicize what happens to men who conceive or nurture mischievous designs against you."

They laughed again, appreciating that they'd be entertaining friends with these stories for many years.

Repeating the story of the mugging of Dennis, one of the most respected among his classmates, he reasoned, will always re-arouse the anger, the pain and the cries for revenge, felt and expressed at the time of the hearing about it and with every encounter with Dennis. The image of his braced jaw, after the reconstruction from the shattering blows with a lead-pipe, the stitches in the scalp, and the thinning face (Dennis could only sip milkshakes or blended liquid nutrients for months) returned to interrupt studying, thinking, and conversing. And the frustration from knowing that the criminals were never caught was oppressive and not likely to give way – not even with the excitement in the preparation of and trial participation in the traditional 'skit' to be staged a few days before graduation.

The skit was a spectacular success. So much talent in this class! His sides were hurting from laughing. His handkerchief was wet with tears. And his heart overflowed with admiration for the satirized Senior Faculty Members who seemed to enjoy it even more.

Helene did not understand everything and did not enjoy it as much. She might have even found it boring, had she known that this would be the "Swan Song," for her (He was going to tell her later; that's why he took her rather than Marian; Barbara had receded in the background and was almost "out of the picture.") Gerry and Edie, his guests, enjoyed it enormously. Gerry stomped his feet as he laughed and Edie was overcome with happiness in her husband's delight.

Searching somewhat desperately, to find a way to tell Helene that this may be the last time they'd be together, he talked all the way to her home (they had to take a bus to the elevated train, then another elevated train, then another bus) about the skit, the weddings coming-up, the dispersion of his classmates throughout the country, the inevitable permanent separations. When he came close to the point, he balked. Was she listening? What was she thinking?

After they arrived at her home, he felt that he had fumbled again, and he hoped that she had drawn her own conclusions. He sat next to her on the stairway, accepting her invitation. They remained silent. He kept thinking, "What now?"

She broke the silence with an abrupt and resolute, "Let's get married!"

He stood up, facing her. He suddenly found the strength. "No. We can't. We mustn't. Not to each other," he replied firmly.

"Why not?" she asked, imploringly and angrily, staring at him. Before he could answer, she reminded him: "We've known each other for six years. We've fought, we've ventured away from each other for long, very long intervals; but we've always been drawn back to each other. It's time we stayed together." She stopped, looking at him intently.

He'd established his position. There was no retreat. "When I, like your parents and my parents, get married, it's *forever*. Hopefully in happiness and bliss, with mutual understanding and respect, sharing joy and toil, following the same path to a common goal." He took her hands in his and looked into her eyes. "Add up all the times we've shared in the last six years, what do you come up with? Very, very little!" He spoke slowly.

"But I've always thought of you, always; mentally, emotionally I was never far from you," she protested.

"We won't last more than six months," he ruled. "We're too different. We'll start fighting. Physical attraction is not enough. We'll remain friends."

She surrendered. He took her in his arms and kissed her cheek gently. "Good night."

He walked to the door, then turned around to wave. She was sitting on the step, holding her head in both hands. He stood for a moment, opened the door, walked out and managed to not look back.

"Goodbye," he repeated aloud, walking down the quiet, deserted streets all the way to the elevated train station.

The train was empty at 1:00 A.M. He felt empty.

The occasional passenger walking in or out of the train, at the stops, did not change the emptiness. Remorse, flashes of the skit – so long ago! - and emergence of thoughts like, "Is she still crying on the stairs? Will her pain turn into hate?" could not fill the emptiness in him. Not now, not through the night. His attempts at escape from the pursuit of the relentless vengeful Furies and at rescue with his appeals to Morpheus for mercy proved futile. He tossed and turned in his bed, sighing and praying for deliverance, blaming and cursing his ineptitude in appreciating his weaknesses, and looked for shelter in pacing from his room to the living room or in trying to read the *Parallel Lives of Plutarch*.

George, apparently aware of his restlessness, pretended he had to go to the bathroom, reminded him, "It's late. Go to sleep." And retreated after his imploring long look was left unanswered. Going for a walk on the Lake-Shore was frightening. He'd be at the mercy of the screeching and hissing vengeful Furies. He went back to bed, lay face down, and listened to the tick-tock of the clock.

He waited for one of the others to rise first. He could not bear to look at his face in the mirror. And the "Good morning" wishes were meant for the others. When asked, "What's wrong?" he recounted the exchanges on the stairway, hoping for relief and understanding.

"That's the price you pay," George pontificated sternly.

"One down, two to go," Nick added, shaking his head in sadness.

"Cut it out," Tony pleaded with understanding and walked to Lampis to squeeze his shoulder.

Lampis stirred his coffee, not raising his eyes. They were right, all three of them. He'd made his bed; he'll have to sleep in it, alone. Maybe alone forever.

"I am going to the Laboratory, he said, standing up. "I have some work to do."

"What about your coffee?" Nick asked.

"I'll see you later," he answered and walked out. He'd check his mice, review some of his slides, go over his tables and graphs; leave them all in order before leaving. He must not disappoint Dr. Wissler or Dr. Fitch.

His mice were all alive, some bigger with ascites, some wasting from the tumor. He inoculated some more with tumor cells, rationalizing his guilt with the reminder that he needed "more numbers, better statistics." He reviewed some of his slides to correlate fluorescence and chromosomes, in the dark room, pulling away from the microscope every time Helene's image sitting on the step holding her head appeared before him. He checked his graphs with columns and lines joining points extending far beyond the margins of the paper. He gave up. He went down to the Cafeteria and sat alone. He could not impose on mere acquaintances. He left. He did not mind that the bus was late. He looked out the window after returning a half smile to a young woman across the aisle on the train. "Yesterday, at this time," he thought and looked at his watch. It was late.

"Barbara called," Nick said compassionately. "She asked that you call her back."

"Not tonight. It's too late," Lampis answered, and sat at the table.

"It's not too late. She wants you to call her tonight. It's important, she said."

He read in George's expression "You got yourself into this, you deal with it."

He looked at Tony for some support, but he only saw confusion. "Did Helene call? Did Marian call?" he asked.

"No, they didn't," George answered.

He was relieved, partly.

"I'll give them a week after you move to Philadelphia, before they forget you," Nick said, half-joking, half-apologizing.

"Thanks, Nick," he countered.

They managed to laugh.

The inevitable call from Barbara found him braced and prepared but left him exhausted. She would not take "no" for an answer. His appreciation of her deep hurt, especially after her declared resolution to change from Catholic to Greek Orthodox before he married her, prostrated him with guilt and remorse. He tried to reason with her, to emphasize the differences between them; to remind her of his irrevocable commitment to several more years of intense study and deprivations; to make her understand that he could not contribute to the happiness that she deserved; to assure her that she'll always have a special place in his heart. She kept reminding him of the strength of her love. His heart ached, and his ears began to hurt from the pressure of the ear-piece of the telephone. In desperation, hoping to arouse some resentment for him, he invented some blatant lies to portray an ugly picture of himself, unworthy of her. He prayed that she did not believe him and that she understood why he did it. They exchanged "goodbyes" and "good lucks" and hung up.

The burden of guilt, remorse and shame was crushing.

The invitations to parties for his graduating class by the Faculty, for all who had participated in Research in the Department of Pathology, and for the close friends of Fraternities crowded his schedule and brought some relief from his conscience pangs. The preparation for the presentation of his research work and conclusions added another welcome distraction. The attempts at rationalization promoted only self-contempt or pity and had to be abandoned. Work was his only salvation.

The cartoons in the Alumni Magazine helped a little, too, especially the one with him running away, with one arrow stuck on his back and two on course, from the pile of those struck down by the arrows of Eros – Cupid, the Latin God of Love, lacked in his mind the passion and overwhelming drive of the Greek Eros. The picture with the caption, "Noon Lecture," and all of the eleven of his classmates fast asleep in it, evoked chuckles and comments repeatedly, especially by those who were not in the picture.

Attending the parties lifted his spirits to near-euphoria. Mingling with friends, faculty-members, and Alumni at these parties or meetings, with Marian at his side every time, raised his spirits and questions, some discreet and some direct, about the role of Marian in his future. The trite answer "We're just friends," did not satisfy anyone and occasionally evoked a subtle shrug of a shoulder or a half-smile. And he just planned for the next party, his schedule for studying and Lab work, and his graduation. The plans to move to Philadelphia were postponed.

The final, comprehensive exams lasted a whole week and were grueling. He developed a sore throat in the middle, taking the Psychiatry exam with chills, fever, and a temperature of 103 degrees Fahrenheit. He was somewhat paranoid, appropriately enough, about some of the Faculty members in Psychiatry, after his experience at Manteno State Hospital, his conflicts with the female Psychologists, and his confrontational inquiries about his grade in the Gift shop. He did not wish these Psychiatrists to suggest that his illness was psychosomatic. (He was told later that he had done very well in his exam). He recovered quickly and finished with a high grade of self-confidence.

The excitement grew beyond bounds of containment. He walked around campus, in the Quadrangles, along and through the Gothic arches, in and out of classrooms and Libraries, to the C-Shop and Mandel Hall. If he could only spend his entire life here to multiply memories and satiate his thirst for knowledge and inspiration! He was stopped in front of the C-bench by a stunningly beautiful, smiling young woman, her long straight black hair blowing away from her shoulders in the light breeze.

"Remember me?" she asked, the smile of self-confidence inviting an answer.

"You look very familiar...and very beautiful," he responded, then adding, "but give me a hint!"

She tilted her head to the left and pushed back a strand of hair from her face. "Miss Houston?" she asked.

He was stunned. "Miss Houston, what happened to you? You grew up, between expounding on Plato, Aristotle, St. Augustine, Thomas Aquinas, Bacon...at the venerable age of thirteen and now, you grew up, to match your brains with beauty."

She extended her hand.

He took it, squeezed it gently and held it.

"Did you ever suspect that I had a crush on you?" she asked.

"I hope you still have," he replied. They laughed. "What are you doing now, did you stay in Philosophy?"

"I am graduating with you next Friday. I am getting my Ph.D. in Philosophy, you're getting your M.D.; I am one of the ushers. I saw your name."

"All these years, why did you wait so long to run into me? And now that I am leaving for Philadelphia."

"I kept looking for you, but you kept hiding from me, and now I am moving to Yale. I have a job there. I must go now. It was so nice to see you again. I'll see you Friday."

They walked in opposite directions, she toward the Administration building, he toward the arches of the Classics building. They turned around simultaneously, as if obeying an inaudible command, smiled, and waved goodbye.

His anticipation of his appointment with Dean Ceithaml stirred so many memories, brought so many emotions to surface again, and re-raised the vows to try to never fail this great man. Would he be able to express his feelings of immense and everlasting gratitude? He'd try! Knowing that Dean Ceithaml heard, very clearly, all and more than was articulated, he felt at ease.

Dean Ceithaml stood up, extended his hand and after a warm handshake, asked him to sit down. "You made it," Dean Ceithaml declared with obvious prided. "We were always confident that you would, and we're equally confident that you will do well at Philadelphia General Hospital." (Dean Ceithaml seldom used acronyms).

"Dean Ceithaml," he started, "I am frustrated in trying to think of ways to express my deep gratitude to this University, and to you personally, for all that I've received from you. How in the world can I do that?"

Dean Ceithaml stretched his long legs, locked his hands behind his neck and looked at him as if he were the only visible entity. "All you have to do," he spoke slowly, "is make us proud of you."

"I will do my best," he vowed aloud.

They stood up and shook hands.

"Goodbye, good luck. Let us hear from you, from time to time."

"I'll never forget. Goodbye. Thank you."

Trying the gown for size and the cap for fitness, he asked Marian, "Is this for real?"

She shook her head, smiling. "Your dream has come true!"

"I wish my parents could be here Friday," he shared his thought.

"Wish I could stand in for them."

"Maybe I'll get another ticket for you."

Her moist eyes sparkled.

"Friday, Friday, Friday," he repeated. She'd be deeply disappointed, if she were not there. He squeezed her hand. He must find a way.

The carillon bells of the Rockefeller Chapel of the Mitchell Tower, and of the Lutheran Theological Seminary were all ringing. The skies were clear. The gentle breeze made the branches of the Dutch-Elm trees, lining the Midway, bow in respect and deference. He walked with his entourage of his brothers, Cousin Tony, and Marian to the lawn in front of the Rockefeller Chapel, shook hands and exchanged "How-do-you-do's" and "Nice-meeting-you's" with his classmates' parents, wives, or fiancées.

He headed for the Chapel's basement, put on his gown and cap, and lined up for the procession. Miss Houston smiled and waved at him and showed him where to go. His close friend David Anderson stood next to him, Ivan Diamond and Phil Eaton a little further back, Charley Park still further. They lined up alphabetically and started to walk slowly, at a signal. They walked out of the north side of the Chapel, to the front and entered.

The organ's celebrant and solemn music competed with the ceremonious tolls of carillon bells at the entrance and transported to ultimate reverence for the occasion inside. The candidates – they were still candidates! – for higher degrees, Masters and above, from the Professional Schools and the various Divisions, lined up separately, along the pews. The guests lined up along the sides. The Faculty, having led the procession, sat in rows at the platform in front.

"Vested with the Authority of the University," the Provost Marshall said, declaring the purpose "this gathering," and called on the President, Dr. George Beadle, to take the podium. The address, eloquent but laconic, emphasized the achievements of and the expectations from the candidates. This marked another beginning, not another milestone. Fortified with knowledge and humility, they must brace themselves for a never-ending pursuit of excellence, truth, and justice.

The conferring of the Degrees, starting with a brief report for the reasons for each Honorary Degree, followed. The names of the candidates and the Degree conferred were called alphabetically from each School or Division. They walked slowly in succession, with the intervals in between long enough for the President to hand the Diploma to the left hand, shake the right hand and congratulate each candidate individually.

Receiving his Diploma, Lampis shook hands with the President, hearing his congratulations on the platform in front of all these dignitaries, accomplished academicians, and bursting-with-pride relatives, made all the sacrifices and suffering unquestionably worthwhile. He stepped from cloud to cloud, down from the platform, scanning through the mist of his eyes the crowd in front of him, for his familial and familiar faces. He saw smiles everywhere, his ecstasy glowing and reflected from every face – every face framed by a halo. He pressed his Diploma to his heart and touched it to his lips. He stayed in a trance until the organ's notes filled the chapel again and people started to move silently and reverently out of the chapel.

His brothers, Cousin Tony, and Marian rushed to him. Hugs, kisses, and tears of joy followed; pictures; the harmony of the carillon bells; the fluttering of the flags and of the banners; the goodbyes; the gradual dispersion.

A New Beginning.

Instead of Epilogue

THE WINDING PATH, sloping up to the ridge and gutted by the torrential rains, was carpeted with thick clover in blossom and blocked by land-slides. He heard the mourning shrill of a hawk piercing the silence, as it dragged its shadow across a slope with charred skeletons of trees. He saw the exposed boulders in disarray, now scorched by the merciless sun and forsaken by the cooling breeze; the gaping gorge below, with cliff-jaws studded by scrawny and ostracized crab-apple trees swallowing sound and shade. The small plane, prostrated at the foot of the mountain, was surrounded by thickets and sentinels of poplars, which guarded its tranquility.

He resumed his ascent, after wiping the sweat from his brow with his sleeve. When did the ascent start? Where did it lead? Why? What provisions did he make? What was the price? A better view from the summit! A shroud with clouds! A stretch of God's hand!

Sweat drops from his forehead were gliding down his cheeks; his mouth dry, parched; his legs aching. He stopped. He sighed. He listened. Water flowed over rocks somewhere to his right. His thirst overwhelming all other senses and needs. He parted the thickets and ferns. He twisted among the pines and leaped over fallen trunks. His thirst, intensifying, drove him. There, the sparkling water over the rocks and in a pool, sprayed the nearby ferns, causing them to tilt and quiver.

He rose and lifted his gaze from the reflection in the dancing wavelets to the pear tree. He climbed the tree, ignoring the thorns, and bracing against a slanting branch, hung with the right hand and stretched with the left to grasp the pear. He measured the distance, timed the swing and lurked. Holding on. One move. It was his. He admired it, kissed it, and deposited it in his bosom, through the open shirt.

Sliding down the trunk, he took a deep breath with a sigh. That fragrance! He took another slow, deliberate breath. Where was it coming from? He scanned and searched along the banks.

There it was, a wild rose, half-open with dew-drops on its crimson petals, guarded by thorny branches. Resolved! He will not pluck it but just draw it closer to inhale all its fragrance without shaking the dew. He didn't care about the thorns stinging and scratching his hands and arms.

A little bird flitted from the rose-bush. Was it a nightingale? His arm still extended for the rose. He watched it perch on a branch of a silvery poplar across the creek and flutter its wings, quivering its tail. It bowed four times to invisible nymphs, swelling its neck and vibrating its open beak with a song of Apollo's tributes to the rest of the Gods and to nature. He chased after the song to the solid cliff across the deep gorge and held his breath until he returned with the echo to the branch with the little bird.

The leaves of the poplar trembled and danced to the song, fanned and tinged the reflection of the sun-rays, and answered with their whispers to the bubbling of the stream flowing in ecstasy over polished and shining rocks.

He raised his eyes, straining to decipher whispers and bubbling, to the top branch. He was arrested and held by bursts of ray-bundles as the tree-top bowed to the breeze. He escaped to the blue dome and rolled down to the soft layers of the clouds compressed in the horizon. The sun blushed. He must hurry.

He wiggled through the thickets and thorn bushes. He slipped. He fell! He grabbed a root and rose. He pushed saplings aside and forgot the scared rabbit in order to find a path. He did not stop to guess the distance to the peak or to count the ditches and the barriers. He silenced the painful cries from stumbling and cast the curses behind. He rushed up the steep path, panting, sweating, aching, hoping, and expecting.

There before him, he saw the ragged, rough peak, inviting, challenging, promising a wider view, a cooling breeze, freedom. He conquered! He spread his arms and raised his gaze heavenward.

Straight across, marking the boundaries of the Horizon, another crowned, majestic peak; the throne of Zeus? He must gather strength and start his new journey now!

THE END

CPSIA information can be obtained
at www.ICGtesting.com
Printed in the USA
FSHW011654070619
58741FS